THIS STUBBORN SELF:

TEXAS AUTOBIOGRAPHIES

THIS STUBBORN SELF:

TEXAS AUTOBIOGRAPHIES

BY BERT ALMON

TCU Press
Fort Worth

Library of Congress Cataloging-in-Publication Data

Almon, Bert, 1943-
This stubborn self : Texas autobiographies / Bert Almon.
p. cm.
Includes bibliographical references (p.) and index.
ISBN 0-87565-266-2 (cloth : alk. paper)
1. American prose literature--Texas--History and criticism. 2. American prose literature--20th century--History and criticism. 3. Authors, American--Texas--Biography--History and criticism. 4. Texas--Biography--History and criticism. 5. Texas--Intellectual life. 6. Texas--In literature. 7. Self in literature. 8. Autobiography. I. Title.
PS266.T4 A46 2002
818'.508099764--dc21
2002003431

Book design by Barbara M. Whitehead
Linoleum cut illustration by Barbara M. Whitehead

For Olga

CONTENTS

ACKNOWLEDGMENTS

All books of this kind are a collaborative effort. I have had some very capable assistance. A number of the writers have helped. A. C. Greene has answered queries about his own work and volunteered information from his vast knowledge of Texas and its writers. I remember warmly an afternoon in Salado on May 16, 1998, when he and his wife Judy offered hospitality and talk about Texas, Texans, and Texas literature. Pat Mora has generously answered questions about her *House of Houses.* The late William A. Owens once helped me obtain copies of some of his out-of-print works. William Humphrey provided information about his writing during his final illness. Gloria López-Stafford sent me a copy of her résumé which helped me get a sense of her career. Ruthe Winegarten and Pat LittleDog gave me insights into the process of creating an autobiography through interviews.

I am especially grateful to Dian Leatherberry Malouf for information about the elusive John Houghton Allen. Emeritus professor of English at McMurry University Patrick Bennett and his wife, Abilene librarian Shay Bennett, passed on information on Gertrude Beasley. Professor Sylvia Grider of Texas A & M University drew my attention to the work of Mody C. Boatright. The late Dadie Stillwell Potter answered questions about her mother. Betty Heath, Hallie Stillwell's cousin, answered questions. Heath and Gardner Smith provided a picture of Hallie with a Mexican water witcher for use in this book. Don Graham, J. Frank Dobie Professor of English at the University of Texas, first told me about Gertrude Beasley and has offered advice and encouragement on several matters Texan. James Ward Lee and Judy Alter answered various questions about Texas from the scene. Four colleagues in the Department of English at the University of Alberta have assisted me: Julie Rak shared her knowledge of autobiographical theory. Ted Bishop offered advice on modernism and the history of publishing; Jo-Ann Wallace, who is writing an intellectual biography of Edith (Mrs. Havelock) Ellis, helped me with the milieu of Gertrude Beasley; and Dianne Chisholm pointed me toward studies of the body in literature. John Charles, head of Special Collections at the University of Alberta Library, made a rare copy of Beasley's *My First Thirty Years* available for photocopying. Jay Gertzman, emeritus professor at Mansfield University, gave me advice on the history of censorship in the 1920s and made a number of valuable suggestions. Robert Burlingame, emeritus professor at the University of Texas at El Paso, discussed his recollections of Gloria López-Stafford and Pat Mora and sent me clippings about López-Stafford from the El Paso papers. Father Michael McCarthy advised me on numerous matters Catholic. David Tonkonogy helped me with details of Russian geography. Margaret Almon, Tatiana Loverso, Vasilis Costopoulos, and Meli Costopoulos assisted in various ways. My cousin, Beverly Mullins, who was a classmate of Charlie Marie Karr at Lamar University, gave me her reminiscences of the Karr family. Caroline Conley Randle helped me to understand changes in Dallas and shared her mother's memories of taking a course with J. Frank Dobie. Bill Whitworth explained some fine points of ranching in the Brush Country. I must especially thank Dudley R. Dobie Jr. for information about his father's experiences selling Gertrude Beasley's memoirs.

Archives were essential to my task, and many archivists assisted me. Carl Spadoni, curator of the Bertrand Russell Collection at McMaster University was prompt and helpful. Betty Bustos, assistant archivist at the Panhandle-Plains Museum, found the letters of John Houghton Allen to Harold Bugbee for me, and then, after I discovered clues that Allen's lost *Tales of Randado* manuscript was in Bugbee's archive, found that as well. Two people at the National

Archives and Research Administration have been most helpful: Aloha P. South and Sally Kuisel. Cathy Hunter, archivist for the National Geographic Society, gave me extraordinary assistance. Judith Etherton, university archivist, University of London Library, verified that Gertrude Beasley did not enroll at the university. Andrew Hannah, acting registrar at the University of Chicago checked the records of Gertrude Beasley for me.

The University of Alberta gave me a McCalla Research Professorship which provided me with the time to write this work. My wife, Olga Costopoulos, made the writing possible through her patience and advice.

As the conventional expression so aptly puts it, the mistakes herein are mine alone.

Photography Credits

John Houghton Allen: *Self-portrait, 1945*

Jewel Babb: *photograph by Ann Savino.*

Gertrude Beasley: *Passport photo, 1924. Courtesy U. S. Department of State.*

J. Frank Dobie: *Photo by Carl Bergquist, Courtesy Southwestern Writers Collection, Southwest Texas State University, San Marcos*

Ray Gonzalez: *Courtesy Ray Gonzalez*

A. C. Greene: *Courtesy A. C. Greene*

William Humphrey: *Photo by Jerry Bauer*

Annie Mae Hunt: *Courtesy of Barbara Bullard*

Mary Karr: *Photo by Ali Smith*

John A. Lomax, c. 1917, *Lomax Family Papers CN 01203, The Center for American History, University of Texas at Austin*

Gloria López Stafford: *Photograph Courtesy of Gloria López Stafford*

Sallie Reynolds Matthews: *Studio Portrait, 1880*

Larry McMurtry: *Photo by Bill Wittliff, Courtesy Southwestern Writers Collection, Southwest Texas State University, San Marcos*

Pat Mora: *Photo by Steve Northrup*

Naomi Shihab Nye: *Photo by Michael Nye*

William A. Owens: *Photo by Manny Warman, Courtesy Columbia University Archives, Columbiana Library*

Hallie Stillwell: *Courtesy Betty Field and Gardner Smith*

John Phillip Santos: *Photo by Dana Gluckstein*

C. C. White: *Photo by Wilbur Holland, Courtesy Dr. Charles Holland*

INTRODUCTION:

IS TEXAS STILL TEXAS?

Texans have produced some extraordinary autobiographies which reveal the state as well as their authors. Writers in this study can be read for their literary qualities, for their profound self-revelations, and for their record of the geography and history of a state often considered unique by its citizens and the world in general. A trove of economic, social, and religious practices can be found in the books in this study. The record is perhaps especially interesting now that Texas, which has always seemed a special case to its natives, enters the mainstream of American life. The writers born before 1925—Sallie Reynolds Matthews, John A. Lomax, Gertrude Beasley, J. Frank Dobie, Hallie Stillwell, Jewel Babb, Annie Mae Hunt, John Houghton Allen, A. C. Greene, William A. Owens, and William Humphrey—offer portraits of a traditional Texas, with detail after detail which now seems archaic or on the point of vanishing. These writers make the world of small towns, farms, and ranches vivid for readers bred in cities, and most Americans are urbanites. But these writers also show an awareness of modernity, especially in its urban form. In one way or another, they register the shocks of a transition to the modern world, and a surprising number of them welcome the changes. The oldest writer in this survey, Sallie Reynolds Matthews, who was born in 1861, embraced technological change, though she spent her life in rural and small town settings.

Other autobiographers record growing up in a newer Texas or reveal a Texas outside the traditional Anglo consensus. During the presidential campaign of George W. Bush, when commentators wanted to understand the candidate through his Texas origins, Benjamin Soskis wrote an article, "Why Texas Looks Like America: Lone Star Joining,"[1] for *The New Republic* on the transformations of Texas that belie its image as a frontier society dominated by petroleum and agriculture. His points would not be news to Texans, but it is interesting to see them made by a Yale graduate from Philadelphia who writes for a left-leaning New York magazine, someone with an outsider's perspective. He points out that "more Texans now work in high tech as work in oil, gas drilling, refining, and agriculture combined" (24). Computer companies have moved into Austin and the Limestone Hills around it on such a scale that the area is sometimes wryly called the Silicon Hills. When William Owens moved to Dallas in 1921, he took his first streetcar ride and saw the black district of Deep Ellum, which he viewed as mysterious. Soskis observes that the internet company, Yahoo, has set up its headquarters in an abandoned warehouse in the district. It is also home to an artistic crowd, one of the hip places to live, with Greenwich Village-style lofts. In *Farther Off from Heaven*,[2] William Humphrey describes returning to his hometown of Clarksville after thirty years and discovering that it had ceased to be a southern agricultural center dominated by cotton. He saw cowboy boots and Stetson hats instead of overalls. Cotton farming had been replaced by cattle operations in a move which, he says, reverses Texas history (239). But the new cattle industry had nothing to do with the old style of ranching once so important in Texas: The cattle were produced in feedlot operations. The succession is interesting: open range, closed range, feed lots.

In "Horseman, Hang On: The Reality of Myth in Texas Letters," Craig Clifford has claimed that, "as I see it, Texas can never really be urban, for our urban centers are suffused with rural myths."[3] Can future Texas writing be truly urban in its myths? The writers in this book give testimony that it can. Soskis points out that the population of Texas shifted from 80 percent rural in 1940 to 85 percent urban in 2000 (25). Nowadays Texas, he suggests, is more like the rest of America: Texas exceptionalism is in decline. In *This Stubborn Soil* and its sequel, *A Season of Weathering*,[4] William A. Owens has much to say about rural life, but he also looks at Sears Roebuck catalog operations in Dallas and the working of the vast Kress five-and-dime operation as he glimpsed it as a lowly employee in Paris, Texas. Indeed, when he went with his mother to the little village of Blossom and saw his first train and first electric lights, his mother asked how he liked town and he replied, "More'n anything I ever seen. I wisht I could go back." In his childhood, Paris was a market town, a place where his family took their peanuts. Now it has a number of Fortune 500 companies, including Campbell's Soup and Kimberly Clark, the makers of Pampers. While Mary Karr talks about hunting and fishing in her memoirs, *The Liar's Club* and *Cherry*,[5] she grew up in one of the most industrialized and polluted regions in the world, the refinery strip along the Gulf Coast, and the rural past survived primarily in her father's memories.

The Big Bend ranching country described so well in Hallie

Crawford Stillwell's *I'll Gather My Geese*[6] might seem impervious to change, but Stillwell became a small-scale industrialist: She and her son supplemented the income of the ranch during a drought by starting a wax-making operation, using "wet labor" and their own candelilla cactus, a fine example of vertical integration in industry, albeit a home industry. She learned to create a media image through radio and television interviews. And she faxed stories about her region to newspapers outside her area. Her ranch is a tourist enterprise with a web site.

Although many of the authors dealt with in this book grew up on farms and ranches or in small towns, the urban world has registered in their writing. Lomax, Dobie, and Owens devoted their careers to documenting the old ways, but only after getting their graduate degrees. Larry McMurtry is an odd case: He says in the foreword to the 1989 reissue of his fine essay collection, *In a Narrow Grave*,[7] that he strove to leave the "mystic plane" of Archer County ranching life behind him for the "metropolis of the muses." In recent years, his "nonautobiographies," *Walter Benjamin at the Dairy Queen*, *Roads*, and *Paradise*,[8] have told the story of a man who moved back to small town life in Archer City, albeit to start the world's largest used-book operation. It has an E-mail address, and McMurtry himself features conspicuously on his town's web site.

Soskis points out that Texas has never been monolithic:

> Ironically, Texans have historically promoted their state's cultural uniqueness because of its lack of true unity and cohesion. In the nineteenth century, the legends of the cowboy (appropriated from eighteenth-century northern Mexican folk culture) and the Alamo held together a fragile coalition of five ministates, each with peculiar culture, topography and climate. (The annexation treaty of 1845, which incorporated Texas into the Union, included a provision allowing the state to splinter into those five regions if it chose to do so). (27)

Part of the mystique of Texas exceptionalism rests on this provision, which was meant to permit the formation of four additional slave states. It would be inconceivable for Texans to take advantage of it, but it can serve as a symbol of the diversity of the state. A. C. Greene, one of the most knowledgeable and astute commentators on Texas, collected his newspaper articles on the state in 1998 under the title *Sketches from the Five States of Texas*[9] to emphasize the variety within Texas. The five states as Greene sees it are East Texas, South Texas, West Texas, Central Texas, and North Texas. All of them are represented in this book, though it would be mechanical to tie each book to one of Greene's regions, and some areas, like the industrial Gulf Coast and the Trans-Pecos, do not fit into Greene's scheme, which is, after all, a playful device for pointing to diversity. Greene's autobiography, *A Personal Country*,[10] is a comprehensive study of West Texas, his own region.

A sixth state of Texas, to stretch the scheme for a moment, is the Mexican diaspora, which has no fixed geographical area. A central fact about Texas in the twentieth century was the enormous migration from Mexico, which accelerated during the Revolution of 1910 and continued at varying rates thereafter. As for the twenty-first century, Benjamin Soskis observes that by 2025 Hispanics will have a plurality in the state, relegating the Anglos to second place. Furthermore, the Asian population is steadily growing. Texas has a population of *Tejanos,* particularly in the Lower Rio Grande Valley, but the majority of Texans of Mexican descent nowadays spring from twentieth-century immigration, and much Chicano literature is marked by that migration. This migrant experience has affinities with the later migrations of Asians and Hispanic groups who have entered the United States, many settling in Texas (Port Arthur has a Vietnamese district), but of course every group has its unique cultural origins and its unique history in America. The Chicano writers included in this book have much to say about the immigrant experience as their parents and grandparents experienced it. Pat Mora, Gloria López-Stafford, and John Phillip Santos are essential reading for anyone interested in the history of immigration to America, a history shot through with ambivalence, tragedy, prejudice, endurance, and success—a fascinating range of stories. Authorities like the Texas Rangers, the Border Patrol, and the Immigration Service (*Los Rinches*, *La Chota,* and *La Migra*) are seen differently by Anglo and Mexican-Americans. For Texans of Mexican descent, figures like Francisco Madero, Emiliano Zapata, and Pancho Villa are as important as Bowie and Travis and Houston. South Texans like Juan Cortina (who raided Brownsville in 1859) and Gregorio Cortez (who killed two sheriffs in 1901) can be seen as outlaws or heroes of resistance depending on the side taken. The diaspora of refugees fleeing Villa is dealt with by Pat Mora and John Phillip Santos, who had ancestors in that mass migration. The Mexican-American uprising in South Texas in 1915, put down with force by the U.S. Army and the Texas Rangers, has not received such treatment.

Black Texans have created another state of Texas and another diaspora. Their ancestors mostly came to the state as slaves or as ex-slaves who sometimes came with their former masters. At the moment they are not well represented in autobiographies. There are about two million black Texans (and four million Mexican Texans). Dorothy Redus Robinson's *The Bell Rings at Four: A Black Teacher's Chronicle of Change*, tells the story of her education and her experiences during the integration of Texas schools.[11] One of the African-American autobiographies dealt with in this book, *I Am Annie Mae,*[12] has a wide scope, almost recapitulating black history in Texas. The woman who began as a desperately poor black child proudly made her way in old age to a presidential inauguration. In *No Quittin' Sense*, the Reverend Charley C. White tells a rich story about life in East Texas.[13] He worked at every kind of job open to a black laborer and became a respected preacher and therefore a de facto community leader concerned with getting a fair deal for his people, especially from the sheriff's office. He participated in the process of desegregation and conveys a good sense of what it was like to negotiate with the white power structure.

The Native-American population of Texas was decimated in the nineteenth century (the remnants of the Comanches live in Oklahoma), and it is not surprising that there are no autobiographies to represent them. Some of the writers are aware of the genetic contribution: Native ancestry is mentioned by Jewel Babb, Annie Mae Hunt, C. C. White, William Humphrey, Larry McMurtry, and Mary Karr. William Owens had no native ancestry, but his Aunt Julie was half Choctaw and he presents an interesting child's-eye view of her: He sensed that she was culturally different, and he could not perceive her as talking like "kinfolks" or acting like them.

It is probably the sense of place which makes Texas autobiographies most distinctive, for all the diversity of the state. Dave Oliphant's *Memories of Texas Towns & Cities*[14] is a collection of poems and falls outside the scope of this book, but it is noteworthy for its approach to autobiography through descriptions of cities and towns where the author has lived. The long poem on Austin is a particularly rich exploration of the history and ambiance of the capital. A. C. Greene overtly focuses on his region as a means of explaining himself, as does Larry McMurtry in *Walter Benjamin at the Dairy Queen*. Even writers who do not foreground their home territory in this way have a strong feeling for regionalism, an acute awareness of local history and conditions. J. Frank Dobie in *Some Part of Myself*[15] and John Houghton Allen in *Southwest*[16] identify strongly with a particular spot of land: their *querencias*, their beloved spots. Allen alone among authors in this book is dominated by nostalgia, and he burns with contempt for the modern world of oil drilling and the welfare system. For Pat Mora, *The House of Houses*[17] of her title is both her family's at 714 Mesita and an ideal house of words in the desert near El Paso which serves as a kind Platonic ideal of the *querencia*, one located in the imagination rather than in a place. Gloria López-Stafford's *A Place in El Paso* records a quest for a different kind of place, a social space in which she can reconcile her multiple identity as the child of an Anglo father and Mexican mother.[18]

West Texas is probably the region best served by Texas autobiographers, although northeast Texas produced William A. Owens and William Humphrey, writers born only a few miles apart. Hallie Stillwell and Jewel Babb chronicle life in the Trans-Pecos in the far west, and J. Frank Dobie and John Houghton Allen reminisce about the Brush Country of the Trans-Nueces. West Texas is the region which in many ways defined Texas for Texans through the Comanche Wars, a point made by A. C. Greene. It is also a region where the oil and cattle industries, definitions of Texas for outsiders, have dominated the economy. The early days were recorded by Sallie Reynolds Matthews, who endured the wars with the Comanches, the Civil War, the introduction of the railroad, the closing of the open range made inevitable by barbed wire (which her father-in-law, Joseph Beck Matthews, introduced to the region), the settling and abandoning of communities like Fort Griffin, and the formation of a progressive settled community around Albany. The West Texans in her *Interwoven*[19] are generous, hard working, eager for knowledge, and very different from the shiftless people in Gertude Beasley's powerful family memoir, *My First Thirty Years*.[20] Beasley's kin are presented as lazy, antagonistic to learning, and given to incest and bestiality, and her family makes a dramatic contrast with the Matthews and Reynolds families, though *Interwoven* suppresses some painful conflicts, including the lynching of her brother-in-law, John Larn. Beasley regards the respectable people of Abilene with the suspicion of a Young Goodman Brown looking gloomily at the worthies of Salem. A. C. Greene, born in Abilene about a decade after Beasley left, calls it the "Village of My Heart" and sees virtue as well as toughness in the people. Greene and Larry McMurtry consider the past but also take in the present. Greene recognized the importance of the highway in modern Texas (the state has an overweening pride in its roads) and his autobiography explores his state of West Texas from a Volkswagen camper. McMurtry expresses some guilt over abandoning ranch life while setting out to turn Archer City, site of three films growing out of his works, into a town of bookstores. McMurtry's story is a paradigm of change in Texas.

The Brush Country is a fine example of the ways in which human settlement reshapes the landscape. This region between the Nueces and the Rio Grande has a distinctive vegetation, mostly thorny, but it was created late in the nineteenth century when overgrazing destroyed the prairie grasses which covered the area.

Dobie and Allen show no awareness of this process. Pat Mora, influenced by ecological awareness, brings that awareness into her work when she writes about the Chihuahuan desert around El Paso. For John Phillip Santos, the desert and mountains of Coahuila, whence came his paternal ancestors, are a landscape offering visionary experience: They are his *Places Left Unfinished at the Time of Creation*.[21] Texas not only borders on Coahuila, it was once part of it: We could think of it whimsically as Upper Coahuila, just as the comic novelist Dan Jenkins calls Texas "Baja Oklahoma."

People do more than contemplate landscape: They work in it. Readers of Texas autobiographies can learn a great deal about cattle ranching from Sally Reynolds Matthews, John Houghton Allen, and Hallie Stillwell, about goat ranching from Jewel Babb, about red-dirt farming from William Owens, about tenant farming and small-town life from William Humphrey, about the oil-drilling business from A. C. Greene, and about life in a refinery town from Mary Karr. These books preserve a body of material practices and customs. Anyone wanting to know how to go through a barbed-wire fence can learn the technique from Beasley and Greene. Owens preserves many vanished practices of poor white farmers in Northeast Texas. Pat Mora likes to describe the making of Mexican herbal remedies and potpourri. No fewer than five of the authors in this book record the making of lye soap. Three of them—Matthews, Owens, and Babb—describe times when it was necessary to make one's own soap. A. C. Greene's great-grandmother, on the other hand, made lye soap when she was weary of the modern world and craved the old ways. Pat Mora describes the soap making in a special context: One of her long dead ancestors prepares it in Mora's imaginary *House of Houses,* where all the generations of her family can meet in the writer's imagination and share experiences and skills. The books by Chicano writers are especially interesting for their preservation of lore not known in the cultural mainstream, like the importance of the *curandero* or *curandera*, the herb doctor. Jewel Babb, the coauthor of *Border Healing Woman*,[22] was a traditional healer in the Appalachian manner, relying on the laying on of hands, and she was also seen as a *curandera* by the local Mexican population from both sides of the border in Hudspeth County.

Cultural practices are described in rich detail: A student of southern Protestantism can learn a great deal by comparing the various revivals in the early books—the Presbyterian "cowboy camp meeting" at Fort Davis in Sallie Reynolds Matthews's *Interwoven*; the Methodist camp meeting under a brush arbor in John Lomax's *Adventures of a Ballad Hunter*;[23] and the Baptist camp meetings and town revivals in Owens's *This Stubborn Soil* and *A Season of Weathering*. Charley C. White, a black preacher in the Church of God in Christ, describes his spiritual struggle as he moved from being a Baptist to a Pentecostal. His description of one of his visions is superb: "When God gives you a vision your whole body kind of soaks up the message, like a biscuit soaks up red-eye gravy" (134). Gertrude Beasley reports rather caustically on the work of the missionary Baptists, and she describes the fervid atmosphere of their religious revivals which she contrasts with the restrained legalism of the Church of Christ.

In the works of the Chicano autobiographers, popular Catholicism is interwoven with the narratives in a way that may seem exotic to Anglo readers. The Virgin of Guadalupe is a recurrent figure: She makes a fantasy appearance in Pat Mora's *House of Houses*, and her miraculous cloak is glimpsed from a moving sidewalk in Mexico City in John Phillip Santos's memoir. In *Borderlands / La Frontera*, Gloria Anzaldúa points out that the key symbolic figures in Chicana writers are three *madres*: the Virgin of Guadalupe, whose appearance to the Indian Juan Diego in 1531 near Mexico City created a symbolic union of Catholicism and indigenous religion; *La Llorona*, or "The Weeping Woman," a ghostly figure who appears near water weeping for her drowned children; and Malinche, the Indian woman who served as interpreter for the conquerors of Mexico.[24] López-Stafford was terrified by the legend of *La Llorona* in her childhood, and Santos meditates on the meaning of Malinche in Mexican culture. Mora's book is a treasury of saints' days and festivals, with a wealth of material from the liturgical year. All of the Chicano authors herein make use of *El Día de los Muertos*, "The Day of the Dead," the unique Mexican practice of communing with the dead in the cemetery on November 2, All Souls' Day. In the writings of López-Stafford and Ray Gonzalez[25] the practice is mentioned in passing, but it is important in the commemorative vision of Pat Mora and John Phillip Santos.

Education is a key social practice. In Texas, the drive toward education was sometimes the instinct of the community, as in the West Texas ranching country on the Clear Fork of the Brazos River. Sallie Reynolds Matthews frequently emphasizes her family's concern for education in *Interwoven*. Gertrude Beasley, who was a remarkably successful schoolteacher at seventeen, has much to say about the violent and authoritarian atmosphere in Texas schools and her own complicity in it in spite of her socialist principles. Her methods included carrying a two-and-a-half-foot strap to school and even in one case teaching with a revolver on her desk. Beasley's own education reveals much about the curriculum and methods of teaching from the primary grades through the university level. William A. Owens describes his region of Northeast Texas as a world with little interest in education, but he struggled to get a teaching certificate: The thought of not getting an education was devastating to him. His first two autobiographies constitute a full and often dismal picture of impoverished public education in rural and small-town Texas in the early twentieth century, and he meticulously describes his preparatory training at the East Texas Normal School at Commerce. J. Frank Dobie and John Lomax first attended small sectarian universities where the staff had too much work and too little equipment, but they sought a better education in the East: Lomax at Harvard, Dobie at Columbia University. And both were victims of political infighting at the University of Texas. Unfortunately, neither says as much as a reader might like about the traumas of being fired by the university. For so many years education appeared to be the key to success in America, and some of these memoirs are Horatio Alger stories in which schooling plays the part of the wealthy benefactor.

Along with major institutions like religion and education, most of these books examine the texture of daily life, its customs, pastimes, and folklore. The three famous folklorists—John Lomax, William A. Owens, and J. Frank Dobie—were especially attuned to folkways. Sally Reynolds Matthews describes archaic practices like "*infares*" after weddings and pseudo-medieval tournaments in West Texas. Lomax and Dobie recorded tournaments as well, and Chicano writers describe Mexican customs generally unknown to the Anglo majority—like the *grito* of freedom on the *Diez y seis de Septiembre*.

Racism is a social practice rooted in the Texas past. The Texas Revolution was fought in part over the desire of southern American colonists to retain slavery after it was banned by the Mexican constitution. Chicanos have bitter memories of racial relations in Texas. They dissent from the traditional view of Texas that was popular among the Anglo majority, for whom San Jacinto and the Alamo were sacred. Ron Rozelle's *Into that Good Night*, set in Oakwood, an ordinary town in East Texas not too far from Reverend Charles White's Jacksonville, describes the entire Anglo school, all twelve grades, being taken to the town of Buffalo to see John Wayne's film, *The Alamo*.[26] Rozelle's book does not receive substantial treatment here because it is more an account of his father's descent into Alzheimer's than an autobiography, but he does preserve the ambiance of an East Texas town on the verge of desegregation. Santos and López-Stafford have narrated their memories of being subjected to aggressive Anglo history in school, and Ray Gonzalez recalls throwing off the cult of Davy Crockett. He dramatizes the problems of being Mexican in El Paso, where the Border Patrol looks suspiciously at anyone walking near the border who might be racially profiled as an illegal alien. Curiously, the strongest emotional attachments felt by Dobie and Allen in their youth were to vaqueros on their fathers' ranches who offered emotional warmth they did not receive from the fathers. For Hallie Stillwell, Mexican laborers, "wet" or dry, are a financial matter. She is not hostile but not especially empathetic.

William Owens writes a devastating *mea culpa* about his complacent racism as a child. Reverend White and Annie Mae Hunt show what it was like to be the victim of racism. A desire to record the brutalities visited on her family on a Navasota plantation was the impetus for her narrative. Gertrude Beasley is particularly interesting because she tells what happened when a young woman of socialist leanings and an unexamined set of racial attitudes went north to the University of Chicago in 1914. She learned that her prejudices earned her the nickname, "Lyncher." Like J. Frank Dobie at Columbia University the year before, she quickly learned to reassess her racial attitudes.

Naturally we read autobiographies to learn about the human being created for us in them, as well as for social and cultural background. In a work which does not quite qualify as memoir, *Hard Scrabble: Observations on a Patch of Land*, John Graves discusses the "individualistic Southern yeoman" as a Texas type, Scotch-Irish or Scottish in extraction. He devotes a whole chapter to a typical "Old Fart, ornery, independent, holding onto a little land at the edge of suburb."[27] Texas autobiographies abound in "originals," as Dobie would call them—distinctive and strong-minded people.[28] Readers of southern fiction and autobiography are familiar with such characters; the South seems tolerant of colorful eccentricity. Stillwell, Dobie, Lomax, Allen, Beasley, Humphrey, and Karr are tough, opinionated people with a strong sense of self. Annie Mae Hunt and the Reverend C. C. White show that such rugged selves are not limited to the Anglo world. Several writers became celebrities on the basis of their highly visible personalities: They were, to use another term from Dobie, "out of the old rock," and they became good copy for journalists. Dobie, Stillwell, and Hunt are good examples of older "originals," and now Mary Karr dines out, literally and figuratively, on the story of her becoming a tough individual in the Port Arthur area.

The terminology for classifying autobiographies is now very loose. As L. L. Langness and Gelya Frank point out in their book on anthropology and autobiography, the old distinction between the confession and the memoir has disappeared.[29] At one time the narrative stressing the inner life was called a confession, while memoir denoted an account of public events. Sallie Reynolds Matthews writes a memoir in this sense: She seems uncomfortable discussing her inner life and emotions; hence she gives us a family chronicle stressing marriages, deaths, trail drives, and social change. The "memoir boom" of the 1990s, which Mary Karr helped to create, was an outpouring of confessional narratives, stories of dysfunctional families and even incest. The terms "autobiography," "confession," and "memoir" are used interchangeably in this book. Two memoirs, the lives of Charley C. White and Annie Mae Hunt, are not normal autobiographies but compilations from taped interviews, while the memoir of Jewel Babb is a combination of taped interviews and materials written by Babb.

While generic terms are unstable, theoretical discussions of autobiography have become elaborate. James Olney's influential study, *Metaphors of Self,*[30] appeared in 1972; Olney's fruitful suggestion was that autobiographers create a self rather than merely record their lives. They search for and create meaningful patterns in their lives, patterns which he calls metaphors, using the term in a very broad sense. In a celebrated letter to his brother and sister-in-law, John Keats called the world a "vale of Soul-making." Memoirists are concerned with conveying just how they made their souls. Some can even define when it happened: for William Humphrey, it was the death of his father and his departure from tiny Clarksville for a new life in Dallas; for Annie Mae Hunt, it was the moment when she decided never to clean houses again. William A. Owens records the time that he first saw and drank from the waters of the Red River and knew he would be changed by the experience.

Paul John Eakin has extended Olney's ideas in helpful ways. Eakin's *Fictions in Autobiography: Studies in Self-Invention* (1985)[31] eloquently puts the case for seeing autobiography not as a factual transcription of a life (though the work will be rooted in that life) but as a storytelling process which helps to create the self. We come to know ourselves by telling our stories. Olney's Wordsworthian formula, often repeated, is that we "half discover, half create" the self. The task of the reader is not to seek empirical verification of what is told (and we hardly ever do that) but to understand the process. Of course, obvious lies and evidence of bad faith must be considered. "Fictions of self" is probably a superior term to "metaphors of self" but may carry the suggestion that the autobiography is somehow false.

The richness of the self-portrait can be troubling to readers who wonder if the details of the life can actually be remembered accurately. This has been the case for Mary Karr, whose apparent ability to re-create elaborate conversations from the past has been questioned by some reviewers. Barrett J. Mandel's "Full of Life Now" expresses the contemporary feeling about autobiography and truth:

> Readers turn to autobiography to satisfy a need for verifying a fellow human being's experience of reality. They achieve satisfaction when they feel strongly that the book is true to the experience of the author and when they are aware, to a lesser degree, that the book is an achievement of literary construction, making use of pretense as a way of highlighting its opposite, reality.[32]

Mary Karr's first memoir, significantly called *The Liar's Club*, re-creates a traumatic event which happened when she was seven years old, an event which she could not remember clearly for years. This is an objection which could be made to any number of autobiographies. Gertrude Beasley's memory of being sexually assaulted by an older brother at the age of four has a claim to accuracy because such a memory is likely to be horrifically indelible. She assures us of her desire to tell the truth by providing examples of cases in which her memory was not distinct or accurate. Mandel observes that "autobiography forges present meaning into the marrow of one's remembered life" (64). His use of "forged" is superbly ambiguous. He observes that real lying in autobiography, as opposed to taking the freedom to re-create events in a plausible manner, is usually found out: The manipulation can be sensed. Mandel's feeling is that "most autobiographers are honest (that's the whole point of the genre) with occasional distortion, honest evasions, discrete pockets of non-communication"[33] The "fiction of self" could be defined as an interpretation of self.

Memory is selective, certainly. Sometimes the text omits things that the autobiographer remembers very well. The omissions are often highly significant but the reader is not aware of them unless perhaps the writer is so notorious or celebrated that the oversight is obvious. This study will identify some important omissions in the autobiographies of Sallie Reynolds Matthews and John A. Lomax. Hallie Stillwell's omissions, her sightings of the Marfa lights, and her husband's alleged knowledge of the whereabouts of the famous "Lost Nigger Mine," are quite understandable: UFO hunters are probably more annoying even than seekers of lost treasures. J. Frank Dobie, who first described the lore around the mine and the Stillwell family's involvement in it, was pestered by treasure hunters, but he could put them in his books.

Several Texas autobiographers are best approached by tracing the metaphors of self (or fictions of self) which they are trying to forge, as Mandel would say, through their narratives. John Houghton Allen sees his defining trait as *coraje*, a Spanish term used in the Brush Country of South Texas to describe an irritable, restless quality, what the archaic term "spleen," which dropped out of use in English in the eighteenth century, meant. J. Frank Dobie's autobiographical essays (he did not live to finish an entire book about himself) define him as a lover of freedom, a man passionate about storytelling, and an academic who preferred storytellers to professors. Hallie Stillwell conceives of herself as the tenderfoot who would meet challenges set over a long marriage by her rancher husband, whose teaching method was to refuse to teach her anything so that she could fail and learn by bitter experience. The rugged individuals are often the people who had to work hardest to create a strong sense of self. Gertrude Beasley traces her course from terrified child to secretive young woman to tough schoolteacher and confident intellectual. Unfortunately, her last known utterance was a paranoid letter pointing to a collapse in her hard-won assurance. J. Frank Dobie mentions two periods when he lost his sense of self, his periods in New York City and in army training camps. Unfortunately, he says too little about them. Larry McMurtry, on the other hand, suffered a deep loss of self after a heart bypass operation, and that experience has been a theme in his autobiographical explorations.

Confessional writers like William Humphrey and Mary Karr see their lives through the wounds, literal or emotional, received in their childhood. Humphrey would grow up to be the child observer turned storyteller, the man who would turn conflicts, especially Oedipal ones, into art in his novels and stories. Karr defines herself in her first memoir as the scarred survivor who has grown tough in the Darwinian world of an oppressive Gulf Coast society and a family torn by conflict and poisoned by a secret. In her second book, she less convincingly ends with a paradoxical notion that she has achieved an understanding that she is "Same Self," an identity which manages to be enduring and yet constantly changing.

The self is so important in American life (the self has inalienable rights to life, liberty, and the pursuit of happiness, after all) that we can easily forget that the individual is nurtured in a context, primarily the family. For the confessional writer, the family is important primarily in relation to the writer: "this is what I suffered, this is what they made me become, this is how I remade myself in spite of my profound wounds." Most of the autobiographies in this study emphasize family, even extended family, the clan. This is probably to be expected in a selection of writers who represent southern and Mexican cultures, which tend to be family oriented. Texas may seem a distinct society, thanks to its special history, but the original Anglo Texans were mostly southerners, and one characteristic of the region is a deep concern with family and family history, as readers of William Faulkner, Eudora Welty, and other novelists know. Most of the Anglo writers in this book were born into families which arrived in Texas from the Deep South, most often from Alabama and Mississippi. Mexican-American writers also show a strong sense of family.

Some of the most exciting current thinking about autobiography in America today explores what Paul John Eakin calls "the relational life," which is a major subject of his most recent book, *How Our Lives Become Stories*. He believes that "relational lives represent the most prominent form of life writing in the United States today."[34] Texas writers like Sallie Reynolds Matthews are in fact pioneers of relational autobiography. Matthews chose her title, *Interwoven*, to convey the subject of her book, the intermarriages of the two pioneering families included in her name, a metaphor of family rather than a metaphor of self: She subordinates herself to the intertwined history of the Reynolds and Matthews families. A. C. Greene, William Humphrey, William A. Owens, Pat Mora, and John Phillip Santos offer excellent examples of relational lives.

An insight from anthropological folklore illuminates a number of these family-centered works. Texas folklore draws on southern, western, and Mexican sources and has produced at least five important folklorists: John A. Lomax, J. Frank Dobie, William A. Owens, Mody Boatright, and Américo Paredes. Perhaps the most important unwritten memoir in Texas is the life of Américo Paredes, who helped create Chicano/a literature in his brilliant book, *With His Pistol in His Hand*.[35]

In "Memories That Never Were: Katherine Anne Porter and the Family Saga,"[36] Sylvia Grider, a specialist in anthropological folklore at Texas A & M, explains the use of autobiography in Porter's fiction through Mody Boatright's theory of the family saga. It seems even more natural to apply it to genuine autobiographies. Mody Boatright formulated the concept in an essay called "The Family Saga as a Form of Folklore." This brief but suggestive work was collected in 1958 with essays by two other writers in *The Family Saga and Other Phases of American Folklore*.[37] Boatright was closely associated with J. Frank Dobie (who got him started in the collection of folk materials), and both were mainstays of The Texas Folklore

Society, although Dobie remained a campfire folklorist, a collector and reteller of stories, while Boatright took a more scientific approach.

The best discussion of Boatright's life and thought appears in James McNutt's fine dissertation from the University of Texas, *Beyond Regionalism: Texas Folklorists and the Emergence of a Post-Regional Consciousness.*[38] A good biographical sketch appears in "Mody Coggin Boatright," an essay by Ernest B. Speck in *The Handbook of Texas Online.*[39] Boatright took a more scientific view of folklore than J. Frank Dobie, who had persuaded him to join the Texas Folklore Society. Boatright was one of the mentors of Américo Paredes and arranged a research assistantship for him to do field work.

Boatright is interested in the way families pass down stories from generation to generation. They are not passed down as folklore but as authentic accounts of the past. The stories may be true, but they still tend to take certain traditional forms: the explanation of how the family lost its money or failed to strike it rich, the adventures of the early settlers, the tales of lost mines. They usually survive because they embody a social value. Such stories can be found in a number of the autobiographies in this book, especially those which take in the family's arrival in Texas. Sandra K. Stahl, who is probably the most important current advocate of applying anthropological concepts to autobiographies, endorses Boatright's ideas but dislikes the term "family saga," feeling that it implies a more connected narrative than oral tradition normally transmits. However, her alternative, "family story," is a broad and ambiguous term.[40] "Family saga" at least avoids the ambiguity.

The family sagas in Sallie Reynolds Matthews, J. Frank Dobie, Hallie Stillwell, William Owens, A. C. Greene, Jewel Babb, Annie Mae Hunt, and William Humphrey will receive much attention here. These writers are in touch with nineteenth-century Texas. In an interesting recapitulation of the pattern, Pat Mora and John Phillip Santos preserve family sagas as well, stories of Mexico before the Revolution of 1910 and of the ways that ancestors came to Texas during it. No doubt other groups will eventually record their own narratives of migration, among them the Vietnamese and other groups from the Orient.

The future is interesting to speculate about, but the question of where to begin a study of the subject is more important. In his recent collection of essays, *State of Mind: Texas Literature and Culture*, Tom Pilkington speaks of Alvar Nuñez Cabeza de Vaca as an originator of Texas writing.[41] He is not entirely serious, but certainly Cabeza de Vaca and three other survivors of a disastrous Spanish expedition to Florida in 1527 were the first Caucasians to cross Texas, and de Vaca left a kind of spiritual autobiography of a conquistador who learned to value the humanity of Native Americans. He became a healer at the insistence of the tribes who passed him and his companions on from group to group. He eventually came through the Trans-Pecos region around 1535. The Spaniard was an odd precursor of Jewel Babb, the reluctant healer of Indian Hot Springs in the same desert area, or perhaps it would be better to call her an odd successor. But it would be whimsical to consider de Vaca's fascinating *Relación* the first Texas autobiography. Texas did not yet exist, and de Vaca only passed through the region.

The first true autobiography in Texas was *Memoirs of Mary A. Maverick*, written up from diaries in 1880, privately printed in 1895, and finally published by the Alamo Printing Company in 1921.[42] Mary A. Maverick (1818-1898) grew up on a plantation near Tuscaloosa and married Samuel Maverick, a veteran of the Texas Revolution, in 1837. He took her to Texas in December of that year, in a party which included their ten slaves. The journey was hard: Two of their horses froze to death in one of those storms she learned to call by the Texas name, "norther." She describes an encounter with a party of Tonkawa Indians. Some of them beckoned at her buggy window for her to let them hold her five-month-old son. She declined, having heard they were cannibals, and let them see her pistol and Bowie knife: Maverick is a forerunner of bold women like Hallie Stillwell and Gertrude Beasley. Not all plantation women were southern belles, it seems, though she seems not to have known that the Tonkawas were loyal allies of Anglos against the Comanches. Her life in San Antonio included witnessing Indian raids and meeting a number of colorful eccentrics that J. Frank Dobie would have prized. Her activities as president of the Alamo Monument Association generated interest in preserving the ruins of the building as a historical site. She painted a watercolor of the ruined Alamo which has considerable historical interest. She was also a prominent member of the Daughters of the Texas Revolution and one of the organizers of the Battle of the Flowers, a festival which commemorates the battles of the Alamo and San Jacinto: In short, as Paula Marks observes, she was one of the founders and guardians of the Anglo-Texas view of history.[43] Her book, which extends only to 1859, falls outside the scope of this study, which concerns itself with relatively modern works, especially ones which record a shift from a rural or small town world to an urban one.

Another interesting early book is Amelia E. Barr's *All the Days of My Life*,[44] published in 1913. Barr (1839-1919), author of an historical novel, *Remember the Alamo!* (1888), devotes a little over a hundred pages out of five hundred to Austin and Galveston. She was an Englishwoman from Ulveston, Lancashire, who came to Texas in 1856 with her Scottish husband, Robert Barr. He worked as a state auditor in Austin. The years before the Civil War were, she says, the happiest of her life. She provides an excellent portrait of life in Austin during the period, with interesting observations of the mores of Texas women. She admired their independence and beauty. Capable of running their farms and ranches, many were crack shots and good riders: She anticipates Hallie Stillwell rather nicely. Mary Maverick's willingness to show her weapons was not a freak. Barr noted with some dismay the widespread use of snuff, a substance not unknown among Texas women in the early twentieth century. Perhaps her finest anecdote is the account of an old Indian fighter who mysteriously grew a new set of teeth in his late eighties. His wife complained that he became bad-tempered when teething, although in the past he had come home once with a Comanche arrow in his back—feathers still attached—and hadn't complained. Texas makes folklorists of everyone, it seems, including English gentlewomen. After her husband and three sons died of yellow fever in 1866, she moved to New York. Like Mary Maverick, she coped with deaths in the family by turning to spiritualism.

Barr was also a racist, and her book is afflicted with a series of stories about her lazy and superstitious slaves. A better start for a consideration of Texas autobiography is Sallie Reynolds Matthews's *Interwoven*, which rather appropriately appeared in 1936, the centennial of Texas independence. Matthews was born during the Civil War and witnessed the transformation of her West Texas from the Comanche frontier to a region in touch with the outside world through modern communications, change which she celebrates in her preface. She ended her narrative just before the start of the twentieth century, with the birth of her son, Watt, in 1899, but she contemplates the twentieth century with pleasure, speaking with approval of radio and aviation. She describes the past for her grandchildren while looking to the future, and we are that future.

THIS STUBBORN SELF:

TEXAS AUTOBIOGRAPHIES

Sallie Reynolds Matthews

1

LAMBSHEAD LEGENDS: SALLIE REYNOLDS MATTHEWS

The first important autobiography by a native of Texas is Sallie Reynolds Matthews's *Interwoven: A Pioneer Chronicle,* a book which has a secure reputation as a Texas classic for several reasons. The appeal of the text is multiple. Matthews (1861-1938) lived through the Civil War, the Comanche wars, the destruction of the buffalo, the era of open range and cattle drives, the closing of the range, the coming of the railroad, the rise and fall of Fort Griffin (one of the most colorful towns in the West) and the coming of the modern age. Ranching is central to the Texas mystique, and she belonged to two West Texas ranching dynasties by birth and marriage: Her book gets its title from the interweaving of the Reynolds and Matthews families. She has written a relational biography, and her controlling metaphor is not a metaphor of self but a metaphor of family. She is associated with one of the most famous ranches in Texas, the Lambshead (the site of the first Marlboro Country cigarette commercials), and her son, Watkins Reynolds Matthews (1899-1997), universally known as Watt, was one of the most famous and progressive ranchers of the twentieth century. Her book, which was privately printed in 1936, the Texas centennial year, was designed by the gifted printer, Carl Hertzog, and his design was perpetuated in the second private printing in 1958 and the commercial edition from Texas A&M University Press in 1982. A similar design was used in the companion volume by Frances Mayhugh Holden, *Lambshead Before Interwoven: A Texas Range Chronicle,*[1] which appeared along with the commercial edition in 1982. The famous Fort Griffin Fandangle, an elaborate musical pageant held on land provided by the Lambshead Ranch, was based on *Interwoven* and strengthens the near iconic status of Matthews's book.

The identification of Matthews with the Lambshead Ranch is a convenient shorthand: Both families held a variety of ranch properties in the Clear Fork area, a region which straddles Throckmorton County and its southern neighbor, Shackelford County. The Lambshead, founded by an Englishman, Thomas Lambshead, in 1847, came into the possession of Matthews and her husband, John Alexander Matthews, in 1885. As Lawrence Clayton has pointed out in his biography of Watt Matthews,[2] owning large acreages was not important for ranchers until the decline of the open range in the 1870s, a development which was initiated in this area by her father-in-law, Joseph Beck Matthews. Among the important geographical reference points for *Interwoven* are Camp Cooper, which is across the Clear Fork from Lambshead, Fort Griffin, which is a little south of it in Shackelford County, and Albany, a railroad town in Shackelford, where members of the two families spent much of their time after it was founded in 1881.

Matthews writes in a clear and serviceable style. Her schooling was intermittent because it was interrupted by moves and difficulties finding teachers. In his introduction to *Interwoven*, a close friend of the family, the Albany historian and playwright Robert Nail, says that she needed no help in composing her work. The text documents her love of reading, beginning with her discovery of Charles Dickens's *The Pickwick Papers* at the age of ten (73). She uses cliches occasionally: A particular cowboy was "one of nature's noblemen, who to know was to love," (74) and California has "golden shores" and is called "that Golden state." But she avoids the pomposities of nineteenth-century journalism and can allude gracefully to Ralph Waldo Emerson and Lord Byron. Her mother, whose reminiscences are quoted early in the book, was clearly an educated and even eloquent person. Sallie Matthews also used the unpublished narrative of her sister, Susan Reynolds Bartholomew (1848-1921), as a source. A travel diary of Susan's first husband, Samuel P. Newcomb, describing a journey from the Clear Fork to the San Saba River is included in the book as an addendum. Concerning the method of composition, Lawrence Clayton says in his biography of Watt Matthews:

> . . . Watt has definite memories about the creation of the original book. He recalls that once his mother started to write the book in 1934, she stayed busy at the task to the extent that she got cramps in her arms from her almost constant writing of the manuscript in longhand. Watt recalls that his father erected a metal bar outside the house so that she could walk around outside and stretch her arms. (90)

According to Clayton, the work was typed by one of Watt's nephews, Joe Blanton, and later the longhand version was divided among the children as a keepsake.

The title of *Interwoven* defines the author's purpose: to trace the interweaving of the Reynolds and Matthews families in the course of telling her own life story. The book is, in effect, a written version of a family saga, particularly in its early chapters, which are based on family traditions. In her preface she explains that the book was written for her children and grandchildren (xiii-xiv), and her tone suggests a sharing of family stories rather than a polished literary construction. Here and there people are mentioned in passing simply because they were encountered at some time, but this is not a serious fault. Like a grandmother sitting on a porch or at a kitchen table, she tells how the family came to Texas and how they struggled and prospered. They prospered in more than material ways: The Reynolds and Matthews families valued education and they contributed a great deal to the enlightened milieu of Albany, the county seat of Shackelford County and the most important town in the area, thanks to its position as terminus of the Texas Central Railroad.

The story begins before her birth in 1861. She has no reliable knowledge of the origins of the Reynolds family, she says: They may have had noble origins, as authors like to claim, but she has no knowledge of that. The story begins with her parents, and their background is typical of the southern frontier: Her father, Barber Watkins Reynolds, was English and Welsh and came from Oglethorpe County, Georgia, "the son of Benjamin Franklin Reynolds and Sallie Barber" (1). Her mother, Anne Marie Campbell, was, in her own statement, "rocked in the iron cradle of Presbyterianism." The migratory habits of southerners brought their families to Alabama, where Sallie Reynolds's parents were married in 1841. And six years later, they moved to Texas. There would be many moves in Texas (and one to Colorado) before the family settled on the Clear Fork for good. After twelve years of farming in East Texas, they realized that "there was nothing edifying or elevating on an East Texas farm" (William Owens might have agreed) and they found their way to West Texas. Their wanderings took them to Golconda in Palo Pinto County, then to what would become Stephens County, where Sallie, the last of seven surviving children, was born on May 23, 1861, about a month after

Fort Sumter and the start of the Civil War. The county had been organized at a meeting in the Reynolds home on the land they bought, the Cantrell Ranch. They were clearly the sort of people who became leading citizens wherever they went. The Reynolds story is not a family saga of hard luck, as many are (the Owens and Humphrey families, for example) but a tale of prosperous ranches and successful trail drives.

In Stephens County, the Reynolds family had neighbors, the Matthews family, whose lives would be intertwined with their own. With a southern care for kinship, Reynolds notes that the father of the family was from Alabama and "knew my mother's people there" (10). The two families eventually settled a little west of Stephens County, in the Clear Fork area, and the number of unions was remarkable. When Matthews describes the wedding of her youngest brother, Phineas, to Roseannah Matthews in 1883, she seems astonished: "This was an unusual union of two families: two pairs of sisters, first cousins to each other, married to my four brothers, and I married to the only brother of one pair of sisters" (155). Two more alliances—the proper term, perhaps—would come. The reader is provided with a list of the various marriages in the back of the book, but a genealogical tree would also be useful for keeping the interrelationships clear.

The weddings give her a chance to discuss the "*infare,*" a form of wedding reception well adapted to the vast spaces of West Texas. The custom was for the groom's family to hold the infare and with the marriage of her brother George to Betty Matthews (daughter of Joseph Beck Matthews and sister of Sallie's future husband John) in 1867, the groom's mother did not attend, which seems very odd today: She was busy for three days with preparations. The whole wedding party rode in by twos, accompanied by three fiddlers. Two other infares were held in 1879, for the marriages of her brother William to Susan Matthews, a sister of John Alexander Matthews, and for her brother Benjamin to Florence Matthews, a cousin of John's. The wedding for William and Susan was held at the ranch of Joseph Beck Matthews on January 1, and the infare was given by Sallie's brother George the next day. A Texas norther came up on

January 2 and the guests had to ride into it for the eighteen-mile journey.

She deals with more public celebrations as well. One of the oddities of Matthews's time was the staging of pseudo-medieval tournaments, which doubtless reflected a nineteenth-century desire for refinement. Matthews describes one which was held in Albany on the Fourth of July, 1876, the centennial of the Declaration of Independence. Mounted cowboys with spears would follow a course of poles which had rings hanging from them. The object was to take the rings off. Matthews says that she "enjoyed this immensely" (117) and could imagine a "spreading canopy with royalty seated beneath it watching the jousts of their knights. . . (117). These events were held in Bosque County during John Lomax's childhood, and J. Frank Dobie and his brother, Elrich, created their own tournament field on the family ranch in the Brush Country.

The two characters most clearly defined in *Interwoven* are her mother and George, Sallie's oldest brother. The mother had real independence of mind. She was a Presbyterian but most of her spiritual sustenance in the early days, the time of Indian warfare, was provided by courageous Methodist and Baptist preachers. In more secure times, a synod of the Presbyterian Church was held in Albany, where she was living. At the synod she was asked to tell about the early days. She praised a hard-shell Baptist preacher named Clarke who came monthly on foot, as well as the Methodist circuit riders, and then stated: "there were no Presbyterians who came in those early days; I do not know if they were afraid of Indians or did not think there were enough of us to be worth coming after" (173).

George Reynolds left no autobiography, but he was a remarkable man and his sister's admiration for his courage and industry is clear. Indeed, she has more to say about his life than her own husband's. George rode for the Pony Express through Comanche territory when he was fifteen, fought in the Civil War and was wounded, and led his first cattle drive when he was nineteen. Right after the Civil War, he shot a white buffalo and sent the hide to the Smithsonian, a gesture typical of the Reynolds and Matthews families: Don't hang the trophy on the wall, send it to the national museum. When he eventually visited Washington, he was disappointed to find that there was no record of his gift. In 1867, he was wounded while pursuing a Comanche party. Many years later he had a dramatic operation in Kansas City to remove the arrowhead. He was the first ranchman to drive a herd to New Mexico, and he made other drives to "Wyoming, Utah, Nevada, Montana, Nebraska, the Dakotas, and Canada," as Frances Mayhugh Holden points out in her article on him in *The Handbook of Texas Online.*[3] He also seems to have been a member of the Tin Hat Vigilantes of Fort Griffin, an affiliation that his adoring little sister does not describe. And he helped found the famous Bloys Camp Meeting in the Davis Mountains, which still attracts 3,000 visitors every summer.

Along with the narrative of the Reynolds and Matthews marriages, the narrator tells her own story, though it is more a narrative of events and customs than a history of her mind and emotions. Some of the best scenes present life in Fort Davis, not the site in the Trans-Pecos region but a defensive expedient on Clear Fork of the Brazos River where families clustered together in a fort of their own making during the Civil War. In 1861, the U.S. Army had to abandon its forts in the area, like Fort Phantom Hill and Camp Cooper, where Robert E. Lee had served as commander for some nineteen months in 1856-1857. The vulnerable settlers built their own crude shelter. Some of Sallie Matthews's most interesting childhood memories (very early ones) come from that period, along with terrifying scenes of Indian raids. The settlers were thrown on their own resources. They were accustomed to making their own lye soap and candles, activities she describes, and her sister Susan made hair nets from the hairs of horses' tails.

By 1866, it was safe to leave the fort, and Sallie's family moved about five miles to the Stone Ranch, a house which had been built in 1856, by a Captain Newton Given when he was stationed at Camp Cooper. Given actually kept a pack of fine hounds while he was stationed at the camp. The Stone Ranch is now part of the Lambshead empire and has been carefully restored by Sallie's son,

Watt. In 1867, the U.S. Army returned to found Fort Griffin on a hill overlooking the Clear Fork, and, bitterness over the Civil War notwithstanding, the settlers were happy to see them.

Ranching was the family's occupation, and the trail drives are described so vividly in the book that a reader almost feels that Matthews herself took part. Her sister-in-law Betty did in fact go on a drive to California with her husband George Reynolds because they were planning to live there. The wife drove their sleeping quarters, a Civil War ambulance converted for the purpose. They lost six horses to an Indian raid and later made haste when George, who took a telescope on the journey, spotted a party of about 150 Indians. Betty implored her husband to shoot her if there was any danger of being captured: This was an age when a number of women and children were taken captive, especially by the Comanches. Matthews has an especially strong account of a trail drive in 1892 when the Reynolds Cattle Company had to take herds through a blizzard in Colorado. Her emphasis is generally on the struggles of trail drives, not on the sort of glamour and adventure which Larry McMurtry's ranching relatives regretted being born too late to take part in. The Matthews family philosophy of ranching has always been to turn grass into beef cattle at a profit.[3]

One serious lack in frontier life was education for the children, which tended to be irregular. The first school Matthews attended was held in the commissary of the new Fort Griffin in 1867. It was taught free of charge by a quartermaster sergeant. But after two sessions, he deserted his post and took $25,000 in army funds with him. He sent back, she tells us, a cheeky message saying, "A swift team, a good buggy with wheels well greased; catch me if you can" (51). In 1869, the Reynolds family moved to Weatherford, in Parker County near Fort Worth, to seek reliable schools. This meant a return to farming, which they found as uncongenial in West Texas as they had in East Texas. Their next move was to Colorado in 1872, where settlement was beginning. Once again they would find farming too much labor of a kind they disliked. Sallie found herself an outsider for the first time, learning that

Texans were likely to be sneered at: ". . .Texas had a hard name, especially the Western part of the state, being the refuge for criminals from all parts of the country, although some of the best blood of both North and South was represented in the founders of Texas." Colorado proved too cold and irrigation was too onerous for people adapted to the aridity of West Texas, and in 1875, the Reynolds family returned to the Clear Fork. They would not leave ranching life again.

A community had grown around Fort Griffin. It had a short life, fading away after the army left in 1881 almost simultaneously with the arrival of the railroad at Albany, the county seat. Downhill from the army post was the "Flat," the area where civilians lived. Matthews clearly liked the social life in the community, which was the center for the buffalo hunters who would end the Indian wars by taking away the animals on which the Comanche depended. She does not agree with the general opinion that the hunters were "scum of the earth." Many of them seemed quite decent to her, which shows a true independence of mind in a Victorian lady.

Some residents of Fort Griffin were in fact the scum of the earth. The town has been described in many books and films. In *Lambshead Before Interwoven,* Holden lists some of the characters who lived, died, or passed through: Bat Masterson, Hurricane Bill and his paramour, Hurricane Minnie, Pat Garrett, Doc Holliday, and Wyatt Earp (102-03). Sallie Reynolds Matthews rather surprisingly liked Lottie Deno, the poker queen, one of the most interesting characters to pass through Texas. Her knowledge of Deno in *Interwoven* is fairly limited: She says that Lottie was a woman gambler, that she was red-haired, intelligent, capable of holding a "masque ball," and not given to vice. One night Deno disappeared, leaving a well-furnished cabin and a note asking that her outfit be sold to help someone unfortunate (110). A poker queen with a heart of gold, it seems.

It is curious to realize that a well-bred young Presbyterian woman of sixteen could view a professional gambler as an admirable person. What Sallie seems never to have known is just how bizarre the career of Lottie Deno was. Cynthia Rose has summed up Deno's life in *The Handbook of Texas Online.*[4] Carlotta J. Tomkins (1844-1924) was born in Kentucky. Known in Fort Concho as Mystic Maud, she acquired her later nickname when a card player said "she should call herself Lotta Dinero." After parting with a lover named Johnny Golden, she had a Frank Thurmond as her companion. Golden, who had proved difficult, showed up in Fort Griffin and was murdered almost immediately, probably by Thurmond, a situation which seems to have been unknown to Matthews. She was, Rose says, the model for Faro Nell in Alfred Henry Lewis's Wolfville books, and in film she was the prototype for Laura Denbo in *Gunfight at the OK Corral.* She inspired, if that is the word, Miss Kitty of *Gunsmoke* on radio and television. It is rather droll that the generally prim Sallie Matthews admired this extraordinary character.

One of the startling omissions of *Interwoven* is the failure to discuss the vigilance committee in any detail. Members of the Reynolds and Matthews families were probably part of it. The Fort Griffin Vigilance Committee gets two brief mentions, one quite favorable: "The best citizens decided it was time to do something so they banded themselves together to protect life and property. The times called for drastic measures and they were used to put down lawlessness of all kinds. The vigilantes were on the alert and law and order were at last brought about" (111). The passive voice is interesting: Law and order were at last "brought about" by "drastic measures." Holden's *Lambshead Before Interwoven* cites Aunt Hank Smith, who kept a boardinghouse. Aunt Hank knew what was brought about, for the boarders would sometimes tell her at breakfast that another man was hanging from a tree. The other vigilante reference in *Interwoven* is to the story of an innocent man who was almost hanged by the vigilantes for murder but was released because the evidence was too slight. The implication is that some form of due process was observed.

The reticence of Sallie Matthews was understandable, for she would not want to discuss John Larn (1849-78), a relative by marriage who is absent from this text, the one in-law she would not want to interweave in her story of happy unions. Larn married

Mary Jane Matthews, a sister of Sallie's husband John. She is mentioned briefly in the text upon her second marriage, to a minister named John Brown. But she was married first to Larn, whose life and demise have been narrated by many, including A. C. Greene in *A Personal Country*, and Frances Mayhugh Holden in *Lambshead Before Interwoven.*

Larn was a vigilante himself and the second sheriff of Shackelford County. It appears that he was also a rustler who found the post of sheriff a convenient cover. Frances Mayhugh Holden, who had access to family papers and traditions, says that Sallie's husband John was strongly opposed to his sister Mary's union with such a dubious character and called him "the meanest man I ever knew" (157). When Larn was finally lynched in the Albany jail by a gang of masked men, it was likely that the ringleader was one of Sallie's brothers and other members of the Matthews or Reynolds families probably took part. Mary Larn was in a nearby boardinghouse with Tom, their son, and heard the shot that killed her husband. She persuaded her second husband to spend much of his time trying to clear Larn's name: He even wrote a book on the subject.

A. C. Greene did extensive research on Larn's death for his memoirs *A Personal Country.* He told me in a letter of October 21, 2000, that his chief source in retelling the Larn story was Robert Nail (1908-1968), founder of the Fort Griffin Fandangle, "who knew more about the old families than anyone, including members of those families." Indeed, Greene says that Nail wrote an unpublished play about the lynching, *Black is the Color.* Greene talked to the members of the Matthews and Reynolds families, and he says "all they know is family tradition and hearsay. None of them doubt that Larn's brother-in-law was among the '13 men in yellow raincoats' who broke into the jail and lynched John Larn."

Naturally Sallie Reynolds Matthews would not wish to discuss the Larn story. Her stance is to present the Reynolds and Matthews families in an idealized way, a joint dynasty without conflict. She concedes in her foreword that "there were some tragic and harrowing experiences that were left out. This family has not been exempt from trial and tribulations" (xiv). Sentimentality is probably inevitable when an elderly woman born in Victorian times recalls the past for her grandchildren. The crushingly frank family revelations of Mary Karr and William Humphrey required a different social and literary milieu.

While vigilantes were an awkward subject, she was happy to discuss camp meetings. Matthews and her family attended some of the traditional "green brush arbor" meetings in her area. "Several families would pitch their tents together, and cook and eat together. This was one big picnic to the children and was thoroughly enjoyed. We took pleasure in it all, especially the shouting and singing" (68). She does not dwell on the emotionalism which is associated with camp meetings but rather stresses the timetable of sunrise prayer meetings: "Service at nine and eleven o'clock in the morning, at three in the afternoon, vespers at sundown and services at early candle-light were calculated to keep people rather well employed." Her real enthusiasm is for the Bloys Camp Meeting, also known as the Cowboy Camp Meeting, held every year in the Davis Mountains of the Trans-Pecos region.[5] It was set up on land provided by brother George. This meeting, run by a Presbyterian minister, William Benjamin Bloys, known as "the Sky Pilot," was—she seems eager to mention—a decorous affair. It seems to have been very different from the Methodist and Baptist camp meetings described by John A. Lomax and William Owens.

An obvious limitation of the work is the genteel tone. She can describe camp meetings and infares freely, but her emotional life is as sketchy as the accounts of vigilantes. She narrates her courtship by John A. Matthews in 1876 (she was fifteen, he was twenty-three) in one vague paragraph, then devotes pages to the description of her wedding dress and trousseau (118-121), which were cut to patterns out of *Harper's Bazaar.* In fact, her husband never comes into focus in the book. She tells one interesting anecdote about him: When he ran for county judge he told people his object was to lose his childhood nickname, Bud. She makes it clear that he was a very quiet individual, a true Marlboro Man. Her narrative of the marriage has some vivid scenes about events, but they are never intimate revelations of feeling. Matthews is extremely reticent about the birth of her children, whose arrivals are simply announced. Hallie Stillwell, the subject of the fourth chapter, discusses her forty-eight-hour labor with her second child, the sort of detail that Matthews would never have revealed in a book. Matthews speaks in one paragraph about the death of a daughter from typhoid fever, explaining the depth of her grief but ending her brief description of the event with a conventional reflection: First losses are the hardest to bear because "we are given more fortitude as we grow older" (151). She is much more forthcoming about her mother and her siblings.

She does describe the physical circumstances of her early married life at a ranch established by the Reynolds brothers and Matthews partnership in nearby Haskell County, the only ranch in an underpopulated area. Living under similar conditions early in her marriage, Stillwell gives a more revealing account of the painful adjustments required of a young wife with a new husband living among cowboys in a difficult country, especially when the husband is silent and impatient.

But there are surprising aspects of Matthews's personality. Her racial attitudes are surprising in a woman who was born at the beginning of the Civil War and grew up on the frontier. Her family had a few slaves—she assures us that there were never many—and several remained in the Reynolds household after the Civil War. She says little about them, mentioning a servant and former slave named Aunt Amelia a couple of times and citing her mother's traditional southern view that slaves liked their masters. According to *The Texas Almanac*, the present black population of Throckmorton County is zero; the figure for Shackelford County is twelve.[6] But she praises the resourceful Britt Johnson, a black man whose family was among a group of captives taken in the Elm Creek Indian raid of 1864. She was too young to remember the immediate impact of this raid in Young County, which was a little northeast of her home region, but she talked to survivors. Johnson is said by some to have spent two years tracking the captives and living among the Comanches in order to negotiate their release. She praises him generously, after suggesting that he had some aid from the government: "But their ultimate return, after two long years in Indian camps, was due to the faithful, courageous persistence of this untutored negro who was not willing to give up his wife and children without a desperate struggle" (49). In an article about the Elm Creek Raid, Kenneth F. Neighbors[7] says that Johnson's exploits have been doubted by some, but as far as Matthews is concerned, he was a hero.

Fort Griffin had a detachment of the now-celebrated Buffalo Soldiers, members of the 10th Regiment, a unit of black enlisted men with white officers. She has no comment on the race of the soldiers, although A. C. Greene in *A Personal Country* suggests that they were resented by the locals (169). She describes without moral evaluation the shooting of a soldier by his commanding officer, a Colonel Lincoln. The soldier, apparently drunk, shoved the officer off the sidewalk, whereupon the officer shot him dead. "It was probably a mere accident but I suppose his pushing an officer was an act of insubordination and very rude, and no Army officer could let a thing like that pass" (115). Lincoln was acquitted by the civilian court in Shackelford and then by a court-martial, and her father-in-law, Joseph Beck Matthews, testified for him. It would be pleasant to think that she was trying to damn Lincoln in his own words when she quotes his explanation for killing the man: "It was the only dignified course to pursue" (115), but there seems to be no irony intended.

Most surprising is her frequently expressed sympathy for the Native Americans. Mary Maverick's memoirs have a different atmosphere: She speaks of "vile Indians" and areas "infested with Indians." Matthews spent much of her childhood in terror of Comanche raids—Indian raiding parties took livestock from her family's ranch—and she knew people who had been killed or abducted. The twelve-year-old son of one of the neighbors was attacked by Indians and scalped alive. The unfortunate but responsible child ran home taking his hat and calf whip. He died a few days later. One of her brothers, Glenn, became sheriff of Gila, Arizona, and was murdered by three Indian prisoners, including the notorious Apache Kid, whom she calls "a fiend incarnate" (177). Her anger at the Apache Kid did not lead her to bigotry. Her favorite brother, George, was, as described earlier, gravely wounded in the stomach by an arrow during an Indian attack in 1867 and nearly died. He had to be taken home on a support of packs placed between two horses, and characteristically insisted on getting on his horse so that the family would see him riding home, not being carried. The arrowhead remained in his body until 1882, when the point had worked its way to his back and bulged under the skin. He went to Kansas City to have it removed. In one of her best scenes, she describes the operation (held without anesthetic) using as her source an account from the *Kansas City Journal.* The celebrated rancher, Shanghai Pierce, was witness to the operation and had to warn the surgeon that he was cutting too deep. The surgeon stopped, and when Reynolds sat up, the arrowhead slipped out. But after describing the operation, she remembers with some shame the souvenirs from the battle, including Indian scalps.

She follows the description of George's ordeal with a three-page discussion of the wrongs done to Indians. The early memoirist, Mary Maverick, who witnessed a harrowing battle between Comanches and the people of San Antonio, was concerned with wrongs done to settlers and thought that Indian prisoners were treated with a humanity they failed to show to their captives: She was an eyewitness to marks of torture and mutilation on bodies of women and girls who had been held prisoner. Matthews claims not to be another Helen Hunt Jackson (the pro-Indian author of *A Century of Dishonor,* 1881) but she persists in taking the Indian point of view and was particularly repelled by the Sand Creek massacre of the Cheyenne by Colonel John Chivington and his troops in 1863, one of the worst atrocities of the long struggle between whites and Native Americans. Her fair-minded approach to the Indian question is remarkable for a person of her time and place.

Her one bit of minor bigotry came when she was a child, but it was not directed at blacks or Indians. Her sister Susan had married Samuel Newcomb, who was born in Connecticut. He died of measles in 1870. A former Union soldier, Nathan Bartholomew, another man from Connecticut, moved into the area after the Civil War, and Susan married him in 1871. Sallie, who was ten at the time, says she was "a hot little rebel" and asked her sister how she could marry a Yankee who had fought against her own brother. Naturally Susan was amused at this effrontery (87). It was not a time and place where a former Yankee soldier would find welcome, and bitter former Confederates were not friendly when he settled in the village of Picketsville, but the Reynolds family took him in (63).

The families of *Interwoven* seemed to possess strong minds, along with a willingness to experiment with new ideas and a desire to build important enterprises. Sallie's father-in-law, Joseph Beck Matthews, introduced barbed wire to the Clear Fork region. Both families, realizing that the open range would come to an end, bought grazing land. Many other western ranchers resisted change and failed. Her brother George, the highly successful rancher, also served as president of the Albany bank. Her own husband was a major force in the eradication of tick fever in cattle between 1915 and 1917: He built dipping vats and made them available to the whole community. He also introduced the grubbing of prickly pears and the digging up of mesquite trees in the area. And while he built an enormous ranch around the Lambshead core which he leased in 1886 and bought in 1909, he also founded an insurance business in Albany, where the family lived much of the time after 1884. Sallie died there in 1938. The two clans held so many offices that Sallie says their dominant position in the community aroused criticism. The two families founded the Reynolds Memorial Presbyterian Church and the Reynolds Academy. The academy offered an excellent education through the college level but a factor in its failure was the tendency of the families to send their children to even better schools. Sallie Matthews chose Princeton for her son Watt. This example led others to go to the same university, so that Princeton graduates were and still are abundant in Albany, a town of a few thousand.

In *Wolf Willow,* his memoir of the late frontier in Eastend, Saskatchewan, Wallace Stegner complains that frontiers suffer from "deculturation," a kind of recrudescence: The arts and learning are stripped away in the struggle to live.[8] But several Texas memoirs reveal a countermovement: to establish schools and churches, to learn music. The Reynolds family made several moves in order to find schools for their children, and Sallie describes the gift of an organ from her father as "one of most wonderful surprises of my life" (100). It now resides in the restored Stone House on the Lambshead Ranch. After she and her husband began living in Albany, they imported a music teacher to teach stringed instruments to the local children. William A. Owens tells how his desperately poor mother traded livestock for a piano, and Gertrude Beasley describes her equally impoverished family's acquisition of an organ. Sallie Reynolds joined the Chautauqua Literary and Scientific Circle in Albany and even tried painting. Recrudescence was sometimes followed by regeneration.

Albany, a town of 1,962, is an unusual center of culture. It has an outstanding art museum, The Old Jail Art Center, placed in a historic building that Robert Nail purchased in 1940 for twenty-five dollars to save from demolition. According to the Albany web site,[9] Reilly Nail, a nephew of Robert, inherited the building and the museum was assembled from work collected by him, his cousin, Bill Bomar, and their mothers. Clearly Albany has an outstanding interest in culture. The museum has paintings by Picasso, Klee, Modigliani, and John Marin, sculptures by Henry Moore, western and southwestern paintings, pre-Columbian art, Chinese terra cotta sculptures—and a Sallie Reynolds Matthews Room established by Watt Matthews and furnished with items from Lambshead. Deculturation in Albany, if it happened at all, was brief. In her foreword to *Interwoven,* Matthews celebrates the developments of technology in the "Machine Age," mentioning radio, incandescent light, the "high-powered motor car and the passenger plane," and the movement from the "open hearth to the electric range."

Matthews and her relatives liked traveling and learning about the contemporary world. She says at one point that "seeing new places and mixing with new people is an asset" (87). The families sent parties to the 1885 Cotton Exposition in New Orleans and to the Columbian Exposition in 1893. The women would attend cultural sites while the men explored markets and made business connections. Both of these large families built ranches and businesses, but one interest in her book is another kind of history, a movement toward creating a civilized society.

Such a society preserves its past. In 1937, Albany began to hold a pageant every June (with a break from 1942-1947 because of World War II), The Fort Griffin Fandangle. The script by Robert Nail, one of those Princeton graduates, has a cast of a hundred or more and involves almost everyone in town. Indeed, one of his works on the pageant is entitled *The Fandangle: A People's Theater.*[10] The script was based on *Interwoven* and much of the music was provided by a local music teacher, Alice Reynolds, an offshoot of the family. From 1965 the performances were held on land leased from Watt Matthews, who used to lead the Fandangle Parade with a group of friends, Princeton graduates. The amphitheater for the performances was built on thirty acres of the Gourd Ranch, one of the Lambshead properties. He also furnished Longhorn cattle for the productions. The Butterfield stage line went through the Lambshead Ranch, though Sallie Matthews mentions it only once in passing (61), and the Fandangle has a replica of a coach, built by G. P. Crutchfield. Crutchfield, a local craftsman, also built a model of a Texas Central train to commemorate a more important transportation link in the area.

The Fandangle adds prestige to *Interwoven,* and the book adds authenticity to the Fandangle. The long life of Watt Matthews, who became a famous Texan for his work in historical and natural preservation, made Lambshead almost as famous as the King Ranch. Matthews died with his boots on, as commentators were quick to notice: He was not thrown by a horse, but his Bronco overturned on a gravel road when he was ninety-eight. Certainly *Interwoven* would have remained a Texas classic without the Fandangle and the high esteem for Watt Matthews and his good works in Texas. But the book is the core of a cultural tradition, one with a family proprietorship. Watt Matthews was the subject of two biographical works in his own lifetime, Laura Wilson's heavily illustrated *Watt Matthews of Lambshead*[11] and Lawrence Clayton's *Watkins Reynolds Matthews: a Biography,* both of which provide useful background for understanding the world of *Interwoven.*

No one in the family has written anything like *Interwoven,* although Carl Hertzog published a brief memoir by Ethel Matthews Casey,[12] Sallie's daughter. She does have an interesting comment on race when she discusses the chuck wagon at the ranch. The cook, Charlie Standifer was a family favorite. "For years he and Pete King from the Reynolds ranch were the only negroes in Throckmorton County. Being a minority, they did not enjoy going to Throckmorton town with herds. Charlie, who had worked with Mexican sheep-herders and knew a little Spanish, would pretend he knew no English—'no savvy' he would say if any strangers spoke to him." The ranch diary of Ethel's brother Watt was published in 1997 as *Lambshead Legacy.*[13] The book covers the years 1951-1980 and is superbly produced, with thorough annotations by Janet M. Neugebauer and a long introduction by Frances Mayhugh Holden which tells anyone who is interested what Watt Matthews had for breakfast every day and what was in his wardrobe. The diary itself has value as a document in the history of ranching but cannot be classified as an autobiography. According to the preface by Neugebauer, Watt Matthews felt that it was "dull as dishwater" (xi). That is too severe a judgment, though most of the entries read like this one from August, 1967:

> Thur 31: 72–78 Norther blew in before 5. A.M. which is a reminder that it is not long before the chilly winds will be blowing & unless we go to getting rain we are going to get caught in hard shape. (169)

Fortunately, his mother's book recorded her times more vividly if less circumstantially, sparing us the weather reports but recounting interesting events. Her reticence about John Larn is understandable. While the book was written for her grandchildren, it has abundant interest for anyone who would like to know how an intelligent woman with surprisingly progressive views saw the movement of history in an area where the development from frontier to civilization was so telescoped. The Matthews and Reynolds families demonstrate that building a civilized society simply requires civilized people. Larry McMurtry, as chapter ten will demonstrate, records an interesting variation on the process. He is a third-generation West Texan who has decided to herd books—a million of them is his goal—instead of cattle. Another West Texan discussed in this study, Gertrude Beasley, came from a family who appear to have cherished their barbarism. Her struggle out of the recrudescent situation was a courageous and tragic one. Sallie Reynolds Matthews presents herself as a fortunate person, a woman who could look back to a pioneer past and forward to a technological future.

John A. Lomax

J. Frank Dobie

2

GATHERING TRADITIONS: JOHN A. LOMAX AND J. FRANK DOBIE

To have gathered from the air a live tradition
or from a fine old eye the unconquered flame
This is not vanity.
Ezra Pound, Canto LXXXI

John A. Lomax (1867-1948) and J. Frank Dobie (1888-1964) were the best-known folklorists to come out of Texas, and both left highly readable accounts of their lives and vocations, though Lomax's *Adventures of a Ballad Hunter* (1947) is uneven and Dobie never got beyond writing the essays which his wife collected as *Some Part of Myself.* Lomax was the most famous song collector the United States has produced. Dobie's activities as a columnist and broadcaster made him a celebrity as well: He was eventually known as "Mr. Texas," the sort of title which inspires iconoclasm, and wielders of wrecking balls have appeared, notably Larry McMurtry. The books are interesting for the rural ways they describe as well as for their accounts of the authors' collecting activities.

Lomax proudly says in the preface to his 1947 *Adventures of a Ballad Hunter* that his book is the first account of the actual work of collecting songs. He is opening new ground, and as a farmer's son he uses the metaphor precisely: "In Texas we call land, grubbed of stumps, freshly broken and cultivated for the first time, 'new ground'" (x). In fact, the preface is built on farming metaphors. He recalls planting seeds when he was six years old on a farm north of Meridian, Texas, in Bosque County, northwest of Waco. Rather appropriately for his later work, he says he chanted a rhyme as he dropped seeds behind a plow drawn by mules: "One for the blackbird, one for the crow, / One for the cutworm, and two to grow." He would spend much of his adult life collecting rhymes, most of them songs of cowboys, blacks, and the poor whites of his own origins. He uses the seed planting image as an adroit apology for any deficiencies in his activities: Farming is notoriously subject to chance and weather. A half million miles (by his estimate) of travel pursuing songs rescued some extraordinary works from oblivion. Some of his informants, whose lives were poor and perilous, did not live much longer.

The autobiographies of several Texas writers are variations on the American dream. Lomax and Owens had careers resembling Horatio Alger stories in which the poor boy is raised up not by a kindly millionaire but by education, and they had to struggle for it. Lomax was born in Goodman, Mississippi, in 1867 among the "upper crust of the 'po' white trash,' traditionally held in contempt by the aristocracy of the Old South and by their Negro slaves" (1). The family came to Texas in 1869: Leaving the Old South for Texas was a common pattern after the Civil War. The father bought bottom land in Bosque County which was hard to clear, in preference to richer black land in Hill and Navarro counties because he was familiar with bottom land in Mississippi. Lomax grew up in a two-room house but does not complain much, except to say that "Life in Bosque was hard—both in work and play" (13). Much of Lomax's childhood was spent outdoors, hunting, fishing, and swimming as well as planting seeds behind a plow. He loved his horse, Selim; he had a number of friends his age, and at nine he formed a close friendship with a black man of eighteen, Nat Blythe. He presents something close to an idyll, the kind of nostalgic view of the past which Dobie feared writing, as we shall see.

James McNutt's very informative dissertation on Lomax, Dobie, and Boatright has an interesting discussion of Bosque County, which he observes was geographically complex, bounded by the Brazos River on the east, divided down the middle by the Bosque River, with limestone hills in the western part, the last outcrops of the Balcones Escarpment.[1] The recent arrivals in the country, like the Lomax family, settled in the limestone hills region, which looked toward cattle country. A branch of the Chisholm Trail ran by the Lomax family farmhouse. The county was a mixture of ex-slaves, ex-plantation owners, independent farmers (mostly new arrivals from the Old South), and Norwegian immigrants. This human diversity offered a pluralistic culture for the future folklorist to absorb. The society was, like the rest of Texas, under a white southern Protestant hegemony and McNutt says the social boundaries eventually grew very rigid. Lomax suppresses one of his most painful childhood memories, one which involved the abuses of the southern power structure. McNutt reports that Lomax witnessed a lynching when he was a boy. He dealt with it in two compositions at Harvard but never wrote about it again. McNutt observes that instead of memories of racial violence we are given an idealized portrait of his relationship with Nat Blythe (30).

The idyll of life in Bosque includes delightful pictures of two social institutions, the camp meeting and the tournament, which are described in far more detail than the similar events in

Matthews's *Interwoven.* The camp meetings in Lomax's area were held by the Methodists in a permanent site, a brush arbor on Spring Creek three miles from his home. The setting was typical of Texas at the time: The permanent improvements for a place of worship consisted of forked posts set into the ground with connecting crisscross poles over the top, on which each year were spread freshly cut branches. The seats devised were puncheons (split logs resting on long pegs) or planks laid across logs. A dry-goods box often served as a pulpit, surrounded by mourners' benches where the penitents came at the urging of the preacher to be prayed and sung over as their friends whispered words of instruction and advice (5). The meetings usually involved three regular services a day and "grove meetings," separate song-and-prayer services for men and women. Sometimes there would be "experience" meetings "where each person told publicly how the Lord had helped him amid the trials and tribulations of frontier life." He mentions Uncle Ben Cooper getting "happy" and shouting: "Whoopee! Hurrah for Jesus! Bully for Christ!! Whoopee!" No one found this exhibition shocking.

The meetings had drama arising from the efforts of those present to soften the hearts of sinners and induce them to repent. Lomax describes what it was like to be the target of such unrelenting love, the same kind of admonishing which some years later would affront Gertrude Beasley in Abilene and provoke her to repeat slanderous gossip about Mathilde Paxton, the woman who tried to convert her. Lomax takes a comic point of view and describes one meeting he witnessed in which a stricken sinner gave endless testimony that he never told a lie, never swore an oath, never cut a barbed-wire fence and never stole his neighbor's wife, and his assertions were always supported by the claim that the highly regarded Thompson brothers, Joe and Bill, could testify to them. When Lomax was thirteen, he was pressured into converting at a camp meeting to please his mother, who was praying fervently for him. He makes it clear that he never really felt saved, merely self-conscious.

The tournament scene evokes Mark Twain's assertion that Sir

Walter Scott ruined the South, although there was clearly a tongue-in-cheek approach to this bit of medievalizing. Sallie Reynolds Matthews witnessed one as part of a Fourth of July ceremony, as we have seen. The scene itself was apparently embellished: McNutt reports that Lomax wrote to one of the participants, Ed Nichols, and expressed the hope that he would not mind the embellishments in the story (33). Such events were odd attempts by horsemen—cowboys in this case—to imitate the courtly customs of the Middle Ages. J. Frank Dobie published an article on the tournament phenomenon.[2] Every-one pronounced the word "toonament," Lomax says. He describes it, using far more detail than Sallie Reynolds Matthews:

> The six-foot lances, carried by the riders at top speed, were not pointed at an enemy, but at five small rings hanging from the arms of upright posts strung fifty yards apart along a track two hundred yards in length. Each "knight" rode down the track three times, and a perfect score meant that the rider must thread on his lance all fifteen rings, and take no more than twelve seconds for each ride. The prizes were three wreaths of prairie flowers which would be worn proudly by the chosen ladies. (15)

There was a master of ceremonies, a Queen of the Jousts, and ladies-in-waiting. The men wore sashes with rosettes and had feather plumes in their hats. Each knight had a title, like the "Knight of the Silver Cross," the "Knight of the Lone Star," the "Knight of Double Mountain," and, most amusingly, the "Knight of the Slim Chance," one Bob Hanna. The Knight of the Silver Cross made a perfect score in his first pass and declared, "Oh, you Knight of the Slim Chance, you ain't got no chance against me!" But Bob Hanna did indeed win the tournament.

The stories and songs of cowboys like Bob Hanna and Ed Nichols shaped Lomax's destiny. Lomax helps account for his song-collecting vocation by describing an important moment when he was four. He was sleeping on his trundle bed by an open window within earshot of that branch of the Chisholm Trail when he was awakened by a cowboy singing "O, slow up, dogies" on "a night of deep darkness and sifting rain" (19). He says that he began to write down cowboy songs even when he was a little boy. His love of reading was nourished by a copy of Eugene Sue's virtually forgotten novel, *The Wandering Jew.*

The story of Lomax's struggles to earn his tuition for a year at Granbury College is like a folktale itself, and he tells the story in a dramatic fashion. His father believed that all the sons should have a year in college "to complete his twenty-one years of service to the family." Lomax so far had not spent a full year in any school, not an unusual situation in a farm family: Gertrude Beasley and William Owens had a spotty education in their early years. James McNutt observes that the hardships of rural life led many to aspire to escape poverty and achieve social status through education, an escape into what Burton Bledstein has called "the culture of professionalism."[3] One of the most accessible professions was teaching, the path Lomax and Owens took. In 1887, at almost twenty, young Lomax was given eleven acres to plant with wheat to pay his tuition, which he arranged to pay in flour. When the grain was ready for harvest, torrential rains and an overflowing Bosque River covered much of his crop. The wheat was eventually threshed but came out of the threshing machine mixed with mud. He tells how he struggled with his brother to carry the wheat to the mill: At twenty miles from home the rains began again and the Bosque River, overflowing again, threatened to drown the brothers and their mules. The round-trip distance was only eighty miles, but it required two weeks to get the job done. He had another journey of thirty miles to the college in Granbury (southwest of Fort Worth) with the flour. And he still had to make up the shortfall in his crop by selling his beloved pony, Selim. He does not mention that he also got loans from his father and a cousin: The narrative would not be as touching, nor would it have its own folktale character. At the end of his "Boyhood in Bosque" chapter, he tells the reader that the county would always be a part of him "for, hidden at the bottom of my trunk, I carried in secret, tied up with a cotton string, a small roll of cowboy songs" (23). The fate of those songs make an interesting twist in the tale.

The "College" chapter gives a fine view of what education was like in Texas in the late nineteenth century: "scant equipment, bare library shelves," and poorly qualified teachers. After Lomax's year in college he taught at a primitive public school in Bosque County, and then, in spite of his own poor preparation, taught in the preparatory department at Weatherford College for six years. Like William Owens a generation later, he brings out the pathos of a good mind piecing together an education as time and money permitted: He spent a summer at Eastman Business College in Poughkeepsie, New York, and was immediately put in charge of the Weatherford Business Department. He was in fact "the entire faculty for two departments." He felt ashamed of his incompetence and stifled by the Methodist atmosphere of the college. He tried to supplement his education with summers at the Chautauqua Institute in New York. Sallie Reynolds Matthews loved the Chautauqua extension programs, but as a teacher Lomax found their usefulness limited because the textbooks were very poor. Chautauqua was good for culture-starved people in rural regions but not for a serious education.

The craving for learning brought him to the University of Texas at the age of twenty-eight. The Horatio Alger figure found a mentor, not a millionaire but a man rich in knowledge. Professor Leslie Waggener, a southerner and a Harvard graduate, raised Lomax from his lowly position and gave him credit for three full English courses on the basis of a huge Shakespeare essay. Waggener's praise made him feel like a serf elevated from the ranks and knighted by the lord of the manor—we can glimpse the spirit of Sir Walter Scott presiding over the "toonament" of education. Lomax experienced immense excitement, knowing that he was on the way to "the magical A.B. degree: An A.B. degree! Never before would I allow myself to dream that I could earn such golden acclaim" (29). He would earn the degree and go to Harvard with a scholarship to work on his M.A.

The most interesting moment in the story, one he often retold and which has become academic legend, is the tale of his roll of cowboy songs. He showed it to Dr. Waggener, who referred him to Morgan Callaway, a scholar in the Germanic tradition of source studies and philology. A generation later, J. Frank Dobie would encounter Callaway, and an acid portrait of the smugly complacent man appears in Dobie's *Some Part of Myself.* Callaway told Dobie that he had never made a careful decision and found himself to be wrong (213). The professor examined Lomax's songs and pronounced them worthless. In Callaway's view, the narrative tradition of cowboy songs had no value in comparison to the oral tradition of *Beowulf.* Lomax says that he made a fire with the roll behind the men's dormitory where he lived. Some doubt has been cast on the conclusion of the story: McNutt speaks of the "fabled roll" and says that Mody Boatright had reservations about the story. It is peculiar that the story should be doubted merely because it is a good one. Callaway was such a blight on the would-be folklorists in the department that McNutt apologizes for presenting him as the villain so often. Stith Thompson, perhaps the most distinguished scientific folklorist the United States has produced, left the University of Texas because of his extreme dislike of Callaway's personality and policies.

But when Lomax went to Harvard to work on an M.A., he had the luck to take a course from Barrrett Wendell, to whom *Adventures of a Ballad Hunter* is dedicated. Wendell complained about having to read endless theses on the same American writers and asked his graduate class to bring in samples of regional writing of their own area. Lomax told Wendell that he would like to write on Negro songs or cowboy songs, whereupon the senior professor came around the table to shake his hand and said he would arrange a meeting with George Lyman Kittredge, Harvard's (and America's) most distinguished literary scholar. It is difficult now to appreciate just how eminent Kittredge was. He had written major criticism of Chaucer and the Pearl Poet, and his edition of Shakespeare is often cited by later scholars. For generations American university freshmen were likely to read G. G. Sedgewick's reverent essay, "Kittredge of Harvard," which observes that Kittredge could never get a Ph.D. because no one was presumptuous enough to examine him. Kittredge became a benefactor of Lomax. He and Wendell signed a circular to all the western newspapers asking for their cooperation in Lomax's quest for cowboy songs, and a career began. To be fair to Morgan Callaway, McNutt records that he gave a favorable response to the circular: Texas deferring to Harvard. With such backing, a fellowship was arranged for field work, the first of many such awards given to Lomax. One of Lomax's proudest moments came years later when he was able to bring Kittredge to the Texas Folklore Society (which Lomax cofounded in 1909) to give a keynote address, and, according to Nolan Porterfield, Lomax's biographer, Kittredge seems to have reciprocated by arranging for Lomax to give a presentation at the Modern Language Association meeting at Cornell University.[4] In this Horatio Alger story, the kindly millionaire benefactor was replaced by the American professor with the greatest cultural capital.

The third chapter of *Adventures of a Ballad Hunter,* "Hunting Cowboy Songs," is one of the best, an account of struggles to gather materials that even the cowboys thought were worthless. On one occasion at the Texas Cattleman's Association convention in San Antonio, a cattleman said, "I have been singin' them songs ever since I was a kid. Everybody knows them. Only a damn fool would spend his time tryin' to set 'em down. I move we adjourn." But Lomax gathered works like "The Old Chisholm Trail" and "Home on the Range" from other informants. Perhaps his prize exhibit is "The Buffalo Skinners," a ballad of violence as understated and powerful as anything in the British border ballads tradition, written by the buffalo skinners themselves and sung to Lomax by an old man who had been with the expedition. He informs us that the song was George Lyman Kittredge's favorite American ballad. The results of his searching appeared in *Cowboy Songs and Other Frontier Ballads,*[5] a book which rescued many superb songs from oblivion. This is the volume which Sallie Matthews quoted in *Interwoven:* the ranch woman getting her text from the farmer's son. On one occasion out collecting folklore, J. Frank Dobie came on a group of cowboys singing songs—but they were singing them out of Lomax's book.

The first three chapters of Lomax's autobiography, a stretch of seventy-six excellent pages, are the best part of the book. His subsequent experiences are fascinating, but the work lacks narrative drive henceforth and takes on a scrappy form. Lomax visited jails, with or without his son, Alan, and, if the warden was willing (and not all were) he gathered songs. He visited black churches. Or he sought out traditional singers in rural areas. The recording machinery often failed. These journeys gathered remarkable material, which he generally deposited at the Library of Congress, where he was made an honorary curator. And he published major works in the field, preserving works like "Dink's Song" for posterity. But there is no direction to most of the narratives, and they fail to tell his own life story very clearly.

One of the puzzling deficiencies in *Adventures of a Ballad Hunter* is the lack of an account of the dramatic days when James ("Pa") Ferguson, governor of Texas, attempted to force the board of regents of the University of Texas to fire six members of the staff whom he considered useless or insubordinate or both. One of them was John Lomax, and the court case which ensued was called the Lomax case. J. Evetts Haley deals with the case in some detail in his biography of the Texas rancher, banker, and philanthropist, George Washington Littlefield, and he observes that for some unknown reason Lomax was the party the supporters of Ferguson found most objectionable.[6] The governor seems to have found it impossible to understand Lomax's job, which was essentially to work as a publicist and fund-raiser: These were relatively new ideas. The chairman of the board was Wilber Price Allen, a Ferguson appointee, and the father of John Houghton Allen, whose *Southwest* is discussed in chapter six of this book. The whole Ferguson/Lomax affair gets a couple of sentences in *Adventures of a Ballad Hunter*: "In 1917, just as the United States entered the World War, a local political explosion on the University of Texas campus catapulted me from the state. James E. Ferguson, the picturesque and dynamic governor, didn't like me" (85). Lomax's account of these days of upheaval (some of it comic) would have been interesting to read. In Haley's book, the affair gets an entire chapter, twenty-seven dramatic pages. Lomax gives much more space to his work as a bond salesman than to his crisis with the governor.

Nolan Porterfield's *Last Cavalier* explains the weaknesses of the later portions of the book. Lomax lost interest in it and had to be implored by his publisher to finish. He ransacked old notes and letters to find material to insert and induced his sons to prepare chapters for him. His editor at Macmillan, James Putnam, actually had to write some of the later material in order to get the book (which had actually been optioned by Hollywood) finished. Lomax's book is silent about many personal matters discussed by Porterfield, like his disputes with his leftist son, Alan. The senior Lomax found even FDR intolerable, and Alan's near-Communist views exasperated him. His complex relationship with his second wife, the woman he always called "Miss Terrill," is hardly touched on. Ruby Terrill was the dean of women at the University of Texas and, as Porterfield says, a single woman of mature years. She, unlike Lomax, was a good Methodist and a teetotaler, and his friends thought the relationship between the two was almost humorous in its complexity. Most telling is the omission of much detail about Lomax's stormy dealings with the most important singer he discovered, Huddie (Leadbelly) Ledbetter, a convicted murderer. Porterfield's excellent biography makes it clear how much Lomax avoided telling. Leadbelly quickly came to resent an arrangement in which two-thirds of the profits from their big tour went to Lomax. At one point he pulled a knife on his white agent.

Race is a subject that Lomax does not avoid—so many of his famous informants were black—but he never gets his feelings into focus for clear examination. He has sympathy for the problems of black people but has the instinctive paternalism of a man of his time. His views seem to have evolved over the years that he collected materials. Porterfield looks with intelligence and fairness at this subject and explains that the chapters in which Lomax did try to understand his difficult relationship with

Leadbelly were omitted by Putnam as "unwise." Putnam actually wrote a draft of the last chapter for Lomax "to demonstrate what he wanted," and the warm commemorative tone of the conclusion is probably Putnam's idea. Lomax praises the Mexican, Cajun, Negro, and mountain folk he got his material from, material he helped to preserve through his arduous journeys with clumsy and unreliable equipment. His work would be carried on by William Owens and by another writer associated with the University of Texas, J. Frank Dobie.

The decline in the reputation of J. Frank Dobie has been so sharp that it is hard to believe that he was once called "Mr. Texas" and considered a major spokesman for the state. Dobie, who received the Presidential Medal of Freedom a few days before his death, was part of a celebrated trio (always referred to in print as a triumvirate) with the historian Walter Prescott Webb (1888-1963) and the nature writer Roy Bedichek (1879-1959). William A. Owens edited their correspondence in 1975 as *Three Friends: Roy Bedichek, J. Frank Dobie, Walter Prescott Webb,*[7] and Ronnie Dugger edited a commemorative volume on them in 1967, *Three Men in Texas: Bedichek, Webb, and Dobie.*[8] Dugger's book contains a tribute by a tree-surgeon entitled, "I Planted a Tree with J. Frank Dobie." No man is a hero to his valet, but he can be a hero to his tree surgeon. The adulation was considerable for some years after Dobie's death. Winston Bode published a pictorial biography in 1965, *A Portrait of Pancho: The Life of a Great Texan.*[9] Lon Tinkle has written an excellent if mostly reverential biography, *An American Original.*[10]

The hagiography in so much writing about Dobie has probably damaged his posthumous standing. In his useful pamphlet on Dobie, Francis Edward Abernethy talks about the legendary status of Dobie and then makes this comment:

> . . . you can be sure that when any group gets to talking about Dobie and his cohorts, Walter Prescott Webb and Roy Bedicheck, someone is going to bet that this Texas triumvirate is presently sitting on the gallery in some mesquite

> Valhalla, sipping Jack Daniel's and discussing the state of the universe. And this sort of primitive mythologizing can come from the most sophisticatedly pragmatic of the group.[11]

Abernethy has it both ways: He has turned Dobie and his friends into good old boys and yet has distanced himself a little from his own creation by attributing it to someone otherwise sophisticated. Now the celebrated triumvirate has almost dropped out of notice, as Don Graham has pointed out in "Pen Pals," an article about their memorial statue in Zilker Park in Austin.[12] Graham, who holds the J. Frank Dobie Professorship at the University of Texas, finds that most students have almost never heard of Dobie, even in the Life and Literature of the Southwest course which he founded.

Mythologizing naturally invites demythologizing, or at least debunking, and Dobie's reputation has certainly fallen. In 1968, Larry McMurtry's notorious essay from *In a Narrow Grave,* "Southwestern Literature?" treated Dobie as if he were the literary equivalent of one of the grandiose sculptures by Pompeo Luigi Coppini at the Alamo and the University of Texas, the statues which Dobie used to ridicule. McMurtry complained that Dobie's writing was often hasty, repetitive, poorly organized, and dull. There was too much of it: "twenty-odd books," on every subject from pioneers to rattlesnakes. Similar comments are made nowadays about McMurtry's twenty-five novels. The most prophetic claim was that Dobie's admirers were mostly nostalgic middle-aged people; Dobie's reputation would vanish along with them. This seems to have been the case. Ironically, McMurtry's *Walter Benjamin at the Dairy Queen* would eventually provide a basis for defending Dobie, though McMurtry might not agree. Another iconoclast is James Ward Lee, who suggested in "Arbiters of Texas Literary Taste" that Dobie suffered from "almost total ignorance of literary matters," that he was "a literary dictator without taste and without serious study."[13] Dobie's reputation has fallen so far that he could be dismissed by Gregory Curtis in the February 1993 issue *Texas Monthly* as a writer of books for junior high school boys, a writer who collected bales of stories by Old Coots.[14] The works of older Texas writers like Dobie are, Curtis says, less interesting than their lives.

The most severe judgments on Dobie have come from two folklorists of Mexican origin from South Texas: Américo Paredes and José E. Limón. In his novel, *George Washington Gómez,*[15] which was written in the period 1936-1940 and published in 1990, Paredes depicted Dobie as K. Hank Harvey, a racist pseudo-scholar who learned a few words of Spanish on a West Texas ranch and then set himself up as an expert on Mexicans in Texas, earning the sobriquet of "State Historical Oracle of Texas." The portrait was probably also a satire on Walter Prescott Webb, whose book on *The Texas Rangers* had negative stereotypes of Mexicans which Paredes attacked in *With His Pistol in His Hand.* In an experimental work on ethnography in South Texas, *Dancing with the Devil,* José Limón's critique of Dobie as a folklorist of Mexican Texas goes to the heart of the older writer's contradictory attitudes.[16] Dobie found Mexican -Americans admirable but patronized them: After all, he was the son of an Anglo rancher and *patrón*. The Chicano scholar patronizes Dobie in turn by calling him by his nickname, Pancho. Limón points out that he has taught Dobie's Life and Literature of the Southwest course at the University of Texas, a way of saying that he is reclaiming the Southwest for Mexican-Americans. Limón prints a map of South Texas for the benefit of his readers. He has deported Dobie from the Trans-Nueces region by a mapping error: In his map of South Texas, the Dobie ranch is placed east of the Nueces River rather than to the west and situated at quite a distance from its actual location.

Even a contemporary admirer, Tom Pilkington, concedes that Dobie's reputation has collapsed. The image of the man proved more durable than his books, Pilkington says, and the image is fading in memory. The image was of an "indomitable, if rather cranky individualist."[17] Pilkington tries to defend *Coronado's Children* by considering subtle ironies in it, and he says that the animal books on mustangs, Longhorns, rattlesnakes, and coyotes use symbolism to represent human moral qualities.

Rather than coming to bury Dobie when there are so many

gravediggers on the scene, I would like to provide reasonable grounds to praise him. The main book considered here for a modest but valuable canon of Dobie is *Some Part of Myself,* a set of essays and notes which his wife, Bertha McKee Dobie, assembled after his death. Another work, *Tongues of the Monte,*[18] offers an interesting supplement to the straightforward autobiography in *Some Part of Myself.* As a kind of fantasy memoir, it deserves some attention as well, flawed as it is by its racial condescension and mannered style. Larry McMurtry ranks it highest among Dobie's books.

The essays provide an excellent retrospect of growing up on a ranch in the Brush Country, a distinctive part of Texas. They reveal a powerful love of place and the sketches of family, Mexican ranch employees, and neighbors are economical, entertaining, and sometimes touching. He has an eye for eccentricity, and that eye was probably trained on his observations of relatives (like his Uncle Ed Dubose and his step-grandfather, Friendly Dubose) and neighbors. These figures were good precedents for a man who eventually wrote about colorful people. The essays also provide a basis for understanding how he developed his stubborn, even willful personality, mainly through maternal influence. He conceived of himself as a maverick and a liberal. Mavericks were more common in his Texas than liberals. Defending labor unions and civil rights was a truly rebellious position in his time.

In her foreword Bertha McKee Dobie quotes a letter he wrote near the end of his life to an English friend: "I don't know if I'll ever get an autobiography completed. All I have of it is many scraps—some long, some short." She misleads the reader a little by saying that the book is mostly made up of scraps and Sunday "pieces" for Texas newspapers. Five of the essays were in fact taken from *Southwest Review,* and these are highly polished, like the essays from the *New York Times Book Review* and the Literary Guild bulletin. But Dobie's ambivalence about writing an autobiography comes through when she tells us that he simply tossed "whatever he wrote about himself" (including notes on bits of paper) into "an autobiographical box." Some pieces, like "Echoes of the All Gone" and "Horses of My Boyhood" are so minor they will not be discussed here. The essays leave out a great deal, like his courtship and marriage to Bertha McKee, and the first fourteen pieces carry him only to the start of his teaching career. The last two essays are not primarily autobiographical, dealing as they do with his other career, as a folklorist. But they contribute to an understanding of the events which determined his vocation and therefore shaped his life.

The opening piece, "Unveiling of a Self-Portrait," published first in *The New York Times Book Review,* reveals such ambivalence about autobiography that it is hard to imagine how Dobie would have written a full-scale one. It does not, in fact, unveil a self-portrait but plants high hedges around the self. He begins by saying "no autobiography is as good as the best biography." He observes that there are limits to how much we can know a real human being, even ourselves: "'Know thyself' is a fine adage, but no self-portrait in literature is so strong, so deep and wide, so rich in both complexities and simplicities, so full and yet so cleared of dross as the created character of Hamlet" (3). Of course, he has chosen one of the most profound characters in literature for his invidious comparison, and he has also picked a character who is notoriously unknowable. The article is full of contradictions. He says that autobiography is terribly limited. "Perhaps the best and worst things lie too deep in a being to ever come out," and his skepticism is profound: "Truth is one thing, justice is another; no autobiography has ever been written that was either"(4). But he also concedes that "the autobiographical medium permits considerable saying about life ruled out by other mediums of writing" (6). He seems especially anxious about the question of ego, seeing an autobiography as a creation of a monument to the author. He quotes the flamboyant and unscrupulous rancher, Shanghai Pierce, who erected a monument to himself on his ranch and gave as his reason: "I knew damn well nobody else would do it if I didn't."

Dobie also claims that he has less interest in writing an autobiography than in writing books on Longhorns and mustangs. The problem he says is "what to select," because he would like to see his early life in South Texas as an idyll. He gives the precedent of W.

H. Hudson, who turned the harsh world of his youth in Argentina into "the distilled innocence of a vanished life" (6) in works like *The Purple Land,* a work also admired by William A. Owens. But such a book does not reverse the loss of that world. The reader senses that such an account would be a falsification. Dobie's disciple, John Houghton Allen, the subject of chapter six, did not resist the temptation to create an idyll in parts of *Southwest,* though he could curse the monotony of their common region as well. Dobie's love of Hudson, who was basically an aesthete, shows a rather genteel love of beauty in a man who liked the company of cowboys and miners. He asks:

> Shall I write of the Far Away and Long Ago as a thing apart or infuse into it some of the stubborn questionings that arise from Now? Those questionings will dispel the aura that is art and delightfulness. I crave to be an artist and nobody values more highly than I the delightful in literature. Nearly all controversial writing is dull to me, even when I am on the side of the controversialist. A writer is forever debating with himself not only the choice of detail but what truth to leave out in the interest of another truth. (7)

The notion that art must have an aura of delightfulness seems dated. On the other hand the final observation about leaving out truths in the interest of other truths identifies a perennial question for the writer dealing with real life. Dobie says he has to resist the desire to write a Texas version of Robert Burns's "Cotter's Saturday Night," which would have been quite easy for him to do, and it would have been as salable as a Norman Rockwell painting.

Dobie also says that his autobiography would have to bear witness to his "passionate belief" in freedom of thought. Various episodes in *Some Part of Myself* show Dobie's independence of mind: This is part of his metaphor of self. He plays the maverick in the academic herd, the critter who would not take a brand. He recalls that he has been charged with being an "atheistic communist" for his skepticism, and he thinks that "controversy defeats its own aims" (7).

In his biography of Dobie, Lon Tinkle discusses Dobie's independence and feistiness by quoting comments recorded in a journal Bertha McKee Dobie kept in 1935. On one occasion when he came home from a Town-and-Gown club meeting, where he had been provoked by a lecture on art and the discussion afterward, he told his wife: "I was fierce; I don't rib myself up to being fierce; I am just naturally fierce about anything I am against—and when I am fierce I am interesting." She noted also that "all his life has been a protest."[19] It soon becomes clear in *Some Part of Myself* that he had a father whose rigidity he needed to protest against. The book manages to convey much about Dobie in spite of all his misgivings in the opening essay.

Dobie was born and bred in the Brush Country, that vast swath of land in South Texas which is technically described as the Rio Grande Embayment. Dobie's family lived just west of the Nueces River. The landscape of the Brush Country has been described by Roy Bedichek in his ecologically minded *Karánkaway Country*.[20] Bedichek consulted his good friend Dobie about the Brush Country, so his book is ideal background for Dobie's work. Bedichek observes that when the area was inhabited by aborigines and buffalo, the grasses were thick and matted, and seeds of mesquite and *huisache* would stay on the surface and die. But with the passing of the original inhabitants and the abuse of the land by ranchers whose cattle overgrazed it, the inexorable march of brush—thorny plants like prickly pear and mesquite—began. The mesquite eventually spread all the way to West Texas. One of the most abundant botanical nuisances is the *huisache,* or sweet acacia, which blooms beautifully but is inedible for livestock and tends to crowd out other plants. Bedichek quotes an early rancher on the Nueces River who saw his first huisache in the 1880s and was so dazzled by its beauty that he went home to pick up his family and drive ten miles back to see it (93). The brush is visually striking but also monotonous.

The first autobiographical essay in *Some Part of Myself* is one of the best: "A Plot of Earth," an account of his *querencia,* the Dobie ranch in southern Live Oak County, west of the Nueces River and about one hundred miles south of San Antonio. The occasion was the signing of a consent form by the Dobie children for the sale of the place, a natural moment for reflection on what it meant to him. And the reflection enables him to give the basic facts of his origins: born September 26, 1888, "in a three-room whitewashed rock house," near Ramirenia Creek, oldest of six children. The nearest town of any size was Beeville, twenty-seven "horse miles" away; the villages of Dinero and Lagarto and Ramirenia were closer. José Limón is annoyed that Dobie does not concern himself with the Ramirez family who left ruins next door: where they went and "*why* they went, Pancho does not say."[21] But in fact Dobie had done exactly this in "How My Life Took Its Turn," an essay of 1931 which Bertha McKee Dobie printed at the other end of the book: He says they were massacred by Indians.

He sketches a childhood in which he and his siblings made up their own games—creating horses from spools, cows from bits of horn left over from dehorning, and goats from snail shells. Dobie and his brother Elrich created a tournament course with three poles and with "tournament poles" in hand would gallop along attempting to spear rings hanging from cross arms. He says that very early he learned to listen to the land talk, but his world also opened up through reading, which his mother encouraged. Besides *The Youth's Companion,* which came on Saturdays, he read such works as Tennyson's *Idylls of the King,* which sent him into a dream world: No wonder he feared turning an account of his past into an idyll. But the world of the ranch, he says, was not romantic, except for Fort Ramirez, the fortified ranch house on the Dobie land that predated the independence of Texas. The abandoned ranch still had some stone walls standing, and there were legends of treasure which brought treasure hunters out to dig for Mexican gold or silver rumored to be buried there. Dobie amusingly relates how his mother's half brother, Ed Dubose, persuaded the family to help him dig for gold on the basis of a San Antonio fortuneteller's tip. After three days they had created a large hole. Such futile treasure-hunting episodes became the basis for two of Dobie's most successful books, *Coronado's Children* and *Apache Gold and Yaqui Silver,*[22] and *Some Part of Myself* ends with "Storytellers I Have Known," an essay which features several treasure hunters. Lost treasures are a motif running throughout the book.

Ranching in Sallie Matthews's West Texas was carried on exclusively by Anglos, but South Texas has a large Mexican population. Some of the ranches have remained in the possession of the descendants of early *Tejano* settlers, and the others are often worked largely by Mexican vaqueros. The WPA publication of 1940, *Texas–A Guide to the Lone Star State,* observed that "the vast majority of Mexicans south of the Nueces River exist in a system not unlike medieval feudalism."[23] In his introduction to *Tongues of the Monte,* Dobie says that he was "about grown" before he knew that "cowboy" was not a literary word. The term in South Texas was always vaquero, the Spanish equivalent. Ranching techniques and equipment were introduced to what is now Texas by Mexicans. The vaquero, Genardo del Bosque, taught him a great deal about roping and riding and tended his injuries when he fell from horses, providing an alternative to Dobie's inflexible father, as he himself says in "A Plot of Earth": "I and my brother Elrich felt freer with him than we felt with our father. . ." (25). John Houghton Allen also depicts idealized vaqueros as a means of overcoming the gulf between the Anglo Texan and Mexican Texan. They were father substitutes for him as well. Dobie's father discouraged his sons from learning Spanish, and the parents feared that they might marry Mexican girls. The "other" often has a magical attraction, as the parents surmised.

Figures like del Bosque can bear an embarrassing symbolic weight. Dobie says that if he were in hell and could be redeemed by a substitute, he is sure that "Genardo, of all the men I know, would without a quiver of hesitation plunge into the furnace" (25), which makes del Bosque seem too much like Kipling's pathetic Gunga Din, who supposedly would bring his British master water in the depths of hell: "E'll be squattin' on the coals / Givin' drink to pore damned souls, / An' I'll get a swig in Hell from Gunga Din!" Del Bosque is the model for the faithful Innocencio in *Tongues of the Monte,* a middle-aged mozo (boy) who is the utterly devoted Sancho Panza to Don Federico and even kills a man to defend him. After Dobie's father died, the mother deeded some land on the ranch to Del Bosque, who wished never to leave, saying "*Yo tengo raíces aquí,*" meaning "I have roots here."

José Limón's essay on Dobie in *Dancing with the Devil* probes into the man's ambivalent feelings toward Mexicans. He observes that Dobie's favored nickname was "Pancho," the diminutive for "Féderico"; he also notes (relying on McNutt's dissertation) that in 1917 he offered himself to the federal government as someone who could help in military operations against Mexico when it seemed that war was likely. He claimed to know Spanish and to understand "the Mexican genius," a statement no sensible Anglo Texan would make today. Two of Dobie's uncles had served in the Texas Rangers, and in 1923 he took jubilant part in a raid of Texas Rangers against Mexican bootleggers and exulted that Mexicans were afraid to come out of their houses for days.[24]

Dobie wrote affectionately of the people on his father's ranch. In the 1947 preface to *Tongues of the Monte,* he sees his parent's role as *patrón* and *patrona* to the ranch employees as part of his warrant for writing "a book about the Mexican people" (x). He always attributed his own career as a storyteller to the impact of Santos Cortez, a goat herder and hunter he met on his Uncle J. M. Dobie's ranch on the Nueces. Cortez was a great teller of ghost stories. But being a *patrón* entails being patronizing. In *A Vaquero of the Brush Country,* his narrative of the life of John Young, a one-time Texas Ranger, Dobie describes battles between bandits and Anglo Texans in 1875 and makes this remark: "Between many Anglo-Texans and Mexican-Texans strong ties of friendship existed. The majority of Anglo-Texan ranchers along the border depended almost exclusively on Mexican vaqueros for their labor; and these vaqueros, generally speaking, proved to be as reliable, as loyal, and as trustworthy as the idealized darkies of antebellum days."[25]

The most touching element in Dobie's "A Plot of Earth" is the way he describes his own roots in that land. His term *querencia* is an excellent Spanish word, derived from the verb *querer,* to love or like. It can mean an animal's normal territory, a spot in the ring favored by a bull, or just a beloved place. A great lover of Wordsworth, Dobie makes his feelings for his home palpable by using the principle expressed in the "Preface" to *Lyrical Ballads:* "I have at all times endeavoured to look steadily at my subject." One of Dobie's best passages describes riding to get the mail in Dinero, a trip set in an era where, as he says, one "traveled instead of being transported" (28). It was possible to see roadrunners and redbirds and judge the soil by the vegetation it supported. He says with some pride, "Yet I don't think everybody who traveled saw particulars" (28). But he had to leave his *querencia,* work and his intellectual interests calling him away. His younger friend, John Houghton Allen, would also find ranch life too limiting for a writer.

The three essays which deal with his family are not tinged with sentimentality, though strong feeling shows through. "The Cowman Who Was My Father" is written objectively, through revealing incidents and astute generalizations. Lon Tinkle recalls in his biography, *An American Original,* that Dobie claimed to have a block against writing about his father, one that took a long time to overcome, and finds no basis for it except for his distaste for authority.[26] Perhaps the real clue is in Dobie's praise for the warmth of Genardo del Bosque. R. J. Dobie (he was actually Jonathan Richard but detested the first name) was an extremely strict Methodist even for a time when the denomination had a reputation for Puritanism. He gave up dancing, and he would not work on Sunday. The elder Dobie actually sang Methodist hymns to quiet the cattle at night, instead of the customary cowboy songs. He is one of Dobie's eccentrics. Dislike of his father's religion doubtless accounts for Dobie's failure to discuss the camp meetings of his youth in any detail.

The portrait is balanced: Dobie assures us that his father's faith was luminous if not joyous. The son does not demonstrate warmth toward his father in the way that he does when he writes about his mother or Genardo del Bosque, but he respects the man's character. Perhaps what he liked least but praises fully is the father's even nature, his failure to get angry more than once or twice in the son's memory. Dobie identifies with his mother: "Regarding him now from the point of view of the volatile temperament inherited from my mother, I consider him about the justest man I have ever known" (69). Justice is a virtue inspiring admiration more than love.

His chapter on "My Mother—Ella Byler Dobie" opens with a bit of family saga, the account of how her father, Rufus Byler, of Fayette, Texas, was probably murdered for his horse and money after the Civil War ended. The mother remarried a man named Friendly Dubose, whose story is told in a later essay, one which provides more of the family saga. Frank's mother, Ella Byler, had a great love of learning and would read Scott, Dickens, *Ben-Hur* and *Tom Sawyer* to her brother and sister and her Dubose half brothers. She became a schoolteacher, and like Hallie Stillwell later, married a rancher. Her love of learning was clearly an influence on her son. After she found a list of the ten best books for young people she obtained them. They included *Pilgrim's Progress, Ivanhoe,* and *Plutarch's Lives.* The Plutarch was a good book for a man whose work incorporates so many character sketches.

What Dobie calls his mother's "impetuous and wildly free spirit" shaped his view of himself. As Tinkle documents in his biography, Dobie always saw himself as a rebel. He also saw a liberal mind as a supreme value, and this he would have picked up from his mother, not his father, whose faith was unchanging. In later years Dobie would lose interest in religion and even enjoy strong drink. But his ferocity in a cause that he considered just might derive from his father's example. Dobie was willing to take on governors and regents at the University of Texas when he thought they were wrong, at the eventual cost of his job, and he spoke up boldly against the climate of McCarthyism in Texas. In 1950 he published "Guilt by Rumor," in *Southwest Review,* an attack on Joseph McCarthy's tactics.[27] The Dallas literary journal was one of the few liberal organs of opinion in Texas at the time. His books and newspaper columns and broadcasts had given him the nickname, "Mr. Texas," and he threw his enormous prestige behind the cause of freedom of thought. Ralph Yarborough, Dobie's friend and a former

U.S. senator of liberal note, wrote a pamphlet on Dobie's liberal politics, listing his stands against censorship and for labor unions.[28]

The brief essay on "Uncle Frank Byler" offers a counterpoise to his look at his father. Uncle Frank was definitely not a good Methodist; he gambled and smoked. He also treated young Frank with generosity when he hired the nephew for a trail drive. Uncle Frank was a friend of the celebrated cowboy writer, Andy Adams, and appears in his book. He also provided Dobie with one of his best stories. Cowboys in the Brush Country rarely packed six-shooters, and that aspect of the cowboy myth is one that Dobie likes to debunk. He tells how Uncle Frank saw a water moccasin at a pool in the Indian Territory and reached for his pistol to shoot it. But the gun was rusty and would not cock: "He threw it at the snake and left it in the mud. He said that unless a man could shoot a gun he had no business carrying it" (84).

The "Ranch Neighbors" essay shows Dobie's interest in turning local characters into subjects for sketches. He describes the people who lived near the Dobie ranch and the nearby villages of Dinero and Lagarto. Lagarto was once a promising town but had been damaged because the new railroad was located ten miles away, a common story in Texas. He says that "the inhabitants of the Lagarto community were worldly, urbane and cosmopolitan" compared with those of the Ramirenia settlement: The redundant adjectives are perhaps a way of emphasizing the point. His family went to church in Ramirenia, perhaps because the Methodists were weaker than the Campbellites (Church of Christ) in Lagarto.

One of his "metaphors of self" is the curious listener, the collector of stories which reflect human nature, and he has a number of anecdotes about the people of the area, though they gave little scope for a Nueces Plutarch. "Ranch Neighbors" captures their speech and ways precisely, recording people like Granny Hinnart, the snuff-dipping midwife whose speech sounded Elizabethan in idiom: When she was offered coffee she'd say, "I'll take a sup." Among the neighbors was Mary Givens, who, like Hallie Stillwell, learned to do all the work on the ranch after her husband lost his health. He also mentions a son of Sally Skull (1813-1867?), the famous pioneer and rancher. She was remarkably tough-minded: One of her husbands drowned in the San Antonio River, and when a ranch hand asked about recovering the body, she said she didn't care about the body but wanted the forty dollars in his money belt. Dobie would pursue the story of Sally Skull when he was in Alpine.

The most amusing story—another treasure-hunting account— is about his great-uncle, Sterling Dobie, who distrusted banks and hid money in small sums all over his ranch. In a scene that could have come out of Erskine Caldwell's *God's Little Acre,* his relatives dug up various caches after his funeral. But the largest sum, a can of gold pieces that his daughter had helped bury, could not be found. Dobie admits that his accounts of the people in his "Ranch Neighbors" chapter are written because he felt an inner compulsion: "They are all gone now, these people I knew as the last century was dying. I do not sketch them with any thought of rescuing them from universal oblivion. I sketch them because they keep coming before me and also because I try 'to make a thing' in order to rest" (88). He is presenting himself as a storyteller by nature. In later years he decided that he was not a folklorist but a storyteller. For a full understanding of Dobie's keen interest in human character, a reader should look at Dobie's "Beeville Talk," another posthumously published essay, collected in *Out of the Old Rock.* Dobie cherished people of tough integrity and seems to have conceived of himself as a character out of the old rock and, to use another phrase he favored, an "original."

One of Dobie's best essays is "His Looks and My Ways Would Hang Any Man." The phrase comes from his grandmother's second husband, Friendly Dubose. Dobie moved to Alice, a fair-sized town in Jim Wells County in 1904 for high school and lived with his grandparents. His account of his step-grandfather (whom he calls "Grandpa") is one of his richest portraits and provides some touches of the family (or step-family) saga, recounting stories of the Civil War and ranching in the early days. Grandpa Dubose was a successful rancher before the drought of 1891 ruined him. One of the more interesting local characters, Pegleg Tumlinson, extends the treasure-seeking motif: Tumlinson was a collector of treasure stories and maps and got local boys involved in digging. Typical of Dobie's eye for the colorful anecdote is the account of Pegleg and his friend Lawrence. Pegleg had lost his right leg, Lawrence his left, and by good fortune they had the same boot size and could buy and share boots.

Dobie is diffident about his high school career, uncertain whether he was valedictorian or salutatorian of his class. But the second-longest essay in his book, "Prose and Poetry," leaves the little world of Dinero and Alice and ranches behind and begins the theme of education. He attended Southwestern University in Georgetown, north of Austin. Some of the essay merely describes classmates and teachers in a routine way (his essay on Columbia University does the same), but the writing comes alive when it deals with Albert Shipp Pegues, the professor who taught him poetry and gave him an intense love for it. He played the role in Dobie's life that Waggener and Barrett played in Lomax's. Wordsworth remained a great favorite of Dobie's, and he tells how the English poet "was my essential self when I walked alone up the San Gabriel River with a volume of Wordsworth, reading him there as I had imagined he had walked and composed by 'sylvan Wye,' and making his lines an integral and abiding part of me" (145). The chapter is a good corrective to Dobie's self-created and polemical image of himself as an advocate of "longhorn culture": For all his interest in Andy Adams and various minor southwestern writers, his literary standards were formed by the classics of English literature. Naturally he took very well to England when he was professor of American history at Cambridge in 1943-1944, a period recorded in *A Texan in England,* a collection of columns he wrote about his experiences.[29] Dobie's alleged conversion to the mainstream of western civilization in the last chapter of that book, "What England Did to Me," is a rhetorical gesture. He had wanted to gain some space for the literature of his region and sometimes overstated the case. Professor Pegues had left him with a deep love for the great works of English literature, which became as important in his life as stories about Beeville or Alice or Ramirenia Creek.

The next essay in *Some Part of Myself,* "A Schoolteacher in Alpine," describes his year in that community in the Big Bend. His stayed there in the 1910-1911 school year, overlapped with the arrival of Hallie Crawford Stillwell and her family. He made a powerful impression on Hallie and the other young girls. He alludes to stories he heard about Alice Stillwell Henderson, the pistol-packing sister of Roy Stillwell, the rancher Hallie would marry. He records an unfortunate loss: Alice Henderson apparently wrote a life of Sally Skull, the colorful woman rancher, but after her death it was left in an old trunk that later disappeared. It appears that her family thought nothing of it. His students in Alpine were very good, he says: "they were for the most part as intelligent as professors," (174), a good example of his antiacademic stance. The stay in Alpine made it possible for him to become a serious writer. His first book, *Vaquero of the Brush Country,* was a collaborative life of John Young, "mavericker, brush-popper, trailer-driver, hunter for the Lost Nigger Mine . . ." (181), a man he met in Alpine. *Coronado's Children,* his first book about treasure hunters and his first great success, was inspired by the whole folklore of the Lost Nigger Mine in the Alpine area. One subject he does not discuss in the Alpine chapter is the growing relationship with his future wife. He is quite reticent about his emotional life, as tight-lipped as Sallie Reynolds Matthews.

After the discussion of Alpine, the book has two pieces about his stay in the East, where he pursued an M.A. in English from 1913-1914. The first, "Columbia University in the City of New York," seeks to trivialize his experience there, part of his tendency to denigrate academic life. He does say that he soon realized that black students were not inferior: He had never experienced racially mixed classrooms. He claims to have spent most of his time attending plays, and he essentially dismisses all of his professors except for Brander Matthews, whom he seems to have liked because Matthews was famous (like Dobie afterward at the University of Texas) for his anecdotes. He went to hear the anarchist, Emma Goldman, who would so impress Gertrude Beasley at lectures in

Chicago. Perhaps typical of Dobie's unease with the intellectual life, he says he took away not ideas but "glimpses of another world and an impression of vitality" (187). He assures the reader that he was always on the side of rebels. A later essay in the book mentions that he had a profound feeling of alienation, a loss of personality, in New York. The other New York piece is a travel diary, "Along Lake George," subtitled by Dobie's widow as "Written in 1913 as a Log Book." It is not a distinguished work, but it shows Dobie in a characteristic way, as a wanderer gathering experiences and listening to people he met on the way.

"No Idea Where I Was Going" presents an author torn between a career in the academic world and ranching. He began teaching English at the University of Texas in 1914. He appears to be making a case against teaching through contemptuous portraits of people like his boss, Morgan Callaway. Further evidence that the academy is full of stuffed shirts comes through in his accounts of the dean of law, Judge Town, who did not believe in public schools, considering them too socialistic, and the dean of engineering, a jingoistic man who eventually produced some superficial and self-published works about the West. In effect, Dobie writes about academics as if they were Beeville or Alice eccentrics. Dobie shared an office with Stith Thompson, who would become a great American folklorist. Dobie claims he did not know what folklore was until Thompson asked him to pay a dollar to join the Texas Folklore Society. Thompson had given him a name for the activity he liked best, gathering and writing up tales by gifted storytellers. He himself induced another rancher's son, Mody C. Boatright, to join the society and begin collecting folklore.

In "No Idea Where I Was Going," he relates his attempt to take up ranching again, at the invitation of his Uncle Jim Dobie, who signed a note for him to buy cows and lease a pasture near the family ranch. He married in 1916 but had grave difficulties with ranching, owing to a severe drought. He entered the army in 1917, where as usual he had difficulty with authority. He devotes some pages to a National Guard colonel whom he despised as much as any professor. His initial reaction to the army was another loss of personality. He had "been too long soaked in poetry and novels" and "a certain refined personality kept me away from my fellows" (225). James McNutt has suggested that a large element in Dobie's flamboyant character grew out of his fear of being effeminate. A college teacher, he suspected, was not manly enough. So he wore cowboy boots and jeans on campus and denigrated professors. Dobie fails to discuss such issues in any detail. A loss of personality and power is an immensely interesting subject for someone writing about his life. It is also a subject that a man who feared being thought effeminate might not linger on. When he got out of the army after service in France (in the artillery, as close to cavalry as one could get in World War I), his cattle, tended by his Uncle Charlie Dubose, had made him a lot of money in spite of the loss of many of them in the drought. The war had boosted the prices for beef enormously. He began teaching again at the University of Texas in 1919.

"How My Life Took Its Turn," written in 1931 for the Literary Guild magazine, *Wings,* as an introduction to *Coronado's Children,* gives a superb defense of his vocation as a collector and reteller of tales. In effect, the essay is a search for a "metaphor of self," his position as maverick folklorist and antiacademic academic. The crucial moment in his life came in 1920, when he left the University of Texas to try ranching. Once again, it was at the suggestion of his Uncle Jim Dobie, who had an enormous ranch in La Salle County, among other holdings. Dobie managed the La Salle Ranch, Los Olmos, which was on both sides of the Nueces River and may have provided the model for the nocturnal storytelling at the imaginary Mexican Hacienda of the Five Wounds *(Hacienda de Cinco Llagas)* in *Tongues of the Monte.* One of the men working on the Texas ranch, Santos Cortez, told Dobie some remarkable stories, including a terrifying account of a *bulto,* a kind of incubus spirit. It became clear that he could do for "the legendary tales of Texas" what his friend John Lomax had done for cowboy songs. He would provide the background of the region as well as the tales themselves. "One day it came to me that I would collect and tell the legendary tales of Texas as Lomax had collected the old-time songs and ballads of Texas and the frontier. I thought that the stories of the range were as interesting as the songs. I considered that if they could be put down so as to show the background out of which they have come, they might have high value" (237).

His approach has been described rather harshly by the scientific folklorists, heirs of Stith Thompson. Américo Paredes and José Limón dismissed Dobie as a "romantic regionalist." Limón says that a "romantic regionalist folklorist ethnographer" represents his material "in an embellished, stylized form usually translated into a standard literary language (English in this case), so as to make the original text sound more like 'high' literature, fit for a dominant literate reading public."[30] For Limón the loss in authenticity is apparent: The "high" value is actually a debasement, a loss of authenticity.

Dobie had tremendous success with stories of lost treasure, and "How My Life Took Its Turn" was written to explain how he came to write *Coronado's Children,* his first collection of such stories. He had long been aware of treasure hunts in the West, beginning with his Uncle Ed Dubose's search for that lost fortune at Fort Ramirez. His epiphany was to understand that the men who told the tales of treasure, and their physical environment, "were the most vital part of the narratives" (232). He tells us that he avoids academicians "with their eternal shop talk" in favor of Mexican goat herders, "lawyers with a an eye for characters and a zest for hunting, trail drivers, and women who know how to cook frijoles in a black iron pot. I belong to the soil myself and the people of it are my people" (238). One lesson he quickly learned was that stories beget more stories, that publishing a story about lost treasure, say, brings more informants, including people who wish to find the lost mines and hidden silver shipments in his stories. Lost treasure turned out to be a renewable resource.

The final essay in *Some Part of Myself,* "Storytellers I Have Known," published near the end of his life in *Southwest Review,* adds little to an understanding of Dobie's personality, aside from affirming his love of eccentrics and good yarn spinners, a love which is a major current in his autobiographical essays. The eccentrics are interesting, some of them having surfaced repeatedly in Dobie's life, usually with new tales of treasures they hoped to find with a little assistance. Dobie realizes that the storytellers he enjoyed belonged "to times when folks had to amuse themselves, before machines to furnish amusement had been invented" (268). Television, the most powerful amusement machine, can wipe out a folk tradition. Larry McMurtry, the scourge of Dobie's reputation, offers a means of defending it, which he might not accept. McMurtry himself is concerned with the loss of storytelling. In *Walter Benjamin at the Dairy Queen,* he cites Benjamin's great essay, "The Storyteller," which maintains that "the art of the storyteller is coming to an end." McMurtry regrets that Benjamin's thesis applies to the ranch country of Texas as well as to Europe. In part this change is because experience has been cheapened and in part because we are subjected to a flood of information which comes with its own commentary: Benjamin says that "by now almost nothing that happens benefits story-telling; almost everything benefits information."[31] At its best, Dobie's campfire folklore preserves the story and respects the humanity of the teller, whom he often evokes as precisely as the tale: Indeed, he realizes that the storyteller is often more interesting than the story. He often strives to provide the context of the teller, the social world, and the physical landscape. In "How My Life Took Its Turn," he says: "If people are to enjoy their own lives, they must be aware of the significance of their own environments" (237). The essays in *Some Part of Myself* put Dobie in his own environment and help his readers to understand that world—and his stubborn, antiestablishment character, the maverick in the academy and the academic in the field.

The most structured literary work produced by Dobie is his *Tongues of the Monte,* a book which even McMurtry praises in his controversial essay, "Southwestern Literature?". This book, which has been touched on above, is not strictly a memoir because, as McMurtry says, it is "frankly fictionalized." The name Don Federico, given to the gringo narrator, is the equivalent of Frank. The book blends traditional Mexican tales of the marvelous and the violent with fine descriptions of the landscape and way of life of the vaqueros and villagers of the State of Coahuila, where John Phillip Santos would later spend some summers at the Rancho Los

Generales. Dobie appropriates, as we say now, figures out of Mexican folklore, telling a story of a *curandero* and the devil and the folktale of Juan Oso, a Bear Man. He also includes an account of *La Llorona,* the ghostly weeping woman so important in Mexican and Chicano folklore. The book is a celebration of storytelling and a symbolic expression of brotherhood with the vaqueros he admired in real life. It ends with the faithful Innocencio performing a ceremony of blood brotherhood, joining his blood and his master's (he called the Dobie surrogate "master"!). He used the knife with which he killed a gringo-hating man who threatened the life of his master. The man was a former Dorado, a member of Pancho Villa's elite guard. As Limón points out, Inocencio is loyal to the gringo, not the Mexican nationalist. In imperialist fantasies, Gunga Din always sides with the Europeans. The book is marred by a romantic subplot about two jealous women adapted from W. H. Hudson's *The Purple Land.* Hudson was perhaps responsible for the purple prose as well. In Dobie's defense, it should be said that the description of a sojourn at the hut of goat herder is a particularly fine piece of atmosphere, an outstanding feat of genre writing in which the man's life is masterfully evoked.

Dobie was disturbed by the relative failure of the book with readers, who were uncertain about his purposes. McNutt speaks of generic confusion. Readers were probably puzzled by the title: *Voices of the Mountains* would have been clear. But he had one imitator, another man who grew up on a ranch in the Brush Country, his friend, John Houghton Allen. Allen would adapt the storytelling format and atmospheric richness of *Tongues of the Monte* to try to enter the imaginative world of his father's vaqueros.

The stubborn and volatile personality whose formation is traced in *Some Part of Myself* led to his parting with the University of Texas. He was certainly an adornment of the university, and his value was not unrecognized: He rose to full professor in record time and without a Ph.D., a unique case in his department. His course in southwestern writing was an important step in providing recognition for regional literature. He expected ample time on leave (unpaid) to write books. In 1947, he had been on leave for four years and requested another year to finish a book. His request was denied; he refused to teach and was dropped from the staff in a kind of procedural firing, exactly the kind of academic technicality that he deplored. The rule against leaves of absence beyond two years became known as "the Dobie Rule." Some thirty years before, the firings at the University of Texas were known as "the Lomax case." Dobie's persistent criticism of right-wing conservatives on the board of regents was probably a major factor. Today Dobie's name is perpetuated in the Dobie Room of the library system and in the Dobie Center, a shopping mall across from the Harry Ransom Humanities Research Center, a center built by coincidence on the site of the antiquarian bookstore run by Dobie's cousin, Dudley R. Dobie Sr. Most fittingly, Dobie's hobby ranch near Austin, Paisano, is made available to two writers each year as holders of the Dobie Paisano Fellowship awarded by the University of Texas and the Texas Institute of Letters. Dobie won the academic war posthumously, though perhaps he has lost the literary fight, his fame with readers having declined. Perhaps his literary reputation will recover, not to the rather exaggerated level it reached in his lifetime, but his merits as a proponent of the storytelling tradition deserve respect. Larry McMurtry has not become a Dobie/Paisano Fellow yet, but it is not impossible.

Gertrude Beasley

3

THE CONFESSIONS OF GERTRUDE BEASLEY

Thanks to the U.S. Customs and Scotland Yard, one of the most daring works of modernism, Gertrude Beasley's *My First Thirty Years,* remains almost unknown, although it had the cachet of publication in Paris by Robert McAlmon's Contact Editions, a small press which issued first books by Ernest Hemingway, Gertrude Stein, and dozens of other modernists.

Beasley's book deserves rescue from obscurity for several reasons. As social history, it portrays farm and town life in West Texas with near photographic detail and then turns to Chicago, showing the influence of what Steven Watson calls a "cradle of modernism" on a young woman from the hinterland. It is also a pioneering confessional narrative, far more frank than the memoirs of her fellow Texan, Mary Karr, who has a reputation for shocking honesty about life in a dysfunctional family. Unfortunately, Beasley paid a terrible price for her frankness: imprisonment, confinement in a mental ward, and, perhaps, a final descent into paranoia. Her fate after January 1928 is not clear, but the trail is not cold.

Information about her outside of her own memoir has been hard to find. Larry McMurtry, with the assistance of Patrick and Shay Bennett[1] of her native Abilene, compiled a number of facts for his "afterword" to the Book Club of Texas reissue in 1989, which came in a deluxe edition retailing at $120. The reprint is used for citations in this study: It is more easily obtained than the fragile and exceedingly scarce first edition, which sells for up to $1,000. The facts known about Gertrude Beasely in 1989 would fit on two pages. Much more will be revealed in this chapter: The National Archives and the State Department have released a torrent of documents to me, including three passport applications, the records of the banning of her book by U.S. Customs, and what appears to be her last deranged letter from the S.S. *Republic* in or near New York Harbor on January 7, 1928. I have also obtained copies of her letters to Bertrand Russell from his archive at McMaster University. The history of the book is perhaps as interesting as the life described in it. For one thing, it is the only Texas memoir written in Moscow within sight of the Kremlin.

The first page, set in Moscow, describes her state of mind this way:

> It is perfectly clear to me that life is not worth living, but it is also equally clear that life is worth talking about. Perhaps talk is the greatest thing in the world. If I could destroy my bump

> of curiosity, I would go on this January day to the river at the Kremlin where Russian churchmen are said to be carrying out religious rites (a piece of idiocy which prevents life from being worth while) and throw my body into its icy depths. But I have curiosity, fear, and that potent enemy of death known as hope. Besides I have enough money (U.S) to keep me going for nearly two years. . . .

She had gone to Russia in 1922 to write an article for *National Geographic*. A letter she received from the editor, Gilbert Grosvenor,[2] accepting an article on Japan seems to have persuaded the American consul in Lithuania to issue her a passport to Russia, when it was against policy to provide such documents for women and children because of the danger: The country was in the aftermath of revolution and the United States did not have diplomatic relations with the USSR.

The most daring aspect of *My First Thirty Years* is her frankness about incest, rape, and bestiality in her own family, events which help explain her claim that life is not worth living. As Don Graham said in an article in *Texas Monthly*, the Beasleys are presented as the "trashiest family west of the Mississippi."[3] She begins the work with a startling paragraph:

> Thirty years ago, I lay in the womb of a woman, conceived in a sexual act of rape, being carried during the pre-natal period by an unwilling and rebellious mother, finally bursting from the womb only to be tormented in a family whose members I despised or pitied, and brought into association with people I should never have chosen. Sometimes I wish that, as I lay in the womb, a pink soft embryo, I had somehow thought, breathed or moved and wrought destruction to the woman who bore me, and her eight miserable children who preceded me, and the four round-faced mediocrities who came after me, and her husband, a monstrously cruel, Christ-like and handsome man with an animal's appetite for begetting children. (1)

She frequently expresses such rage against her family, even a desire to strike some of them dead. The memoir constitutes a symbolic enactment of such destruction by revealing their secrets. On the second page, she describes her oldest memory, being held down in the stalls of her father's horse lot by three of her elder brothers while the oldest, Wiley, who was about sixteen, at least tried to rape her. It is not clear if he succeeded on this occasion. She describes incest among most of her older siblings (her sister Emma remembered being tied up by her brothers to facilitate an attack), and three of the brothers committed bestiality, two of them with cows and one with chickens. Her four younger siblings were not sexually depraved, but they are presented as lazy and ungrateful, resistant to any self-improvement.

The source of the incest pattern was "ole Alice Beasley," as Gertrude's mother referred to her, an aunt by marriage who had seduced the older brothers and encouraged them to have sexual relations with their sisters. On one occasion when she was four, Gertrude was so severely injured by a sexual attack by her brother Rush that she thought she'd never be able to walk again (33), and later she learned that her fourth brother Ruel had been caught poking at her with his finger when she was "a mere baby" (196). Emma, her third sister, had "nearly spanked the skin off him" in retaliation. The mother seems to have suspected that Rush was molesting Gertrude but did nothing except warn him to "treat her right."

She seems to have no problem with sexual experimentation among children. It is rape and abuse which she abhors. When she describes hearing from her mother years later that Rush had tried to arouse Emma when she was "a great big girl, of thirteen," the implication is that sexual interest is wrong after the onset of puberty. Gertrude's comments on the older brothers have a psychological interest: ". . . I would not have liked to sleep in the same room with one of them overnight, alone. Perhaps any highly sexed girl feels that way about an older brother. I disliked having them around on account of that feeling; I was afraid of them. I was afraid of my own wish too, and found all sorts of reasons for hating them and being glad when they left home" (113). She says that her excessive sexual energy began to decline when she learned to read at about five, an odd slant on the latency theory which Freud had formulated about infantile sexuality in his *Three Essays on the Theory of Sexuality*,[4] a work which was available in English and discussed in avant-garde circles in Chicago when she was living there.

Late in the work she mentions her pleasure in these experiments again, and then corrects herself, as she does elsewhere in the book: "It may be due to something that I read in Havelock Ellis, that I write the last sentence" (193). Her background had made her very interested in reading the new works in "sex psychology." Along with Havelock Ellis's discussions of early sexual feelings, Freud's essay on "Infantile Sexuality" in the *Three Essays* had made the unthinkable thinkable by suggesting that children have sexual awareness.

Beasley is a pioneer in exploring such feelings, as when she describes an attempt by her second brother, Reuben, to arouse her when she was about eight and he was eighteen. He came to her where she was sleeping "and lay by me and tried to wake me for some sexual communication." She says she was terrified by the size of his penis, and she escaped his attentions by feigning sleep. During this time she had strong physical desires herself: "I remember that I had a strong sexual desire at this time, a desire which I experienced at the age of five or six when sexual energy was so great in me that I used to press something against myself trying to gain gratification, but this desire was also accompanied by great shame, and horror that made one's flesh shrivel up or appear to crack as with some dreadful malady" (31). Freud and Havelock Ellis had discussed autoeroticism in the young. Gertrude Beasley must have felt she had permission to deal with such matters.

Her sensational charges have no independent corroboration, of course. But they are astonishingly detailed and show a convincing knowledge of the dynamics of family abuse which she could hardly have acquired from her reading in the 1920s, as when she attributes the pathology in the family to the seduction of the older brothers by the corrupt aunt, "that ole Alice Beasley." Such an explanation of family dysfunction is commonplace now but was not in 1923. There are cases in which she repeats hurtful and dubious gossip about other people, but the family stories are far more circumstantial.

Beasley describes the appalling explanation that some of the family eventually found for their dysfunctional state (which they themselves could recognize) was that they must have "Indian blood." Her sister Corrie once told her that "we cayn't be nobody nohow," because they were of the supposed ancestry (121). Gertrude was incensed by the crudity of the comment, which was also untrue as well as racist. Later, brother Wiley made the same claim and his mother went over the Beasley ancestry—she had met so many of them, back to a great-grandfather—without being able to find any Indian forebears. The mother said that she'd rather have "nigger blood or dawg blood" than Indian blood. "There was no use to reason with her; sometimes I felt my mother the most repulsive and ignorant woman I had ever heard of. She was incarnate vulgarity and looked upon it as a mark of superiority" (200). More appropriate was another remark by Corrie that there "was never a speck of love in our family" (158).

The Beasleys were poor southern whites, the sort of people who would be made notorious in the fiction of Erskine Caldwell and William Faulkner. H. L. Mencken, the only American reviewer of the book, loved any opportunity to sneer at the backwardness of the South. He said in *The American Mercury* that the book was "a social document of the utmost interest. It presents the first genuinely realistic picture of the Southern poor white trash ever heard of."[5] He spoke of Beasley as "a none too intelligent woman, lifted out of the lowest levels of the Caucasian race." He does show admiration for the mother, whom he sees as the most impressive figure in the book.

"Poor white trash" is a loaded term, succeeded now by the equally pejorative "trailer trash." Beasley encourages such sneering judgments on her family by citing her father's gross behavior (urinating on the front step, to choose just one example) and by expressing her own embarrassment with their speech. Her mother, she tells us, said "nedcessity" for "necessity," "hope" for "help," and "remlent" for "remnant." Connoisseurs of racy idioms might well enjoy her mother's favorite saying about people who chatter "like the clatter bone of a duck's ass" or her descriptions of busybodies in her church as razorback hogs and scissorbills. After moving to Abilene, the children realized that city children say "Mother" instead of "Maw" and adapted themselves. Gertrude strove vigorously to overcome her country ways and speech.

The mother, Lucy Jane Fickling, was born in Butler County, Alabama, on April 17, 1862, the daughter of Thomas Fickling and Margaret Pharoah (or Farrow). Thomas Fickling became an overseer on a plantation and was a fervent convert to Methodism. Gertrude gives the family name by its variant, Ficklin: She may be rendering it as pronounced in the family. He moved to Navarro County, Texas, when Lucy was fourteen. There she met William Isaac Beasley (born March 17, 1854), the son of a Texas pioneer, Dr. Wiley Beasley. Dr. Beasley came to Navarro County from Mississippi when he was about eighteen. Lucy Jane and William Isaac married sometime between 1879, and their oldest child, Wiley, the first of thirteen children, was born around 1880. Gertrude believed her mother had considered her husband a "Beau Brummel" when they married, but that feeling was succeeded by hatred.

The father was one of those compulsive wanderers who helped drive the westward movement. Gertrude was born at about the time when, according to Frederick Turner's famous claim, the frontier had closed. But William Isaac Beasley was a frontiersman at heart. Wherever they settled, he would find the "grubbing too difficult and requiring too much time, or the grass too dry, or the summers too hot, or the cotton crop too little, or the water too mineral or gyps," so that "something or other was always wrong with the big central *taps* of the resources of life" (16). When he was a boy, he had shot off two fingers while playing with a six-shooter while his parents were out. He managed to be a competent fiddler anyway, a left-handed fiddler, she says, holding the bow in his left hand so that he could use the right on the strings (71). He worked variously as a cotton farmer and, in spite of his handicap, as a blacksmith, but his real vocation seems to have been engendering children, which was an enormous source of conflict with his wife, who had to bear them and raise them. When after ten children she told him they should have no more, he replied: "There'll be more wimmen in hell for trying to keep from having babies than for any other one thing" (155).

Freud's work would have introduced the concept of the Oedipus complex to Gertrude, and she seems to interpret her experience with that pattern. The Oedipal drama that she endured was ferocious, and her mother was the winner. Whenever the father asked his little daughter to kiss him, she would remember the mother's low opinion of his character. Gertrude had firsthand evidence of his meanness, saying that her father beat her brothers as if they were cast iron. On one occasion he beat a balking mare with chains and knocked out one of its eyes. He also occasionally beat or choked his wife, and he drank heavily. When the children went off to Sunday school, their mother liked to warn them that their father might kill her while they were out. The wife's weapons were verbal, a constant harping on the detestable Beasleys and the noble Ficklins.

The couple eventually had thirteen children,[6] and Gertrude learned years later that her mother had induced abortions three times before the last child was born. After the third abortion, we learn, "a terrible thing appeared to her. The image of a child was clutching at her skirts and pleading with her; it had the saddest face of anyone she had ever seen. She vowed before her God that she would die before she would ever do a thing like that again. After that she had her thirteenth child" (186). Knowledge of birth control was rare in the period, and the subject became an obsession with the daughter. When Gertrude was in her teens, her sister Corrie, who had once sided with their mother against their father, suggested that their mother had so many children out of laziness: It was a common belief that douching was an effective method of birth control, and Corrie thought that her mother was just too lazy to get up after sex and "wash herself." Such frank writing would have been unique in 1925.

The Beasley family had a cotton farm in Coleman County at the time Gertrude was born on June 20, 1892. The daughter remembered little about that period, except that there was a German colony nearby where the men did not beat their wives and the households were not squalid. When she was not quite five, about 1897, her father sold the farm and the family began years of wandering through West Texas in three covered wagons, the traditional prairie schooners. Her view of the first trip, which ended in Scurry County, near the town of Wheat, has her signature overuse of the semicolon:

> This trip did not require a very long time or else my memory is very dull with reference to it. I recall the cold; brush heaps piled around the herd after they had gathered and lain down for the night; fires being made to keep the cattle warm and those for preparing the food; black pots, skillets and kettles; my mother's rolling out the biscuits by hand; that the food was good to eat; and that I did not like the mineral water which we were forced to drink. (8)

She also recalls with horror the sandstorms which covered everything with dust.

It was at Wheat that she got her first experience of school: two weeks. By the time she started school in Abilene at ten she had completed only eighteen months of education. In Wheat she learned the basics of reading by phonics almost immediately, creating pride of her in her siblings. She had been afraid of being taken for an idiot: Her family's biggest term of contempt was to call someone an "ee-di-ut." They all went home through the dry gray grass typical of West Texas, crossing under barbed-wire fences in the classic way which A. C. Greene would later describe in humorous detail in *A Personal Country.* She was ecstatic, and when the news of her ability was repeated to her mother, the mother's reaction was swift: "W'y, she'll be a-teachin' school by the time she's sixteen"

(12). Gertrude speaks of immediately wondering about the word "W'y" which "I could make nothing of but a plain 'y.'" Not long after her first encounter with reading, she had a daydream:

> There was a great gathering of women among whom I was the principal figure, as I am eventually in almost everything I dream of, sitting or standing in some open space, all dressed in white, including myself, and all intensely interested in my directions or speech or whatever was happening. I can only suppose this to be the heavenly host for whom I am to sing the contralto. At any rate this was the beginning of my various ambitions which have gradually consumed me during the last quarter of a century and virtually incapacitated me for supplying my quota of seven sons and six daughters (no twins) to the state. (13)

In Scurry County Gertrude became aware of religious differences. Religious life in West Texas has always been heavily Protestant, and the dominant churches are the Baptists and the Church of Christ; she refers to the latter as the "non-progressive Christian Church," the conservative group in the Restoration Movement which rejected instrumental music in worship. These churches engaged in formal debates, often about the theological nuances of baptism, and Beasley recalls they debated this topic in Scurry. "On such occasions long-haired preachers were invited to the country homes for chicken dinners" (14). One elderly preacher held ten-year-old Emma, the third sister, on his lap and seemed too familiar with her, kissing her neck and getting his whiskers tangled in her braids. Her mother told her never to let it happen again. Gertrude, who was about five, had the sexual awareness of a molested child and says she felt a "tremendous sensation" with "some sexual feeling mixed with it" (17-18). This is a common pattern for her: an ambivalent obsession with sexual words and actions.

After the family moved to Mitchell County around 1898 her repulsion for her prolific father was increased by the whipping of

Corrie, the second sister. Corrie had become aware of boys, and she was seen kissing one in school by Emma, the third sister, and Gertrude. Emma, apparently jealous, told, and the mother insisted that Corrie should be whipped, lest she go too far and be ruined. The father performed this duty with a heavy horsewhip. Afterward, Corrie took refuge in the outhouse. In one of the most disturbing scenes in the book, Gertrude mentions going into the outhouse and catching a glimpse of blood and excrement (22).

After Mitchell County, the family spent another period camping out and hunting for farmland. In 1926, *The American Mercury* published a piece by Beasley called "Moving,"[7] which tells about this period in much more detail. It is probably an extract from the original version of her manuscript before the cuts made at the suggestion of Havelock Ellis and Bertrand and Dora Russell. In the magazine version, she presents a vivid picture of the father, a man who loved nomadic life and would shoot rabbits from the high seat of his prairie schooner:

> At least he was more pleased at traveling in the open road. . . . But he was black-passioned and of a violent temper, too, and the slightest inconvenience or oversight sent him into a rage. At that state of my life, I was more afraid of my father, I think, than of any person I had ever met. Yet, as he stood by the wagon in a big gray Stetson hat, a red bandanna at his throat, with his hickory shirt, his familiar jean pants, and his high boots—as he stood with one foot on the hub of the wheel, elbow on knee and chin in palm, I could see even as a child how picturesque he was, and knew that curious fascination sometimes broke through one's dark fears. . . . I was ashamed that my father chewed tobacco, but somehow it seemed to me manly to be able to spit as far as he did. (228).

This was also a family in which the mother took snuff, a habit which Gertrude did not admire.

On this trip, they encountered an old man and his granddaughter (or perhaps daughter). The old man was said to be an infidel, an extraordinary thing in fundamentalist West Texas. Later when she was teaching in Mulberry Canyon, she heard about another infidel (and thought it worth mentioning), a scholar of Latin and Greek. In the full version of her early encounter given in "Moving," Gertrude describes talking to the little girl who traveled with the old man. The child was her double—scrawny and poorly educated—but Gertrude shows no awareness of any similarity. She was offended that her family thought they should be friends: "What a scraggy, scrawny, stunted child she was! A road rat. Hers was the voice of the ignorant, shiftless and low-down of her class, pitched too low for a little girl, with a grating note in it" (229). The child had more schooling and tried to teach Gertrude reading by giving her words and asking how they should be spelled. But Gertrude complained that the girl's diction was very bad, that she said "uv" and "ef" and "frum," and expected Gertrude to know how to spell them. "'Ah k'n spell,' I told her, offended at being told to my face that I wasn't clever, 'but you cayn't pronounce.'" Already Beasley was hoping to climb out of the lower classes, and despising one's fellows is a common strategy. She sometimes seems similar to Faulkner's Colonel Sartoris Snopes, the little boy in "Barn Burning" who glimpses a world of elegance at a plantation house and turns against the squalor of his sharecropping family. There is a similar scene in *My First Thirty Years,* an occasion when Gertrude went to a fine white house with her mother, who was taking in laundry, and witnessed her mother being snubbed by the woman of the house.

In "Moving" she also provides some idyllic pictures of life on the road in West Texas, like the pleasure of making biscuits in a frying pan. Jewel Babb, who also spent her early years in a prairie schooner, presents similar scenes in *Border Healing Woman.* Babb's childhood was far happier: She had parents who were close to one another, and her one sibling, brother Hollie, was not a rapist. In one of the best scenes in "Moving," Gertrude describes a successful water witch finding water in land he wanted to sell William Beasley. The water witch asked the father to play his fiddle. He did, but Gertrude was embarrassed by his missing fingers and the simplicity of his jigs, some of which she knew had indecent lyrics (230).

The family made their way to far West Texas, to San Angelo, which she found beautiful. They camped in a pecan grove while her father negotiated to buy land. He eventually decided that the seller was trying to "skin him" and canceled the deal. The next stop was in nearby Eldorado, which turned out not to be a city of gold but a town full of saloons, which appealed to her father. The Beasleys settled there for a while and the father worked as a blacksmith. All the while tension had been growing between the parents, and the eldest son, Wiley, declared that the situation would end in a killing.

After yet another move, to Roscoe County, the thirteenth child was born. Fed up with the situation, the second and third sisters, Corrie and Emma, helped their mother keep the father away by sleeping in her bed. Gertrude says they may have armed themselves with a poker and shovel. H. L. Mencken, who seems to have read the book carelessly, says that the mother's final method of birth control was to take a shotgun to bed. The confrontation with the father was remarkably dramatic. It happened in 1902, when Gertrude was ten, and deserves lengthy quotation:

> My mother was bathing the baby before breakfast one morning and going through her usual rigamarole out loud of how badly she had been treated since she had been in the Beasley family; and was doing what she called in other people, "throwing out slurs" about the man who had begotten her children and who was lying in a bed in the same room. Finally someone dropped the water basin or somebody received a good slap in the face and was sent away crying, which roused my father who sat up on the side of the bed, began putting on his clothes and swearing in most violent tones. In his fury he exposed himself and I caught a glimpse of his private parts, the size of which frightened and awed me. He was cursing my mother and saying, "I never have cared a damn about you. . . I ought to have my God damn throat cut for ever living with you." My mother replied quietly that she had known that for many

> years, and then she began raising her voice and shouting that she would never live with him if he cut her throat that minute. A terrible scene of talking shaking fists and threats ensued, but my sisters backed themselves toward pokers and knives in the next room, the kitchen, and my father did nothing, though on several occasions during their twenty-five years of married life he had struck her or choked her on such occasions. (37-38)

After that he would sit outside the bedroom at night, chewing tobacco and cursing. The family finally escaped by a ruse, pretending to go off to pick cotton but actually settling in Abilene, where the mother obtained a divorce on the grounds of nonsupport. It was a dubious plea, since they were in fact hiding from William Beasley. The mother kept a boardinghouse in Abilene, and for a while the family supplemented their income by raising vegetables on a rented plot of land.

The daughter's comment on the marriage is remarkably bitter. She knew her mother considered the father "the sorriest man that ever lived" and had meant to leave him for years:

> She hadn't done it because she thought it was such a disgrace; she had no place to take her children; and she was afraid he would kill her as he threatened. Twenty-five years of married criminality, official monogamous prostitution, between "a damn fool woman" and "the sorriest man that God ever let live" ended after becoming the parents of thirteen legitimate bastards. I have never understood how my parents could be so heartless. I shall protest against having been brought into the world without any heritage, mental, moral or physical to my dying day. (41)

Divorce was indeed a social disgrace at the time, and the family was terrified that the truth would come out. To avoid lying, they would reply to questions about the father by saying "he is not now living," meaning "he is not living with us," a pathetic attempt at a white lie.

More disgrace awaited them soon after the flight to Abilene: The oldest daughter, Willie, went off to Baird to work. Eventually she turned to prostitution and became pregnant, more facts to conceal. The phrase "disgrace, disgrace, disgrace" kept running through Gertrude's mind, increasing her nervous terrors. And one night the mother attacked her fourth son, Ruel, with a horsewhip, having caught him in sexual congress with the old cow in the backyard. The mother revealed that Rush, the third son, had done the same in his time. We learn much later that Reuben had once tried to satisfy himself sexually with the chickens—and that the father had made a joke of it when his wife complained that the hens were not laying (195). By this time, Freud's discussion of "The Sexual Aberrations" in his *Three Essays* had revealed to the world that bestiality was not uncommon in rural areas, but Beasley was doing something remarkable by discussing bestiality in her family and identifying the members so clearly.

In 1902, Abilene was still a fairly new city, having been founded by the Texas & Pacific Railroad in 1881. The railroad advertised it as "The Future Great Town of West Texas." By 1900, it had reached a population of 3,411, somewhat short of greatness. A. C. Greene's view of Abilene in the 1920s and 1930s presents a much happier city. Gertrude Beasley's town is one of hypocrisy, secret pregnancies, and abortions. It is hard to imagine that they are writing about the same place. Some of what she reports is merely gossip, but her mother witnessed some aberrant behavior in the boardinghouse, like the miscarriage suffered by the mistress of a prominent citizen. On one occasion, William Beasley, suspecting that his daughters were being prostituted, put a man up to inquiring if there were women available at the boardinghouse. Lucy Jane pulled a six-shooter on him and made him beg for forgiveness. The first boardinghouse was on Willow Street, not an elite address, but later they moved to the most prestigious part of town, Butternut Street, the equivalent of "Silk Stocking Street" in William Humphrey's memoir, *Farther Off from Heaven.* Gertrude was socially insecure, understandably, and on one occasion when she was driven home by a schoolmate, she pretended that a more expensive house was her own and got out in front of it.

Gertrude seems to exaggerate the family's role as social outcasts. She herself had some socially prominent friends, and her brother Roger was a friend of the mayor's son, (William) Hale Kirby. Roger went into the navy with Hale, who married one of Gertrude's sisters, Martha Washington. Emily married into a respectable ranch family near Sweetwater, west of Abilene, though it may be significant that the in-laws insisted on taking the couple off to El Paso for the wedding and honeymoon, and the Beasley family was not invited. On the other hand, Gertrude mentions scornfully that two of her brothers married ignorant, snuff-dipping, cotton-picking girls.

The Ladies' Aid Society of the First Baptist Church of Abilene quickly targeted this fatherless family for charity (which was resented) and salvation. The church was part of the Missionary Baptists, a fervent group (as William Owens's *A Season of Weathering* shows), and the South Side Mission of the Ladies' Aid came by frequently to offer personal prayer meetings. The mother told them that she had already experienced her religious conversion, which she recounted with tears streaming down her face. Gertrude was disturbed by the excessive emotion shown: There was too much weeping. She was also offended by her third sister, Emma, who had gone out to work for a "sanctified" Methodist woman and came home "sobbing and blubbering, for she was the champion weeper of the whole Beasley connection, and announced that just that afternoon she had been converted. . . ." (56). Gertrude came to prefer what she considered the lack of emotion among the Church of Christ and always distrusted her family's church.

She eventually gave in to pressure and converted to the Baptists. As she slyly puts it: "Two things happened when I was fourteen. I had nervous prostrations and I joined the church" (124). The nervous breakdown was triggered by one of her father's visits to town, while joining the church was something she thought inevitable, as her mother and sisters had already joined. She walked down the aisle one Sunday night, out of a vague sense of duty. When she was baptized some time later, she was offended that Brother Lee Scarborough, the preacher, had to ask her name. The choir began to sing the traditional hymn, "Just as I am without One Plea." The conversion made her afraid that her Sunday school teacher, Mrs. Paxton, would ask her to pray in public. It was two years earlier, when Brother Scarborough was asking sinners to come forward, that Mrs. Paxton had spoken the words Gertrude found so offensive, "Little girl, why not give your heart to Jesus? Why not follow Christ *now?*" The reaction to this plea when she recalls it in the memoir seems excessive, an expression of pride and vulnerability: "I hope I shall learn to explain how this hurt my pride and the sense of degradation it gave me" (92). In her essay on "Birth Control in Russia,"[8] published some sixteen years later, she summons up the incident again when she describes being told that she was not a Marxist. She would have her revenge on Mrs. Paxton and Lee Scarborough by intimating that they had an affair. In the book, Scarborough's name is spelled Scharborough, whether through Gertrude's ignorance or a printer's error is impossible to say. The proofreading of her book was disrupted by the British mails, as we shall see. One disturbing element in the accusations against Mathilde Paxton is the fact that her daughter, Mary, was a good friend of Gertrude's.

In 1927, the reformer Dan Moody was elected governor of Texas, and Mrs. Paxton was his mother-in-law. The book became even more unacceptable in Texas than elsewhere. As we shall see, in her last paranoid letter in 1928, Gertrude suggests that a conspiracy in Texas was aiming to bring her back to the state. The subject was so sensitive that the outstanding rare book dealer in the state, Dudley R. Dobie Sr., was hauled off from San Marcos to Austin by a Texas Ranger on one occasion in the 1940s to face an investigating committee on smut led by Senator George Moffett.[9] He had obtained four copies of the book at the suggestion of his cousin, J. Frank Dobie, and sold one to the University of Texas Library. Moody was still alive and apparently the book was under an unofficial interdiction.

Beasley presents Scarborough (1870-1945) as an ignorant man, possibly a womanizer, who kept his wife "in mother-hubbards" (pregnant) all the time. Scarborough did in fact have six children, not an extraordinary number for the time. He was not an ignorant man: he had an A.B. from Baylor and a second A.B. from Yale, where he was elected to Phi Beta Kappa.[10] He wrote a number of books and was greatly respected among the Southern Baptists. She also insinuates that he and his father were cattle thieves at one time. A. C. Greene had this comment on Scarborough in a letter to me: "As for the Rev. Lee Scarborough being a cattle thief in youth, the George Scarborough family was famous as Southern Baptists and some as law enforcement officers. They were also big ranchers in the Abilene and Jones county area" (March 19, 2001).

Eventually Gertrude's father came to call with Willie and her illegitimate child. The passage is extremely interesting as an approach to memory, which is always an important issue in autobiography. Quite early she had stressed the unreliability of memory, wondering why her memory of Wheat, Texas, provided her with two quite different images of the house in which they lived. Willie's visit carries this kind of self-correction to an extreme. One day William Beasley appeared in Abilene in his covered wagon with Willie and the child. Willie asked if the "little children" could come and see her and the child in the wagon. The mother refused, saying that the older boys could go but that the smaller children (which included Gertrude) should know nothing about her and the baby. So the children were herded into a room with the blinds pulled down. Gertrude remembers that she and her mother peeked out the side of a window. The oddly punctuated passage which follows is worth quoting at length:

> Here I find it difficult to distinguish between images and realities. I have a picture in mind of seeing a partial outline of my sister and her baby as a side curtain of the covered wagon was raised; and yet as I think of this childish image which flitted through my mind then, (The shape of the child in what I now believe must have been only my fancy was that of a regularly cut rag doll with arms extended.) My mature intelligence tells

> me that it could not possibly have been a baby I saw. There was emotion and curiosity and something of hate, scorn, pity, fear, a little skepticism and perhaps myriads of other states out of which to manufacture a picture of a woman and a baby. My creation, if it were merely a fancy and not a reality, was certainly not a happy one and far from beautiful. (73)

Along with the image, she recalls a scene, which she suspects was also created by her mind: "I seemed to remember that my brothers said that my sister was crying and said that God would forgive her for He knew her heart. This again, I am afraid, cannot be taken as authentic. It may be only that kind of imagination, which makes one what America calls a sob artist." She suspects that she created this memory from other details of the sister's disaster, details reported to the family by the oldest brother, Wiley, who was present at the birth of the child.

Such passages support Paul John Eakin's claim in *Fictions in Autobiography* that the materials of the past are shaped by memory and imagination to serve the needs of present consciousness."[11] Eakin praises Mary McCarthy for questioning her own recollections in *Memories of a Catholic Girlhood,* a book which queries the reliability of early memories. One of Eakin's points is especially relevant to Beasley: "self-invention refers not only to the creation of self in autobiography but also to the idea that the self or selves they seek to reconstruct in art are not given but made in the course of human development" (Eakin 8). In her book, Gertrude Beasley evolves from a terrified little girl subject to nervous prostrations into a ferocious schoolteacher who met violence with violence in the classroom. She recalls that in childhood her "little white cords called nerves" were under enormous strain and she was subject to fits of terror and nervous prostration. She reports several times on the way that others noticed her shaking or white as a sheet. She grew from a nervous overachiever into a confident intellectual who wrote controversial articles about education for West Coast papers. She would react to perceived maltreatment with angry letters, threats of legal action, or—to her eventual downfall in 1927—with acts of vandalism.

One of the pioneering aspects of her book is the frank treatment of every area of a woman's sexuality. She tells us about coming of age as a woman in West Texas, and she freely discusses her mother's experiences with menopause. Six years after the publication of Gertrude Beasley's book, Virginia Woolf published her lecture, "Professions for Women."[12] In it she said there were two tasks a woman writer had to perform: to slay "the Angel in the House," the image of woman as modest, self-effacing and pure, and to write the truth about the body. Woolf felt that she had succeeded in slaying the Angel but not at "telling the truth about my own experiences as a body" (288). Beasley tries to tell the truth about her body by reporting in detail on sexual sensations. She repeatedly describes "movements" or "sensations" in her sexual parts, triggered by sexual desire or by obscene stories or words. Her models were probably the personal anecdotes in Havelock Ellis's huge multivolume series, *Studies in the Psychology of Sex.*[13] Ellis's anecdotes were anonymous accounts in the name of medical research, not a signed memoir, and he avoided serious trouble with the censors.The genteel and romantic ideas represented by the Angel in the House lingered in her mind. She eventually had a daydream about a dean at the University of Chicago in which she literally played that role, though with a mild sexual overtone: "I recall distinctly that I once fancied myself on the portico of Dr. Butler's residence. The figure was aerial and graceful, and wearing flowing white garments. I was in his house as an angel or a fairy or simply as an amorous woman in her night dress" (202). At the end of her work, she describes her departure from the United States for Japan in 1920, and says "a secret wish hid in my heart. I hoped I was going to find someone. . . . (231). As Larry McMurtry comments in his afterword: "Thus with the admission of a common dream—to find romance—her earnest, lonely book ends" (238).

One of the barriers to her fulfillment was her endless ambivalence: toward her mother, toward sex, toward her self-image. Her mother was the most important person in her life. In psychoanalytic theory, the mother is the primary love object and it is necessary to detach the self from the mother to achieve self-development. The usual agency for the change is the Oedipus complex. Near the end of her book, she discusses her early attachment to her mother: "once when I was a child I felt a sexual impulse while observing the baby sucking at her white breast" (211). More often she felt repulsion toward her mother's body, which she describes several times. It was heavy and distorted by constant childbearing. She recalls a time that her mother, who usually wore "mother-hubbards" which could serve as maternity dresses, went into Coleman City and had to be crammed into a corset with the aid of all three of the older sisters. The daughter was repelled by her own looks, and she feared that she might come to look like her own mother if she married and produced children, hence her sexual repression and her preoccupation with the birth control movement. Kissing, she thought, led to babies.

The sexual education offered by the mother was minimal, and Gertrude had to blunder into maturity. She was told that the doctor brought babies in saddlebags. Just before the last child was born, she saw baby clothes being made and was told on one occasion that they were for the neighbor's baby, and on another that they were for her little brother: "if I questioned too much I was sure to be sent away with a smack" (37). She was warned that she would be getting her "monthlies" without being told very clearly what they were. In a revealing passage Gertrude talks about the rage she felt when her mother smacked her with a cloth and told her to "put this in the ragbag, it will do to go between your legs" (67). When she was having "the pouts," her mother would say, "I think she got a flea *up* her crotch," a statement to which she reacted physically: "I would feel some sex movement in me, mixed with the most violent hatred of her."

She got some sex education by talking to her peers. A little girl next door provided information. Gertrude says "she was of a very ignorant and scrubby family of cotton-pickers and small workmen, that is the father engaged in blacksmithing during the winter" (65). This description fits the author's family rather closely, which explains why she eventually felt ashamed of having such a friend, one who was laughed at by teachers and students for "her bacon-greased, yellow hair and her queer manner of speech." The little girl met on the road comes to mind. Before the friendship ended, they had discussions of sex:

> One day when we were playing together in our backyard, riding broomsticks, she began to talk to me about sex matters. She said she had had sexual relations with her brother (we were both then about eleven years old) and asked me if I knew that I had a rather large opening at the place where one urinated; and then when we were sitting astride a bench she poked at me with the end of the broomstick through my underwear and recommend that I take a mirror and look at myself. As far as I can remember I was very careful to conceal from her the idea of having had any of the experiences which she referred to, while at the same time being perfectly willing to let her prod at me with the stick. I believe someone must have almost discovered us at this, as I have a recollection of terrible shame. (66)

Her greatest rage came over a demeaning reference to her breasts. She does indeed seek to write the truth about the body:

> Already when I was ten years old my nipples had begun to swell and when I was eleven there appeared a very small lump under them, sufficiently inflamed so that I felt it when I lay flat on my stomach on the floor. I never mentioned this to anyone in spite of the fact that it troubled me a lot. But I was immensely curious, uneasy and a little melancholy when I thought of it. One day when I was in my underwear my mother noticed my sprouting breasts and remarked that they looked like "little risings" and that after a while they would be as big as pin-cushions. I was so incensed that I began to blubber and cry, and before I could control my tongue had called

her a fool. (67)

Gertrude remained self-conscious about her appearance. She was told frequently that she was ugly, by her mother and by members of the community, and she says that she was twenty-five before she thought she could be attractive. Her passport photos reveal a normal enough face, though she says that her nickname in the family was "little Wiley" because she had the widely spaced teeth of her hated brother.

Since she was very small she could remember her sisters whispering about "turning thirteen," which seemed to be their term for the onset of puberty. Her period began when she was working at a soda shop. She walked home with one of her sisters who told her that it was dangerous to run or get her feet wet. When a friend, Nora Powers, went swimming in the country during her period, Gertrude's mother said that "it would kill ennybody in the world except a horse." Along with her accounts of coping with the menstrual cycle, she describes her mother's change of life at about forty-seven, which she says led to endless talkativeness and fits of temper.

Her descriptions of sexual repression are vivid. In early adolescence, she imagined getting into bed with a seventh-grade boy, but "beat it down with mental blows like those of my father's sledge hammer against the anvil, or like the lashes of the whip on a boy's back for some sexual crime" (96). The use of imagery associated with her family is not surprising. When she began teaching school at seventeen, she was courted by a young man named Vernon Trout. He kissed her hand one night: "A sexual emotion swept through me; but I composed myself and bradded down the head of the demon within me" (193). "Bradded" is another term from the blacksmith's trade, meaning to beat down.

Corrie and Emma were less inhibited. Corrie eventually married a man named Jack West, whose attractions rested on his dangerous character: He was said to have killed a man and may have had a wife and children in Louisiana. Sister Martha found some kind of device that he left behind in the bathroom of the house once, and the family feared that it involved the treatment of a venereal disease. Corrie was proud of Jack's bullying nature and his ability to talk to "fast women." When he scorned her abilities as a musician, she seemed to consider this a manly trait and sold her piano. They moved to Idaho, and Corrie reported that Jack took up with some local whores. Gertrude was living in Chicago at the time, and she received a letter from Corrie about the situation. The letter appeared to have been opened, and Gertrude was terrified to think that the landlady might have read it, for Corrie said that one of the whores had told her that it was easier to have sexual relations with a dog than a man.

As Gertrude got older, her mother talked more freely about the alleged sexual misdemeanors of the neighbors, like Ada Blake, who was ruined by a young man. After he took her off on his bicycle and seduced her, she bled "lak' a stuck hog." When Corrie took turpentine to bring on her period, the mother readily assumed that this was an attempt at abortion. After Mrs. Powers, a wealthy farmer's widow, paid Gertrude's first year of tuition at Childers Classical Institute, an act of charity which seems to have rankled mother and daughter both, Mrs. Beasley claimed that one of the benefactor's daughters had gone away not for medical treatment but for an abortion. Reproduction was made as squalid and lurid as possible by this bitter woman. Later Gertrude's brother Sumpter married a young woman named Pansy Eudaly, who had injured herself by sitting on a china-headed pin that had entered her vaginal canal and required surgery to extract. The mother was certain that this story was a cover for being "ruined" by an affair with a young preacher (151). When Gertrude's flirtation with a soldier during a holiday in Galveston went nowhere, Lucy Jane consoled her daughter by saying that, like all soldiers, he surely had syphilis. Lucy Jane also liked to make deflating remarks of a nonsexual kind: When Gertrude expressed admiration for the president of Simmons College, the reply was that he had "nigger blood."

Yet Gertrude also loved her mother and was outraged by her life, which she says was the hardest she had ever heard of. When

Gertrude was seventeen, her mother showed her a book on sex by a woman doctor. The object was not sex education for the daughter but an assessment by the mother of her own life. What struck Lucy Beasley was a reference to the importance for children of having parents who loved one another. She was devastated after reading this claim. Her husband's reaction to any attempt at a show of affection had been to "give her what she wanted" immediately, and he never addressed her with any terms of endearment. Her comments were put in a humiliating perspective for her daughter: She showed Gertrude the picture of the woman doctor (a "for-ig-en" woman) and said, "Just look at that face; she looks like you; how ugly she is! But, God, I'll bet she's smart" (205). After this appalling compliment, she assured Gertrude that she too would have degrees after her name. The conclusion of this scene helps explain the daughter's motive for writing her memoir:

> "Ah, God," said she, "what a different woman I would-a been if ennybody had ever cared for me." I wanted to throw myself at her feet and clutch at her skirts, "But, Mother, I'm here: don't forget, I'm here." I wanted to cry out. Once when she talked like that I made a vow: "I will do something about it, I will tell, Mother; I will tell; I swear I will tell your story." (147)

After Gertrude's move to Chicago, they began to have a rapprochement induced by their first really frank conversations, and at the end of one of Gertrude's visits home they "cried like two old peasants."

The author dealt with the wretchedness of her family in two ways: She sought education, and she conducted her life with extreme secrecy, never confiding in anyone. She learned to read almost immediately on starting school in Wheat, Texas. Her mother was full of stories of people who "riz" in the world by education and encouraged the younger children to go to business college, a plea mostly unheeded. Gertrude herself thought she would be a "Joseph" for her family, leading them to prosperity and self-improvement. Corrie, who had musical talent, was offered a scholarship by the president of Simmons but refused it, as she refused Gertrude's efforts to get her to become a schoolteacher. When Gertrude offered to send Roger to business school, he turned on her, saying that her career was built on his suffering, because their mother had sent him out to pick cotton while Gertrude continued in school. Gertrude and her mother pointed out that he in fact failed in school. He told Gertrude that he was embarrassed to have such an absurdly studious sister, and he shunned her when he passed her on his delivery wagon. Reuben told her that she was not intelligent, otherwise she would not have to study so much, and contrariwise, Corrie said that she deserved no credit for doing well in school because God had given her a bigger brain than most people. Gertrude could have her pick of demeaning theories about her achievements.

The generosity of Mrs. Powers had enabled her to take a year of high school at Childers Classical Institute, a school which would evolve into Abilene Christian University. Gertrude, as ready as her mother to make sneering comments, says that the school was known as "Childers' Christian Idiots" to students of other institutions. The Baptists were upset that she was attending a school associated with their biggest rivals in West Texas, the Church of Christ, so a scholarship was arranged in 1908 for Simmons College, now Hardin-Simmons University. She graduated from Simmons in 1914. Her education there gave her the basics in mathematics, literature, German, sociology, and psychology, and she describes the courses and teachers in detail, offering a real opportunity for anyone doing research on the history of Hardin-Simmons University or Texas higher education as a whole. But real intellectual excitement came only when she began graduate work in Chicago

At school she kept her feelings to herself. Her closest friend in the Classical Institute, Adelaide Klingman, the daughter of an eminent Church of Christ theologian, told her that one professor was so attractive that "sometimes I wish he would put his thing in me." Gertrude carefully refrained from reacting, which hurt Adelaide, though not as much as the reporting of the incident in the book must have hurt if she read it. The pattern of listening to other people's confidences while keeping her own persisted through her years at the University of Chicago, where she made many friends among female students. The memoir is her way of finally telling the truth, even if it meant betraying numerous confidences. The Angel in the House became the truth-telling Demon.

Her schoolteaching days were another way for a young woman full of anger to express her rage in violence. She was hired at seventeen to teach at Mulberry Canyon for sixty-five dollars a month, ten dollars less than Hallie Stillwell received in Presidio a few years later. Texas country schools looked for one qualification above all in teachers: the ability to keep order, which meant corporal punishment. In *A Season of Weathering*, William A. Owens describes his disastrous first job, one he lost because of reluctance to beat the students. Gertrude Beasley arrived with high ideals as a teacher, but when order broke down she went to school one day with a bag holding a two-and-a-half-foot strap and a copy of the school laws. She began what she calls her reign of terror, and she punished most often for bad language and behavior outside of school. At the same time she was reading William James's enlightened *Talks to Teachers on Psychology* (1899). She was soon in demand as a teacher and taught in several districts, each one paying her more than the one before. In one community, the previous teacher, a man, had been chased around the school by a student with an ax. She placed a tree limb in easy reach and when the same student gave her a black eye, she hit him so severely that he claimed his arm was broken. His younger brothers came toward her with knives drawn but she faced them down. The community approved, though the boy's family talked of tarring and feathering her—and of pouring tar in her "other end." She responded by sending to Corrie and her mother to bring her a revolver. She made it clear that she would use it and she had no trouble.

She brought the pistol with her when she started graduate work in education at the University of Chicago in 1914, fearing that white slavers would kidnap her between the train station and the YWCA. She arrived a socialist, having read Eugene V. Debs's famous work, *An Appeal to Reason,* at the very time she was appealing to the strap at Mulberry Canyon. Texas is not considered a center for socialism, to put it mildly, but the Snows, the farm family she boarded with at Mulberry Canyon, read socialist papers and talked about the ideas in them. Two of her brothers, who had become itinerant laborers, returned home to Abilene converted to socialism. Before the Red Scare in 1919 put an end to socialism as an electable alternative, there was strong grassroots support for Debs and other socialist leaders Gertrude admired, like Scott Nearing.

Her socialist principles of brotherhood and justice were quickly tested. She had never examined race from a socialist point of view and was accustomed to demeaning views of blacks from her family. In her first job, at an Abilene soda shop, she angered the owner by serving an ice cream soda to a handicapped black man, which might have damaged the business by outraging the white clientele. With this background, she was astonished to see a black student, a "mulatto," in one of her classes in Chicago. She decided at first that he was merely aping his instructors but finally had to acknowledge his abilities. When she saw young black women in the swimming pool, she hesitated before entering but then applied the cliché, "when in Rome." One of her new friends at the Elinor Club, a rooming house for young women in the professions, asked her about a lynching in Texas: "Beasley, ain't your people civilized yet?" Gertrude replied with the usual southern ideology about the necessity of lynching: "I told the most gruesome horrors I could remember, of negroes raping white women and cutting off their breasts" (166). For a while she had the nickname "Lyncher." A peer group exerts powerful pressure, and she soon adjusted her attitudes. Later her mother visited her and mentioned that the razorbacks and scissorbills in the church were afraid she might be teaching black children, which was not the case.

In his study of the first American avant-garde, *Strange Bedfellows,* Steven Watson says that Chicago was a beacon to those who were "dissatisfied with midwestern towns where cultural life was limited to Booster Clubs and potluck suppers in the church basement"[14] Cultural life in Abilene was on the level of the small towns of the midwest, if not below them. In Chicago, Beasley could attend operas and exhibitions at the Art Institute. In *American Salons: Encounters with European Modernism 1885-1917,* Robert Crunden makes this point about Chicago intellectuals in 1917:

> [Chicago's] most talented artists were firmly committed to sexual liberation in some form, thought of themselves as sympathetic to socialism but were most likely to be anarchists suspicious of political involvement. They sometimes read psychoanalytic literature, and talked about its ideas whether they had or not.[15]

Gertrude Beasley was at home in this environment.

She heard Margaret Sanger lecture on birth control and bought Sanger's *What Every Woman Should Know,* which she hid in her room in the lowest drawer with her underclothes, though she could imagine her mother saying, "A helluva lot of use you'll ever have for such a book" (177). She was delighted with talks by Emma Goldman, the celebrated anarchist, especially a lecture on atheism—strong stuff for a Texan raised in a fundamentalist world where an "infidel" was a curiosity—and she visited the home of the late Frances Willard, a temperance leader and suffragette. She organized meetings for the newly formed Woman's Party in 1916. She and her journalist friend, Hume Whitacre, visited the Chicago headquarters of the most controversial socialist group, the Industrial Workers of the World, the IWW, or "Wobblies," many of whom would be imprisoned or lynched when the First World War began.

During the Chicago period she was preoccupied with her own work. She put herself through the demanding program at Chicago by taking night and summer school, working during the day as a teacher. She had more humane principles now. One of her influences was Ellen Key, the Swedish educator who had made a strong case against corporal punishment for children in books like *The*

Century of the Child. The head of the Chicago schools was Ella Flagg Young, whom she had admired for years, having read about her in *The Normal Instructor.* Young, like Gertrude, had begun teaching at the age of seventeen and eventually made $10,000 a year. Gertrude met Young and was impressed by the way that men deferred to this influential woman: Principals and superintendents were nervous when talking to Young, "big husky men," too. "It was high time the tables were turned; we had had enough of men's superior leadership" (241).

She herself was becoming steadily more assertive. She argued about the marking system with Charles Hubbard Judd, the eminent head of the education division. Hubbard was the author of a book she greatly admired, *Genetic Psychology,* a classic work anticipating evolutionary psychology by applying Darwinian thought to education, something Gertrude had learned about in Texas in a very practical way. He raised her average from a C to a B minus and approved her master's thesis (on "Educational Legislation and Administration in Texas 1820-1860") in spite of her insubordinate attitude. She was learning to be independent.

However, she worked far too hard, suffering from the overachiever's terror of failure, the fear of having to go home to Texas where she would be laughed at for her presumption. Her life of secrecy and obfuscation of her background was telling on her. She advocated atheism in her discussions with other young women and then would go to her room to pray against failure. Ruefully, she says that in her last year as a teacher in Texas she had become a "praying gun-toter, who had sworn to shoot to kill," but now "I was a praying atheist." Exhaustion and anxiety must have been factors in the facial pain, headaches, and back pain she describes. She came close to collapse and took tonics and treatments from a woman osteopath.

On a visit to Texas, she visited Emma, who was now married and living in Sweetwater. There Gertrude had treatments from another osteopath, a married man who treated her in an unorthodox way, by massaging her breasts. Some physicians had been treating neurasthenia by massaging women to orgasm,[16] but she was sure that he was sexually interested: "Why didn't I stop him and say that my thin flat breasts need no attention. No, I liked it; I let him do it." (182). He discussed her "sex energy" and said that "all intelligent and brilliant people were extremely passionate." When he would put his hands on her legs or come "too near my sexual parts, I nearly burned up with sex energy." He kissed her, and she says, "I liked it; but I drew away as if I were horrified and told him to stop." She finally told him that "this had been a course in experimental psychology; he was really very interesting under certain stimuli, I told him" (183).

She tried writing a short story about her low-key romance with the soldier in Galveston. An editor who had offered assistance with her writing for a fee told her that the story was too romantic: It appeared that wedding bells would be ringing. She lacked experience of life, was his implication. "I ought to make a sex story of 'Texas and Sexes'; as it stood it sounded as though the wedding bells were going to ring" (186). In the streetcar after the conference he sat very close to her, "and I thought he meant to suggest that he would give me all the experience I required. The incident cured me of short story writing for a long, long time." She reread the story when she was writing about the episode in her memoir. She realized that she had lived on a mass of lies, "half lies, expediency lies, and black lies." She had tried to make her Chicago friends believe that she came from a "jolly and care free family" that she was extremely fond of, and that her mother was "an adorable old-fashioned type," but voices would cry in her ears sometimes, "liar, liar, liar!" Her autobiography tells the truth about her family, as well as passing on gossip about others in Abilene.

Her mother visited her in Chicago, which caused great apprehension, as Gertrude had never told her friends that her mother was poorly educated and crude. But the visit went reasonably well and strengthened the relationship. Her mother decided that Gertrude was getting better looking because "education sure did improve the human countenance," and she told her that Emma, the sister she most envied, "was not pretty anymore; her neck was long and full of wrinkles and she was getting to be fat" (214). Gertrude must have delighted in this news: Earlier she had mentioned that men sent Emily enormous boxes of candy. By this time the mother's boardinghouse had shared in the prosperity of Abilene, which was having an oil boom thanks to a refinery, and she was hoping to sell the oil rights to some land near Ranger which she had inherited from her father, Thomas Ficklin. One might hope that she was rich when she died in Pomona in 1948. Her death certificate indicates that she moved to California in 1925 or 1926. Emma died there also, at the astonishing age of ninety-nine, and McKinley, the baby of the family, died in California at ninety-one. It is tempting to speculate that the publication of her daughter's book caused Lucy Jane to leave Texas but there is no evidence.

Gertrude Beasley left Chicago in 1918 after receiving her degree and took up a job training teachers at the normal school in Bellingham. She seems, at least by her own testimony, to have been a success. She soon had to seek medical advice for ailments, some of which sound emotional in origin: headaches, neck aches, sore shoulders and spine, and "terrific pains at menstruation." The doctor suggested that her genitals were not functioning properly: She needed to get married and have a baby, he said, though she overheard him saying that her womb was too small and that she probably could not have a child. Judging from the treatment recommended, she must have had a tipped uterus, a condition which often does improve with pregnancy. She discussed her allegedly shrunken womb with the head of the normal school, Miss Earhardt, and explained that she had spent ten years in strenuous study. Miss Earhardt assured her that she once had the same problem. "Nearly all women who worked with their brains shared my difficulties." This was a common notion, and the eugenicists, many of whom were women associated with progressive causes like the birth control movement, had themselves in a bind. Educating women was important, but the development of the brain was commonly thought to cause atrophy of the womb, which meant that the most educated women might not reproduce.

In Bellingham she began to write radical articles about politics and the poor pay given to teachers. She quarreled with the president of the normal school, who actually called her doctor to try to get damaging information about her stability. She was appalled that it might become known that she had been seeking treatment for her sexual organs. "I marvel now that a woman twenty-seven years old could be so distressed and hurt by the thought of such gossip" (228). She must have felt humiliated when she discovered that the editor of the Bellingham newspaper thought that her father had once been the governor of Texas! After a long controversy, which becomes boring to read about in its circumstantial detail, her contract was renewed. The terrified young girl who watched bitter conflicts between her parents and kept her family's secrets had evolved into an aggressive woman willing to take on the educational establishment. She was still vulnerable: When she applied for her passport for her trip to Japan, she was so deeply embarrassed over the marital status of her parents that the clerk had to say it was no one else's business.

As she packed to go, she was ashamed to find her revolver in her trunk. Once she had even envisioned shooting the president of the normal school after she discovered his attempt to get information from her doctor. She decided that she was not a person to be entrusted with a gun. She was, she realized, a socialist and a pacifist: "The whole theory of guns, armaments in general, as a protection, was a fallacy; the idea was revolting" (231). The author is showing some awareness of the rage she has accumulated.

She left from Vancouver on the *Empress of Japan* on June 23, 1920. She visited many sites in Japan and sent out articles about them to the *National Geographic,* which accepted (but never printed) "Some Things about Work in Japan," an essay which expresses sympathy with Japanese workers from a socialist point of view. In December, 1920, she met Bertrand Russell on his brief trip to Japan. She had read his *Why Men Fight* on a train trip back to Texas during the war. Her travels included Korea, which was then a Japanese possession. Her application for registration as a native citizen, filed with the U.S. Consul in Tientsin on March 3, 1922, indicates that she went to China on July 27, 1921, and obtained secretarial work at the Peking Union Medical College, an institution set up by the Rockefeller family. The form contains the only surviving record of her father's exact date of birth and gives her height as 5' 4" and the color of her eyes, blue, as well as the Chinese form of her surname, Pien Ssu Li Shi. On May 23, 1922, her application for a passport to Russia was approved by the U.S. Consul in Lithuania, who handled all such requests. The consul wrote on the front of the application that she was not likely to embarrass the government. He did not know her, obviously.

She went to Russia soon after, undoubtedly on the Trans-Siberian Railway, and visited Siberia and the Crimea before Moscow. In Moscow she interviewed Soviet officials about birth control for her two-part article in Margaret Sanger's *Birth Control Review.* She had scathing things to say about the men and praised the women. In the January installment of the article, she mentions that she published articles in *Izvestia* and *Ogenyok (The Flame)* about Sakai Toshihiko, a socialist whom she says was killed by the police during the chaos of the great earthquake of 1923. Her facts are wrong: Toshihiko lived until 1933. She was disturbed when she realized that the articles had been abridged, leaving out Sakai's views on feminism. An article on "The New Movement in Japan" was rejected by editors of *Novie Vostok (The New East)* because they said, "You are not a Marxist." This offended her, causing her to comment on the "old woman" in Texas who said, "Little girl, you are not saved." She described herself sarcastically to a Communist as an old maid, but she made no revelations about her personal life in the article.

After a trip which included Italy and France, she arrived in England on October 10, 1924, according to her 1926 passport application. Her intention was to take courses at the University of London. They have no record of her attendance but she did obtain a reader's ticket for the British Museum on December 3, 1924, on the recommendation of Bertrand Russell. She said in the application that she wanted to do historical research. She showed the memoir to one of her favorite writers on sex psychology, Havelock

Ellis, and to Russell and his wife, Dora. Beasley cut the work on the basis of their suggestions. Ellis suggested that she send it to Robert McAlmon's avant-garde press in Paris. McAlmon, who was the husband of convenience of "Bryher" (Winnifred Ellermann), as a cover for her relations with American poet H. D., published extraordinary writers with the aid of a subsidy from his immensely wealthy father-in-law. McAlmon's nickname among writers was Robert McAlimony. The book was printed by Maurice Darantière, the same printer who prepared Joyce's *Ulysses* for Sylvia Beach's book shop, Shakespeare and Company. Beasley would eventually write a furious letter to Beach, accusing her and McAlmon of swindling her. *Ulysses,* which had powerful literary friends, eventually triumphed in spite of censorship. The fate of *My First Thirty Years* was different. The association with the printer of *Ulysses* would do her damage.

Robert McAlmon's brief comment on Beasley in his 1938 memoir, *Being Geniuses Together,* adds some background, though he leaves out important details, such as her arrest in London:

> Wanting to get a copy of Gertrude Beasley's *My First Thirty Years,* while in America, I was asked $40 for a book for which we had charged $2.50. Some three hundred copies of that were lost in America. The author, not having registered her residence in London, got into trouble with the authorities at the time proof was being sent to her. The ensuing newspaper publicity made it impossible to attempt distribution of her book in England. In the publishing of some twenty books only two authors got "temperamental," and they were both Gertrudes, Stein and Beasley, and may it be said, both megalomaniacs with an idea that to know them was to serve them without question about their demands.[17]

McAlmon only tells part of a dramatic story. Much more is contained in letters she wrote to Bertrand Russell. Naturally she looked him up in England. Five of her letters to Russell have survived in his papers at McMaster University, and one of them was included in the second volume of his autobiography,[18] with the annotation, "Miss Beasly [sic] was a schoolteacher from Texas, who wrote an autobiography. It was truthful, which is illegal" (176).[19]

Her first letter, a handwritten one from the Gresham Hotel in Bloomsbury, dated November 27, 1924, mentions that Russell had read the manuscript and made comments on it, and that Russell's wife, Dora, was reading it also. Russell annotated many of his letters when he was preparing his autobiography. On the original letter, he wrote: "Gertrude Beasley was a Texas schoolteacher who wrote an autobiography that Scotland Yard considered obscene. I tried to help her." On a typed copy preserved in his archives, the comment was more colorful: "This lady was a schoolteacher from Texas, whom I first met in Japan. She said some of her pupils were rather tough, so I asked if she ever had any difficulty in keeping order. 'Oh no,' she replied, 'of course I always had a loaded revolver on my desk.'" Carl Spadoni, the curator of Russell's papers, has told me in an E-mail (March 7, 2001) that Russell remembered her into his old age and mentions her in the taped reminiscences he prepared in 1950 as background for writing his autobiography.

The next letter, dated June 21, 1925, the one printed in Russell's *Autobiography,* has a startling opening: "Shortly after you left in March I found a publisher for my book, a semi-private company in Paris. Several weeks ago a few of the proofs reached me. Yesterday morning I found myself before the Magistrate at Bow Street after a night in prison." She goes on to tell Russell that on the night of June 21, 1925, "an officer of Scotland Yard called to see me bringing with him a bundle of the proofs of my book which he described as 'grossly obscene.'" He told her that she would have to appear before the magistrate on a charge of "sending improper matter through the mails." The proofs had been intercepted because they were sent by the printer of *Ulysses.* When the detective examined her passport and found that it was unregistered, he took her to the Bow Street Court immediately and she was jailed. Released on ten pounds bond, she was told that she would have to appear on June 27 to be considered for punishment and deportation. Ellis had thought of writing a preface to the book, but finally decided not to do so after the trouble began.

Russell arranged a lawyer, and several of his friends assisted her. One person was definitely not helpful: Russell received a letter (June 30, 1925) from a leading psychoanalyst, Paul Bousfield, whose support he had solicited. Bousfield, a Harley Street physician, replied in a pompous letter siding with the police, suggesting that the work was useless and even harmful because it was not the product of an analysis and would be published without the proper scientific annotations. Beasley got off with a fine for having an unregistered passport. The total cost was twenty-five pounds. Russell sent her a check for that amount (at a time when he was by no means well-off). She returned it, Robert McAlmon (who had Bryher's wealth to back him) having paid the amount. In her letter of June 28, 1925, describing the trial, she says that she had asked the arresting policeman, Inspector Draper (a name worthy of a detective novel), if he would have imprisoned her for sending the Bible or Zola or Swift through the mails.

> He informed me that Zola's translator was prosecuted in this country. Besides he thought it extremely important that when one wrote an honest book, one ought to die before publishing it. "Swift and Zola are dead," he remarked as though to convict me of wrong doing. Furthermore I am told that you are free only "to do good" in this country. I do hope we can meet before long for a talk. This case has been frightfully interesting.

In her biography of Havelock Ellis, Phyllis Grosskurth quotes a letter which Ellis wrote to his common-law wife, Françoise Lafitte, about the trial: "I can think of nothing else. The world is such an evil place that I have only one wish now & that is to get out of it as quickly as possible."[20] He goes on to mention, in a passage which Grosskurth does not quote, that she "is not specially attractive" and says of her work: "It is a *remarkable* book though one cannot exactly *like* it, & one feels that G. B. is too much obsessed by her family. She needs a lover to make her forget her family,"[21] a typical Ellis prescription. The case was prosecuted by the improbably named Sir Archibald Bodkin, Grosskurth says, a moral zealot.

Her troubles did not end with the Bow Street trial. U.S. Customs seized many of the books when they were sent to the United States. The National Archives and Records Administration has a thick file on the disposal of a shipment of twelve books sent unsolicited to Brentano's Book Shop in New York in 1927. E. W. Camp, director of customs, issued the order by letter on March 7,1927.[22] In an earlier letter to the collector of customs in New York, Camp noted that the book had been seized in every case in which it came to the attention of the department (May 13, 1926).

Along with slander of the governor's mother-in-law, the book used raw Anglo-Saxon terms abundantly. Jim Sanderson's "Art in the Desert," an essay in his *A West Texas Soapbox*,[23] deplores what he considers excessive prudery in contemporary West Texas: It is hard to imagine the shock her language and subject would have created in 1925. Dudley R. Dobie Jr. heard from his father that the book was taken off shelves all over Texas.[24] Beasley apparently expected an English audience for her work anyway, and her glosses of what she considered American vulgarisms are amusing. She identified "ass" as "arse" several times, and she has one unintentionally hilarious definition of the favorite southern term of abuse, "shit-ass," telling the supposed English reader that it might suggest a donkey continually producing excrement but might also mean a person with his buttock half covered with dung. She even thought it necessary to define "turd" (spelled "tird") and "fart" to the countrymen of Chaucer. She meant to be absolutely frank.

One of her psychological problems is a simultaneous horror of and attraction to obscenity, and U.S. Customs must have been horrified but not attracted to a passage about her early schooldays in Abilene when she saw "Fuck me you whoar" carved into a seat in the outhouse used by the female students and teachers (58). As a future teacher herself, she reacted to the misspelling as much as to the obscenity. At times she seems to be using the traditional four-letter words as an act of purgation. She was always repelled by them and even as an adult was made ill when she heard a perfectly respectable woman use the word "shit."

Whether or not she was the megalomaniac of McAlmon's description is not clear. He was married to Bryher at the time, a remarkably confident and self-assertive woman, so he would not easily overestimate an ego. Her letter to Sylvia Beach on August 6, 1927, reveals a strong temper. The letter is preserved in Bryher's papers at Yale: It was probably forwarded to McAlmon and Bryher by Beach.[25] The royalties on the book would not have been substantial even if most of the copies had been sold rather than destroyed, but this was not Gertrude's view of the situation:

> Madam,
> I write to ask you to get the remaining copies of my book which you have on hand ready for the American Express Agent. McAlmon wrote in reply to the last letter which I wrote you concerning my book that Miss Beach . . . did not even care to stock it. Please see that these books are handed over at once.

She then quotes more of McAlmon's letter, which must have been exasperated: "Further correspondence is useless. As you have been told repeatedly, if you wish, or an agent of yours may collect the remaining copies of the book in Paris." She ends her letter to Beach with an accusation and an insult:

> I write also to declare that I believe you have acted as accomplice in the grossest theft of the profit made out of my book. There is not legitimate reason for your refusal to tell me how many copies of my book you have sold. I cannot believe that you are the imbecile which you represent yourself to be in your letters.

Egomaniac or not, the terrified child from Coleman County had grown up to speak for herself, perhaps unjustly in this case. Her profits from a book issued in 500 copies selling at $2.50 each could not have been much, especially when U.S. Customs had destroyed most of them. In her own autobiography, published in 1956, Beach discussed the Contact Press. Her only comment on Beasley reads: "My *First Thirty Years,* by Gertrude Beasley, a Texas schoolteacher, was anything but dull." [26]

The U.S. State Department has searched its files at my request, and clues about her later predicament in England have turned up. She sent a postcard to the U.S. vice consul from the Gresham Hotel on August 19, 1927. According to Sally Kuisel of the National Archives and Records Administration,[27] the postcard is bound into a large volume and cannot be photocopied, but is addressed to "The American Councler" and reads: "Sir will you kindly come to me at once I am in distress." It is signed "Miss Beasley." The consular office called the hotel the next day but was told that Beasley had been evicted for nonpayment of rent.

Her last known message came a few months later. On January 7, 1928, she sent a four-page letter to the secretary of state from the S. S. *Republic,* a liner headed for New York harbor. The letter had no return address so it was never answered: It was filed away nine days later and has literally never seen the light of day until now.[28] She was refusing to leave because she thought she would be killed or prevented from completing a work of the utmost significance. The letter is written in what must have been intended to be an objective, factual style. It is highly repetitive and obsessive. Some of her charges may well be true, but suspicion and terror led to some extreme statements.

She was writing the secretary of state to inform him of a claim for compensation (5,000 pounds or $25,000) against the British government and the British police for "a conspiracy against myself, a conspiracy which has spread to other countries." She says that she was evicted from the Gresham Hotel by the landlady on August 19, 1927, although she had an agreement valid until September 15. The landlady was assisted by two men she believed to be a British secret agent (from the Central Intelligence Division) and "a counterfeit London policeman." She says that the landlady and the secret agent beat her unmercifully and "gave me many strokes across the head and neck which I found later were calculated to incapacitate me mentally." On the day that her lease was supposed to run out, she returned to the hotel and poked holes in two tiny windows with her umbrella as a protest. The scene is painful to visualize; this woman, who says she was destitute and starving, wielding her umbrella in a symbolic gesture. She was arrested and taken to Holloway Jail, where she claims that the police made attempts on her life.

She was remanded to the mental ward at the Holborne Institution at her hearing at Clerkenwell magistrate's court. To obtain her release, she had to provide names of people who might help her financially. She suggested two publishers who owed her money: Robert McAlmon (who detested her) and Samuel Roth, a publisher of erotica. She also gave the names of two Abilenians. One of them is not surprising: J. D. (Jefferson Davis) Sandefer, the president of Simmons University, who had been friendly to her. The other name was, astonishingly, G. L. Paxton, the father-in-law of the governor, a man whose wife she had suggested was an adulteress with Lee Scarborough. Later in her letter she says she had been told by Miss Jones of the American Relief Society that persons in Texas (blackmailers, Beasley says) had written to the British police and were trying to have her sent home. They were, she said, aiding and abetting the British police in attempts to take her life. It is hard to imagine that a stable person would want help from someone likely to be her enemy.

She makes various other charges. At one point her rage was so great that she used southern vernacular, referring to a "jackass journalist." She outlines the conspiracy:

> The British Home Office and the British Police tried to find a charge of murder or manslaughter or attempts at such crimes against myself with the object either of having me executed or sentenced to long term imprisonment. It is the British Secret Police who are at the bottom of the references

> in the European press to myself as an anarchist and the British Police, for reasons best known to themselves, have endeavored to classify me as a politician rather than an artist or a scientist. It is the British Police who have inspired a jackass journalist to mention my name in the same sentence with the roué, the hypocrite and the spy Casanova.

Some of her account may be true: The British government would have seen her as a writer of obscene works and may have regarded her as a subversive, as she was a journalist who had been to Russia and a friend of Bertrand Russell, who had been imprisoned in World War I for his anti-conscription activities. It is not inconceivable that someone in the British government encouraged her landlady to evict her, and considering that she was doubtless *persona non grata,* a C.I.D. agent may have been present at the eviction. As for people in Texas conspiring against her, Governor Moody and the Paxton family would certainly have seen her as a slanderer, and letters may have been written about her to the British government. As for her status with the United States government, the staff of the National Archives and Records Administration has searched the files of the Department of Justice and the Bureau of Investigation (forerunner of the FBI) and have found no references to her.

Her reference to Samuel Roth is a clue to a previously unnoted printing of her book. Roth's complicated publishing operations have been traced with great care by Jay A. Gertzman in *Smuthounds and Bookleggers: The Trade in Erotica 1920-1940.*[29] Some of the works published by Roth were pornographic by the standards of the time. One of his many imprints was what he called "The Magazine Adventure of the Century," his journal of high-class erotica called *Casanova Jr's Tales.* Beasley's *My First Thirty Years* was serialized in four installments in that magazine, an appearance previously unnoted.[30] The notoriety of *My First Thirty Years* would have interested him in Beasley. Some of the ads for *Casanova Jr* in his *Two Worlds Monthly*[31] mention that the book was selling for twenty to fifty dollars, which would help explain the impoverished author's rage at Sylvia Beach, though neither Beach nor McAlmon was responsible for the used-book market. One ad calls her book "a story which is still the sensation of Paris." Her book was serialized along with extracts from *The Memoirs of Casanova,* which explains why that "jackass journalist" compared her to the spy and roué. While this particular publication was not sleazy, appearing in it would have encouraged the authorities to think of her as a morally dubious writer.

At the end of her complaint, she states: "I must protest against leaving this boat until my case is settled. The British are very shrewd and the Americans unusually stupid where plots such as the one laid against myself are concerned. I naturally do not wish to leave this steamer to lose my life or to give up the opportunity of completing a work which I believe to be one of the most significant of its sort ever written." She ended by saying: "I hope to hear if the State Department will take up my claims against the British Government." But her call for help was filed away. No doubt the desperation and claims of an international conspiracy made it appear the work of a crank. The trail of this remarkable author is by no means cold, and more may emerge to explain her absolute silence after 1928.

Hallie Crawford Stillwell

4

FROM GREENHORN TO CHILI QUEEN: HALLIE CRAWFORD STILLWELL

Hallie Crawford Stillwell was born in 1897, some thirty-six years after Sallie Reynolds Matthews. By the time she died on August 18, 1997, two months short of her hundredth birthday, she had become a media star. She was adroit at creating an image, and her activities helped support her family's ranch in the Big Bend region during times of drought and bad cattle prices. Her first unusual enterprise was a wax-making operation on the ranch, using the local candelilla plant. She also worked as a barber and coroner at various times and operated an RV park at the ranch with a "Hallie Stillwell Museum." When she died she not only appeared on the cover of *Texas Monthly,*[1] she received an obituary in *The New York Times,* a longer one than a much finer writer, William Humphrey, received a year later.[2] She started out as a schoolteacher and wound up an original in the J. Frank Dobie sense, a character out of the old rock. But she achieved her stubborn self through a long series of ordeals, mostly at the hands of her husband, though drought and hard times contributed as well.

Stillwell and her family are the subjects of an excellent documentary about ranching in the Big Bend area, Alan Fisher's *Change in the Bend,* produced by Austin Community College, and she was included with two other ranch women in a film by Heather Gilmour, *Not a Clinging Vine.*[3] Her later career is fascinating as an example of image-making, but her autobiography, *I'll Gather My Geese,* describes a substantial career as a ranchwoman and feminist trailblazer. In a way she recapitulated several phases of history moving from the pastoral life of ranching to proto-capitalism with the wax-making industry, then created a role for herself in the information society as a tongue-in-cheek celebrity.

Born in Waco on October 20, 1897, she could remember her family moving from place to place in covered wagons. Her memoir is written in a colloquial style and presented in a rather choppy fashion. She was the kind of narrator that Walter Benjamin described in "The Storyteller," a woman who valued experience and expressed a wisdom gained from it, although at times her loyalty to her husband, Roy, seems misguided. She polished her stories for years in columns, public lectures, and frequent radio interviews. Some of her anecdotes first appeared in interviews published in 1955 in Virginia Madison's *The Big Bend Country of Texas.*[4] She later collaborated with Madison on *How Come It's Called That? Place Names in the Big Bend Country.*[5] The audiocassette of radio interviews by "Tumbleweed" Smith, *Hallie Stillwell 1897-97*[6] overlaps with the book. By the time she sat down to write her book in her nineties, the material had been carefully refined. Indeed, the cassette shows how routine some of it had become. On one track, it is clear that she does not know what town she is in. Stillwell's anecdotal tone at its best—earthy, irreverent, proud but self-deprecating—comes through in the written versions of some of her narratives in *I'll Gather My Geese.* Occasional slang expressions like "I could have fought a room full of saws" and "I had flubbed the dub again" give a regional flavor to her style.

Her father was a restless storekeeper who moved the family often. They wound up in Brewster County in the Trans-Pecos region, where she spent the most of her life, with a brief sojourn as a teacher in Presidio, to the west. The family arrived in Alpine in a prairie schooner in 1910, the same year that J. Frank Dobie came to teach. She graduated from high school in Alpine in 1916. According to a letter to me from her daughter, Dadie Stillwell Potter, Hallie knew Dobie from the school in Alpine, an interesting conjunction of two writers who would become Texas legends as much for their images as for their writings. Potter says, "He was so handsome and all the girls were in love with him" (November 2, 2000). After high school, she took a six-week course in a normal school, a very good route for a woman wanting a job: "Teaching was certainly the most respectable job for a woman in the West Texas area" (11). She found the job in Presidio on the Mexican border, in the county west of Brewster. Presidio is across from Ojinaga, a city which had fallen to Pancho Villa. Her father did not approve of her move and uttered the phrase which she used for her book:

> My father thought this place was too dangerous for a young lady. He didn't want me to go, and stressed this point often.
>
> "Daughter I think you're going on a wild goose chase," he said.
>
> I finally replied somewhat flippantly. "Then I'll gather my

> geese." Even though my father disapproved of my going to Presidio, I armed my self with a six-shooter, my father's favorite and most dependable weapon and one he was very glad to lend me, took my teaching certificate, and headed for Presidio. (11)

The six-shooter is a cliché of the Old West and has a special place in Texas history, thanks to the Texas Rangers: In her memoirs, Mary Maverick rather jubilantly describes the first use of the weapons against the Comanches in 1844. The guns which figure in this study belong to women: Hallie Stillwell, Alice Henderson Stillwell, Lucy Jane Beasley, Gertrude Beasley, Jewel Babb, Charlie Marie Karr (mother of Mary Karr), and Tía Pepa, the great aunt of John Phillip Santos. Only Pepa is recorded as firing one, a silver pistol given to her as a wedding present.

Hallie Stillwell represented a change in the behavior of American women, one which had been accelerating since the turn of the century and would speed up even more with the First World War, which made employment in offices and factories easier to obtain. Women were changing their ideas as well as their cumbersome fashions. A six-shooter makes an unusual women's fashion accessory and challenges the mystique of the western male. After her marriage, Stilwell's husband told her that when he was away she should shoot any stranger who walked through the front gate. He told her that she would only have one chance and should shoot to kill. Fortunately, she only needed firearms for hunting.

Her most dangerous moment in Presidio did not involve Pancho Villa: She was followed one day by two drunken U.S. soldiers from the unit assigned to protect the town. She also had her first encounter with the customs agents after she bought a "wet" horse, one brought in from Mexico illegally. She seems to have charmed them: They gave her twenty-five dollars for the horse, probably out of their own pockets. Because she would marry a rancher who needed Mexican labor, there would be other encounters with federal agents—mostly the Border Patrol. Ranches in the Big Bend, like the ranches in the Brush Country where Dobie and John

Houghton Allen grew up, frequently used workers from Mexico, and this led to problem with what Chicano writers call *La Migra*, the Immigration Service. The term for the Border Patrol in Stillwell's book is the *chota*, also a common slang expression among Mexican-Americans.

Stillwell's fine opening chapter skillfully integrates her background, her time in Presidio and Marathon, and her courtship by a rancher, Roy Stillwell, whom she met in Marathon and married in 1918. Much of it is a flashback set into a description of her first night at Roy's ranch, a primitive place twenty-two miles north of the Rio Grande and "forty-six miles from Marathon, the nearest town" (13). In 1944, the Big Bend Park would be established, with a main gate only six miles from the ranch. Hallie would learn to profit from tourists. In the opening chapter, she describes spending the night in a bedroll on the floor with Roy, in the one room, which was twelve feet by sixteen. The three sullen cowboys who normally slept there had to move to the barn. Stephen Crane's great story, "The Bride Comes to Yellow Sky," had dealt long before with the upheaval created by the introduction of a woman into a western male environment. Subsequent chapters explore her dealings with the cowboys and with her equally sullen (as in the root meaning, silent) husband. She ends the chapter with daybreak; Roy brought her coffee and she took it outside to a rock on a sand dune behind the house, where she contemplated the sunrise on Stillwell Mountain. That rock was a firm point in her emotional life, a place to which she went over and over to relieve her frustrations and sorrows by contemplating sunrise or sunset in an area of austere beauty.

She leaves the reader in suspense about her new domestic life by interposing a chapter about her husband's background, "Roy in Mexico." The chapter, a pure example of the family saga, is based on stories told to her by Roy. The Stillwell family's sojourn in Mexico is a tale of conflict with the Mexican army, ingenuity in dealing with the conflict, and, of course, considerable personal courage. Roy's account is hard to reconcile with history: His father, John, was supposedly devoted to Maximilian and Carlota and received a land grant in the Coahuila, near the Big Bend. It is difficult to imagine that the government of Mexico would have honored this grant after the fall of Maximilian. The story goes that the family moved to the grant and prospered, but they eventually had trouble with the Mexican army, which colluded with a rich American named Cheesman who wanted their land for his cattle empire. The story sounds very much like a stale western movie, but Hallie Stillwell says in her preface, "I had no reason to doubt Roy, and therefore I offer to you, the reader, what I believe to be true based on what I was told or experienced" (xi).

An important figure in *I'll Gather My Geese* is Roy's sister, Alice Stillwell Henderson (1866-1914). Alice is the woman Roy admired without reservation, and she must have served as a role model for the young bride who wanted to prove her worth as a ranchwoman to her demanding husband:

> Alice was a fearless woman who was highly respected in Texas and Mexico for her ability to ranch, work cattle and ride horseback as well as any man. She took her troubles into her own hands and never backed down from any problems. She rode beside the men, worked as hard as they did, and produced quality work that any cowboy would acknowledge as the "best." (20)

Alice is said to have retrieved her husband's favorite gun from the Mexican army by riding into their camp and seizing it at gunpoint. When pursued by the soldiers she hid among a corral full of horses. "This is just one of the incidents that gained her the respect of anyone who had ever questioned her ability to be equal to any man. From that time on, most stood in awe of this tiny Texas woman" (21). Alice also taught school in Marathon and dressed as a lady in town. Her sister-in-law observes that she would often "catch myself wondering if I could follow in her footsteps" (22).

Mody Boatright says that family sagas use incidents to teach social values. One of the Stillwell values was to act warily in Mexico: Much later in the book Hallie Stillwell describes the misadventures of her son Guy after he and a friend crossed the Rio

Grande illegally. They went over the river to pick up a wetback worker who was attending a wedding. They had several misadventures, including a brush with members of the old Stillwell nemesis, the Mexican army. As she tells the story, she provides her rules for surviving in Mexico, principles she had failed to teach her son. They were: Never cross the river in the first place, never buy liquor in Mexico, and always say "*si, si*" to avoid trouble. The rules clearly grow out of the Stillwell family saga.

There is no skeleton like John Larn in the Stillwell closet, but Stillwell omits one interesting story from the saga, the "Lost Nigger Mine." In *Coronado's Children*, J. Frank Dobie tells a story from the Big Bend Country about Bill Kelley, or Seminole Bill, the "nigger" of the legend, a man half Seminole and half black, who showed up in the Reagan Brothers camp in Brewster County with a piece of ore.[7] After leaving the Reagans, Kelley went back to Mexico and rode into the Stillwell ranch in the Coahuila Mountains with rocks that Roy's father John (said by Dobie to be a former mining engineer) recognized as gold. Kelley was vague about the location of the mine. Years later, one of John Stillwell's children, Will, who had become a Texas Ranger, wrote to his brother Charley and said that he had located the mine, but he was killed by a gunshot in the back from a Mexican outlaw soon after.

This is Dobie's account. In *The Big Bend Country of Texas*, Hallie Stillwell's friend, Virginia Madison, says that Will had visited his brother Roy in Marathon, Texas, and disclosed the location of the mine, which was near a particular boulder in the mountains of Mexico. Madison, who knew Roy Stillwell and used him as a major source in her account of the Big Bend, puts it this way:

> Roy Stillwell, then, was the only man living who could go to that certain boulder, but he was not particularly interested in gold mines. He had made a little wager with himself, when he got out of Mexico, years ago, with his life and a whole hide, that he would never go back. He had experienced too many brushes with death to press his luck too far. And why should he? He had all a man could hope for in life—a vast range

> stocked with good cattle, and Roy Stillwell was a cattleman. When a magazine writer asked Roy, at the age of seventy-one, why he didn't try and find the mine, he said, "I'm saving that little job for my old age."[8]

Betty Heath, a distant cousin of Hallie's who is editing the sequel to *I'll Gather My Geese,* suggests in an E-mail to the author (August 29, 2000) that Roy did not want his sons wasting their lives pursuing a lost mine and therefore he refused to divulge any details.

Hallie Stillwell also omits any mention of another sensational legend of the Big Bend: the Marfa Lights, mysterious white lights often seen in the area and of great interest to UFO enthusiasts, as are the corresponding "red lights" often seen in the desert around Hudspeth County where Jewel Babb lived. In an article by Rosemary Williams in *Texas Highways,* Hallie Stillwell was quoted as saying she had seen the lights since 1916, but that she was not particularly interested in them: "The Marfa Lights are a mystery," says Hallie. "Let 'em stay a mystery."[9] Stillwell was even interviewed briefly in a television program, "Unsolved Mysteries." Clearly, her aim in her book was to talk about her marriage, the ranch, and the landscape, not to indulge in stories about lost mines and UFOs.

Hallie Stillwell's narrative resumes the story of her marriage after her excursus into the Stillwell saga. She presents much of her experience as a series of trials in becoming a rancher. On her arrival the three cowboys on the ranch immediately showed skepticism about her ability to handle ranch life: "Hell, that woman schoolteacher won't last six months down here in this godforsaken country," one said (5). The first meal was marked by cutting comments which strengthened her resolve to stay. She presents herself as a woman aiming to win her spurs—her metaphor. She endeavored to overcome her greenhorn status in a traditional way, accepting the male standards of ranch life. The cowboy tradition of scorning the tenderfoot presented a challenge that this tenacious woman strove to overcome. Her lowest point with the cowboys was the time she decided to perform traditional housewife's chores by washing the walls of the bunkhouse and the foul coffeepot. The cowboys were outraged: She had scrubbed off wall scribbling with important ranch information, and the long unwashed coffeepot made coffee exactly as they liked it.

This was a region often raided by Pancho Villa's forces, and she could not remain in the ranch house alone. But riding with the men required practical clothing, and Roy thought her split riding skirt—a garment which came into use once the sidesaddle was supplanted—was not practical enough. Jewel Babb was struggling to ride in such a skirt over in the Langtry area to the west at this time. Roy was sure that only pants would do for the rough and tumble of working with cattle. In one of the most amusing episodes in a book which is often humorous, she describes her mother's outrage at the thought of Hallie walking around in front of cowboys in pants. This was 1918. Her mother sewed her a pair of very modest pants with a stride so full and low that they caught on the back of the saddle the first time she tried to wear them. After this humiliation, she wore normal pants. She did protect her femininity by wearing gloves and makeup, which irritated Roy: He thought gloves impeded work and applying makeup was a waste of valuable time. Like Babb at the same period Hallie was preoccupied with finding ways to preserve her skin in a bone-dry environment. Hallie wore her favorite bonnet out riding only once: Roy insisted that she wear a Stetson, which may have been more practical.

The initiation of this female greenhorn was made difficult by her husband far more than by the cowboys. One fascination of the book is the unresolved ambivalence in Hallie Stillwell's feelings about her taciturn and demanding husband. He gave her minimal instruction and never revealed his emotions, leaving her uncertain about her progress. In fact, the cowboys sometimes had to explain things to her. Early on she laughed when Roy fell onto the doubletree of a wagon. He soon sent her on a tough errand, to bring back a huge cake of feed for a bull, and he had her ride a very bad horse which wouldn't stand still to let her mount with the cake. She had to use great ingenuity to return with the feed, and when a cowboy told her how contrary the horse was known to be, she concluded that this was Roy's way of getting even with her for laughing at him.

She went through a number of ordeals that suggest figures like Patient Griselda in medieval literature, the woman who patiently endures irrational behavior by her husband, or Psyche in Apuleius's *Cupid and Psyche*, who was put to terrible tasks by Venus. Roy's behavior was absolutely brutal in one episode late in the marriage: She was kicked when roping a calf and thought her jaw was broken. After she spent a painful night without even an aspirin, Roy decided to let her have an easy day, in his conception of ease: She could go hunt for a buck he had seen. She rode off in agony and missed her shot. His response on her return was anger for her failure. She seems at cross-purposes in her handling of Roy: She knows that the interesting stories are about his orneriness, yet she wishes to present him as an admirable person and herself as a devoted wife. On a goat and sheep ranch in Langtry a hundred miles to the west, Jewel Babb learned about the cowboy life from a family whose tactics seemed to have been kindness and patience.

On another occasion Hallie found beautiful wildflowers on the range and picked herself a beautiful bouquet. When she and Roy located a missing cow and calf, the cow was difficult to bring back. Roy's angry theory was that the flowers on Hallie's saddle spooked her. Hallie believed that once again she had "flubbed the dub" (102). He never apologized for his outbursts and silent spells, but two days after the flower incident he sent Hallie off for a bit of sport: hunting a mountain lion. She succeeded, and he showed pride in his face when she returned. Her conclusion at the end of the lion episode was that "life would always be bittersweet as long as I was married to him" (105). Later she describes life with Roy as a roller coaster, but she rarely shows any of the exhilarating moments.

It appears that she could project a great deal on a silent man. Her chief rationalization was that he was teaching her by letting her fail. On one occasion during a cattle drive she spent an entire day trying to keep a recalcitrant cow in the herd. Only at the end did Roy tell her that the cow was not one of theirs, and that it had been trying desperately to return to its calf. She was immensely unhappy and had to spend time after supper contemplating the mountain sunset to restore her calm. One of the cowboys told her that Roy was trying to teach her what she needed to know about cattle by letting her make such a big mistake (40). She accepted this view of Roy's behavior and let it guide her in the future whenever he behaved perversely. She would join in when he laughed about her mistakes.

Some of the behavior she describes was clearly mean-spirited. He refused to put in a sink given to her by a neighbor because sinks could clog up: Water in a house was trouble. This was, after all, merely a convenience for his wife. She had to wait a long while before a nephew came over and installed it. When she bought a refrigerator in Alpine he insisted that she return it, but she threatened to return herself to her hometown along with the appliance. Perhaps the most humiliating moment from a contemporary viewpoint is the corral episode: She wanted a bathroom but Roy refused to give her lumber from the demolished barn because he wanted to build a corral with it. She resorted to removing boards from the corral as he built it in order to continue with the bathroom. Such episodes seem out of the traditional "war of the sexes" and are hard to square with Hallie's general independence of mind. She eventually felt that she had won her spurs, a metaphor which shows the model defining their relationship: She was the tenderfoot; he was the gruff and tormenting mentor. At least he never sent her on a snipe hunt, though the episode with the feed cake comes close.

For all her deference to her husband's traditional domineering ways, she showed a frankness that Sallie Matthews would have found shocking. Certainly Hallie's own mother was mortified when she heard her daughter answer a son's question about the castration of calves. Her mother not only objected to the explanation of the process but to the use of the word "bull." Unlike Matthews, Hallie Stillwell talks about her pregnancies quite freely. She so adapted to what she thought was the male attitude that she was quite surprised that the cowboys were more excited about the arrival of her first child at the ranch than they would be over a new calf. But she found it hard to tell her husband about her second pregnancy, fearing he would disapprove of the expense so soon after the first child. She was surprised that he was overjoyed. Clearly the husband and wife are somewhat isolated from one another by the husband's Marlboro Man image.

Her three children were born in Marathon, some forty miles from the ranch. She and Roy maintained a house in the town, as childbirth far out in the countryside would have been dangerous. Roy hired Rita, a fourteen-year-old Seminole Indian, to assist his wife during her pregnancy and after. The house in Marathon made it possible to send the children to school.

Her chief outlet, aside from the contemplation of the mountains and wildflowers was the exploration of archaeological remains in caves on the land, a pursuit which Roy, the practical rancher, naturally found a waste of time. Her achievements, shared with a professor at Sul Ross State College in Alpine, were considerable and she was concerned with conservation of the remains as well as discovery. Hallie's finds became a source of income for the ranch when the Big Bend National Park brought tourists to the area: The ranch still offers tours of the caves.

In "Hallie and Farewell," a *Texas Monthly* essay celebrating Stillwell, Helen Thorpe observes that she "was really more representative of the new Texas than the old one."[10] Her commitment to doing what was called men's work and her small feminist rebellions within a very traditional marriage represent a new spirit. Eventually she would learn to foster her media image: the mystique of the old Texas marketed for the new. She and her eldest son, Roy Walker Stillwell (called "Son") started a business to gather and process wax from the candelilla plant, a kind of low-key entrepreneurial enterprise which broke with the cattle-ranching tradition. Roy reacted by ignoring this kind of foolishness. Hallie eventually made the enterprise more her own than Son's.

The essay on wax-making by Joe S. Graham in the Texas Folklore Society publication, *Some Still Do,*[11] is interesting to read in the light of Hallie's account: In both cases there is an emphasis on cultural differences between Anglo-Saxon and Mexican workers. Stillwell complains that the Mexican workers were always looking for reasons to quit work, while Graham, a professor at Sul

Ross University in Alpine, says that for most Mexicans "time, like any good Mexican clock, walks; it doesn't run." He does suggest that there is a collision of values between Anglos and Mexicans and that the Mexican commitment to tradition over inventiveness has its own value. Graham's abundant photographs make his essay a good supplement to Stillwell's account of wax-making.

After Roy's death in a feed-hauling accident during the drought of 1948, the worst the Big Bend ever experienced, she was forced to send the cattle to market. But as the last truck was pulling away, rain started, and she made the driver stop. She ends her book dramatically at this point, with a tiny herd as a basis for rebuilding the ranch. Her independence and intelligence would make her own account of the second, post-Roy half of her life immensely entertaining. When she died, she was working on a sequel to *I'll Gather My Geese,* to be called *My Goose Is Cooked.* On her audiocassette, she joked there would be a third, *I Eat My Goose.* There are ten chapters in the unfinished sequel, and Betty Heath is supplementing them by soliciting reminiscences from people who heard Hallie's stories.

The subsequent life was fascinating. She in effect saved the ranch by her other economic activities: her beauty shop and her work as a barber, her job as justice of the peace and coroner, and her newspaper columns (handwritten but faxed) for the *Alpine Avalanche* and other papers. She became a press favorite through the Terlingua Chile Cook-Offs. Terlingua is a ghost town on the western edge of Big Bend National Park. One year at Terlingua a creek was jokingly renamed Dirty Woman Creek when she was alleged to be a biased judge—the incident was a joke, but the Texas legislature capped it by passing a resolution annulling the name. The governor named her "Yellow Rose of Texas," a picturesque accolade also held by Annie Mae Hunt, whose story is considered in the next chapter. The Stillwell Ranch still offers four-wheel-drive tours to her archaeological sites as well as tours of the Big Bend National Park. Perhaps most appropriate to her spirit is the Hallie Stillwell Museum on the ranch grounds. The Stillwell Ranch lacks the resources of the Lambshead Ranch, but the family showed tenacity and ingenuity. The future of the ranch is unclear: Her rancher son, Guy Stillwell, died in 2000, and Dadie Stillwell Potter, who managed most of the ranch activities, died in 2001.

Hallie Stillwell had no difficulty being who she was. The public image was not far from the reality, surely, though the image has to be taken with a grain of salt, or a pod of chile. She defined herself through her anecdotes, without needing Freudian concepts of the psyche like Gertrude Beasley, nor is she concerned with a tortured childhood like Karr and Humphrey. No other writer in this book is as unselfconscious. Dobie could never write an autobiography because he feared egotism. Because of the loss of self that he experienced from a heart bypass operation, Larry McMurtry fears that he has no real ego to express; Mary Karr describes achieving a self as an endless process. We can contemplate Stillwell on her horse in the *New York Times* obituary photograph or smile at her, rifle in her hand, in the memorial cover of *Texas Monthly* and feel that we know who she was. She could pass for an original out of Dobie's "Beeville Talk."

Stillwell published her book when she was ninety-four. The record for nonagenarian autobiography in Texas is actually held by another woman, Bess Whitehead Scott, who published *You Meet Such Interesting People*[12] when she was ninety-seven. Scott's friend, Lou Letts, "prodded" her to write about her experiences and said, "Start this way: 'I was born in Blanket, Texas, twelve miles from Comanche.' That will sell a hundred books" (xii). Scott, who died at 107, had a fascinating life: After attending Baylor Female College (now Mary Hardin-Baylor) in Belton and Baylor University in Waco she became the first woman reporter on the city desk at the *Houston Post* in spite of a severe hearing impairment. She later tried writing in Hollywood and did meet interesting people, including Clark Gable. But the work is bland without the narrative skill that enlivens Stillwell's work.

Hallie Stillwell and Sallie Matthews make an interesting pair. One was a pioneer in a Texas filled with conflict: Comanche wars, the struggle of vigilantes against lawlessness. She was part of the creation of one of the most successful ranches in Texas. Hallie Stillwell was also a pioneer, a woman assuming a role as working rancher inconceivable for a nineteenth-century lady like Matthews. Hallie's narrative benefits from the kinds of social change she represented: She too was writing for her grandchildren, but she did not find it necessary to be genteel (gentility was an obstacle to overcome, if we recall those pants with the enormous stride), and she can admit marital conflict, even make it the basic pattern of her work. Matthews fails even to discuss her courtship, though the matter of sewing a trousseau is described at length. The reader who wants to learn something about the cattle industry will find out about trail drives from Matthews, who reported on what male members of her family had done, while Stillwell describes the intricacies of bulldogging from the bulldogger's point of view. The interest in Matthews lies more in what she has witnessed than in what she conveys about her emotions, but of course she witnessed remarkable times. She never needed to forge a persona and seek publicity, to become an original like Hallie Crawford Stillwell. One of the subjects of the following chapter, Jewel Babb, whose life has striking parallels to Hallie's—both started as greenhorns, both improvised a living in the Trans-Pecos when ranching became difficult—never developed a marketable public image.

Annie Mae Hunt

Rev. C. C. White

Jewel Babb

5

AUTOBIOGRAPHY BY INTERVIEW: JEWEL BABB, CHARLEY C. WHITE, AND ANNIE MAE HUNT

Most autobiographies are written narratives, and unless the subject is an athlete or film star, we assume that the author has prepared the narrative, choosing what will be discussed and what will be overlooked. Jewel Babb (1900-91), the Reverend Charley C. White (1885-

1974) and Annie Mae Hunt (1909-) differ from other figures in this study because their stories were prepared from interviews which reflect the oral style of individuals who had little schooling: five years in the case of Hunt, six for Babb, and four for White. The works taken down and arranged by their collaborators preserve unusual personalities and some remarkable phases of Texas life. Babb, the subject of *Border Healing Woman,* became a sheep and angora goat rancher and then learned to be a healer in the desert of the Trans-Pecos and was celebrated in *National Geograpic.*[1] White, the speaker of *No Quittin' Sense,* was a black man born in Shelby County in the Piney Woods region of East Texas, who wanted to be a preacher since he went to a "baptizing" when he was three years old, became a Church of God in Christ minister and founder of a food bank. *I Am Annie Mae* tells the story of Annie Mae Hunt, the granddaughter of slaves, who lived both in rural Texas and Dallas, and moved from picking cotton and cleaning houses to becoming a businesswoman and political worker. All three became media figures as a result of the articles and books about them. The fame seemed to benefit White and Hunt, while Babb had her life seriously disrupted by the attention.

All sorts of questions arise when those who are poorly educated collaborate with individuals who have superior writing skills. L. Langness and Gelya Frank devote a whole section of their *Lives: An Anthropological Approach to Biography* to ethical issues arising between the interviewer and the informant.[2] The three autobiographies considered here make an extensive use of the actual words of the subject, though choices had to be made about the reproduction of accent and pronunciation. The intention was to facilitate autobiography. Ada Morehead Holland and Ruthe Winegarten excluded themselves from their books on White and Hunt, except for introductions (and annotations, in the case of Winegarten). Pat LittleDog is present in the body of the work, describing her encounters with Jewel Babb and her family and providing linking passages. But she does not intrude into the transcripts of Babb's words: Her subject's voice comes through clearly, without interruption. In a sense LittleDog writes an autobiography of the autobiography, a highly personal and frank narrative of her dealings with her subject.

Pat LittleDog (1941-) was an aspiring fiction writer and member of El Paso's counterculture when she heard of Jewel Babb, "who was living in the desert approximately thirty miles from Sierra Blanca and six miles from the Rio Grande" (xv) in a tie house, a less than wind-tight shelter made from railroad ties. Such structures were once common in treeless regions of the Southwest. LittleDog has written an article on them. They are forms of vernacular architecture like the shotgun houses and dog-run houses built by settlers in areas with trees. Babb had once operated a rundown therapeutic bath center at Indian Hot Springs, not far away. She had been eking out a living in the desert, raising goats and healing people for voluntary donations, mostly of water, peanut butter, and graham crackers.

Babb had been discovered for the El Paso counterculture by a hippie identified as Greg T., who asked her for water when he was in the desert looking for peyote buttons. She discouraged him on the subject of peyote. Her skills as a wise woman and healer became well known, and LittleDog (known then as Pat Ellis Taylor) decided to investigate. They got on well and LittleDog's then-husband, the Texas poet Chuck Taylor, received treatments for a bad case of hepatitis. The two women eventually agreed to prepare a book together, and LittleDog made several long visits to Babb, who by that time had left the desert tie house for Valentine, a small town in Jeff Davis County. Valentine is a little east of the tie house and about sixty miles east of Alpine, where Hallie Stillwell had her house in town. Babb hoped to make enough from the book to pay her basic expenses and buy some pedigreed goats. The collaboration began with taped interviews, but LittleDog has told me in a very informative letter (August 21, 2001) that the tapes disturbed Babb: "After the first few tapes were made, I played them back for her, thinking that she might think of additions and gaps as she heard herself talking. But in fact, all that she heard was the inadequacy of her own voice, and then she didn't want to be taped anymore." She rejected the recorder, and LittleDog would makes notes after the interviews. Babb would also provide written texts and some of her long letters to LittleDog were incorporated in the work. Her style had limits, of course: She quit school very early.

LittleDog's letter explains her working methods in rich detail. I had commented on the flow of the transcripts. She points out that the flow was achieved by hard work:

> I'm glad you like the flow of the transcripts. In fact they were very much pieced together. Jewel was somewhat repetitious, as is most everyone—and sometimes I would have four or five versions of the same incident, some on tape and some written. I worked by topics, which I arranged in the old style of making sense of diverse notes, B.C.—Before Computer (I still don't have one and still work this way). Make a circle around yourself, sitting in the middle of the floor, of your topics cards; place your bits and pieces of thoughts and notes and photos and all under the notecards they adhere to; chop the transcripts into ribbons of sentences and paragraphs and rearrange them in more orderly sequences. When gaps appeared, I wrote Jewel questions, just like you're writing me. When answers came, I slid them into the places I wanted to fill. When the rough draft was put together, I sent it to her and she went over it and added more and corrected. . . .

In her preface to *Border Healing Woman* she says, "I have tried to edit her writing as little as possible, other than to arrange the spoken and written segments into orderly sequence, editing no more than was absolutely necessary in order to preserve the enjoyable way of telling which is Mrs. Babb's unique 'voice'" (xvi). The paradox of oral history implied here is interesting: It is sometimes necessary to edit to preserve the unique voice.

LittleDog's skills as an ethnographer are thoroughly professional. She had a folklore minor in her graduate work at the University of Texas at El Paso, where she worked with John O.

West, author of an important book on Mexican-American folklore which deals with *curanderismo* and other customs.[3] She also studied at the University of Arizona with Jan Brunvand, one of the most eminent folklorists in America. She points out in her letter to me that "the universit[ies] gave me the academic trappings necessary to write a book acceptable for a university press."

Anthropologists and folklorists are increasingly aware that their projects may not fit the expectations of their subjects. In the original 1985 edition, LittleDog was quite aware of this problem. She explains that her emphasis on the story of Jewel Babb as a healer was not one her subject might have chosen "because, to her, goats are at least as large in her life as is faith healing" (105). With admirable honesty, LittleDog says that while she chose to title the book *Border Healing Woman,* the word goat or mother might have been used. She did in fact publish a thirty-page work for Babb called *Goat-Lore: A Book of Folklore & Folklife from the Rio Grande*[4] and set the book in type herself. But this book too disappointed, as the financial returns were tiny. The book has rather limited interest but does reveal Babb's love of the desert landscape and her deep feeling for animals. An interesting supplement to *Border Healing Woman* is LittleDog's short story based on the start of the collaboration, "Acquiring Point of View," collected in *Afoot in a Field of Men.*[5] In the story, she evokes the desert setting with power and dramatizes the narrator's ambivalence about the healer she is going to work with, wondering if she is only a silly old woman. She also feels uncomfortable when she realizes that the champagne she has brought to mark the event is the first alcohol the old woman has ever tasted.

LittleDog was not only a good ethnographer but a person willing to take her subject's unusual occupation seriously. LittleDog still has counterculture loyalties and reviews books on the hippie period for *The Texas Observer.* She has a willingness to accept practices as exotic as faith healing and is untroubled by Babb's visions of luminous objects and tiny spirit physicians. However, she is not simply a bohemian but a Dobie Paisano Fellow (1986) and a distinguished writer of fiction: *Afoot in a Field of Men,* was published by Atlantic Monthly Press. Her afterword presents an excellent review of the literature on *curanderismo,* the Mexican practice of folk healing, and on traditional American folk healers, and she has annotated Babb's reminiscences with information on history, geography, ethnology, and folklore. She presents herself as an open-minded but not credulous listener and provides glimpses into her own life and her reactions to Babb, her family, and the overpowering Trans-Pecos landscape. The epigraph to the book, from Carl Jung, reveals something of her point of view: "We no longer ask, 'Has this or that been seen, heard, handled, weighed, counted, thought, and found to be logical?' We ask instead, '*Who* saw, heard or thought?'" The point of view is perhaps scientific subjectivity rather than scientific objectivity.

The reminiscences begin with Babb's memories of her family and childhood and incorporate some of the family saga. Jewel Wilson was born on August 13, 1900, in Juno, Texas (present population: ten), in Val Verde County, less than a hundred miles south (and a little west) of Eldorado, the farthest point that Gertrude Beasley's family roamed in their years in a covered wagon. She was the daughter of Luke Wilson and Norah Bosworth. Her parents and paternal grandparents were itinerant well diggers and until she was eight camped all around West Texas and the Mexican border region, digging wells in some of the driest and emptiest counties. The Wilson grandparents (Doc Wilson and Lucindy Belle Starr Wilson) came from Tennessee. Lucindy was "a tiny old thing, with black hair and blue eyes" (13). She was one quarter Indian, but her granddaughter did not know the tribe. Lucindy's father and two brothers were killed by Indians in Tennessee. Others in the family brought her in a wagon to Starr County, deep in South Texas, a country on the Rio Grande near the Gulf. On the way, the wheels would be muffled with some kind of cloth when passing through Indian territory.

The family saga of the other grandparents was less detailed. The grandmother was English but Jewel never knew from where. She hated to travel but her husband, Woody, was one of those restless frontier males, like Gertrude Beasley's father, and she spent twenty-two years in a covered wagon, which may be a record. Finally the husband wanted to move to New Mexico but his wife refused to go on with him, stopping at the state line. She settled in a little house in Ozona but was not able to rest even in death. Her grave was washed away by a flash flood. The grandfather reputedly died in Mexico. The story is redolent of family saga and *Coronado's Children:* "And then my grandpa wandered just here and yon and finally he came to Big Bend. He was killed in a cave down in Mexico, and they always said Pancho Villa and his men killed him. They thought he was looking for a treasure" (12).

Jewel Babb remembered her first eight years living out of a covered wagon as an idyll. She and her brother Hollie had little beyond their Barlow knives to play with but could always whittle a sotol stick or occupy themselves scraping cow horns. The cow horns passage has her customary use of "takened" for "took":

> Then if Hollie and I wandered a ways from our camp, we might find where an old cow had died, and her horns were lying around. We were always glad to find a horn. We takened them back to the camp, got a piece of glass that our parents had picked up somewhere, set down in the shade, and spent many hours scraping these horns. It might take several days of work on the horn. Then when our grandfather looked at it and thought it was ready, he sawed off the sharp point of the horn and, with a red hot wire, he would burn a hole through the small part of the horn until it went through into the hollow of the horn. Then we had a horn that we could blow on. And it would make a noise! (14)

They played with old horseshoes found in the grass, and their father would make stick horses from sotol for them. She notes that her parents "never fought or quarreled in front of us children. That way we were never upset or unhappy," a situation not shared by writers dealt with in this book like Gertrude Beasley, William Humphrey, and Mary Karr.

She and her brother were immersed in nature and her love for it comes through clearly. She gives lists of bird sounds. Like Gertrude Beasley, she knew the kildeer as a "kil-dee." She catalogs wildflowers and talks about such pursuits as hunting for armadillos in their holes or lying under a live oak tree observing the animals which lived in it. The wild pigs, or peccaries, sometimes ran with the dogs, she says. She and her brother would find nests of baby rabbits and try to raise them. Her attunement to the natural world was surely a factor in her learning about folk uses of plants from Mexican culture. During her years of poverty and privation at the tie house, she was sustained by a love of natural beauty, particularly the beauty of sunsets seen from her hill (103). She puts a mystical spin on the sunsets, imagining herself stepping off her hill and walking into the heavens, but the feeling still suggests Hallie Stillwell's love of the sky seen from her own little hill behind the ranch house.

Her descriptions of daily life in West Texas and the Trans-Pecos are thick with detail. She describes the wild plants used by her parents and grandparents: pursley (purslane), horehound, and careless weed (more often known as pigweed). She gives meticulous descriptions of the preparation of hominy and some attention to candle-making and—of course—lye soap. In the chapter entitled "A Ranch Marriage," she details the making of jellies from prickly pear and *aguavilla* berries. In the same chapter she explains how cowboy stew is made on a campfire with jerky and "cowboy bread," biscuit dough fried with grease in a skillet. She describes ranch work like treating goats and sheep for lice in sulphur water and vaccinating livestock for sore mouth. The major industrial operation of washing all the clothes on a large ranch is covered, including the posting of guards to make sure that the cattle didn't eat the clothing hung out to dry. Perhaps the most interesting customs she deals with pertain to pre- and postnatal care. It was unthinkable that a woman should get up for twelve days after childbirth. Her first child, a son called "Dixie" (Walter Dillard), got gravy as his first taste of adult food after being nursed for six weeks. Baby-sitters not being available, children would be taken along on horseback with their mother or tied to a burro when ranch tasks like checking traplines had to be performed.

Most of Jewel's early life was spent in Val Verde County. The parents eventually settled in Del Rio, the county seat, when she was about eight. After a childhood spent on the range she detested school and had to be followed to make sure she got there. At the age of fourteen, her schooling ended: Her parents gave up on it when she was in the sixth grade. Her lack of schooling shows in the grammar of the transcripts, the double negatives, the archaic forms like "takened," and expressions like "learned him" for "taught him," but her descriptions are eloquent nevertheless. She left Del Rio in 1916 to get married in Langtry, famous for its justice of the peace, Judge Roy Bean (?-1903), "the Law West of the Pecos." According to *National Geographic* her husband, Walter Isaac Babb, appears as a little boy in a well-known photograph of Roy Bean. Wayne, her third son, had the full name Judge Wayne Babb. Jewel first saw Walter on the street in Del Rio. He was staggering along with another boy, and she thought they were drunk but they were only laughing. Walter was as reticent as Roy Stillwell, and the courtship was quite short.

Walter Isaac Babb was the son of two people on Jewel Babb's list of the seven people she most admired. The others were her parents, her Wilson grandparents, and Walter himself. The in-laws, William Isaac "Bill Ike" Babb and Laura Alice Lewis Babb, had an enormous ranch near Langtry. At one time it was five hundred sections, but by 1916 it was down to two hundred. These are vast stretches of land, but the area is extremely dry. Typical of the area from San Angelo southward, the livestock was mostly sheep and goats, especially angora goats. Jewel immediately wanted to take part in the ranching. Unlike Roy Stillwell, the owners of this ranch thought the work was not fit for a woman, but the young bride insisted. She needed proper clothes and her sister-in-law sewed riding skirts for her.

Jewel set off armed, a precaution against "varmints" and "the different classes of men who worked on the ranch" (32). Like Hallie Stillwell, she had been given a pistol, her grandfather's "cherished forty-five, a 'hog-leg,' as it was called." But a .22 caliber pistol was more suitable and could be slipped into a pocket of her skirt. She describes greenhorn adventures similar to Hallie Stillwell's—trial and error seems to have been the pedagogical approach—but without the sadistic element in Roy Stillwell's instruction. She describes a series of attempts by the Babbs to find a horse which she, a town girl from Del Rio, could ride successfully. "Only time I ever heard one of the cowboys say a word was when I was getting back in the saddle after one of my falls. He said, 'She's got what it takes.' I thought that was silly. After all, getting back in the saddle again was about all you could do miles from anywhere" (34). Some of her adventures have a Hallie Stillwell quality to them, like being sent to shoot a flock of ducks on the water tank and managing only to hurt herself with the recoil of the shotgun.

Her mother-in-law won her loyalty for having confidence in her: "Thought I could do anything" (35). Indeed, she recalls that the entire family was patient with her and never criticized her for her frequent mistakes, a real contrast with Roy Stillwell's harsh methods. There were conflicts on the ranch: Some of the Babb brothers were always fighting, and on one occasion two of them showed up bleeding because they had gone at each other with knives. But Jewel decided that these conflicts were none of her business.

People reminiscing often recall the catastrophes, comic or otherwise. There are so many in Jewel Babb's narrative of the days on the ranch that the reader wonders about the intelligence of the persons involved. She mentions times that her infants fell off horses through carelessness of the parents, and on some occasions cowboys would ride through the breakfast campfire smashing coffeepots and dishes either because they could not keep control of the horses or because someone threw a hat under a horse as a prank. She herself managed to give her family sore mouth by failing to wash her hands after vaccinating the livestock, and on one occasion when dipping sheep she came close to falling into the sulphur water. Later in the book we are treated to an anecdote of Walter lowering his son Wayne into a dark hole on a rope to finish off a wounded mountain lion. The animal attacked in the dark and only a reflexive firing of the gun saved Wayne (55). Perhaps the oddest miscalculation comes late in the book when Jewel and "a man from across the river" spent three days painting the main building of her Indian Hot Springs resort because a group interested in holding a retreat was coming to look over the place. It was cold and there was no firewood so she decided to burn a *tire* in the fireplace, filling the freshly painted headquarters with acrid smoke. The visitors arrived and very quickly left (81-82). After, Jewel Babb looked at herself in a mirror and saw that her face was completely blackened.

Times were so hard after a while that, after a period of ranching on their own, Jewel and Walter moved eastward to Sierra Blanca to run a trailer court. The oldest son, Dixie, eventually bought the abandoned Indian Hot Springs facility, which had been established in the late 1920s and failed during the Second World War. Walter Babb, who his wife admits was a solitary man, even misanthropic, went off to Torreón to hunt mountain lions. He had the notion that his health would improve in the solitude of Mexico. He died of a heart attack and was buried in Mexico, Jewel was told in a telegram. Shortly after, in what a reader may perceive as a mysterious coincidence, all three of Jewel's sons were involved in a cattle-smuggling scheme. Two of them, Irvin and Wayne were sent to jail for three years, and Dixie hid out in Mexico for a decade. The Stillwell family saga comes to mind: the problems over herds of cattle and the border. Jewel found that all her friends dropped her, and she was destitute. In 1952 she moved to the Springs to live.

One of the sons, Wayne, appears in a narrative chapter by Pat LittleDog about her stay in Valentine with Jewel. LittleDog is very circumspect in dealing with him. He and a crew had a profitable business trapping animals for ranchers: ringtails, panther, lynxes, skunks, badgers, foxes, coyotes. They also spent much of their time digging cactus out of the desert to sell to nurserymen in El Paso, a controversial practice even in 1976. Wayne's conversation tended to glorify guns and dogs, and LittleDog permits herself one comment that Jewel Babb had already made it clear that she detested guns and dogs. Such discretion is sometimes necessary when preparing a collaborative book. LittleDog could hardly have enjoyed Wayne's demeaning comments about hippies either. Wayne mentioned that his family had set up a wax-making enterprise at the Hot Springs, an interesting affinity with Hallie Stillwell.

Her years at Hot Springs turned Babb into a healer, a vocation more or less forced on her, just as the most famous traveler to come through Trans-Pecos Texas, Cabeza de Vaca, found himself healing people at the insistence of his Indian captors in the mid-1530s. The springs, which are in Hudspeth County some twenty-five miles from Sierra Blanca, had been used by Native Americans since prehistoric times, according to William A. Cloud.[6] The area was patrolled by Buffalo Soldiers, and Cloud reports that a detachment was killed by Victorio's Apaches on October 28, 1880. The springs are remarkably rich in minerals and have a high level of natural radiation. Babb merely wanted to live there, isolated as it was, but people kept showing up to use the stone tubs, and she found herself pressed into service to help them. After a while she learned the properties of the twenty-two springs, some of which have a folk poetry in their names: Stump Spring, Soda Spring, Squaw Spring (of course), and Chief Spring.

Babb was drawn into being a healer through her empathy with the suffering. She learned Anglo techniques of healing, including the use of the hands, visualization, and the form of zone therapy which uses massage of points on the bottoms of the feet to treat other parts of the body. LittleDog includes an account of a treatment undergone by her then-husband Chuck for aftereffects of hepatitis. Eventually Babb learned that healing could be done at a distance. LittleDog's afterword to *Border Healing Woman* has an excellent discussion of the folk-healing tradition in the United States, which flourished in the Appalachian area whence Babb's paternal ancestors came. Possible influences LittleDog does not mention are the radio broadcasts from XERA and its successor, XERF, stations across the river from Del Rio which used 1,000,000-watt transmitters to transmit offers of faith healing and goat-gland rejuvenation therapy over much of America starting in the 1930s.

Along with faith and natural healing techniques from the Anglo world, Babb learned *curandero* methods and was sought out by many Mexicans from both sides of the border. The *curandero/a* is an important figure in Mexican folk culture, a practitioner who treats a variety of ailments, including folk diseases like *mal de ojo* (the evil eye), *susto* (separation of the soul from the body as a result of fright), *empacho* (a supposed ball of food in the intestines), *mal puesto* (sorcery), and *caída de la mollera* (a fallen fontanel). The *curandero* is also consulted about what Anglo culture would call depressive illnesses, and of course ordinary sickness is dealt with as well. As Joe Graham points out in a sympathetic but by no means credulous article on the *curandero* in West Texas, practitioners like Don Pedrito Jaramillo have had enormous followings.[7] J. Frank Dobie's preface to the 1947 edition of *Tongues of the Monte* discusses a pilgrimage to Don Pedrito made by a woman who worked on the Dobie ranch. Ariel Kiev, director of the social psychiatry program at Cornell University, deals with the *curandero* as an analogue of the psychiatrist in mainstream medicine in his book on *Curanderismo: Mexican-American Folk Psychiatry.*[8] The *curandero* has generally gotten favorable assessments from the scholars, though Graham discusses some shoddy practitioners. Mexican Americans are not always so reverent: Américo Paredes collected jokes told by South Texas Mexicans ridiculing *curanderos.*[9] The enthusiasm shown for the *curandero* as symbolic figure in Chicano/a literature is natural enough (Pat Mora offers good examples), but not everyone in the culture has confidence in them.

The *curandero* makes more use of herbs than the Anglo folk healer, and Babb was aware of desert plants from her childhood. She told LittleDog about the uses of star cactus, bloodroot, and aloe vera. H. L. Hunt bought the Hot Springs after Babb had to give it up, and he tried commercial plantings of aloe vera, a powerful natural healer. LittleDog perhaps assumed that readers would realize that this eccentric man who bought the springs was the immensely rich Texas oil man, notorious at one time for his extreme right-wing views, which were disseminated in radio broadcasts.

Jewel Babb healed people of all races, which did not please some citizens of Sierra Blanca. As LittleDog says in her afterword, the springs were "a place where Mexicans, Negroes, Creoles, and Cajuns came together, many times speaking different language, came together to be healed" (105). The book describes the semi-occult experiences of many of these people, but unfortunately the stories are banal or pointless, involving odd dreams or mysterious visions of lights and spirit dogs.

Some of the proto-New Age qualities of the book may irritate skeptical readers. The mysterious red lights of the area around Sierra Blanca are discussed, a phenomenon similar to the Marfa lights to the east: The rugged Trans-Pecos region is known for UFO sightings, and the road from Sierra Blanca to Indian Hot Springs is called Red Light Draw. Legend has it that the lights are the spirits of Native Americans; Babb believed that blankets infected with smallpox had been given to the local Indians and that the red lights were their souls. LittleDog was fascinated by the red-light folklore but did not see any herself. Jewel Babb describes seeing a mysterious multicolored object the size of a football descend to the ground outside her tie house. It disappeared with a puff. A few nights after, some unseen force seized her arm and side. Most interesting is the vision she had of spirit doctors when she was learning healing at the springs:

> I was praying and asking what this was that was happening. And I saw something like a vision. I saw these little men with something like flashlights. And whenever someone was sick they'd shine their light on it. They were the prettiest men you ever saw. They have the roundest little face, their cheeks was red, and their skin was a light gold color; And their heads were just so round, pretty heads, and then they had a band around their head, and then their light. And ever time they was going to heal anybody, then they shined that light on that person. And they weren't friendly. (80)

They appear to be the equivalent of the shaman's familiar spirit but translated into modern terms.

LittleDog visited the hot springs alone, Babb refusing to go back again. She found the area frightening. The desert is unusually harsh in this region. After looking at the remains of the Hot

Springs resort, she found a rope bridge over to the village of Ojos Calientes. She walked across but could not bring herself to enter the village. Suddenly feeling isolated and vulnerable, she rushed back to the veranda of the hotel, "which had become in those minutes a symbol of life and civilization for me" (88). She sat there realizing how solitary and wild this area was, a place where Jewel Babb had lived alone for so many years. It is a powerful moment, the Anglo writer confronting the otherness of Mexico and the austerity of the desert and being driven away by both. On her return drive, she was forced to stop by an obstinate wild burro which seemed different from the burros she had seen on the streets of Juarez.

The new epilogue to the book, "Jewel Babb: Her Legacy," has a melancholy tone. It is a final collaboration, LittleDog says, a reconstruction through letters and photographs of the impact of the book as well as an account of Babb's death from lymphoma. LittleDog realizes that not only did the book fail to bring in money, it made Jewel Babb's life difficult. The *National Geographic* article on the Trans-Pecos had a fine picture of Babb practicing her healing touch on a child. She was terrified that she might be targeted by the law for practicing medicine without a license. She was sought out constantly in her eighties and nineties by the sick and feared arrest for medical quackery. Her destitution and ill health weighed on her. She was frequently interviewed by the press, who took her time and gave her nothing in return. The two times she was featured on a regional program, *The Eyes of Texas*, were no help to her. Hallie Stillwell played the role of colorful character very astutely, but Babb had no desire for it. Her family, knowing nothing of the realities of publishing, thought that their grandmother had been cheated by a sly author. LittleDog's final affirmation of her collaborator comes through quotations from old letters to LittleDog in which Babb states her faith in a kind of psychic economics, a feeling that unselfishness ultimately brings its own reward. She was buried with her head toward the mountains which she loved and which she said gave her a look into eternity.

Pat LittleDog is a major character in the story she tells, creating an autobiography of sorts alongside Jewel Babb's story. Ada Morehead Holland, who prepared the life of Charley C. White from tapes, has kept herself out of the text, though Reverend White discusses the articles about him she published in *Ebony* and *Texas Magazine*. He mentions approvingly that she divided the money from the article in *Ebony* with him and gave him the whole sum from *Texas Magazine*. The publicity was good for his charitable activities. Her role in the book was to encourage him to talk "in vivid, smooth-flowing vernacular," and to get him to follow up on interesting incidents he mentioned. She makes it clear that she had an extensive role in bringing order and chronology to his mass of anecdotes and her comments in the preface sound very much like Pat LittleDog's remarks on her methods in the letter to me:

> After each recording session I would go home and listen to the tape, and make notes, and try to push the material into a logical, readable form. Many good incidents had to be eliminated, and others had to be condensed. Transitions had to be fixed. At last I was able to string together the incidents in a way that I believed accurately reflected the life story of this man. It was done largely in his own words. When I had to fix transitions or move the story, I went back and listened to the tape until I found expressions and clauses that would logically fit my need; I tried to keep it in his vernacular.

She got his approval and corrections for each chapter and his approval of the whole manuscript.

Jeffrey David Titon, an important theorist of the "folkloric personal history," has written in an essay on "The Life Story"[10] about the issues involved in this approach. The suppression of the interviewer's role may give the impression that the work represents the conception of the person interviewed, although a process of splicing and arranging has gone on. Titon admits that his first "autobiographies" of musicians involved more editing than a reader would realize (285-286), and he has chosen to use much rawer material in his later books and avoided the illusion of straightforward authorship. The words of Reverend White are valuable testimony to the nature of black life in East Texas: We wouldn't want to lose them out of some sense of ethnographic correctness. But it is also valuable to know how the book was prepared.

White's story is a powerful one expressed in effective black American vernacular. He was born in Shelby County and lived his whole life in the three adjacent East Texas counties: Shelby, Nacogdoches, and Cherokee. He was raised in a single-parent family along with an older brother and sister by a tiny but strong-willed half-Indian woman, Alice White (born Cartwright), who worked extremely hard as a domestic servant while raising vegetables to support the children. Her grandmother had been a "full-blooded white Indian," which may have meant that she belonged to one of the families who had been assimilated into the Cherokee or other "civilized tribes" in the Old South. His mother knew how to jerk meat the Indian way and gather herbs. He received large measures of love and corporal punishment (with the switch broom) from her. The family was even poorer than that of William A. Owens: He remembers on his seventh birthday that his mother brought home the table scraps of the white employers. His brother and sister got partially eaten pieces of chicken: Because it was his birthday, he got a whole drumstick. Hunger was a constant of his childhood. Once his mother managed to kill a deer with an axe as it ran by when she was washing clothes. Unfortunately, she knew how to dress a hog but not a deer and had to give an old man three quarters of the meat for doing the job.

White wanted to be a preacher from the age of three and conducted church services and baptisms with homemade dolls. Soon he preached sermons to other children. He had to quit school at ten because his mother's health was too bad for her to work. She died when he was eighteen. His life entered a new phase: He sought out his long-missing father in Nacogdoches, the county just west of Shelby. Charles C. White Sr. was an enormous man with a libertine lifestyle. The father lived with two women and had some sixteen other children by them. The father is brilliantly characterized as an eccentric domestic tyrant. This unorthodox establishment was supported by his farm, which was a large one for a black man. He had 593 acres and a number of tenant farmers.

After young White quarreled with this patriarchal figure he left for Center back in Shelby County. Charley White entered a phase of hard drinking and womanizing, which he calls "my mean years." He became a licensed preacher later: The classic pattern set by St. Augustine's *Confessions* is followed in the book, with the sinner and reprobate becoming a man of God. The path was rather torturous, but he eventually became a Baptist preacher, asking for and receiving a license to preach. He started a church in a small town near Nacogdoches.

His first marriage, to a woman named Lucille, appears to have been in part inspired by his desire to rescue her from a violent stepfather. White managed to farm in partnership with a white man named Chuck Richards: "He never said, 'Charley go do that.' He always said, 'Let's do that.' I worked with him ate with him, slept with him. We was just like brothers. We stayed partners for seven years" (118). He voted for the first time in 1920, a big event for a black man in Texas, where voting was legal but frowned on by whites. It was the first year women could vote, but Lucille was not ready for such a step. White went to the poll with Chuck Richards and was given no trouble. Voting would eventually win some leverage for black people in city councils and sheriffs' departments. White never plays down white injustices and abuses of power by deputy sheriffs, but he writes without prejudice.

His conversion to the Pentecostal Church of God in Christ came slowly. His wife turned to it first. The text details his resistance and its slow collapse. He attended a meeting and while kneeling in prayer felt a shock in his body. He was startled and looked about, having heard that members of this church could put a spell on a person by touching him. But no one was near. In spite of this sign and growing attraction to the church, he was not converted immediately, in the sense required: a baptism by the Holy Spirit. He and his wife were able to give up snuff, and he quit drinking. Finally, after a long struggle during which he wanted the spirit but could not experience it, the moment came. He was almost immediately made a preacher by the church.

The book is stronger on the social side of his religion than on the inner experience, nor does he say much about speaking in tongues and faith healing, which are doctrines of his church, the second-largest Pentecostal denomination in the United States—and a leading black organization. He did have visions from time to time, and he struggles to convey the experience:

> It's hard to explain about a vision. It's not anything you can touch, of course, but you know it's there. It's about the only thing that is real to you while it's going on. I guess it comes closer to being like a dream than anything else, but it's not exactly like that neither. When God gives you a vision your whole body kind of soaks up the message, like a biscuit soaks up red-eye gravy. And sometimes you can hear the message as sure as feel it. And sometimes you can see it. But generally can't none of the people around you see it or hear it. Leastwise, none of the people around me ever did. (134)

One vision, on New Year's Day, 1928, led him to move to Jacksonville and start a church there. He kept hearing a voice saying, "Jacksonville, Jacksonville." The town was about fifty miles from Shelby County. In the 1930s and 1940s it was a leading center for the growing of tomatoes. He moved into the community with the assistance of a man named McBride (but known to everyone as "Black Man") and a man he calls "Professor Howard," a retired schoolteacher who owned many rental houses. White's second wife, Malindy, was a highly successful midwife, a "baby catcher," and he supported himself with multiple jobs. Malindy would take the children with her to make money picking tomatoes.

The book naturally has much to say about the organization and growth of his church. White has a sense of humor and tells the story of threats to his life by a woman he ordered out of church one night because she was immodestly dressed and intoxicated. One of his members, Sister Tilley, started coming to church with a knife in her hand to protect her minister, who was not supposed to fight. Nor was she, he told her, whereupon she declared that she would "get out of the church." She would come to every service and say, "He won't fight for hisself. I come to fight for him. I ain't saved" (151).

He eventually took on a large role in the community. He started God's Storehouse, a grassroots organization to feed the hungry among the black population and among any white people who would break caste and ask for help. He found himself slaughtering and dressing many hogs at his own house without a permit. He became adept at raising money from both blacks and whites for this work, and he also started a blood bank, as black people could not afford the cost of transfusions. He gave everything he could to the work and raised his annual car license fee by trapping raccoons and selling the skins.

The dominant metaphor of self is summed up by the title, *No Quittin' Sense*. It is taken from a scene in which White's third wife, Marthy, gives her scant meal to two little girls who come by needing food. White said to his wife, "Marthy, you're just as bad as me. You ain't got no quittin' sense, either" (161). White demonstrates over and over again his deep commitment to providing for the hungry and doing other acts of mercy in the manner of Matthew 25:33-36 (King James version), which could have served as an epigraph for the book: "For I was an hungred, and ye gave me meat; I was thirsty, and ye gave me drink; I was a stranger, and ye took me in; Naked, and ye clothed me: I was sick, and ye visited me: I was in prison, and ye came unto me." Every one of these actions is performed by Reverend White, most of them over and over, tirelessly. Jewel Babb's acts of charity were performed almost in spite of herself, for her vocation as a healer was imposed on her rather than sought: She never presents herself as a person with a mission.

One of the most revealing aspects of White's narrative is the dramatic re-creation of the role of a black preacher in the community. He never left small-town East Texas, but that does not mean that he failed to adapt to or even bring about change. He acted as intermediary for the poor and for people in trouble with the law: Visiting prisoners was part of his biblical job description, after all. The franchise was one means for putting pressure on sheriffs whose deputies questioned black men by putting a boot on the prone suspect's neck and beating him with a rubber hose. White felt that policing was essential and understood that a sheriff had to be hard, but he pressured the authorities into giving up beating suspects into confessions. He could deliver votes if reforms were made, and the town council and sheriff knew it.

When integration came, he was for it, and he found that the white community leaders were eager to have the process go forward without the sorts of rioting often seen on television in the mid-sixties. He presented suggestions for reform to the town council. Most of his ideas were readily accepted, but they told him they had to think a while about colored policemen, though they did come around. His book is a meticulous portrait of life before and during the civil rights movement. It is not surprising that James W. Lee has praised the "brilliance, accuracy, and simplicity" of Charley White's narrative. The observations of life, are, as Lee says, "clear and real and unsentimental."[11]

White's book offers a powerful re-creation of rural poverty at the start, the kind of hopeless struggle with the stubborn soil which William A. Owens describes in his more famous work. Like Owens, he also re-creates the intense religious emotions of the poor. He naturally has insights into racial discrimination closed to Owens, who was, as we shall see in the next chapter, well-meaning once he outgrew the prejudices of his time and place. White worked as effectively as he could within the white supremacy framework of East Texas before the civil rights movement. Once change began—and the book was started in 1964, during the period of upheaval—he was enthusiastic about the possibilities at a time when many older black leaders condemned change. The book ends with regret and modest hope: "There's one thing here in Jacksonville I don't like. When I drive past the school, and see the children out at recess, I see all the white children playing together, and a little bunch of colored children way over in a corner, playing by themselves. That ain't right. I ain't said nothing yet. I'm just gonna watch and see how it goes" (216).

In spite of its small-press origins, *I Am Annie Mae* sold far better than *Border Healing Woman* and *No Quittin' Sense*. It has been picked up by the University of Texas Press and has had new incarnations as an ensemble musical by Naomi Carrier and Ruthe Winegarten and as a one-woman play with Carrier as Annie Mae Hunt. In 1993, Cynthia Salzman Mondell and Allen Mondell produced a video about Hunt, entitled *Guts, Gumption and Go-Ahead*.[12] The success of the book is not surprising. It describes the African-American experience in Texas with remarkable scope, from plantation days in Washington County to Annie Mae's transformation from cotton picker and domestic servant to political organizer and small businesswoman in Dallas. As Ruthe Winegarten says in her introduction, "Her grandmother Matilda Boozie (c. 1846-1947) was a slave; her daughter Leona operates a computer" (xii).

The work was prepared between 1977 and 1982 on the basis of a partnership contract between Winegarten and Hunt. Winegarten excluded herself from the text but has provided extensive annotations at the back of the book. She is a historian of black women in Texas, the author of a huge work, *Black Texas Women: 150 Years of Trial and Triumph* and the compiler of *Black Texas Women: A Sourcebook*.[13] One function of the annotations is to provide background through documents for Annie Mae's understanding of the past, which rests on oral tradition and the memories of an elderly woman who struggled to raise six children under desperate conditions. At least one contradiction in the narrative is quietly noted and the areas where research could not establish facts are indicated.

In an E-mail to me (August 28, 2001), Ruthe Winegarten has described the process of assembling the book. Only five or six hours of interviews were taped: Mrs. Hunt was clearly a good raconteur. The transcription was not easy because of her form of spoken English:

> She had a good memory and was very articulate. My children helped with the transcribing, which was very difficult as Mrs. H speaks Black English. In the days before xeroxing, we made multiple copies of the transcripts (I had help of a friend, Frieda Werden, with the editing), and we cut and pasted till we got the ms the way we wanted it. As in all other oral histories, Mrs. H gave several versions of the same anecdotes, so we patched together the best language, plus sometimes we had to fill in missing words. This is typical.

There are only a few traces of Winegarten's questions, as when Annie Mae says, "Yeah" or seems to be rhetorically repeating a question she was asked. Holland worked very hard to turn many conversations with Reverend C. C. White into full chapters. Winegarten's work is in fact more readable and less circumstantial: Annie Mae's life is provided in relatively brief chapters, each with a colloquial title taken from the text. The reader can get bogged down in Reverend White's lengthy discussions of his charitable activities and family life, though these have tremendous documentary value. It would be unfair to say that Annie Mae's story is told in sound bytes, but it certainly has brevity and each episode makes a strong impression.

It is possible that some of Annie Mae's discussions of women's issues, which seem to obtrude a little into the chronological narrative of her life, were more a concern of the interviewer, a concerned feminist, than of Annie Mae. Annie Mae's colloquial style has been retained, with punctuation for clarity and orthography which captures some of her pronunciation, like the dropping of the terminal "g," something which Holland did not attempt to do. Winegarten has deposited the tapes and other materials at the Dallas Public Library, and a scholar of oral history might someday examine the process by which the book was created.

One of the outstanding features of Annie Mae's book is profusion of excellent photographs from family albums. It is fortunate that a woman whose life was full of vicissitudes and moves managed to preserve so much. In later years she was often in the press for her political activities, and pictures and newspaper articles from her scrapbooks appear in the book. The violent tenor of life for black people in America is introduced almost surreptitiously in one picture of Annie Mae's niece, Georgia Mae Hall. The caption to her funeral program reads, "She was killed in her house; had her head beaten." The broad margins contain occasional glosses, mostly of dates.

The book begins with a declaration of identity: "I am Annie Mae Hunt. My name now is Hunt." But while her identity is clear to her throughout, names are problematic: Women, after all, change their names when they marry. "Hunt" is the name of a third husband. She was born Anne Mae McDade. Her children by her first husband, John Robert Prosper, did not want her to give up the Prosper name, so she defines herself as "Annie Mae McDade Prosper Hunt," which in fact omits a second husband, George Darden. The husbands seem incidental in the book.

The narrative starts with a family saga passed on by Annie Mae's maternal grandmother, Matilda Boozie. Before she came to Texas, she was a slave on a plantation in South Carolina. According to Ruthe Winegarten's annotations, the place and the details of the Boozie family who owned her are so far untraceable, not an unusual situation for an African-American family. Matilda was a house slave of the Boozies, one of the favored few, but her experience when she was not quite thirteen was marked by horrifying events which were quite normal in the slavery period. Her mother and her siblings were sold. Annie dryly records that "Old Mistress hugged her and told her, 'Don't worry, Tildy. I'll take care of you.' And she did. She took care of her" (5). How well she took care of her was demonstrated when Tildy was raped by the son of the family:

> Grandma say that she were near 13 years old, behind the barn *tee-'teein'* when Young Mawster come up behind her. She didn't see him, but he put his hand up under her dress, and said, "Lay down, Tildy." They called her Tildy, but her actual name was Matilda. And so this thing happened, and her stomach began to get big.

> One day, Grandma and Old Mistress, they was puttin up the clean clothes. Old Mistress had a pair of socks, or two pair, in her hand. She said, "Tildy, who been messin wit you down there?" Grandma say, "Young Mawster." Old Mistress ran to her, and crammed these socks in her mouth and say, "Don't you never tell nobody. If you do, I'll skin you alive." (9)

The rape is presented in squalid terms, no bodice-ripping or moonlight sex on the plantation: Young Mawster interrupts Tildy in the act of urination, which is described with a southern vulgarism. And Old Mistress's fondness for her house slave does not prevent her from enforcing silence with a domestic object, a pair of socks. The product of the rape was Annie Mae's Uncle Theodore, whom she refers to as a white man. Certainly judging from his picture he could have passed for white.

The Boozies moved to Texas, to Mount Pleasant in Titus County, but exactly when is not clear to Annie Mae, who relies on oral tradition rather than documents. Then there was a move to Washington County, near Brenham, perhaps after the Civil War. There the grandmother married Eli Randon, who had Seminole ancestry. Matilda was part Cherokee, not at all unusual in South Carolina where she was born. The ceremony took the traditional form from the slavery period, jumping over the broomstick. The Boozie family gave a large tract of land to the couple, in some kind of compensation for the child fathered by the son of the family. Like Charley White's father, Matilda and her husband had an unusual situation for blacks at the time: They had sharecroppers working some of the land, and they had paid workers as well, at the rate of fifty cents a day. Like Reverend White's second wife, she was also a highly successful midwife—a "baby catcher"—and had a clientele of white women as well as black. Annie Mae takes great pride in her grandmother's work, describing it in some detail, and boasting that "she caught everybody in that country, white or black. You better know she did. She had a name for herself. She was good and she was recognized!" (21).

The text provides an interesting picture of life in a sharecropping operation: The grandfather, who seems to have been very lazy, paid his tenants with scrip which could be cashed at a particular store. She covers such matters as cleaning globe lamps and advances in well buckets. The perennial subject of lye soap appears. Clothes were cleaned (as on the Babb ranch) by boiling them with lye in big basins beside the smokehouses. The chapter entitled "Grandma didn't believe in no dingy clothes" ends with a kind of prose poem on her grandmother's housekeeping:

> I remember the time Grandma's well went dry, and we had to tote the tubs of water from the spring fore we went to work. She always had lots *rinch* waters. This first *rinch* water wasn't good enough, she'd wash with the third *rinch* water. Always *rinchin*. And my grandma had a wash *pit* there. She used lye. She put them clothes in that lye water. Boiled them clothes like boilin beans. Boil them clothes, juice em down like that, and wash them clothes. Grandma had pretty white clothes. You didn't see nothin dingy in her house till they got to be rags. A whole lot of times, today, they got polyester, it just turns dingy. But a long time ago, they had pure cotton, and Grandma's clothes didn't get dingy like see some people's clothes. She didn't believe in no dingy clothes (31-32).

Annie Mae suggests that her mother, Callie, had a beautiful childhood, and she herself displays strong affection for the family estate. Callie was the youngest of sixteen children. She eloped with George McDade when she was sixteen: "And always in our house it was a joke about Grandmother looking for Daddy with a shotgun across her lap. She was going to shoot him for *stealing* her baby. Yeah, she was mad, but she got over it" (35).

There were three children in the McDade family: George, Annie Mae, and Dora. The father, who was abusive to his wife, deserted the family when Annie Mae was seven. The mother became a cook for oil-field crews, then when Annie Mae was eight moved near Dallas. She and the children chopped cotton at

Mesquite for fifty cents a day. Annie Mae could recall when the pay went up to a dollar a day. They survived because her grandfather would pay their rent and come visiting with supplies. Black family solidarity in the face of hardship is dramatized by this story. The seasonal work and the visits to the grandparents till late in fall made it difficult for the children to attend school, and Annie Mae only finished five grades. She remembers vividly the "school closings," her term for the school programs in the spring.

In 1922, the mother took her family to Navasota in Grimes County. Annie Mae's first impetus to tell her life's story dates from that time: She wrote an account of "a little tragedy" which befell them and kept it in a cardboard box for fifty years. Her children, not realizing the value of the contents, threw the box out. Telling her story to Winegarten was probably a way of making up for this loss and making the story public. Her stepfather "said something out of line that wasn't for black people to say at that time" (49). He was warned by the overseer, Mr. Kirk, that white men would be coming that night "and whup you up." He fled across the Brazos. Five white men came to the house and slapped Callie Randon around, asking where her husband was. She decided to leave town and sent to her family for money. But in the middle of the night before their departure, the plantation owner, Old Man Morrett, came with a group and whipped her mother: She was unable to walk for thirteen weeks. He also broke Annie Mae's arm and broke her little sister Dora's nose with a pistol.

On a later occasion in 1924, after Annie Mae's marriage to John Robert Prosper, her mother, who had moved away, brought her a sewing machine. Old Man Morrett demanded it, but Annie Mae's husband refused. He seems to have survived because he had a white protector, his boss, Steven Moore. But Annie Mae's sister, Dora, who had married, was raped by Morrett and her husband, Buck, was taken away one night by Morrett, who sent in a black employee named Bud Jones (whose wife was Morrett's victim also) to bring him out. He was never seen again. These events took place sixty years after the end of the Civil War but were not uncommon in Texas in the early twentieth century, as Winegarten establishes in *Black Texas Women*. Annie Mae, like a Holocaust victim, demands that the facts be heard: "That's the truth. This can be verified. It's people living knows this—Buck mother's dead, but his stepdaddy's still livin" (54). Part of the tragedy is that she cannot appeal to the court records for verification: No one was called to account.

Annie Mae's story has some interesting contradictions and gaps, which show up in a startling way in a chapter called "I was prejudiced toward men." She married John Prosper at fifteen, a marriage that broke up after three children. She says that he was a good man in one paragraph: She didn't know how to live with him. The next paragraph begins, "He was about the meanest man; he was mean; he was a mean man," a statement followed immediately by, "If I'd had any sense I'd have stayed with him, with all them children" (55). She left him with the children to go cotton picking. Her marriage had elements of reciprocal violence. He would hit her; she would scratch his face. She attributes her violence toward men to seeing her father beat her mother. Not long after, she got in serious trouble, doing "an ugly little thing in Houston." She "hit a boy with a knife pretty hard, and the boy slapped me, and had called me an ugly name." She decided to leave town and went to her father for money. They had a frank talk about his bad treatment of her mother and that seemed to have helped her deal with her own violent streak. This intuitive approach to healing the effects of a dysfunctional family shows real insight. She would hardly have been able to pay a therapist to tell her to resolve conflicts with her father.

Her story is in fact inspiring. She managed to raise six children on pitifully low wages. The book gives a detailed account of the struggle of black people to survive during the Depression, when even starvation wages were hard to find. As she says with bitter humor, there were thirty or forty applicants for every job as a maid, and "the *pickanniny* didn't know who was gonna be picked" (68). She seems to have known the Depression was over at last when housemaids' wages went up to $3.50 a week. One way that she was able to raise her children under such conditions was through the help of her neighbor, "Big Mama," who watched out for the children. She had a support network of friends.

Along with the description of the labor situation, the book discusses women's issues and customs. There are discussions of menstruation (known in the black community as "coming around"), birth control (inaccessible to impoverished black people in her youth), and abortion. She was brought up to believe that "the more children you had, the better it is for you." Only later did she learn that "the more children you had, the more it tear your resistance down" (65). Late in the book she has apparently been asked about the women's movement. Her response is amusing. She says she wouldn't join it but then goes on to make it clear that she believes in equal pay for equal work. She also notes that men do not have babies.

Most of her life has been spent in Dallas except for a stay in West Texas, in Lubbock, which she hated because of the sandstorms. Her turning point came one day when she was going out to clean a house on a rare icy day in Dallas. A girl at the bus stop told her that if she put socks over her shoes she wouldn't slip. She went into the Seals and Grant store and bought socks. When she got back to the bus stop, she had her epiphany: If she continued to clean houses for five dollars a week, she deserved to freeze to death. She resolved never to be a domestic again. Her chosen occupation, Avon Lady, is a traditional route to independence (or at least to supplementing income) for working-class women. She sometimes cleared three hundred dollars a month, an enormous increase over five dollars a week. She eventually managed to have a house built for herself. When a loan was needed, she called Mr. Julius Schepps, a well-to-do man for whom she'd worked when his children were small, and persuaded him to use his influence to have the loan approved. The reader can sense her growing confidence.

The latter part of her book has much to say about children and grandchildren, but she also deals with the institutions which have made an enormous difference in her life: her church, her political party, and her social club. The social club, the Daughters of the Improved Benevolent Society of Elks, illustrates the way that black people have created their own institutions when excluded from white ones. The main body of the Elks refused admission to their organization, so blacks not only created their own body but satirically called it "improved." The formula "separate but equal" was long used to oppress black people in the South. The black Elks club implies a "separate but improved" rule.

For American black people, churches have been institutions with profound significance over and above the spiritual life. They have offered mutual support, economic and psychological, in a hostile world. Annie Mae Hunt's favorite church is the Good Will Baptist Church in Brenham. She describes the annual barbecue and other activities at the homecoming every fall. One startling passage talks about a preacher in Dallas, Richard MacNeal, who comes from Brenham. When he preaches there, "boy, every *nigger* and his brother is there" (134).

Annie Mae became involved with another institution in the 1940s, the Democratic Party. Blacks could in fact vote in Texas, though it was not until 1944 that they could vote in the all-important Democratic primary. She was involved in selling poll taxes in the 1940s, and after the poll tax was abolished, she issued voters' certificates. The poll tax tended to keep black people from voting, which was no doubt one reason it was retained so long. She details a wide range of her activities for the Democratic Party, including membership in the Democratic Women of Dallas County, a group for which she has worked as a telephone solicitor. She was also involved with a multiparty group, the Texas Black Caucus. One of the great events of her life was attending the presidential inauguration of Jimmy Carter. She got a ticket through her congressman and proudly let him know that she did not expect him to pay for it. She took a Greyhound bus to the inauguration and had a splendid time. She was eventually named a "Yellow Rose of Texas" by the governor and given the keys to the city of Austin (xi).

The final chapter of her book contains her musings on whether or not she needs another man in her life. The answer: no. She "put out" her last husband after discovering that he was "shackin out" with a woman seven or eight blocks away. Her attitude toward men seems to have been pretty sanguine, another reason that her book has popular appeal: The Billie Holiday attitude of subservience to "My Man" is now obsolete. She is not ashamed of her mature body—she says she is "built like a buffalo" in the shoulders. At the end of the chapter, she says that a man who wanted her for herself would be acceptable, but she has no interest in cooking and cleaning: "I been loose so long till I been set to my ways that I couldn't do that no more. I don't want no man to tell me nothin no more" (138). A quadruple negative is ungrammatical but makes her point.

The course of her life—from chopping cotton to entrepreneurial independence and political activity—really does encapsulate a remarkable and representative history of working-class black life in Texas. In his book on *Black Autobiography in America*, Stephen Butterfield points out that "the 'self' of black autobiography, on the whole . . . is not an individual with a private career, but a soldier in a long, historic march toward Canaan. The self is conceived of as a member of an oppressed group with ties and responsibilities to the other members."[14] The pattern, he suggests, is "a bid for freedom, a beak of hope cracking the shell of slavery and exploitation. It is also an attempt to communicate to the white world what whites have done to them" (3). The stories of Reverend Charley C. White and Annie Mae Hunt perform all of these functions. Their ties to their community and supportive friends were essential. Hunt's individual story moves toward the personal Canaan of a life of relative security and meaningful political activity, and at the same time she communicates what the white world has done to her and her family, especially that "little tragedy on a plantation in Navasota." The "metaphor of self" in her work is certainly a move toward self-sufficiency. Reverend White had God on his side spiritually but also worked immensely hard for his community. Both of these black writers have defined freedom through the economic gains they could register: for his people, in White's case, for herself in Hunt's. The conclusions of their stories are indeed uplifting, whereas Jewel Babb's life, interesting and positive as it may have been for others, ended with poverty and fear. Babb and White were each entrusted with a power beyond themselves. Hunt found ways to empower herself.

William A. Owens

6

BAPTIZED IN EARTH: WILLIAM A. OWENS AND NORTHEAST TEXAS

The first of William Owens's books about his life in Texas, *This Stubborn Soil,* is a Texas classic. Mody C. Boatright's review of the book puts its merits succinctly: "This is a profoundly human document which with unerring art details the struggles of a poor Northeast Texas farm boy to get an education and depicts in vivid scenes and language a rich folk culture."[1]

According to William Pilkington's study of Owens, the book was begun in 1947, but the author's agent "told him he was not old enough to write an autobiography,"[2] so the work had to wait nineteen years for completion and publication.

Owens (1905-1990) writes a reverberant book for anyone interested in the social, educational, and farming history of Texas, though the power of the work rests in its portrait of a boy growing up in a close and impoverished family in red-soil farming country. The place of his birth in 1905 was the laughably named Pin Hook, sometimes passed off as "Faulkner," a village about twenty-five miles from Paris, the county seat of Lamar, up in the northeast corner of Texas. One of his recurring problems in the book is to explain to people he meets just where Pin Hook might be. The opening chapter of his memoir explains the physical setting (tortured by weather), and the social history (settled by the Witherspoon family just before the Texas revolution), establishing the character of this margin of southern agrarian life. The land was poor: Lamar County could support plantation agriculture in the black soil of the river bottoms, but Pin Hook had thin red soil which wore out quickly, leaving the inhabitants scrabbling for existence on little farms where they could raise cotton, corn, and black-eyed peas and make "a living submarginal, exhausting to mind and body" (3).

It was fifty years before Pin Hook had a schoolhouse, and it was open only three months of the year, which was not uncommon in rural Texas, where the students would be needed to work on the farm most of the year. Gertrude Beasley showed up for her teaching job in Mulberry Canyon and discovered that the cotton picking had not been finished, which meant that she had to go home again for three weeks. The other public institution was religion, mostly Methodist and Baptist. For entertainment, people would sing the old Scottish and English ballads brought from Britain many generations before. Church, education, and folklore are particular interests in this book, and Owens has much to say about each.

The story begins with the death of Owens's father in 1905, only a few hours after a fifth child, William himself, was born. The father's illness was probably worsened by the incompetent treatment he received from the local quack. The ordeals of people who could hardly afford even quacks run through the book, culminating in the family's sufferings during the influenza epidemic of 1919, during which Owens almost died. Owens's one sister, Linnie, died after bad medical treatment. Owens gives considerable space to his brothers: Monroe, Dewey, Charles, and Roy. The poor in Owens's time often named children for public figures: Monroe was named for the nineteenth president, James Monroe, and Dewey was named after the celebrated admiral of the Spanish-American War.

Owens never knew his father, then, and the family matriarch, Missouri Ann James (nee Cleaver) died when he was not yet two. Missouri Ann, his mother's grandmother, was a real force in Owens's life, although he could not remember her. She was born in Alabama and eventually lived in Arkansas, where she married a distant relative of Frank and Jesse James. Missouri Ann is the focus of Owens's family saga. He grew up on tales of her experiences during the Civil War when, widowed after her husband died in the Confederate army, she had to take care of her children with almost no resources. On one occasion she hid the last food, corn pones, under her skirts, to keep them from being taken by Yankee soldiers searching for provisions. This kind of story is common in the South. In Faulkner's story cycle, *The Unvanquished,* Rosa Millard hides two boys under her enormous skirts when a Yankee detachment comes to arrest them. No doubt fashions in the Civil War permitted such subterfuges, though a skeptic might wonder how hungry Yankees missed the smell of hot corn pone in Missouri Ann's case. Later she sheltered a young man who she believed was Jesse James. The family naturally came to admire James, the Robin Hood of poor farmers, and at one point Owens's grandmother told him that she hoped he would grow up to be as good a man as Jesse James. A third story from the Civil War period told how a starving Yankee soldier was given the family's last food, a pail of molasses, and downed it without stopping.

The values taught by these stories are clear: Women need

ingenuity and courage to survive without men; outlaws are admirable if they have a just cause and serve the poor; and compassion is a virtue even if the beneficiary is an enemy. Part of Missouri Ann's value for young Owens came from his awareness that she was a link to a different life, one which once seemed to offer more prospects. She was educated, prosperous—she even brought an ex-slave, Mose, to Texas with her. She helped Owens's mother write verses, something that became important for Owens in forming his sense of himself as a writer. He sums her up by recalling her portrait which hung on the wall: "She was a woman of strong body, strong face. What did not show in the picture was that she was a maker of verse, a teller of stories, stories that from the time I could talk belonged to me" (19).

At the end of the war, Missouri Ann and her family moved to Texas, with a few cattle and a wagon for the younger children to ride in. Her story serves as the culmination of Owens's *A Fair and Happy Land,* his full-length family saga which traces his Cleaver ancestry back to 1685. *A Fair and Happy Land* does not fall within the scope of this study, for it is all family saga, much of it conjecture, without any autobiography. Owens pays little attention to his paternal ancestry in *This Stubborn Soil:* His imagination is fired by the self-reliant (another word for "desperate" in rural Texas) women in his youth, widows like his mother, his grandmother, and his great aunts, Nellie and Vick. Only his mother's sister, Niece (for Berniece) Kitchens, had a living husband, Charlie. The struggle of the family to survive is the focus of his first autobiography: His own development is important, but the family story is foremost.

Owens spent his first year literally in the stubborn soil. His mother had to put in a crop, so as she plowed he played nearby, tied to a stake so that he wouldn't crawl into the woods. "My toys were the dirt, and a stick to dig the dirt. No one could live closer to the earth than I did. I dug the sand, I rolled in it, I covered myself with it" (12). Throughout the autobiography he conveys his experience of nature in powerful images, but he also reveals his desire to escape from bondage to the soil. He became painfully aware of the suffering that poverty created in his family. But they were not dehumanized. The autobiography of Charlie C. White depicts even more desperate rural poverty, and a similar survival of the human spirit.

The theme of family loss is strong in the book, creating the greatest pathos when his great-aunt Nellie returned with her younger daughters from a stay in Oklahoma. She had been roughened into a masculine-looking figure by hard work and pellagra, and she was exhausted by the work and by grief. Her oldest daughter, Bessie, had died in a buggy accident not long after marriage. There was no photograph of her alive, so Nellie had a photographer take pictures of the young woman in her coffin. One picture was retouched to make the eyes look open, but the photographer did not get the color right. The scene of Nellie passing the photograph around for the family to see is told with a restraint that intensifies the effect.

Such episodes affirm the rich humanity of Owens's family. They are not flawless, especially in the matter of race. This is made quite clear in a visit with his grandmother to see her son-in-law, Uncle Jack, and his wife, the half-Choctaw woman, Julie. Aunt Julie still had many Indian ways after two marriages to white men. Young Owens perceived her as different: "I could see that she had too much Indian blood to be like kinfolks, or talk like kinfolks" (81). And when Aunt Nellie returned from Oklahoma, she had nothing good to say about the Choctaws she met.

The most wrenching looks at racism arise from Owens's own shameful experiences, which he reports fully and without excuses. He came to know the elderly black neighbors, Parson Perry and his wife Betty, and treated them with condescension. They responded politely to his ignorant rudeness, but when he told them that slavery was not a bad thing—a common southern white belief—the Perrys, who were born in slavery, were deeply hurt and responded vigorously, telling the boy that nothing could have been worse.

The worst incident was his setting a fire in the meadow while playing with matches. He had been warned beforehand by Betty Perry, and in defiance he struck a match on his white duckings. The resulting blaze nearly destroyed his family's farm. Owens covered his actions by saying that he saw Old Betty set the fire. She was profoundly hurt when she told her side of it and discovered that the word of a little white boy was taken over her own: "You believing him? You believing him when I seen him with my own eyes striking matches on the road? You putting his word before mine?" (164). Her husband was also appalled: "I never would have believed it." The incident leaves young Owens with a bad conscience: "I knew that my word was better than a nigger's any day, but I did not feel very good about it" (165). And the failure of his brother to ask him any questions about the incident indicated a racial code of silence.

His prejudices did not survive his education, and his activities as a collector of folklore gave him a more intimate knowledge of black life than he could ever have experienced in Pin Hook. He eventually wrote a novel about race in Texas, *Walking on Borrowed Land,*[3] in which he tried to see the racial situation from the black point of view; he also wrote a book on the celebrated *Amistad*[4] case in which Africans who had taken over a slave ship sued for their freedom. Like Gertrude Beasley and J. Frank Dobie, he learned to transcend his attitudes during his university education. In his case the change was initiated by his interest in African-American folklore when he was attending Southern Methodist University in Dallas. He began wandering through the black district around Thomas and Hall, listening to the speech, and even attending a movie where he had to sit in the balcony, a reverse of the usual southern pattern.

This is a book of "remembered aspiration," to use John Graves's term from the introduction to the latest edition (ix). The family had impulses to escape the cycle of poverty and the degradation of spirit. Love of music runs through the book. The mother played a parlor organ and the songs, simple as they were, had enormous significance for them all. The mother even bought a piano from a traveling salesman, trading a beef cow for it. And she wrote a little column about Pin Hook for the newspaper in nearby Blossom. The family's multiple moves in Owens's childhood represent an attempt to achieve a better life, though the farms they rented were not good and the children's schooling suffered. The tendency of Owens's relatives to move to Dallas or to work in the oil fields is another sign of aspiration. In fact, they were taking part of the shift from rural to urban life in Texas, a change brought about by economic forces. T. R. Fehrenbach points out in *Seven Keys to Texas*[5] that the urban growth in Texas came mostly from within the state, not from other states or other countries.

Owens's own early aspirations are symbolized by the moment when he went pecan picking with his Aunt Niece and Uncle Charlie and saw the Red River—the northeast boundary of Texas. He longed to cross over into Oklahoma. The whole party drank the water (54). The epiphany is understated, but it was clearly a major moment for a boy who had seen little of the world: "we had crossed over from before to after drinking it" (54). The area was so backward in the years between 1910 and 1920 that he is able to report on his first experiences of telephone poles, automobiles, trains, and electric lights, moments as significant as seeing his first great river. He saw telephone poles long before he encountered a phone, and he assumed that the humming of the wires in the wind represented the blended voices of many people. Once when he was about seven his mother took him to the little town of Blossom, where he saw his first train and electric lights. Lomax saw his first train at the age of ten. As mentioned in the introduction of this book, when Owens's mother asked him how he liked town, he replied, "More'n anything I ever seen. I wisht I could go back" (67). Even more exciting to him was the first trip to Paris, the modest-sized county seat. He was permitted to accompany his brother Dewey to sell a load of peanuts. His experience of the town was limited to a ride on the wagon along Lamar Avenue and a little time spent on the sidewalk outside the wagon yard gate, but he was smitten by urban life, even on the modest scale of a small town like Paris, which bills itself cheekily as "the second largest Paris in the world."

His deepest aspiration was for schooling. The family moved

seven times in a few years, to communities like Linden and Blossom, making Owens's education very spotty. Indeed, he did not begin regular attendance until he was eight. He taught himself a fair amount from books used by his brothers, including a history of America. The schools did not offer textbooks: Children learned from whatever books they could find and bring to school. The elaborate accounts of schools in *This Stubborn Soil* and its sequel, *A Season of Weathering,* provide a full picture of the running of early schools, and the second book describes the system of training and employing teachers. The old saying that "Texas is hard on women and horses," which Sallie Reynolds Matthews says her mother heard in the 1850s, clearly applies to teachers as well: A strict teacher, like the very admirable Mr. Jessee, might be driven out of Pin Hook by the antagonism of students and their parents, and Owens expresses shame at having failed to defend the man, who finally gave up on inducing students to learn and kept order with beatings, much in the style of Gertrude Beasley. Owens, who had to go to school barefoot, was impressed from the start not only by Mr. Jessee's intelligence but by his good brown shoes. He wanted to be a teacher someday and have shoes himself.

Owens's family was aware that education is necessary for a start in life. In a plaintive scene, Owens helped his illiterate grandmother learn to read and write. She was finally able to write a letter to her sister Vick and niece, Maggie, who had moved to Dallas. She began the letter with the formula used by her mother, Missouri Ann: "I seat myself with pen in hand" (94), though she had no pen, only a pencil. She found reading books beyond her, but she stressed to Owens that he would never get anywhere in life without an education. On another occasion, the family discussed a teacher at Linden, George Haley, who started in poverty and raised himself to a permanent teaching certificate with tremendous efficiency. Owens's mother said, "No need'n staying behind a plow all your life unless you want to" (104). Burton Bledstein's "culture of professionalism" is the pull here. Teaching was a way to escape from farm drudgery.

Like other writers who tell their life stories, Owens records his early love of words: Education was not solely a way to escape the plow. When his family moved back to their place near Pin Hook after years of renting other people's farms, the neglectful tenants had plastered the walls with copies of *The Saturday Evening Post,* and Owens delighted in reading the stories. He began memorizing poems very early, and when his mother almost died of the Spanish flu, he longed to find words to express his feelings.

He had more opportunities to read when he met a mysterious man who lived in a two-room shack with a badly educated and grotesque-looking woman and their child. The man was a tiehacker. He made his living cutting crossties but never talked about the woods, something that young Owens found surprising. He was proud of his collection of twenty-five books, ranging from *Treasure Island* to Booth Tarkington's *Penrod* to Jack London's *Martin Eden*. The man's wife said, "He'd druther read'n eat," and the man's comment was, "They ain't nothing like reading" (218). The tiehacker loaned Owens books, after explaining that he always washed his hands before reading and put a cover on the book. The boy borrowed a series of books, but one day he found the shack empty and no one in the area knew where the family had gone. The anecdote is self-contained and has no sequel, but it conveys with great pathos the hunger for reading among those who might seem too oppressed by work and poverty to have any intellectual ambitions.

Owens's own ambitions were treated with cruelty by the popular teacher who replaced the persecuted Mr. Jessee. DeRhon Stuart was well-dressed and had the new fashion of bobbed hair. She made school fun: "every day was like a play day," and she succeeded where the more scrupulous Mr. Jessee did not. When Owens wrote a brilliant essay for her, she read it to the class and then humiliated him with an accusation of plagiarism. When he said that he could show her his honesty by writing more papers, she made a statement unforgivable in a teacher, "You can't teach me a thing I don't already know" (227). While John A. Lomax was induced to burn his roll of cowboy songs by smug contempt of Morgan Callaway, young Owens had his essay thrown into the woodstove by the teacher. And when he returned home, he found that the family had taken for granted that he would be quitting school that year to help on the farm, the attitude that Gertrude Beasley faced down in her own family.

His determination would lead Owens to a Ph.D. from the University of Iowa and a distinguished teaching career at Columbia University, but it was full of detours and potholes. He went to Dallas at fifteen to find work and lived with Aunt Vick and Maggie. The young man going off to seek his fortune in the big city is a perennial American subject—and a subject of folk tales; the appeal is eternal. At one time every school reader in America included Benjamin Franklin's account of walking down the streets of Philadelphia with two loaves of bread under his arms. Owens's experience was more rustic: His mother gave him a chicken so that he could stop off in Paris and sell it in order to buy a pair of socks. His entrance into Dallas left him dazed. He was especially impressed by the lights on the stores and movie houses on Elm Street as he went down it on the streetcar with Maggie. The illuminated sign which impressed him most (and he returns to the image) was the splendid moving bird on the *Majestic Theatre*. The streetcar soon passed the black district, pronounced "Deep Ellum," the future home of a Yahoo internet operation. In 1941 Deep Ellum was described in the WPA Guide to Texas as "the congested Negro shopping and amusement district" where one could buy "anything from a threadbare cloth-of-gold evening gown" to a "folding bathtub."[6] The guide notes that the Negroes regarded it as something different from other Negro shopping areas. It seems to have been as mysterious in 1920 when Owens took that streetcar ride.

Owens did find a job packing parcels at the Sears Roebuck catalog operation, where he amused his fellow workers because he wore clothes from their own company. One worker showed off his own fifteen dollar pants and said that he would never buy "anything made to sell to country folks" (248). These experiences added to Owens's awareness of the world outside Lamar County, but he still craved education and moved back home to attend school under the radical Mr. Swindle, who "with all Pin Hook against him, had put in the study of algebra and Latin" (261). He eventually got a job on Mr. Swindle's farm, but he let him down by falling in with an evil companion, Swindle's own son. The betrayal was intensified because Swindle had offered to loan Owens money to pursue his dream of going to the state teachers' college at Commerce, now known as East Texas State University. Owens is very frank about his shameful acts: his false accusation of Betty Perry over his own arson, his failure to support Mr. Jessee, and his shabby treatment of Mr. Swindle. One of the pleasures of the sequel, *A Season of Weathering*, is to see him reestablish warm relations with the Swindle family when he returned to the Pin Hook area as a teacher.

He moved back to Dallas, hoping that he would be able to save money for an education. He was an absolute failure back at the Sears Roebuck catalog operation—he practically destroyed the women's underwear department when put in charge of it. He got behind and began to make wild substitutions when he could not find the right product. His next job, the last one in the book, was at the University of Dallas, a Catholic institution, where he was hired as the priests' scullery boy in the communal kitchen. His hiring came about by mistake: The employment agency should have sent a Catholic. As a Baptist, he faced a new kind of temptation after his boss, Father Carney, told him that the university would be able to help a Catholic boy go to school, and then asked him if he would like religious instruction. After a Dickensian experience stripping and revarnishing floors, he left the priests' kitchen for Commerce, where he hoped to finish high school and take courses at the East Texas Normal School to qualify for an elementary school certificate.

His final ordeal awaited him. The rules at the normal school had been changed from the previous year, and his scanty education no longer offered him a hope of entering high school, so it seemed. He pleaded desperately with the dean, the registrar, and the president in turn. The reader shares his devastation as he was repeatedly turned down. He was only a year too late, but like the sinner in the popular invitation hymn, faced the prospect of "Almost, but lost." However, he showed up to take the entrance examination anyway, and the president permitted him to try. The book comes to a fine ending. He had the second-highest score on the examination, and therefore an exception could be made.

Along with its narrative, *This Stubborn Soil* offers an exhaustive but never tiresome look at daily life in northeast Texas. Farming was the mainstream of Texas life deep into the twentieth century, as T. R. Fehrenbach makes clear in his magisterial history, *Lone Star*. Owens has become such a Texas classic that Fehrenbach's chapter on agriculture is titled "The Stubborn Soil" although Owens is not mentioned explicitly.[7] It would be possible to extract a systematic view of Texas farm life from *This Stubborn Soil*: The book covers cotton picking and ginning, making a crop with a hoe (the family's horse died, and they were reduced to this extreme), the application of Jerusalem oak to control chicken mites, the cultivation of peanut crops, and the use of the thresher ("thrasher") to deal with the vines; the list goes on and on. The making of lye soap by the same process used by A. C. Greene's great-grandmother gets full attention, not to mention the preparation of sweet cider. The reader even learns how a "toothbrush" for dipping snuff is made from a twig. The smallest details are here: the making of a grater for corn out of a molasses bucket, the effects of eating the poverty food such as poke sallet, a toxic weed. The desperate treatments given to a bloated mare to "scour" it are elaborated. A chapter is given to Uncle Charlie Kitchens's construction of a new clay chimney for the Owens family. These details are introduced in a natural way as part of the narrative of everyday life.

Owens, an experienced folklore collector, naturally has an interest in rhymes, songs, and folk customs. The rhymes and songs are everywhere in his book. He brings in a number of proverbs and sayings as well: When the family had to move three times in a year, his grandmother said, "three moves means a fire" (52). Later, when they lived in a secluded area where "niggers" were perceived as a threat, the grandmother took an axe into the house for protection. Later she was careful to carry it out of the house backward to ward off the traditional bad luck for bringing an axe inside. When the oldest son, Monroe, went into Paris in a buggy to get married (a common practice at the time), it was the mother's turn to be apprehensive: She believed that it was bad luck to get married on wheels. "Start out rolling, keep on rolling, they say" (224).

The book is also a compendium of social practices. After Owens's widowed mother married a Mr. John Rhodes, the neighbors gave the new couple a traditional "shivaree," with noise made by shotgun blasts and cowbells. The participants quieted down when the new couple came onto the porch and gave out the customary treats: a bag of candy and teacakes from the store. Incidentally, Owens, unlike Beasley, makes nothing of the eventual divorce of Mr. Rhodes and his mother. Owens also describes Christmas festivities, which for the poor were often just noise made with fireworks and gunshots: He remembers visiting his Aunt Niece and Charlie one Christmas. Fireworks were customary at Christmas in the Texas of the time, and Charlie bought a good selection. He carried his merrymaking to the point of blasting the gate with his double-barreled shotgun, an act in which four of his guests joined in. Owens's grandmother did not approve, but Charlie's wife came out with a peeled orange (a fruit few ate except at Christmas). Charlie gave the traditional southern Christmas greeting, "Christmas gift," which obliged the other person to give money or a treat. His wife, who seemed to understand Charlie's need for an outlet, responded without antagonism: "She went up to him and stuck a slice of orange between his teeth. They were both laughing without making a sound, and once he leaned over and kissed her. 'I had me some Christmas,' he said" (76).

An interesting set of folk beliefs centers on Old Christmas, the twelfth day of Christmas, January 6. Little Owens was told that the horses talk at midnight and the cattle walk on their knees on that occasion. Ghosts were also likely to be seen. He goes beyond Thomas Hardy, who says in his great poem, "The Oxen," that if someone told him that the oxen were kneeling, he would go. Owens actually went to the barn without prompting, and was disillusioned to find that the animals were doing nothing unusual. He went so far as to kick Old Reddy, the cow, to induce her to get up, but she wouldn't walk on her knees.

Games are covered as well. Near the end of the book, a farewell party was given for Monroe, who had been drafted. The game played at the party was "snap," which should merely be a form of tag played between couples, but at the party it quickly turned into a kissing game. Rolyholy, a game of marbles, was a diversion that captured not only boys but adults. We are told that grown men "wore the knees out of their duckings and their fingernails to the quick" playing rolyholy. The blacksmith eventually changed the nature of the game by emerging one day from his shop with a steel ball taken out of a bearing. He proceeded to smash everyone's agates and then sold some bearings for two bits each. "Soon it was steel balls at school, steel balls at the store, and rolyholy stopped as fast as it started" (258).

Immensely more important than marbles and snap games and Christmas fireworks was religion, one of the few emotional outlets for the poor of rural Texas. Owens has two fine scenes of camp meetings. Emotions ran high at camp meetings, part of a tradition started at the famous Cane Creek Meeting in 1801, at which people were profoundly moved and marked for life. For the rural poor, the meetings were not only spiritual experiences but social events full of drama as preachers and members of the audience worked on notorious sinners and young people who had never been "saved."

John Graves's introduction to the latest edition of *This Stubborn Soil* singles out one episode from a revival as an example of the power of understatement in the book: At a "union revival" of Baptists and Methodists, a man overcome by conviction of his sins beat his head against a tree. Graves observes that Owens does not state that the moment is comic, rather he demonstrates it. On the last night of the revival, Aunt Nellie Haigood, a woman who had neglected religion, was persuaded to attend. She was one of the numerous widowed relatives who had to raise a family without a grown man to do the backbreaking work of farming, and she had three daughters whom "she was raising to work like men" (29). She did not respond to the invitation call to the mourners' bench, much to the regret of Owens's family. But in a poignant scene, on the way home in a wagon, she and her sister, Owens's grandmother, began talking of hard times, the daughters started to sing a hymn, and Aunt Nellie finally leaped out of the wagon and ran down the road, "shouting, crying, crooning, begging God to have mercy on her and help her." The scene is powerful because the moment of religious fervor is not induced by social pressure and emotional manipulation, and it ended laconically with the aunt climbing into the wagon and saying, "I had me a good shout" (31), which perhaps is as important as having some Christmas like Uncle Charlie.

The other revival scene in the book also has comic touches. The Baptists of Novice held a meeting one August, at a time when the men of the area were too tired to build the traditional brush arbor to protect against the heat. The meetings were therefore held at night. They were presided over by a famous preacher, Brother Cummings, whose status was not damaged by his illiteracy. One night, at the invitation hymn, "a notoriously stiff-necked sinner" was converted. But when baptism day arrived, and the community gathered at a rather filthy "hole of yellow water in a cow pasture," the preacher had great difficulty with the sinner, whose instincts caused him to resist the total immersion dictated by Baptist theology. And worst of all, a snuff tin floated out of his pocket, a sign that he had not changed his worldly ways (178). The incident gave the local people much to think about: Is baptism valid if the immersion is a little short of total? The humorous tone taken by Owens in describing these revivals foreshadows his own ambivalent attitude toward religion after he is converted: Much of the drama of his second autobiography, *A Season of Weathering*, is created by his simultaneous craving for salvation and his resistance to it.

Owens's book deserves its high reputation as a Texas classic. The depictions of folk life, which were praised by Mody Boatright, are introduced in a natural way, and the impoverished, badly educated characters have, as Boatright said, "an innate dignity." Further, the book has a startling objectivity about the author's less admirable actions, though it is not confessional in the way we are accustomed to today: This is not the moral universe of Mary Karr, who details her sexual and drug experiences. Nor does he present his family as a hotbed of deviant behavior in the way of Gertrude Beasley. They are tough, certainly, fond of the country saying, "they c'n kill me but they cain't eat me." But they care for one another.

The successor to *This Stubborn Soil* appeared in 1974. It is an interesting work, though even the title, *A Season of Weathering*, suggests that it will be a more even book, one less concerned with sheer survival but depicting hardship nonetheless. It is worth reading but does not rank as a classic. Owens continues the story of his education and dramatizes his struggle by presenting two tempting alternatives which might have kept him from his goal of becoming a teacher and writer. One was religious fanaticism, the other was capitalism in an evangelistic mode.

The early chapters describe his life at the teachers' training school at Commerce. They are not especially engrossing, but they do give a good glimpse of higher education in Texas at the time. J. Frank Dobie's long essay on Georgetown University in *Some Part of Myself* is a good complement to these pages. After finishing the eleventh grade, Owens found it too late to get a teaching job for the year, so he followed the suggestion of his mother and visited her at Gem, Texas, in the Panhandle area, where she had married again, to a rancher appropriately named (or nicknamed) Lank Smith. Owens found the wind and flatness intolerable, but they were nothing compared to a song everyone in the region sang or hummed or picked out on the piano: "I Ride an Old Paint," also known as "Cowboy Jack." The sandstorms and cowchip fires were not as oppressive as the song. He decides he cannot stay: "All [Gem] had to offer as far as I could see in music, literature and drama was 'I Ride an Old Paint.'" The episode has an irony that Owens must have relished, as he became an expert collector of cowboy songs.

He decided to seek work in Paris and quickly met his two tempters. One was David Phillips, a boy evangelist who was quickly building a reputation in the Missionary Baptist Church, an especially fervent branch of the Owens family religion. The other was Mr. Watkins, who hired him at the Kress mercantile store. While the Kress stores now seem archaic in the age of Wal-Mart, they had a tremendous impact on American business life. The founder, Samuel Kress, had some original ideas. He micromanaged the stores in an unheard-of way, sending out inspectors frequently. Even the cash registers were preset to avoid petty embezzlement, as Owens learned one day when he played with one back from the repair shop and cost Mr. Watkins a week's profit for nonexistent sales. But the most original feature of Kress was the practice of giving a share of a store's profits to its manager. The path to being a manager was set out in a philosophy which divided employees into learners, who were the elect, and non-learners. Owens quickly detected elements of "Pelmanism" in Mr. Watkins, the philosophy of mind training invented in London in 1898 at the Pelman Institute. Pelmanism is an ancestor of any number of mental development and motivational schemes designed to help the ambitious get ahead. Kress managers were required to take a twelve-part course from the Pelman Institute of America.

Mr. Watkins quickly picked out Owens as a learner and encouraged him to consider a career with the company. He offered training in such mysteries as window dressing and assured Owens that he could rise in the company. At the same time, Owens's growing friendship with the boy evangelist (who was, in fact, eighteen, not quite a boy, and a year younger than Owens) led him to a religious conversion at a revival in the Immanuel Baptist Church. The conversion was an act of will in the face of tremendous emotional pressure. Gertrude Beasley too felt that her conversion was more expectation than fervor. But for some time Owens's life was shaped by a three-way conflict: to accept a religious vocation as a Baptist preacher, to become a learner at Kress, or to pursue his goal of education. The education would have limited use for Kress, and David

Phillips believed that it would merely get in the way of spiritual development. Owens, whose self-conception pointed toward becoming a teacher, was being offered two alternative metaphors of self, as a learner or an evangelist.

Fortunately, Owens took courses at the new Paris Junior College, and he met a third influence to balance the pressure of Mr. Watkins and David Phillips: Miss Hudson, a fine English teacher, who encouraged his efforts in reading and writing. As he says, "Before a month had passed I found myself pulled by three different people: a Baptist, a Pelmanist, and, though she may not have applied the term to herself, a humanist" (85). She introduced him to the essays of Robert Louis Stevenson, which he admired, and then to the work of another Hudson, William Henry. W. H. Hudson, whose *Green Mansions*, *Far Away and Long Ago*, and *The Purple Land* were tremendously successful, has now been almost forgotten. The works are romantic in tone and exotic in setting. J. Frank Dobie, as mentioned in chapter two, was also an admirer of Hudson. He and Owens had taste formed on pre-modernist writers.

Miss Hudson was an Episcopalian. She invited Owens to a young people's group at her church. He was pleased by this, but he knew that there would be dancing, which was forbidden in his church. When he consulted David Phillips and the pastor of Immanuel Missionary Baptist Church about the invitation, they reacted with anger and shock, the pastor in particular, as he saw the evil hand of Episcopalianism beckoning a Baptist into sin. Gertrude Beasley's attendance at Childers Classical Institute had aroused sectarian feelings among the Baptists: Why was a Baptist girl attending a Church of Christ college? Not long after, Owens witnessed an appalling church trial of a young girl who had failed to leave a party after dancing started. The brutal tone taken toward the girl—who was browbeaten into repentance—disturbed him.

He remained active in his church nevertheless, and assisted David Phillips in giving lessons in churches in the area. The scenes of religious meetings and missionary work in towns like Direct (present population: seventy) are vivid and give an insider's view of fundamentalism in Texas in the 1920s. Owens found that he had a gift for sketching and provided the pictures for chalk talks with his colleague. He was so successful that it was announced at a revival meeting that the church wanted him to become an ordained preacher. This conscription without consultation did not please him: His emotions were really committed to education. Indeed, he showed a humanist regard for art when a preacher decided to deliver a message against a new statue at the junior college, a classical work depicting two nude wrestlers. Owens reported to the preacher that nothing revealing could actually be seen, and interest in the statue faded quickly.

Of course neither Pelmanism nor revivalism captured Owens's permanent allegiance. He had to let both his mentors down—the Kress manager and the evangelist. It seems a flaw in the work that he never tells us what became of David Phillips. Perhaps he did not know. Phillips is a sad figure: He confided in Owens that he suppressed the desires of the flesh until his marriage, but on his wedding night literally ripped the clothes off his bride, leaving her standing terrified by the relentless force of his lust, and alienated her permanently. Some sketch of his later career would have been interesting, if Owens knew anything about it.

After Owens at last qualified for a full teaching job, he had the task of finding one, and the book depicts the low regard felt by many rural people for teachers. He was treated rudely by trustees: He describes one who was patching his fence and asked, "You know enough to hold this [wire] while I steeple?" (115). Owens finally got a job in his native Pin Hook, a sentimental and idealistic choice. He put his heart into the work and strove to visit and even spend the night with all of the families in the district. One visit led to a comic misadventure. He had squirrel stew, and the squirrel's head kept bobbing up in the serving bowl with its eyes looking right at Owens, who became understandably uncomfortable. At school the next day the daughter of the family giggled in class and said, "Old Squirrel Eyes," a nickname that Owens admits "stuck far longer than I wanted it to" (200). He was a good sport and once he even let himself be led into a possum hunt, which was more like a wild goose chase.

The chapters on Pin Hook describe the activities of the school year in rich detail, particularly the all-important events: the Christmas program and the school play. In depicting community life, he includes an account of a "play-party." His first published work was a study of the play-party,[8] a southern social event now virtually extinct, though anyone familiar with *Oklahoma!* is likely to remember the play-party scene. Strict fundamentalists did not approve of dancing to music, but at the play-party the same dances were permitted as long as no fiddle, piano, or other instrument was used. Owens evokes the happy atmosphere of the play-party and quotes from the songs.

He had enormous trouble over questions of discipline, with the parents wanting corporal punishment and the teacher refusing to give it. His attitude was radically different from Gertrude Beasley's, but perhaps he had fewer frustrations to work out on his students. He was finally pressured into giving a "whipping" to two boys who were caught smoking at school. He could not bring himself to make them roll up their pants for a whipping on the legs, so he gave it to them on the hands. This turned out to be his doom: The community found "whupping on the hand" intolerable because it might cause permanent damage. So he wound up without a job and without a recommendation. He decided to hitch a ride to Dallas from Paris and rather symbolically was offered one by the George Graves family, who had left Pin Hook and moved to the "blackland." They succeeded; Owens apparently had failed. He declined the ride and took advantage of their destination to make a dejected pun: "They were only going to their farm at Glory, and for me that was off the main road" (258).

He would find his own forms of glory in time. Some of his later story is covered in *Tell Me a Story, Sing Me a Song. . .*[9] which he calls a third volume of autobiography. The first volume, he says, dealt with place (the farms of East Texas), the second, with time (his movement out into the world), the third, deals with people, through the songs he collected in his work as a folklorist. The book is only marginally autobiography: Like the second part of Lomax's *Adventures of a Ballad Hunter*, it is a series of short chapters about collecting songs and lacks the kind of plot which would give a coherent picture of his development. It quotes the songs liberally (including "I Ride an Old Paint"), a delightful feature. But it is arranged by ethnic category and the emphasis is on the people and not their historian.

The book does tell how he became a folklorist. In 1930 he was pursuing a degree at Southern Methodist University. His English professor was Henry Nash Smith, who was a year younger than Owens and already an academic success. Owens took Smith to a play-party in Forest Hill, near Pin Hook. The professor suggested that he should collect play-party materials, which led to his first book. Seven years later, while pursuing his Ph.D. at the University of Iowa, Edwin Piper, who had contributed materials to Carl Sandburg's *American Song Bag*, immediately took to Owens and encouraged him to record Texas folk songs to be housed at the university. Owens was able to write a dissertation on Texas folk songs, and Piper actually gave him seventy-five dollars (and this was during the Depression) of his own money to buy a Vibromaster Recording Machine, which made aluminum disks playable with a cactus needle, replacements for which are readily found by the roadside in much of Texas. The songs he collected were from every ethnic group, and he clearly learned to understand other races in ways far beyond Pin Hook's prejudices.

In 1941, he decided to pursue his collecting from the University of Texas, where he met the celebrated trio of Texans: Roy Bedichek, J. Frank Dobie, and Walter Prescott Webb. Dobie was responsible for his getting a job with the University of Texas as a folklorist. Many years later he would coauthor a book on the folklore of the Texas oil industry with Mody C. Boatright.[10] He met John A. Lomax at the University of Texas, but felt that Lomax was merely interested in getting hold of his materials, not in a genuine cooperative effort. Eventually Owens become a professor and dean of the summer school at Columbia University. He moved to upstate

New York, where he lived not too far from another Texas writer, William Humphrey, who grew up in Red River County, the county east of Lamar. They became great friends, and Owens's autobiographies were an influence on Humphrey's brilliant memoir, *Farther Off from Heaven.*

One postscript is worth making as an example of an interesting conjunction of people in the cultural history of Texas: In *Tell Me a Story, Sing Me a Song. . .* , Owens describes going with a young student, a poet, guitarist, and journalist, Américo Paredes, to collect songs across the river from Brownsville in Matamoros. They found an old singer in a cantina who would perform songs for a dime each and a beer. Owens could not bring recording equipment into Mexico, so he relied on Paredes to learn the songs. One of them was the "Corrido de Gregorio Cortez," a true story of a Mexican who shot a Texas sheriff in self-defense and had a standoff with the Texas Rangers. Paredes would base his celebrated book, *With His Pistol in His Hand*, on the story, and in doing so he illuminated Texas history from a Mexican point of view, in effect initiating the Chicano movement. Paredes's book, growing out of that moment in a cantina in Matamoros, had an enormous impact and helped prepare the way for other Chicano writers. The conjunction of a writer from the stubborn soil of Northeast Texas with one from the southernmost tip of the state was a fruitful one.

John Houghton Allen

7

AN ANGLO VAQUERO OF THE BRUSH COUNTRY: JOHN HOUGHTON ALLEN:

O land that lost your horseback men!
Remember you the riders, the long gone riders.
The gray dust riders in the far off music
Of the dreams of El Randado!

Tom Lea, *Randado*

John Houghton Allen produced one book, *Southwest,* a kind of elegy for his own *querencia* in the Brush Country, the Jesús María Ranch down in Jim Hogg County, one of the emptiest quarters of Texas. He commemorates a lost simplicity, writing the sort of idyll which his mentor J. Frank Dobie feared creating, an idyll of little villages and vaqueros who were honest and manly. And he rages against the changes in the region although most of them were introduced by gringos like himself.

Allen was born in Austin in 1909, the son of Wilber Price Allen, the Texas Midland Railroad executive and University of Texas regent who would take the lead in firing John A. Lomax and five others at the University of Texas. According to Dian Leatherberry Malouf's *Cattle Kings of Texas*, John's mother, Josephine Houghton, was given a ranch in South Texas by her father, John Henry Houghton, vice president of George Littlefield's American National Bank, who acquired 30,000 acres for a mere dollar an acre, the sort of bargain available to bankers.[1]

Immensely important for *Southwest* was the ranch adjacent to the Jesús María, the Randado, which was founded by Hipolito García in the 1830s and once had 100,000 acres. It got its name, according to Elmer J. Edwards in *The Handbook of Texas*, "from the highly ornate lassos, called *randas*, that were made on the ranch."[2] Catarino E. Garza, a Mexican dissident, camped near the ranch when he was preparing his invasion of Mexico in 1891, an unsuccessful attempt to overthrow the Porfirio Díaz regime. When Richard Harding Davis, the most eminent journalist of his time, came to the area to cover the Garza rebellion, he visited Randado and described it in his work of 1892, *The West from a Car-Window*: "It embraces eighty thousand acres, with twenty-five thousand head of cattle, and it has its store, its little mission, twenty or more adobe houses with thatched roofs, and its little graveyard"[3] He also noted the post office and "a school, where very pretty little Mexicans recited proudly in English words of four letters." Davis also described the Brush Country at length, calling it the "back yard of the universe," which sounds like a euphemism, and remarking that "it is a country where there are no roses, but everything that grows has a thorn."

J. Frank Dobie visited Randado in 1940 with his friend, Tom Lea, who wrote a poem, *Randado*,[4] published in a limited edition by Carl Hertzog in 1941. In *Tom Lea: An Oral History*, Lea observed that the locals pronounced the name "Randa'o" and that the ranch produced "a great strain of Spanish horses."[5] In *Randado*, Lea claims rather romantically that the ranch was founded by a man named Viscaya in the eighteenth century when the region was called the Wild Horse Prairie and that anyone wanting a horse would toss a silver coin onto an Indian blanket and then take the first mount cut out of the *caballada*. He says in his prefatory note to the poem, "Nothing now remains of El Randado but the crumbled hacienda, the watering tank and the name, slurred by all tongues of the *campo* to the musical name 'Ran-*dow*.'"

Clearly the Randado has an aura. It has been well covered in writing by Lea, Davis, and Allen. It also has a full chapter in Joe S. Graham's *El Rancho in South Texas*.[6] The ranch has declined from its great days, which leads Allen to some melancholy reflections in *Southwest*, where it appears as the San Juan, presided over by the gargantuan and mythical *patrón*, "Don Juan." Edwards dryly observes that "in 1968 Randado consisted of an estimated fifteen residents and the chapel, a cemetery, and a business. In 1983, the business, the chapel, and the cemetery remained." Naturally the almost deserted ranch is a subject of melancholy reflection for Allen, who begins his book by placing himself in a cantina near the ruins of the once-grand hacienda.

Allen's *Southwest* is a memoir of a person and a region, with interpolated tales, a little like a Brush Country *Decameron*. Allen the man is a mysterious figure, a wanderer, who appears in no reference works on writers, so it is worthwhile to fill in some of his story. Orlan Sawey's introduction to *Southwest*, the only substantial discussion of his work, mentions that he attended a half dozen universities as well as going to an art school in Paris around 1928.[7] In the issue of *Southwest Review* that printed Allen's story, "The Long

Ride,"[8] the editor's note quotes him as saying that he would be spending time in Denver "or Gulf Shores, Alabama. . . ." But the editor observed that when the magazine last heard from him, "he was in Tucson, where he had come from a stay in Nevada. Still, he tells us, he has his spiritual homes in Monterrey, San Francisco, and particularly New Orleans." And his permanent mailing address at the time was Gilchrist, Oregon. Restlessness was, in fact, one of his "metaphors of self," an interpretation of his own character.

The best source of information about him outside of his writings is his correspondence with Harold Bugbee from 1944-1963. Bugbee was the Texas artist who prepared the drawings for the privately printed *San Juan*. He was to have illustrated *Southwest* and prepared a number of plates before the publisher decided on Paul Laune, an inferior western artist who also illustrated Hardy Boys mysteries. Allen's forty letters survive in the Bugbee papers at the Panhandle-Plains Museum in Canyon, Texas. At one time Allen's many unpublished manuscripts (mostly of novels) were in Bugbee's collection at the museum, sent there by the wandering writer for safekeeping, but in a letter of June 6, 1960,[9] he told Bugbee to destroy most of them, though one, *Tales of Randado*, a sequel to *Southwest*, survives in a bound typescript. The letters confirm that he moved about restlessly, and they enforce his view of himself in *Southwest* as a man who drank heavily and had a difficult temperament. In one letter he apologized to Bugbee for a visit when he drank all of the host's whiskey and told him that as an artist he was myopic. In the same letter he admits that he has had "multiple vision" and may have hallucinated some of the events for which he was apologizing.[10] Allen told Bugbee that he came from three generations of Methodist preachers, and he seems to have thought that background was a good reason to drink.

He got in touch with Bugbee in 1944 because he liked the illustrations Bugbee prepared for J. Evetts Haley's *George Littlefield, Texan*, the 1943 biography of the famous rancher, banker, philanthropist, and member of the board of regents of the University of Texas. In his most revealing letter, on November 27, 1944, Allen told Bugbee with some embarrassment that he had to admit to being a Texan: His father and grandfather were in Haley's book. The account of Wilber Price Allen's handling of the Lomax case would have been painful to the son: No one wants to see a circumstantial account of his father's subservience to a corrupt politician like Governor James Ferguson. Even Littlefield, a supporter of Ferguson and a conservative, turned on the governor because his sense of fair play and his love for the university took precedence over political loyalty.

Allen rather strongly disliked his father. A curiosity of his book is that it deals with his childhood and youth with hardly a mention of his parents. The only family saga in the book is the thoroughly fictionalized story of "Great-Uncle Beverly," which is loosely based on the life of a distant relative, Sterling Price, a Confederate general. Price did not move to Mexico and die there, as in *Southwest*: His life is merely a starting point for a wild story about a branch of Allen's family supposedly extant in Mexico. Allen published an autobiographical essay in *Southwest Review* about his hatred of ROTC at Texas A&M, where he was a disgruntled student at fifteen.[11] In it he mentions that his father thought a military school would do him good, and he clearly disagreed. In "That Was Randado," an article written for *Holiday*, rancor against his father is intense: "Father was a little fat roly-poly man the Mexicans called *La Cucaracha*."[12] "Roly-poly" could be taken as affectionate, but the cockroach nickname is not. He says that his father had no understanding of the Mexican vaqueros who worked on the ranch and would force them to rise at four in the morning, when work was impossible. They would ride into the brush, then nap for a few hours, but the father, who thought that Mexicans had no sense of humor, never understood this tactic. The father knew only three words of Spanish, *Gracias a Dios*, and thought they meant "thank you and good-by," but the son observes, "It was never boring when my father was in the country." The father's way of being in the country was not on horseback. He would follow the vaqueros in a car (with the terrified chauffeur sitting in the passenger's seat), tearing up the brush. It is not surprising that Allen came to hate a certain kind of pushy gringo. Allen's sympathies were with the vaqueros, who became his models of masculinity. They were "grace spilled into action," he says in *Holiday*.

As an adult, Allen had to leave the Jesús María Ranch. It is clear from his letters to Harold Bugbee that he felt isolated in Jim Hogg County, as anyone who looks at a map of Texas might deduce. The area is remote and thinly populated, with only three small towns: Randado (population: fifteen), Hebronville (population: 4,465) and Guerra (population: seventy-five). Allen liked living in artists' colonies like Laguna, California, and Tubac, Arizona. Malouf tracked him down to his last place of residence, Tubac, Arizona, near the Mexican border, a town which is proud of being an artists' colony. He could barely talk, as he was still suffering from a fall from a polo pony many years before.[13] Any reader of *Southwest* or his brilliant pieces in *Holiday* about rodeos and polo[14] will not be surprised: He seems to have ridden hard. He was also, she reported to me in a telephone conversation, drinking heavily, which also would not surprise readers of *Southwest*. The need to cope with the disillusionment of a decaying Brush Country world by drink is a common subject in his book: "the best way to see the southwest is through the bottom of a glass. You can take it after a half a dozen beers" (13). He told her that he had left the ranch because he couldn't write there. But he seems to have been perpetually discontented. Numerous letters to Bugbee express a desire to find new places to live—even to leave the United States for Central or Latin America, but his wife did not want to emigrate.

In a telephone conversation with me, Malouf has expanded on her written account of visiting the ranch with Tom Murray Allen, John Houghton's half brother. John Houghton Allen had built himself a mansion on the Jesús María in a European chalet style with the sort of roof meant to stop the build-up of snow, a quixotic feature in South Texas. At some point in the late 1940s it had simply been left behind, falling into ruin. Her book has fine photographs of the area. She found family portraits and expensive furniture, paintings by Allen himself rolled up and lying on floors, and a library full of books. One cabinet contained the private and small-press printings of John's own works—and a nest of very large squirrels. Tom Allen invited her to take what she wanted, and she reached into the cabinet and retrieved a few copies of a very scarce work, *The Poetry of John Houghton Allen.*[15] Clearly, Allen had cut his ties to the world he loved. He gave several reasons in *Southwest*: It had been corrupted by the oil industry and the welfare system, and the gringos he despised had taken it over. There may have been some sour grapes in his dislike for oil riggers: In 1944 and 1945 he wrote several letters to Bugbee about his hopes of recovering his fortunes by an oil well being drilled on the ranch. However, the well finally turned out to be a dry hole. Another attempt at bringing in oil failed in 1947.

Allen first wrote about the region in three privately printed books, *Song to Randado*, *Four Tales* (1943), and (with Bugbee's drawings) *San Juan* (1945).[16] The nineteen poems in *Song to Randado* are mostly written in archaic diction with a few images (mostly of plants, like the huisache) from the Brush Country they celebrate. Jerald Underwood has written admiringly of the poems in a brief article, "The Vaquero in South Texas with an Interpretation by John Houghton Allen."[17] The first of the *Four Tales* was "San Juan," which became the privately printed 1945 book of the same name, with some poems added as choral interludes to the action. San Juan, of course, is a version of the Randado. Allen's narrator is Ernesto Acuña, a vaquero said to have worked on that ranch. The setting for the storytelling is Margarita's cantina, and the stories he tells are expanded in *Southwest.* Unfortunately, the interpolated poems in *San Juan* (which are the narrator's, not Ernesto's) are poor: They resemble the early works of Ezra Pound, poems which owed much both to Browning and the *fin de siècle*, a mixture of world weariness and loud gestures.

These exercises in poetic diction were fortunately dropped when *San Juan* was incorporated into *Southwest*. Allen imitated one of Pound's idols, François Villon, in another privately printed book, *The Minor Testament of John Houghton Allen*,[18] a dreadfully written defense of American isolationism dedicated to the best-known isolationist, Charles Lindbergh. Allen seems to have shared some of Pound's extreme political views and attitudes. The poem attacks the New Deal from what seems to be an anti-immigrant and racist point of view and suggests that Germany would be welcome to conquer Europe. With remarkably bad timing, it appeared shortly before Pearl Harbor. But like his other privately printed books, it had little circulation.

Allen's prose often has an ambiance suggesting Baudelaire and the Symbolists, especially the former. He was, after all, an art student in Paris, where, he told Bugbee, he spent all his money on one of the "gladest ladies" anyone would want to meet.[19] That ended his artistic career, but he said that he did not regret it. In *Southwest*, he treats Nuevo Laredo, where he liked to carouse with his lawyer friend, Hugo Corrales, as if it were a kind of Mexican Left Bank. He is as likely to use French phrases (*frisson*, for example) as Spanish ones. His favorite term to explain the emotional ambiance of South Texas is *coraje*, which he defines in *Southwest* as "blind hardheaded rage," which he suggests grows out of the "terrific ennui" of the area (30). It seems very close to Baudelaire's notion of "spleen" and the medieval notion of the choleric temperament dominated by yellow bile. In "The Low River," an essay published in 1963, Allen defines *coraje* as "the feeling of helpless rage, futility and ennui."[20] The abandoning of a mansion and a library containing his own works seems a gesture of spleen, something that Baudelaire would appreciate. In his letters to Bugbee, Allen frequently mentions his uncontrolled hypertension which seems to have been related to his emotions. He said to Bugbee that he would have liked to illustrate his own books but that ten minutes of that kind of work would make him ill from the stress. The term for spells of hypertension he used in several letters was "blow my top." In that same letter, he described himself as a dragon, which he said was hard work, and admitted to having a bit of a persecution complex.[21]

One aim of *Southwest* is to explore the sources of Allen's own *coraje*, his restlessness and discontent. Through the concept of *coraje* he is creating his own "metaphor of self." Malouf recounts one local story about Allen: He encountered two hunters from the county seat at Hebbronville and invited them to come to his mansion for dinner. He met them in full evening dress and served them drinks in the library. The dining room table was beautifully set, but each plate contained an open can of sardines.[22] The dinner was doubtless an expression of the *coraje* he suffered from. In the conclusion of *Southwest* he mentions his "Chateaubriand complex," alluding to the heroes of François René de Chateaubriand's Atala and René, with their introspective, melancholy, and restless world-roaming ways. The Chateaubriand complex complements *coraje* in his self-creation. A constant theme of his correspondence with Bugbee is his compulsive wandering, never finding a "comfortable place," to anticipate Gloria López-Stafford's term for her own unease.

The mood of *coraje* dominates the opening chapter of *Southwest*, which, like the one which follows, is set in the cantina just outside the remains of San Juan. The narrator is hopelessly ambivalent: The landscape of the Brush Country is presented as fearful, desolate, and monotonous. He has affection, deep affection, for the Mexicans of South Texas, but the area has been taken over by gringos that he despises—oil riggers and men with fancy boots who drive Fords and believe that they have a White Man's Burden to carry. "They are usually gross Falstaffian fellows, but without humor, about their melting faces a petulant and perennial cast of grievance. They have black hairy noses sticking out of their pumpkin faces like the beaks of manta-rays" (16). He particularly hates their loudness. In his rage and disgust he contradicts himself freely. The land was once "a fine place to live," before the decay of the society. But he also talks of the "damned brush, the dry jungle creeping, heart-rotten, that gets you down" (15). He ends his first chapter by describing a village that he loved: "there was never anything so beautiful as this village in a barren land. . . ." It was razed for caliche to build the county roads. The most beautiful sights in the monotonous Brush Country were the Mexican villages, especially at dusk. The chapter is dominated by bile (his term) and the melancholy brought on by drinking beer as an anodyne in a world where he says, "the Mexicans today are no better than the gringos—both races make you want to go out and eat grass" (17).

Sitting in the cantina, he presents us with a return of the native, "but all the nostalgia I feel is for the land I knew as a boy. Before the land had spoiled the people, and the people had spoiled the land" (19). That unspoiled land and people constitute the lost land of his idyll, a landscape where traditional activities are carried on by pastoral people, the Mexicans who worked the ranch.

He describes an old man in the cantina, the keeper of the local store, who shares his memories of the past. The man, a family friend, is said to be "very gracious and dignified, one of the Old Men, a type of Mexican that existed before the wrong kind of gringo came to this land" (18). The man is more a symbol than a person. Significantly, Allen was never able to define what was special about the Mexicans of his childhood, except for a dignity found in illiterate people (110). He likes to say that they were "more human" than other people, but that begs the question of what constitutes the human norm. In the fiction of Rolando Hinojosa which began appearing in Spanish and English during the 1970s, the voices of the people of the southern Rio Grande Valley would find a spokesman of their own, an unsentimental spokesman who understands the lives of the border *Tejanos* from within. The postcolonial question, "Can the Subaltern Speak?" asked by theorists like G. C. Spivak,[23] would be answered efficiently by a number of Chicano writers in Spanish and English. Allen's work would yield some interesting insights to postcolonial theory, as his *patria*, as he likes to call it, has been a colony through most of its history, first of Spain, then of Mexico, then of Anglo Texas.

The second chapter, nominally set in the same cantina as the first, is made up of memories of his arrival at the ranch from Laredo, where the Texas & Mexico railroad line came down from central Texas. The region was known on the old maps as Wild Horse Country, he says, and though the horses on the ranches were technically not wild, the boy was plunged into a daily life of dangerous rides which might end in death, as in the story of Felipe in the third chapter. The area was "splendid and mad," a phrase he uses like a choral line in the early parts of his book. The boy heard lurid stories about people like Don Sebastián, who went beyond

Othello by killing his innocent wife because someone had defiled her by looking at her. Later he would castrate his own son. And yet Gutierrez, one of the vaqueros, suggested to young Allen that Don Sebastián was still admirable because "somehow you couldn't get away from the fact that he was a man" (29). Allen attributes his own tendencies toward instability, intemperance, and ennui (*coraje*, in short) to immersion in the raw and extremist world of the Randado region.

In Dobie's *Tongues of the Monte*, Don Federico and his faithful *mozo* ("boy"), Inocencio, hear many stories, some realistic, some supernatural. Allen's interlocutors are Javier Chávez, his mentor on the Jesús María, Guiterrez, who has tales of Maximilian's Mexico, and the old vaquero, Ernesto Acuña, the last living cowboy from Don Juan's days at the San Juan. The stories vary from range realism to overcharged romantic tales with rather stereotyped señoritas involved in melodramatic plots. His third chapter begins the telling of such tales, one of the ways that a man who has a "head like a gringo and the heart of a Mexican" (30) can try to bridge the gap between himself and the vaqueros. There are two stories in a row by the old vaquero, Ernesto Acuña, anecdotes first published in *Four Tales* and republished in *San Juan*. These are among the best, lacking the melodrama of some of the later tales. Ernesto describes the death of Felipe, a cowboy who was strangled by his own rope in a freak accident while pursuing a *ladino*, a stray, in the brush. The work of cowboys in the area differs from ranching in the open grasslands. It is exceedingly dangerous, and the cowboys were referred to as "brush poppers," according to J. Frank Dobie in *A Vaquero of the Brush Country*. The narrative of Felipe's death is dramatic but not overstated. It is followed by Ernesto's account of the way the vaqueros of the San Juan, overcome by grief, went on a spree in the nearby town and tore a cantina up after they were ordered to leave by an insolent deputy. A few chapters later he tells the story of his old boss, Don Juan (the remaining story from *San Juan*), and the style is racheted up in celebration the *patrón's* wealth and the splendor of his wedding to a spirited woman he found in a cantina in Monterrey during a brawl.

Allen's problem is that he is an outsider in the Mexican world, hankering for communion with the Other, as we say these days. He considers the Mexicans of his youth to be the most honest and admirable people he has ever met, and, of course, he could never be one of them: He is always the *patrón,* forced into a relation of master and servant, perhaps, like the headmaster of a boys' school. Condescension is inevitable, in spite of his admiration for what he considers the superior humanity of the Mexicans. In the fifth chapter of his book, he explains that he would be a Mexican if he could, because "all of them, good and bad," were "human to a vivid degree" (55). He begins the chapter by confessing "there might be something wrong with me, but I couldn't help loving Mexicans." For a man who was born in 1909 and grew up in a world where Anglos called Mexicans "greasers" or "Mesikans," the statement must have seemed radical. It is repeated in one of his late essays, "Always a Brave River," published in *Southwest Review*: "Maybe I'm contrary, but I always liked Mexicans." He goes on to say that they may be the only people in Texas who have character.[24] But when he describes Mexicans in chapters five and six of his book, he sees them in stereotyped terms: The Mexican is a Puck figure, Mexican women like for their men to be triflers. His case studies are José, who has a contrary temperament (he has the *pendejo* in him, an untranslatable term literally meaning "pubic hair"), and two men that he particularly likes, Chávez and Luro. He describes them as clowns (his own term), and tells a rather demeaning story about the death of Luro's wife from overeating. Chávez and Luro left the ranch and became successful in Zapata, but he undercuts their achievements by speaking of them as "cattle buyers and horse dealers *san peur et sans reproche*," applying the epithet of the Chevalier Bayard in the *Chanson de Roland* to them in what can only be seen as ridicule (63). Clearly they would have to remain simple vaqueros to retain his admiration: Change spoils them; they cease to be quaint and charming. He admires the Mexicans of his youth for their childlike qualities and their trust, the usual view of those who patronize a whole group from outside. He never really escapes from being the *patrón* in *Southwest*.

Beside Ernesto Acuña, he has another storyteller, Javier Chávez, the foreman of the Jésus María. During the revolution, Javier had ridden with Rodolfo Fierro, whom Friedrich Katz, Pancho Villa's biographer, refers to as an executioner.[25] Javier was often called "The Butcher" or "Little Blood." Javier rode with Villa's elite troops, the "Dorados," or "golden ones," so called from their glittering ornaments. Allen recalls seeing a group of them on a raid in his area when he was nine, c. 1917. They rode by without attacking the ranch, close enough for him to see their shining rosettes.

A story told to the narrator by Javier describes the capture of Chihuahua City by Fierro. The head of the local council, Santos, was forced to surrender the city. He signed the document with the added proviso that he signed for three reasons, "from fear, for fear, and of fear" (116). Later he was forced to agree to let his amorous daughter marry Fierro's gringo aide, Reilly, and he signed the marriage document with the same avowal. This tale is not a vaquero narrative in its origins: Allen is borrowing it from a Peruvian tale collected by Ricardo Palma and translated in Allen's own limited press book, *A Latin American Miscellany*.[26] Another tale of Javier's is the story of one of Fierro's raids, this one on the hacienda of Don Santiago in Hidalgo. The purpose was revenge for a slight on Javier himself. In the story, the wife of Don Santiago's son tried to save her husband's life by offering her body to Fiero. The husband is outraged and denounced her as he was about to be executed: "you slut . . . you dirty slut!" (128).

The limitation of most of the vaquero stories in *Southwest* is their lurid romanticism, their world of elemental passions, proud men and dangerous women. Although Allen spoke of his art to Bugbee as similar to the watercolorist rather than the oil painter,[27] these tales of lust and violence are presented in the stark colors of a bullfight poster. One of the most extreme is the tale of Isabel, who lived in a high tower on the San Juan. She and her brother had escaped from the massacre of her family by the Kiowas, protected by a great grey wolf. One night her brother and her lover fought over her honor on the balcony, and the brother fell from the tower and died. She, of course, went mad and never responded to the gifts that her lover constantly sent her. Another story told in his own voice is as extreme as any of the vaquero stories. The beautiful *femme fatale*, Barbara, a half-Dutch half-Peruvian heiress from Surinam, lives a lonely life in Monterrey because of an indiscretion. At seventeen, she had an affair with an escaped prisoner from Devil's Island, an artist from Fontainebleau who repaid her love by creating and selling nude images of her.

One of his own narratives is a tale supposedly told to him in Nuevo Laredo by a half-mad journalist named Mike Judy, who claimed to have trekked through the jungles of Honduras to find the camp of the deposed president, Gómez. The tale was as good as Conrad, Allen says, and after pages of vivid narrative he finally realizes that the man is a liar. The story has been lifted from one of Allen's early works, "Extravagance," which was published in *Four Tales*. The original version was set in New Orleans. Allen was given to recycling.

Horse cavalry were stationed in the border area during Allen's youth. They came to a post which he declines to name and stayed until 1930 in what he likes to call "the lost world." As A. C. Greene has discussed in an article, "Polo Fever, 1904," from his *Five States of Texas*,[28] Texans took up polo enthusiastically in the early twentieth century. The cavalry were naturally avid players, and in their matches with Allen and the Jesús María vaqueros, the game took on a Brush Country style, with nothing aristocratic about it: He speaks of it as "like a damned rodeo or hockey on horseback" (75). He wrote a vivid account of polo, "The Gentleman's Game," for *Holiday*, and one of the best essays of his later years, "Little Pinto,"[29] is an elaborate life story of a polo horse from the Jesús María, a horse he discusses often in his letters to Bugbee, whom he engaged to paint it. The soldiers tended toward melancholy and alcoholism, confirming his theory that gringos on the border go bad. They were a lost regiment, neglected by Washington, a hopeless anachronism. He ends his chapter on them with another of his romantic tales, this time about Jerry Calahan and Pete McBride, two young officers who fell in love with a cantina dancer named

Conchita and fought a duel (the first in the army since the Civil War, Allen says) over her, which left both of them dead. Their story helps to advance Allen's view that gringos go wrong on the border. The view of Conchita provides a completely stereotyped image of the *femme fatale*. More interesting than the story of this triangle is the interpolated narrative of a broken carousel in the little town where the officers met Conchita. One day a drunken vaquero rode the blue carousel horse and, after getting off, took a few steps in the square and vanished.

This bit of magic realism anticipates the two chapters about the dope addict who comes into camp at Aqua Dulce in a "futurist landscape" and tells a long and fantastic story. The description of the man as a "marijuana addict" now seems quaint. The story is something out of Rider Haggard crossed with Sleeping Beauty, a tale of an enchanted city in the Sierra Madre filled with people in suspended animation. The man had supposedly been educated at the University of Salamanca, which might account for his description of the city as "cubistic." The *marijuanero* leaves the city and can never find it again: An influence here may be J. Frank Dobie's tales of lost mines.

The most revealing cluster of chapters is set across the border in Nuevo Laredo. The first two are a kind of elegy for lost youth and describe his wild binges with his friend, Hugo Corrales, a remittance man in exile from Mexico City. The two found the company of whores and cutthroats honorable: "They were just like everybody else, only a little more human" (155). He becomes Hemingwayesque in remembering the wild times: "And the women we laid, fine brutal women, the love we demanded arrogantly in those days, the Youth breaking out all over us—even the books I put by to write another day, because in Mexico it was the living that counted and not the books, and who wanted to write books when he could live?"(155). He has an amusing account of being taken to a whorehouse by a friendly prostitute after he was rolled and left in the gutter. He learned after a period of pleasure in the woman's company that he was being held for ransom by her and the one-eyed madam and the pimps in the kitchen. He was rescued finally by his friend Hugo, who gave the culprits a tongue-lashing, which they listened to more out of respect than fear.

The third chapter in his portrait of Nuevo Laredo gives a fine story of a bullfight which paired two great matadors, Silvano and Gallo. The spirit of Hemingway presides over the prose, but the writing is dramatic and thoroughly visualized. It presents the psychology of the crowd astutely and has an unexpected twist: The spectators treated Silvano scornfully, and in retaliation his good friend Gallo showed deep contempt for them by refusing to kill the bull after a brilliant series of passes with it. He simply walked out, leaving the crowd hushed and ashamed.

In the final chapter of his book, Allen writes an elegy for the Jesús María, seeing it as "an idyll, a colonial dream violent and colorful, with bitter things to love" (211). Dobie's temptation to write his childhood idyll comes to mind. Allen is concerned for the truth of his impressions rather than for the truth of fact: The realism of Dobie's sketches of ranch life and the neighbors is not his concern. Allen's memories of the old days among the vaqueros serve as a contrast with what he sees as the corruption of the area by oil money and the spreading Americanization of the Southwest:

> I don't know what happened to the Jesús María, to the Hispanic southwest. It was absorbed, it disappeared, or it turned sour. For a hundred years the vaqueros had resisted what they considered with rude insularity the sad decay of Americanization, but installment buying and gadgets and the cinema got them finally, and in this connection got is a good word—and they were to clutter the highways with second-hand Fords like white trash, these splendid hoary-handed horsemen. They listened to the radio wide-open, their sons learned English and pomaded their hair and they could not throw a mangana, skidding through the dust as the thousand pounds of horse hit the end of the lariat. (214)

His nostalgia includes his own youth, when he could go on vaquero sprees "where we drank prodigiously and fought over gringa whores, and as the young padrone I had my choice." But he admits that "I, exquisite young man, I had found it for the most part, tedious" (213). At the end of such sprees he would return to the Jesús María, "the ever lovely and crumbling Jesús María on the great *laguna* where the huisache spread its green and yellow scattered lace. . . . (213).

And so he turns from the gringos of the present—whom he abuses as "choleric, loud, cowardly, pathologically garrulous tenantry civilized by Sears Roebuck" (218) and ends his book with memories "of the Old Time, to remember the rich raw words of another world" (218). The last pages of his book are given to recollections of campfires where the vaquero Gutierrez would talk of the days of Maximilian. Gutierrez too remembers a lost world, and the book ends with a coyote howling: "That was all, but it was enough to remember—Oh the raw rich words, the rich lost words" (220).

J. Frank Dobie described the book in his *Guide to Life and Literature of the Southwest* as "a chemical compound of highly impressionistic autobiographic nonfiction and highly romantic fiction and folk tales," and he noted the author's "passion for superlatives."[30] The parts do not fuse perfectly, and after almost fifty years the romantic view of the vaqueros and señoritas seems quaint. But the atmosphere of the lower Brush Country, one of the most isolated and distinctive areas in the continental United States, is powerfully evoked. Dobie's comment that "that author has a passion for superlatives" is correct: The country is mad and splendid, the people are sour, the horses are grand. These terms and others are ridden hard. There is no striving for objectivity, as we sense in Greene and Dobie. We witness a man trying to explain his restless and extreme temperament through the country where he grew up. While the book has its flaws, it does present an unforgettable portrait of his lost world.

Allen continued to write, always drawing on the emotional capital of his home country. He tried to write novels in the 1940s at the insistence of sympathetic publishers, but as he told Bugbee metaphorically, he was a watercolorist with a talent for impressionistic stories, not an oil painter who could create big canvases. He worked on a sequel to *Southwest* in the 1950s, a book to be called *Tales of Randado*. Two of the stories, "Horse Cavalry"[31] and "Little Pinto," were published in *Southwest Review*, and the entire manuscript survives in the Panhandle-Plains Museum in a bound typescript with the title stamped in gold on the spine.

But the most interesting works of his late career are the two passionate essays in *Southwest Review*, "The Low River" (1963), and "Always a Brave River" (1965). They are a continuation and development of his feelings about the land and people of *Southwest*. The first essay defines the Brush Country landscape once again—huisache and mesquite, arid soil, and blue northers, and says, "My roots are here, and a man never gets away from his *pátria*, really."[32] The *patria*—which he calls a lost land, as in *Southwest*—and its people are evoked in a series of brief impressions. He still has traces of condescension in his views, saying that the Mexicans of his youth appreciated the *patrón* for saving them from the *rinches* (Texas Rangers) and usury. He turns elegiac in a passage which social change has made ironic: "The rust of the moon has eaten the implements of the village, nor do I know why, except for love, I am the late laureate of these lost Israelites, and I am not even Mexican"[33] The Mexicans would find their own laureates, but the intention is honorable.

In "Always a Brave River" Allen writes a powerful indictment of American policy toward Mexico and the Mexicans of Texas. This piece does not seem dated: It is almost a Chicano manifesto, from a surprising source, an Anglo rancher. He details the outrages of the Texas Revolution and the Mexican War, the killings by "anointed Texas Rangers" and the land grabs—what he calls sixty years of genocide. He celebrates the men who resisted, in this "*otro Mejico*" between the Nueces and Rio Grande, like Abrám de la Garza and Juan Nepomuceno Cortina. Much of the essay is a celebration of Cortina (1824-1894), who grew up in the Rio Grande region in South Texas and took on the Texas Rangers, a man who was denounced as an "archfiend, horsethief, cattlerustler, renegade, ravisher, assassin and *peon*."[34] Cortina received considerable space in Dobie's *A Vaquero of the Brush Country*. The Rangers pursued him after he shot a marshal and attacked Brownsville to defend the rights of Texas Mexicans. Not even the famous ranger, "Rip" Ford, could capture him. In this essay, Allen finally achieves a true kinship with the Mexicans of South Texas, as a critic of their oppressors, as a chronicler of their heroes. His attitude is more satisfying than Dobie's sentimental melodrama in *Tongues of the Monte*, with an ex-Dorado stabbed and a blood brother ceremony performed with the same knife. Allen no longer speaks as a *patrón*. His anger on behalf of the Mexican people of the Trans-Nueces region has more weight than his sentimental view of them as childlike and loyal. His imagination has gone some way to bridge the gap between Anglo rancher and vaquero.

A. C. Greene

8

THE JOURNEYS OF A. C. GREENE

If Gertrude Beasley's autobiography is a horror movie set in West Texas, A. C. Greene's book is a documentary about the same region prepared with a care for the facts and a generally warm tone, especially when he writes about their common town, Abilene. He has no scores to settle. Greene (1923-2002) describes unhappiness in his family but no scandals or child abuse: nothing more than the incompatibility of his parents. In a letter about Beasley's *My First Thirty Years*, he remarked that "there are local incidents in the book that aren't factual" (February 27, 2001). Greene's respect for fact is one of his strengths—he likes to explore places and find artifacts that record the past—but he does more than accumulate details in *A Personal Country*. Greene's valuable interview by Patrick Bennett in *Talking with Texas Writers* is appropriately called "Molding the Past into Art."[1] Greene does not merely compile; he shapes.

Chris Ohan has called Greene the Dean of Texas Letters on the website for the A. C. Greene Papers at the University of Texas at Arlington. Ohan lists the activities that justify the title: the books, his work on the *Abilene Reporter-News*, his direction of the editorial page of the *Dallas Times Herald*, his column of "Texas Sketches" in the *Dallas Morning News*, his activities in the Texas Institute of Letters and the Texas Historical Society, his radio programs, and his appearances as a book reviewer on the PBS news program, "The MacNeil/Lehrer Report." Greene was also codirector of the Center for Texas Studies at the University of North Texas for some years.[2] No one since J. Frank Dobie has been such a spokesman for Texas, and the title of Dean of Texas Letters has been widely accepted.

As he explains in his afterword to the 1998 edition, *A Personal Country* came about by chance, with a meeting between Greene and Angus Cameron, J. Frank Dobie's former editor at Little, Brown and Company (330). Cameron asked Greene, one of the most experienced newspapermen in Texas, if he had a book. The newspaperman of the stereotype has a smudged manuscript in his desk drawer, but Greene did not. But, in 1968, with the aid of a Dobie Paisano Fellowship from the University of Texas, he stayed at the former Dobie ranch near Austin and wrote *A Personal Country*, the first of his twenty-seven books on Texas.

Greene's newspaper background serves him very well in his memoir. He has a tremendous appetite for facts. He prepared for the book in 1967 by traveling over his native country in a Volkswagen van. The second part of his book can serve as a supplement to *Interwoven*: He explores the history and archaeological remains in West Texas, including important ones in Shackelford and Throckmorton counties. He brings together historical and geographical fact with the facts of his own family saga and his own life to establish (within the horizon of his own understanding) the characteristics of modern West Texas, with due regard for the role of the past in shaping it. For Sallie Reynolds Matthews, the region was primarily ranching country, though she and her family did eventually move to the small town of Albany. Greene grew up in a small city, Abilene, and he can take for granted the Machine Age she praised in her preface: Indeed, he knows that the automobile on the paved highway, not the horse on the open range, is the new epitome of West Texas. In effect, he is defining a major region of Texas, and the specifications include aspects of geography (particularly rainfall), economics, and cultural traditions which grow out of the past and involve folklore as well as verifiable events. His West Texas is marked by a frontier history which left an inheritance of values, including a paradoxical individualism and willingness to help neighbors and strangers. It is not the savage world of Gertrude Beasley, in which incest and abortion are widespread and respectable people are hypocrites.

The first half of *A Personal Country* explores the austere landscape and the equally austere character of the people, beginning with three chapters on place. At the end of the first chapter he suggests that the book will be a journey. The mode in chapters four through eleven is a journey in space, sometimes a literal one along Highway 80 (now coextensive with Interstate 20). But there are also remembered journeys along that route as well as some imagined detours to describe places not along the axis of the highway. In the second half of the book, after he has considered the approximate terminus of West Texas at Midland, he ranges freely through the history of the region. Near the end he finally describes his own family in detail, telling us about the pioneers in his past and his own family's history in Abilene. When I wrote to Greene suggesting that I would use his journeys as an approach to his book, he endorsed the idea in a letter (October 21, 2000):

> I think your idea of "journeys" is excellent. When I taught S'west writing at UNT [The University of North Texas] I chose about six books tied to the cattle trails north and posited the underlying theme as seeking, moving forward, changing your life, because at the end of each trail book things have changed, even with the reader, and no one can be the same at the end of the journey. My students loved the idea. I also suggested that John Graves's *Goodbye to a River* was not really about a man taking a river voyage—it's about how the journey of life changes the man and the reader, how the river changed every mile, never being the same river and John (or the narrator) never being the same. I believe this is one of the purposes of literature: changing the reader. I hope APC can fit that journey theme. Thanks for finding it.

His preface, called with deliberate modesty "Some Words," defines the purpose of the book: "I have not set out to write a history of West Texas, neither have I tried to do a guidebook. If this is a history, it is an emotional history of a boy and a man in a place, and part of that place in them" (xv). He says that the book is often autobiographical, but not because he sees himself as important. Rather, he is an example:

> No, the purpose of this book (and discussing purpose is a deadly pursuit for an author) is simply to find out, from one life in one region, if all of us are not gifted from the soil whence we sprang, seeded by the people, and watered by the times. And if I seem to spend too much time searching my own recollection, it is only to help the reader find the same identity. (xvi)

His introductory chapter, "A Place Called West Texas," emphasizes that he has moved away from the region with its "barren grandeur" (3). He realizes that the place is part of his consciousness, that even his voice, a nasal drawl, and his pronunciations ("git" for "get") identify him as a product of this world. In a time when sectionalism has faded and economic necessity requires mobility, he has removed himself from his region, and yet has the perspective to understand his inheritance, which includes ethical notions and a certain rigidity of character: "West Texas was, and is, as demanding a social environment as its natural elements are demanding" (7). Greene is probably influenced by the celebrated Texas historian, Walter Prescott Webb, who asserted in *The Great Plains*[3] that society and technology in western America were shaped by the geographical setting.

His second chapter, "The Boundaries of Its Life," indicates the approximate territorial boundaries of that setting: east and west, the borders are the Brazos and Pecos rivers; to the north, the Cap Rock area is a reasonable demarcation. The southern boundary is harder to fix. He suggests that San Saba (where his Poe ancestors lived) and Brady mark the approximate limit of early settlement. An all-important measure of West Texas is climatic: It can be defined as the area of rainfall from twelve to thirty inches annually, which determines the possibilities of land use. And there is a psychological boundary with the Brazos River, west of which was traditionally the Texas frontier, where the Comanches made life difficult in the early settlements. The frontier, Greene observes, was an area where people felt tested. He recalls the contempt the old timers of his childhood had for people who "went back" because they could not endure the difficult life. One of his great-grandfathers, he says, was among them, the schoolteacher and poet he discusses in "So All the Generations," his family saga chapter. This great-grandfather, Lytle Craighead, was beaten by the drought of 1884 and retreated to a store in rainy East Texas, where Greene suggests the sound of the rain may have killed him by reminding him of his failure. We can see the macho culture of West Texas in such attitudes.

The succeeding chapter, "Some Arteries of Time," is masterly in exposition and leads quite naturally into his journeys through the region. The arteries are highways: "In West Texas 'where you are' starts with a highway," (120) one which the West Texan is likely to drive at high speed. The fences, which were introduced to the area by Joseph Beck Matthews made the modern ranching industry possible. Through the fences, beyond a border of domestic grasses sown by the highway department, the native brown grasses (which fatten cattle so well) can be seen. And sometimes there are oil fields.

Mesquite trees are also visible through the barbed-wire fences, and Greene provides a brief essay on this unwanted fixture of the landscape. He calls the mesquite the national flower of West Texas and says that its tenacity, rough bark, and thorny branches make it a symbol of West Texas. He also talks about cedar trees, which are not as common as the mesquite. They once provided a livelihood for fence-post cutters and charcoal burners, people whose wandering way of life reflected the independent outlook of West Texans. Cedar, in fact, is an interesting minor theme in Texas writing: In his book on central Texas, *Hard Scrabble,* John Graves has some interesting pages on "cedar people," individuals who still make a living by cutting trees for fence posts,[4] and John Phillip Santos has a brilliant depiction of making charcoal from cedar. The chapter finishes with a description of the methods for passing through a barbed-wire fence, as Gertrude Beasley described less systematically some forty-six years before. He suggests something of the traditionalist attitudes of West Texans by mentioning that a woman in a skirt is likely to present an interesting view to an accompanying male and then dryly observing that "West Texas ranch women were among the last in the country to take up the wearing of pants" (37). Women in Hallie Stillwell's Big Bend were not so tardy.

Chapters four to eleven take a kind of composite car journey from the east, from Weatherford just beyond the Brazos, to Midland and Odessa in the far west, with two chapters devoted to his hometown of Abilene and a third digressing to talk about religion in West Texas before he wraps up the journey in a chapter on far West Texas, "Beyond the Old One-Hundredth." The journey is a composite because not all of it took place in 1967, when he rented that Volkswagen van: Some of it involves memories of travel in his childhood. The starting point of Weatherford, just outside the boundaries of the region, is the town where the Reynolds family moved in 1869 to seek better schools for their children. It is also the place where John A. Lomax taught college for six years. And northwest of Weatherford, John Graves began the canoe trip along the Brazos which was commemorated in his 1959 classic, *Goodbye to a River.*[5] In his interview with Patrick Bennett, Greene described Graves as "far and away his favorite" living Texas writer (Bennett 39). Graves's journey and Greene's both interweave stories about the past with the personal narrative. But Graves is not striving to characterize a region in a systematic way or to explore its history in depth. He is an elegiac narrator contemplating a river threatened by dam building, and his tour moves steadily east, away from the edges of West Texas toward Somervell County.

Greene begins with Weatherford for personal reasons. He got married there after virtually kidnapping Betty, who became his first wife, in Dallas and returning to Abilene with her. The incident is told with humor and some retrospective desperation. Highway 80 (now Interstate 20), the route from Weatherford to Abilene, goes through the heart of West Texas. All of the important towns, with the exception of San Angelo (and Albany, in its miniscule greatness), lie along a line defined by the Texas & Pacific Railway. The towns which did not have the railway declined or died. Two of them were actually shifted to the railroad area: Red Gap, which became Cisco, and Ranger Gap, which became just plain Ranger. Gertrude Beasley's mother inherited her potential oil land near Ranger. The railroad laid out towns every twenty miles or so, and one of them was Abilene, named for Abilene, Kansas. Greene has pointed out that the name means "grassy plain," which is appropriate for West Texas.

Much has been written about journeys in prairie schooners: Greene has vivid memories of early automobile travel. The most amusing memories come in the long seventh chapter, "The Ominous Journey." By that chapter his imaginary journey westward has gotten to Cisco, forty-five miles from Abilene, and he recalls that all family journeys began by covering that ground. He builds the chapter around some of those trips, without worrying that most of the scenes described came from trips eastward. The journeys were ominous because his mother, grandmother, and great-grandmother were all prophets of disaster, sure that the house would burn down in their absence, that bridges would collapse, that one of the notorious tornadoes which often hit the little town of Clyde would strike. Greene attributes this pessimism to their fundamentalist religion, which assumed that anyone whose guard went down might be subject to mischief by the Devil.

On one journey, the family members were his parents, his Uncle Grady, and Aunt Pat. The story takes place on a rainy night in Cisco. A bent oil plug created the emergency, and the only way to obtain a replacement was to awaken the blacksmith. The description of the night is vividly atmospheric, especially when the blacksmith crawled under the car (the jack used was a curb) with lantern:

> I see in my mind the chiaroscuro surrounding the car, him partially under it, the lantern protected so the hot glass wouldn't break in the rain, the other men peering down under the car, only their faces visible in the yellow lantern light, my uncle holding the lantern, turning it one way or another as the blacksmith directed. (89)

As he points out, this was long ago, the relatives have died, the shop has gone, and "the night around the lantern, in the rain, the waiting, is all mine now."

The chapter ends with the prospect of Abilene, his hometown, and he makes a stop there for chapters eight and nine, dealing with the city in his childhood, and before resuming his journey writes another chapter on the fundamentalist religions so influential for him and West Texans in general. At his birth in 1923 (to Alvin Carl Greene and Johnnie Marie Cole) he was thought to be stillborn, and in the rush to save his mother's life, a nurse discarded his body in a corner of the delivery room. The family tradition held that he was placed on a pile of newspapers, which certainly would have been prophetic, but he doubts (a typical doubt) that a delivery room would have old newspapers in its corners. The hospital where he was born was a temporary one set up in a former boardinghouse, which Greene believes just might have been one of the boardinghouses operated by Lucy Jane Beasley (Letter to author, February 27, 2001).

He devotes two chapters to the town of Abilene, "The Source and Since" and "Village of My Heart." Although the city began as a railroad town in 1881, it was long haunted by the spirit of the frontier, as was West Texas in general. He is proud of its progressive ways, citing the early installation of water and telephone systems and electric lights. His sketch of Abilene in an anthology called *Growing Up in Texas* [6] stresses the urban nature of the town and describes its manufacturing and processing plants. It had an important role as a transportation center. There were three railroads and American Airlines had Abilene on its transcontinental route. Yet it was not that far from the values of the early days: "But it remained a frontier town because its gods were frontiersmen" (109). The frontier mentality valued strength, and modern West Texas still does.

In "Village of My Heart," his chapter on the values of Abilenians and West Texas in general, he suggests the moderating influence of Christianity inculcated values of friendliness and willingness to help one's neighbors. Yet at the same time, he suggests "religion is the least tolerant area of West Texas life." God is too important to be left to whimsical personal concept. There is a way, each denomination believes, and you either seek it or are forced to acknowledge its existence" (124-25). The reflections on God and values in "Village of My Heart" lead into the succeeding chapter, "God in West Texas," one of Greene's best. It was this essay, published in *Arlington Quarterly*, which persuaded Angus Cameron at Knopf that Greene could write a book. Greene thinks that the dry, harsh setting of West Texas, with its similarity to the biblical lands, encourages a fundamentalist attitude, one of severity toward sects other than one's own and a suspicion of Catholics. In a series of paragraphs which are very close to poetry in imagery and rhythm, he makes an imaginative if not factual case for the environmental influence. "The loneliness of the high sky makes men see God. But he is seen in the fiery sunlight and not the cool moonlight which bathes the countryside in a supernatural coating so wonderful and confusing that men draw indoors to avoid it," suspecting a "pagan infection" could overtake them from being under it (128). Larry McMurtry has similar reflections on the West Texas sky in *Walter Benjamin at the Dairy Queen*.

Greene provides a taxonomy of the leading Protestant denominations in West Texas: the Baptists, the Methodists, and the Church of Christ. These groups are the great defenders of the odd dry laws in Texas, the laws giving communities the right by referendum to prohibit the sale of liquor in their boundaries. The Presbyterians are the arbitrators, Green claims, a small group with more moderate views and membership drawn largely from the professional classes. The "iron cradle of Presbyterianism," to use the phrase from Sallie Reynolds Matthews's mother, did not nurture teetotalers.

Greene looks most intently at his family's own group, the Church of Christ, the rural and conservative wing of the Restoration movement of Alexander Campbell. The Church of Christ split from the more liberal Disciples of Christ and Christian Churches on the issue of instrumental music, which the conservatives believed was an unscriptural addition to worship. The Church of Christ appealed to Gertrude Beasley because it lacked the emotionalism she saw in the Baptists, although she did not like the a capella singing. Like Gertrude Beasley (and John Graves), Greene calls the Church of Christ "Campbellites." Greene's own mother split from her church after she was criticized by a well-to-do woman at a prayer meeting. Her offense was petitioning the deity for a refrigerator. It was condescendingly explained that God could not be approached in such personal matters. The mother decided that such a distant God was not for her and found another church. Even the eventual acquisition of a Frigidaire "with a motor on top" did not change her mind. The departure from the church occurred when Greene was twelve, so he never became a member, not having reached the "age of accountability" in a church which deplored infant baptism.

Greene received his education at Abilene Christian College

(now University) where, he told me in a letter, his original article on "God in West Texas" got a mixed reception (October 22, 1981), though any animosity seems to have died down. His essay has the advantage of being written by a former insider. What he sees as the rigidity of fundamentalism is based on his own knowledge. Thanks to the association of well-known evangelists with right-wing conservative causes or television huckerstering, fundamentalism tends to be mocked rather than understood. Greene's feelings are ambivalent: He says in the interview, "Molding Past into Art," that "I began to pull away from the fundamentalist code. But morality is at the bottom of everything I write, the ambiguities and ironies of it" (45).

After his stop in Abilene and his digression on religion, Greene resumes his tour, heading further west on Highway 80. Not far from Abilene the highway crosses the 100th Meridian, the line often used to indicate the transition to western America, the boundary where truly arid regions begin, with annual rainfall below twelve inches. He has a great deal to say about the shifting landscape, which begins to approach desert, and the wind, a powerful presence even east of the line. The harsh winds drove the windmills for the irrigation needed to raise stock in dry regions. Like Sally Matthews, he talks about the destruction of the buffalo herds in the 1870s. The end of the buffalo finally broke the power of the Plains Indians and opened the frontier for secure settlement.

He also turns figuratively off the main road to consider San Angelo, the one important city lying off the Highway 80/Interstate 20 corridor. It is anomalous because it is the center of the wool and mohair industry in the United States, an industry which reaches to the Mexican border regions, where Jewel Babb ranched goats and sheep near Langtry. The myth of the cowboy, as William Humphrey called it, is so strong that Texas is identified with cowboys and ranches the world over but never with sheep or goats, although the state produces ninety-five percent of America's wool and half of the world's mohair. Greene observes that the consumption of mutton and lamb in West Texas is virtually zero. The tour of Highway 80 resumes after the side trip to goat-and-sheep country and comes to an end with the twin cities of Midland and Odessa, which have produced enormous quantities of oil and an American president. Greene notes that the oilman has been added to the pantheon of Texas gods but without really replacing the figure of the cowboy. There is too much greed involved in the oil business to engage the emotional sympathy felt for the cowboy.

The rest of the book is a different kind of journey, one into the past, an excursion through documents and historical sites mixed with Greene's family history. There are some journeys by car, but the most effective moments are peripatetic: Greene on foot at Fort Phantom Hill, or searching out ruins of Butterfield Stage outposts, or searching for the grave of a man killed by the Comanches. Much of the territory covered is in the cattle country north of the highway and railway axis, the ranching county of Shackelford, the Clear Fork region that Sallie Reynolds Matthews told about in *Interwoven*.

In "What Time Owns" Greene calls Shackelford a "historical laboratory," because it has remained a ranching region with few changes in population (mostly descendants of the early settlers) and no real influence from the oil boom. He considers Shackelford and the surrounding area in Throckmorton and Anson Jones counties "the cradle of West Texas," because the area represented the frontier, Comanche country. The heart of the area is the Lambshead Ranch, where he takes the reader on an imaginary walk around the Stone Ranch, the oldest part of the enterprise, the house where the Reynolds family lived briefly from 1866-1867, until the opening of Fort Griffin nearby. The desire to preserve history sometimes undoes the work of time: The ruined house described by Greene in 1971 was restored years later by Watt Matthews as a tribute to his mother and her family. What time owns it is sometimes forced to give back, if only as a replica.

The narrative moves from the Stone Ranch to Albany, where much of the population takes part in the "Fort Griffin Fandangle." And quite naturally the next journeys are to Fort Griffin, where he provides a less rosy picture of frontier life than Sallie Reynolds Matthews gave, and to Camp Cooper. Matthews said little about

Camp Cooper because it was abandoned a few months before she was born, its commander having surrendered to secessionist forces. But her family did live on the site most of the time between 1877 and 1882 on a ranch they called Tecumseh. Robert E. Lee was Camp Cooper's commanding officer from April 9, 1856 to July 28, 1857. It was Lee's first actual command, and Greene suggests that his time there helped build his character and give him essential experience as a commander. The tragic story of the famous Comanche captive, Cynthia Ann Parker, has a link with Camp Cooper too: She had been carried off by the Comanches when she was nine, in 1836, and in 1880 she was captured by soldiers who took her to Camp Cooper. Cynthia Ann Parker's story is mentioned but not discussed in detail by Sallie Matthews because she felt it was too familiar, and she strangely mentions Robert E. Lee without placing him at Camp Cooper, the site of her own Tecumseh Ranch.

Her biggest omission, of course, was the story of the vigilantes and the fate of John Larn, subjects that Greene looks at in depth. The remains of John Larn's house, built for his bride, Mary Matthews, and usually referred to as the Honeymoon Cottage, are not far from Camp Cooper. Greene, always ready to explore history on foot, recalls that on his first visit to the cottage, "the romantic interpretation was enhanced by a large flowerbed in the front yard, the bed carefully shaped with rocks in the form of a heart." However, he and Robert Nail, the founder of the Fandangle, dug in the yard and established that it had four flowerbeds, in the shapes of diamond, heart, club, and spade, a less romantic layout.

Sallie Reynolds Matthews mentions the Butterfield Stage only once in passing, saying that "the old Butterfield stage route passes through our ranch, the route which so many wagon trains took during the famous gold rush to California; it has its share of graves" (61). The stage route (properly known as the Overland Stage but always called by the name of its Utica, New York, founder) closed down with the Civil War, which began a month before Matthews' birth. Greene devotes his longest chapter, "Butterfield and I," to his quest to find the old stage stations. The name of the Lambshead

Ranch, he points out, comes from the name of an Englishman named Thomas Lambshead, who managed a station there in 1858. Running through the chapter are citations from Waterman Ormsby, who took the first stage ride for the *New York Herald*. He closes off the chapter neatly with the story of Anson Mills, a Texas state surveyor and Union sympathizer who left Texas on the last stage ride as the Civil War was beginning.

Between those trips through the pages of Ormsby and Mills, Greene describes his own journeys to several of the old stage sites. He went to Chimney Creek in search of Smith's Station, driving with two friends, Robert Green, a rancher, and Robert Nail. Their old Chevrolet moved through high grass and then slipped into the ancient ruts of the stagecoach trail, controlled by them, as he says, until they literally bumped into the past: the dressed stone of the station. But the stone corrals were gone. At the gas station down the highway, Greene learned what happened: The proprietor, who was once the foreman of a ranch on the site of Smith's Station, said complacently that he had told the builders of Highway 351 that some convenient stones were available for the road, and so a portion of the past has been crushed for the convenience of the present. Maybe it was appropriate, despite the injury to history. "Using a Butterfield ruin to create a new road is gloriously just, as symbolism goes" (206). In this chapter Greene describes finding a flint "humpback scraper from the Clear Fork Indian culture of 3,000 years ago" (235), a discovery mirrored by his finding a triangular flint scraper during a search for the grave of Philip Reynolds.

The long episode about Fort Phantom Hill in the middle of the chapter combines historical research and family memory. The fort was built in 1851 and abandoned in 1855 because water was too scarce, and the site was taken over in 1858 by the Butterfield Stage line. One of Greene's finest sketches, this focuses on a Fourth of July family fishing trip at the fort and prepares the reader for the family saga two chapters later. The picnic is vividly described, with a fine cast of family characters like the eccentric Uncle Stub, who followed the old Texas (southern, really) profession of trading. He would trade anything for anything. The fishing was done mostly with trot lines, though the older generation favored bamboo poles. A comic scene depicts Uncle Stub's encounter with a cottonmouth snake, and we learn about Greene's initiation into alcoholic beverages. A member of the family gives him a drink of home brew (passed off to the pious at the picnic as iced tea). The whole episode is a good evocation of a Texas family institution, comparable to William Humphrey's descriptions of Graveyard Decoration Day in his novels.

The next chapter, "Sandstone Sentinels," taking its title from the old and easily eroded tombstones in West Texas cemeteries, is another journey through the past. The focus of the chapter is a field trip on a cold February day when Greene and Robert Nail set out to find the grave of Phillip Reynolds near Albany. Reynolds was not a member of Sallie Reynolds Matthews family, which must have been unusual in Shackelford County. He was an employee at W. H. Ledbetter's salt works, which is mentioned in passing in *Interwoven* (20, 116). The Brazos River has several Salt Forks as well as a Clear Fork, and Ledbetter started a salt gathering operation at one of them. Greene and Nail stopped at the salt works, where Greene's feeling that presences from the past were hovering nearby got confirmation by his instant recognition of an artifact that outdated even Ledbetter: an ancient flint scraper. Anyone who visits Greene's home in Salado, Texas, as I did on May 16, 1998, will see a house hung with western objects and pictures accumulated over many years, Western without kitsch. Such material reminders of the past seem especially important to Greene. He tells us that the taste of the salt water at Ledbetter's abandoned works is his equivalent of Proust's madeleine, giving a similar sensation of timelessness.

At first it appeared that Reynolds's gravesite would be inaccessible because of vast tangles of mesquite, but the area around the actual grave had been cleared by bulldozers. It was not cleared for archaeological reasons but because mesquite will take over an area if not controlled. One of Greene's unforced historical ironies is here: The past has been inadvertently made available by heavy machinery, balancing the situation in the previous chapter, the destruction of the stagecoach corral to build a modern highway.

The cemetery chapter is an implied introduction to the next section, "So All the Generations," which begins with Greene's family saga, the story of his maternal ancestors (the ones who were Texas pioneers) and then goes on to talk about his own nuclear family. The family saga commences with a characterization of the Scotch-Irish, the group to which his mother's family belonged. The Scotch-Irish were the irascible, land-hungry driving force in the westward movement: In his massive history of Texas, *Lone Star*, T. R. Fehrenbach begins his discussion of Anglo settlers in Texas with a chapter on the Scotch-Irish (the "Anglo-Celts").[7] Greene's description of the Scotch-Irish as "highstrung, hot-headed and brave; obstinate, opinionated and moralistic" (275) fits Fehrenbach's analysis of the evidence. By implication, this group helps to explain the origins of the rigidity and individualism of Texans in general and West Texans in particular.

When telling the family saga, Greene writes like a professional folklorist testing the plausibility of what he has learned and with a good knowledge of the folk tradition. He states in his introduction to *A Personal Country* that some of the stories in his book belong to "those universal classics of folk heritage" (xv). He undoubtedly benefited from knowing Mody C. Boatright, a friend who visited Paisano several times during the writing of *A Personal Country*. Greene recalls that his daughter Meredith named a stray Spanish goat at the ranch "Mody Goatright" after the folklorist, who dryly stated that his name had been used to name a grandchild, a goat, and a jackass (Letter to author, February 17, 2001).

The oldest story that he cites is the tale of his great-grandmother's grandfather, Grandpaw Poe; it dates to the 1850s. Possible alterations in transmission are likely in a story handed down from so long ago, and Greene is aware of that it may be full of inaccuracies: He points out some of them. But he says that the story "exemplifies not just my own bloodline's adamantine tendency but that of a whole social era" (279). Boatright would have liked this statement: It confirms his notion that an event in a family saga reflects a society and one of its values. The value implicit in Grandpaw

Poe's story is perhaps rather unusual outside of West Texas, the danger of stubbornness carried to suicidal lengths.

The story involves an old man on the San Saba frontier at the southeastern edge of West Texas, who insisted on taking part in a buffalo hunt more than a hundred miles to the northwest. His insistence on going, in spite of the dangers of the coming winter and his advanced age, is attributed to his Scotch-Irishness. The tale is virtually a short story. When the old man insisted on returning home in the middle of winter, he eventually wandered unhorsed and sick in the wilderness. He finally took refuge in a cave which happened to be a den for rabid skunks. Like an experienced folklore scholar (or a good journalist), Greene doubts that there was a whole nest of skunks. One would have been enough, he says, but he concedes that there may have been more skunks in the wilderness back then: "so we may presume this to be true, I think" (282). The final "I think" is an essential part of the tone. The old man was discovered by his sons, who in remorse and concern tracked him down. He died weeks later in misery. Greene says that his grandmother could never condemn the old man for his foolish actions: He had a right to be stubborn, even to the point of self-destruction. This may seem an unusual social value, but Greene makes it clear that on the West Texas frontier, it was acceptable.

His next tale is closer to the present, and its central figure, his great-grandmother, is someone he knew, a veteran of those family car journeys. He affirms his own social values by handing down to us the story of her killing a panther with an ax when she saw it threatening her child. He mentions that she discovered a den of rattlesnakes on the family farm. He shows some skepticism in this case by telling us that she was *said* [emphasis added] to have been the one who killed the snakes. Her husband, Lytle Craighead, was mentioned earlier as a man who gave up and went back to East Texas, incurring social disgrace.

After the first husband died young, the widow was married—married off, in family legend—to Campbell Longley, a man of seventy-three, the father of a notorious outlaw, Bill Longley. Campbell wanted to send her three children to an orphan's home, and the family legend even says that he tried to poison them. Two died of a fever, and Greene's informant, his grandmother, nine years old, was the survivor. He gives her grisly account of the death of a brother (his eyes supposedly popped out of his head and dangled on strings of flesh) but notes like a good folklorist that the story may not be accurate. Greene himself in telling the story of his great-grandmother affirms his own social values by emphasizing her courage and independence. She stood up to the malevolent Campbell Longley and in a wonderful twist received recognition and a pension in her old age as the last surviving widow of a veteran of the Texas Revolution. His summary of her marital history helps to define the West Texas ethos—"Hers was a tough philosophy, I suppose: a philosophy of take what is offered and evaluate few things on the balances of pleasure and happiness" (292).

The end of her life showed a lack of adaptability. Women like his great-grandmother could not adjust to the changes in the 1880s and 1890s, the extension of technology with devices like the telephone, electric lights, and home appliances. She never learned to use the telephone correctly, and in her seventies she began making her own lye soap and brooms again, though the store-bought products were cheaper and more effective. Greene sees her attitude as a reflection of something in the West Texas pioneer's frame of mind. Self-reliance was a frontier value, as was a stubborn insistence (like Grandpaw Poe) on making your own choices. He believes that even modern West Texans tend to be doers rather than planners, and he thinks this is a flaw.

With Greene's grandmother, his family history moves from saga to personal observation. His grandmother, a librarian, was not only a custodian of books but the author of one: Maude E. Cole's *Wind Against Stone: A Texas Novel* (1941) deals with a pioneer woman in West Texas.[8] Greene's admiration for his grandmother is intense. After all, he spent much of his childhood in the Carnegie Library over which she presided. His pages on the library and the characters he met there (like the elderly sisters who spent years copying the *Encyclopedia Britannica* into notebooks) are among his best. He concludes his penultimate chapter with pages on his parents, lamenting that his mother seemed blocked from joy in life by her religious upbringing and its inhibitions, and regretting that he never got to know his father, Carl, as a friend. Carl was a generous man who suffered from being clamped in a box of moral strictures. Greene characterizes his father effectively by citing the time a friend came into his father's shop and asked urgently for the shirt off his back: The father gave it, and the friend went out to tell people waiting for the outcome outside the shop. The marriage of these two people, the openhearted man and the inhibited and pessimistic woman, might have been joyful if it had not been spoiled by repression and incompatible outlooks.

Greene has told us about "the ropes of blood and human time that reach down and up and back into unknown territories of inheritance" (311), and it only remains for him to return to Abilene in "Bring Me to . . . ." for a return and farewell. He writes the chapter in the present tense to give it immediacy. He believes that a regional identification like his with West Texas means that it is possible to find a city, a region, a people, and a history within the self, which constitutes extra birthright. He has found his inheritance not in goods and gentility but in the land and people and (even) the beliefs of his region. Not everyone has this regional feeling, he understands, and many people are more concerned with their social class or their jobs (314). But as his living relatives have almost all vanished, the awareness of place, which has always been important for southerners in general and Texans in particular, has become important to him.

It is common enough for individuals to wonder what they might have been if they had not left. Greene describes having coffee in a motel coffee shop with a friend who stayed in Abilene and "missed his turn at the dice" (316). His friend had ties that could not be broken, while Greene found it just as impossible to stay. After coffee he made a tour of the town, sketching its layout for the reader and explaining the changes that have occurred since his childhood. Five years later, William Humphrey would provide a similar tour of Clarksville at the end of *Farther Off from Heaven*. The high point in Greene's return was the discovery of rows of bricks in a vanished brickyard of the 1890s, another moment of discovery like the finding of the scrapers in "The Butterfield and I" and "Sandstone Sentinals." Appropriately enough as a symbol of change, the bricks were removed two weeks later when construction began on one of the ubiquitous features of American life, a pancake house. The trip around Abilene was as much a trip through time as through space, with a host of vivid impressions coming into Greene's mind, like the atmosphere of barber shops long ago and the odors of farm wagons coming into town with earth and grass on the moldboard. The journey, the last tour in the book, turns when the West Texas Everyman drives down a gravel road and enters the Cedar Hill Cemetery.

Before describing the graves, he makes a survey of objects which he left on a shelf in his office, souvenirs from his last archaeological walkabout in West Texas, things like flint artifacts from early native hunters, bottle glass left by the later white hunters of buffalo, square nails from an early house, a brass pipe fitting from a later day, "chips of time, all of them, signs of human habitation in the earth, none of them rare or valuable, but pieces of West Texas" (327). They help define his personality as a man who likes to sense the nature of the past and feel himself part of the continuity of life in his region. "A place is something you can't scrub off your soul," he says, which could be a motto for most autobiographies of Texans. The affirmation of continuity through physical traces of humanity are a subtle preparation for the moment when he looks down on two graves, covered with the red West Texas earth. The reader understands implicitly that these are the graves of Greene's parents. "And I know how my journey ends" (328). It is the end of the journey for us all: Greene said at the outset that his experiences were meant to be typical, not exceptional. But his book is exceptional in its wide-ranging voyages through West Texas space and time and blood kinship.

Greene says in the first chapter of his book that he is like "millions" of others, but one fact makes him exceptional. In 1988, at the age of sixty-five, he received a heart transplant. He was unusually old for the operation and has survived remarkably long. While *Taking Heart*,[9] his book about transplant surgery is not strictly an autobiography, it adds some personal touches to the austere self-portrait in his earlier memoir.

The book is a kind of survivor's journal, as he puts it (11), and anyone undergoing a heart transplant operation would learn much about the history, procedures, and aftermath of the operation. The reader wanting to learn more about Greene will find that he has a moderate religious faith: He thinks the metaphysical impulse is a strong part of human nature. The book also reveals an open secret; this prolific author was devoted to work. His strong feeling for his family and his desire to cultivate a positive attitude in response to his original heart disease also tells us much about the man. He is particularly good on two parts of the transplant experience: the sense of disorientation in the early weeks after the operation and the tremendous sense of new life, even rebirth, that follows for many patients, including him. Fear of death decreases, and depression and caution about such matters as money seem unimportant. Strangely, heart transplant recipients have fewer experiences of depression than by-pass patients. Greene's fellow West Texan, Larry McMurtry, is one of the victims of by-pass melancholy.

It is fitting to end with two dreams that he had during his anesthesia. Such dreams are a common experience for those who have had such a massive operation. One dream is typical of a writer: He dreamed being given a book called *Alphabets*, a work by a Swedish writer and calligrapher, as an aid to the psychological exploration of death. In the dream he saw vividly the color and design of this mythical book, the brown letters, and creamy paper, and he saw photographs and calligraphy explaining the letters of the Swedish alphabet. For a writer, bookmaking is one of the basics, and the alphabet is the start of it all.

The other dream was archetypally Texan in its imagery. He found himself in the Alamo, in a round stone room filling with water. The imminence of death was overwhelming. The significance of the setting of the dream is obvious: While the Alamo is said to be the cradle of Texas liberty, none of the defenders got out alive. Just as doom seemed about to occur, a 1936 Ford V-8 burst through the wall and let the water out. Greene perhaps felt it was unnecessary to tell his readers that 1936 was the centennial of the Battle of the Alamo and of Texas independence. At any rate, a group of Baylor University drama students entered the room and congratulated him on passing the test. In typical self-deflating mock-heroic style, he mentions that during his second day after the operation he was unconscious but ripped the ventilator out of his throat and muttered, "I want Paul Newman to play my part."

In *Taking Heart*, Greene describes his most interesting personal adventure as an adult. In *A Personal Country* he set out to put his typical experiences as a boy and man in a unique region and therefore to speak for us all, wherever we may have begun life, whatever circumstances form us. He says in the afterword to the 1998 edition of his book that it has been readable for thirty years and that he hopes it will remain readable for "at least thirty years more" (334). The prognosis is good.

William Humphrey

9

ALL THE TIME IN THE WORLD: WILLIAM HUMPHREY'S CLARKSVILLE

William Humphrey's *Farther Off from Heaven* is the only Texas memoir written by a major novelist. The prose is luminous, the design is intricate and absolutely clear, the characterization is absolutely convincing. Humphrey (1924-1997) received the Carr P. Collins Award from the Texas Institute of Letters for the work. But the book failed to gain readers and soon wound up on remainder tables in Manhattan. The English edition from Chatto and Windus also failed. Humphrey's English publisher, Ian Parsons, was so disturbed by the book's failure to sell that he actually wrote a letter to the trade paper, *The Bookman*, complaining that a book he ranked with Fitzgerald's *The Great Gatsby*, Hemingway's *A Moveable Feast*, and Faulkner's "The Bear" had gone unsold. "I want to know why,"[1] he wrote. Such questions are difficult to answer, but the critical and popular failure of *Proud Flesh*, Humphrey's confused and melodramatic family saga of 1973 may have been a factor. Humphrey's American publisher, Alfred A. Knopf, had, in Humphrey's view, failed to promote the work, probably because the novelist had offended Knopf himself. Whatever the reasons for the failure, *Farther Off from Heaven* remains out of print and mostly unread.

William Humphrey was born on June 18, 1924, in Clarksville, the county seat of Red River County, a town of about 3,000 north of the Sulphur River. He died in Hudson, New York, on August 20, 1997. His place of birth is central to almost all of his writing, and his long residence in New York represented a need to distance himself from his native soil in order to write about it. Clarksville, which he left at the age of thirteen and revisited only once, remained as vivid in his mind as Dublin did in Joyce's. Separation from his place of birth preserved it forever. Thanks to its native son, Clarksville is one of the most palpable towns in American literature. It is the setting for three of Humphrey's novels, *Home from the Hill*, *The Ordways*, and *Proud Flesh*, and for the frame story of a fourth, *No Resting Place*,[2] a novel which attacks the glorification of Anglo Texan history in the revolution and republic, the "Myth of Texas." Many of his short stories are set in Clarksville or in nearby towns.

A recent work similar to Humphrey's is Horton Foote's *Farewell: A Memoir of a Texas Childhood* (1999),[3] which gives a good picture of life in Wharton, a small town southwest of Houston, during the period from his birth in 1916 to his departure in 1932, when he went to Hollywood to seek a career. Foote, a Pulitzer Prize-winning dramatist and Academy Award-winning scriptwriter, provides a full picture of life in a small town, with a chilling look at the Ku Klux

Klan. The town of Wharton has been the inspiration for much of his work, just as Humphrey came back to Clarksville fictionally again and again. Foote is strong on dialogue, as might be expected, though Humphrey surpasses him in creating an imaginative town systematically and deeply. In describing relatives, Foote accumulates detail, while Humphrey is concise. Humphrey, who left Clarksville at only thirteen, creates a more vivid sense of the setting and the people of his birthplace, perhaps because he had a traumatic parting with it.

Humphrey's decision to deal with his father's mortal accident in a car crash early on the morning of July 5, 1937, led to some difficult problems of narration. He keeps to something like the three unities of time, space, and action, building his narrative around the three days when his father, Clarence, lay dying in the hospital in Paris, thirty-five miles away, and the day of the funeral. Chapters two through six begin with stages in the father's dying, and chapter seven deals with the funeral, which Humphrey did not attend. Each chapter goes on by some process of association to deal with the background, childhood, and marriage of Humphrey's parents and then Humphrey's childhood. He elaborates, without losing track of the primary action, the tragedy of July 1937.

A problem of point of view arose in narrating all these events. The background of his parents could be presented from an adult's point of view, but there was the question of how the author would present his younger self. Humphrey's 1975 notebook[4] for *Farther Off From Heaven*, which can be found in his papers at the Harry Ransom Humanities Research Center at the University of Texas, contains pages of speculation about the proper way to handle this material. As I explain in my *William Humphrey, Destroyer of Myths*, Humphrey had difficulty naming his work, trying out *Father of the Man* and *Growing Pains*.[5] He was not sure how to classify the work either, pondering subtitles like "a memoir" and "an evocation." He would have stressed the subjective element if he had called it an evocation. He rejected *Growing Pains* after his wife said it was too much like Booth Tarkington, but the title was apt for a work depicting his initiation into the tragic world of adults. His longest working title was "Father of the Man," from the famous epigraph to Wordsworth's Immortality Ode: "The Child is Father of the Man; / And I could wish my days to be / Bound each to each by natural piety." The thrust of such words is ambiguous, and rightly so: Humphrey intends to tell the story of his own childhood, but he also tells the story of his father and of the father's childhood. He stresses in the notebook that the memoir will be as much about his father as himself. He also resolves to let the details of the tragedy speak for themselves, like the powerful scene in which the father, being carried in the ambulance to Paris, keeps screaming for the lights to be turned off, even though it is dark.

But the phrase, "the Child is Father of the Man," raises questions of point of view. The memoirist could write as a child, but sustained naiveté and stylistic simplicity would become tedious and rob the narrator of the chance to employ adult insights, all the wisdom the man has gained since leaving childhood. There are precedents in American literature for taking a child's point of view: *Huckleberry Finn* is the most famous. But his notebook shows Humphrey thinking about Wordsworth's poems written in a child's language and deciding that emulation would lead him to create a mere hat trick. He worked out for himself the insights of Barrett Mandel and Paul John Eakin, the understanding that an autobiography represents not the historical self but that self as created by the adult "forging" a self (Mandel's phrase) in the act of writing. The French theorist of autobiography, Phillipe Lejeune, has emphasized in his writings what Humphrey discovered in practice, that there is a duality in an autobiography between the author and the way that the author is presented in the text: "A person is always *several people* when he is writing, even all alone, even his own life."[6] Lejeune speaks of "gaps of information, gaps of appreciation" which are masked by the use of first-person narrative, but the gap between the two is most obvious when an adult writes about childhood and imputes adult understanding to the earlier version of the "I." Humphrey avoids such imputations: it is clear that he is interpreting his earlier self, not re-creating it, as Mary Karr often does. He is not masking the differences between child and adult.

He turned to a novelist for examples, not to the theory of autobiography. Proust's methods in *Remembrance of Time Past* proved to be a better model than Wordsworth: The child is presented using all the insights of an adult in an adult rather than childlike style. Humphrey says in the notebook that he will use all of his adult wisdom and vocabulary to understand his younger self, and it is clear when he is commenting on rather than narrating his experiences. He is careful not to emphasize the gap between adult and child by attributing adult insights to his childish self. He does not make the reader stop and query whether the younger self could be thinking like the older one. Mary Karr's memoirs sometimes cause the reader to wonder about exactly that question: In an admiring review William Harmon wonders how a juvenile narrator can use terms like "porcine."[7] Humphrey never falls into such inconsistencies. In the epilogue to his book he presents his return to Clarksville after three decades, and then he consciously measures the gap between adult and child.

The image which liberates the past for Humphrey is not a madeleine but the chimes of Old Red, the clock on the Clarksville Courthouse. The clock is not a symbol of mortality for Humphrey, but an image of his childhood liberation from time: Its ringing at the end of the book makes him reexperience a setting in which he felt he had all the time in the world (242). The book shows how wrong that feeling was. The Clarksville presided over by Old Red was, in the memory of the autobiographer, a paradise. The title of the book comes from a poem by Thomas Hood, "I Remember," in which one stanza concludes, "But now 'tis little joy / To know I'm farther off from heaven / Than when I was a boy." In the poem, the speaker used to think that the fir trees came close to heaven, an indication that he was naive in thinking that his childhood universe was small and cozy. Humphrey knows in retrospect how small Clarksville was, but he still longs for a life shut for him by his father's death, which forced him and his mother, Nell, to move to Dallas right after the funeral so that she could find work. The fact that the memoirist-narrator is now an adult is conveyed effectively by Hood's poem, with its use of the changing perception of the fir trees as an emblem of the gulf between the child who is father to the man and the man who is writing as father of the child.

The power of Humphrey's memoir arises in large part from the sheer sensuous detail of the setting he knew as a child, a world defined socially by the poles of Niggertown and Silk Stocking Lane. He charts the town for us by describing his walks to school. The one area that frightened him was the street of hovels behind the cemetery. As in many East Texas towns, the town square was the center of social life, a place for Saturday markets and a gathering place for men who whittled and gossiped, a place where vendors sold tamales and popcorn in the shadow of the traditional Confederate monument. Clarksville is presented as a happy world for the boy, far different from Owens's Pin Hook. Adults like Humphrey's parents had to worry about the devastating effects of the Depression, but children can be fairly isolated from want by self-sacrificing parents. Humphrey suffered indirectly from the Depression, through the tensions between his parents which were created by growing financial hardship. The tensions in the marriage grew steadily as the financial hardships of the Depression took the joy out of their lives.

But Humphrey was a novelist steeped in Freud and, like Gertrude Beasley before him and Larry McMurtry and Mary Karr after, he was acutely aware of the deep tensions between his parents, which gives his memoir a psychological depth. Like Karr, he is the child of parents who loved one another and their child but fought ferociously. Children in such families witness parental wounds and are wounded by what they see. This kind of dysfunctional family narrative is almost to be expected since the beginning of the so-called memoir boom, a boom for which Mary Karr is credited or blamed, depending on how much a critic admires confessional writing. Humphrey's narrative is tame compared to Karr's *The Liar's Club* and *Cherry*, much less Beasley's *My First Thirty Years*. His parents fought but not on the scale of Karr's.

Humphrey skillfully alludes to several mysteries early in the book, a strategy common in memoirs. He intimates that he died in childhood; he alludes to a fire which destroyed his childhood souvenirs and his death certificate; and he describes his sadness at the vanishing of the house where he was born. He is puzzled that even the plot of earth where the house stood seemed to have gone, so reticent were his parents about the location (141). He also tells the reader that the Fourth of July was always his unlucky day. He waits until the book is almost over to explain these matters. Humphrey shares with many contemporary memoirists (including Mary Karr) a strategy of withholding and then revealing family secrets, usually about parents or some suppressed childhood experience. Only in the last chapter does the reader come to understand fully the hints and puzzles placed in the text. The secrets are not the cause of the family's dysfunction as they are in Mary Karr's *The Liar's Club* and in John Phillip Santos's *Places Left Unfinished at the Time of Creation*. When the Humphrey family secrets are revealed, they illustrate anxieties—about young Humphrey's health and about the family's social status.

Humphrey devotes much of his space to exploring his origins: his grandparents' background, the childhood of his parents, and their courtship. A fair proportion of the book deals with events that happened before he was born. The Humphrey side of the family was impoverished: His paternal grandfather, Will, was a sharecropper who lived on a succession of cotton farms near the settlement of Lone Star. The grandfather's own father, Star Humphrey, was a Native American, but no one knew from which tribe. The family saga records that his wife was a gypsy and a fortuneteller. Mary Karr and Jewel Babb both speak of native ancestry, again, with no certain knowledge of which tribe. Anglo Texas is not as Caucasian as Anglo Texans would believe, and multiracial origins are erased from memory. Humphrey tells one story about his great-grandmother's fortune-telling prowess and says that this is his "total trove" on her (67). He complains that there seemed to be no paternal family history to transmit to him: All his forebears seemed to have done was "get born, breed and die" (68). Here Humphrey touches without emphasis on a theme of his work, the family which keeps secrets. We never learn just why Humphrey's father kept a gun in the house near the end of his life, and only in the final chapter of the book do we discover several secrets in the nuclear family of father, mother, son. It is a truism in America today that secrets haunt dysfunctional families, and Humphrey's family was no exception to this rule.

Humphrey's father found life with his parents oppressive, and he frequently ran away to his Aunt Suzie Sample's house, where he found warmth. The routine of farm work was too demanding. Like Owens, who was undoubtedly an influence on the younger writer, Humphrey devotes some interesting pages to describing the work on the family farm: There is a fine scene on slaughtering a pig; and the cutting and cording of firewood are meticulously detailed. In the chapter on his father's childhood, he quite skillfully moves from his father's early hunting prowess to the ways that young William learned to hunt such game as mourning doves (a Texas favorite) and wild ducks. One day, Humphrey tells us, Clarence saw his first automobile, which would be his way out of rural poverty. He became a "shade tree mechanic" and eventually opened a successful garage in Clarksville. But the means of his success became his way to failure with the Depression, and he met his death in an automobile accident.

The mother's parents, the Varleys, had a happy if impoverished household. Ed Varley was born in England. His contribution to the family saga lay in his emigration: He was treated as a servant by his older brother, and one day lost patience after being ordered to polish the brother's boots. He refused and was cuffed by his brother; he complained to his father and was cuffed by him. He ran away and eventually turned up in Boston. Family sagas can be highly selective. Humphrey had only the one anecdote of this family's past and says that his grandfather must have arrived in America and started breeding right away, as he had three children by his first wife and nine by his second. The amusing part of his sketch of the Varleys is his portrait of the way that the parents turned their adoring children into slaves by doting on each other: The children would constantly be asked by one parent to do things for the other, and neither parent wound up doing anything.

The whole family adored the youngest child, Humphrey's

mother. Her special position grew out of a terrible accident when she was only three. The older children had been riding the rope used to lift hay into the loft in the barn. They encouraged the child to ride the rope up, but she was terrified and couldn't turn loose. She mangled her hand in the pulley, losing her middle finger and permanently stiffening her ring finger. Humphrey notes that she became skilled at concealing the injury. Most people never saw it: Indeed, Clarence Humphrey did not perceive the mutilation until five years after his marriage, and William only "spied it" at the age of eight. The concealed injury is a subtle motif in the work. In the revelatory last chapter, we learn that Humphrey himself had a defective foot at birth and that his mother refused to accept the permanence of the injury and made a brave journey to Dallas to see a specialist. The foot was cured by the age of three and the son learned of the injury only when he sprained the ankle of the same foot much later. His mother's terror was so great that she confessed that she had always feared that the ankle would fail him. She had blamed herself for the birth defect, accepting the old superstition that a baby would be born with a defect if the pregnant mother slept on her side. Nell was sure that she had caused the problem by failing to sleep on her back often enough. After learning the truth about his foot, Humphrey notices that in all of his baby pictures the defect had been concealed, just as his mother concealed her own handicap. Humphrey's implication is that concealed traumas breed fear and anxiety. The theme of physical injuries (which represent psychic traumas) is reinforced by a serious injury Humphrey had on the Fourth of July, 1933: He fell on a pointed stake in the grass and tore off his kneecap.

Humphrey's book serves as a fine complement to Owens's memoirs, providing more genre painting of the lives of sharecroppers and citizens of small East Texas towns. But all this is backdrop to the real story which unfolds as Humphrey tells about his parents. They had a volatile courtship and married in spite of her parents' disapproval. The culmination of their courtship was a country dance, the atmosphere of which the son describes so vividly that the reader has to remember he was not even conceived yet. A man paid too much attention to Nell, and Clarence took him outside for a fight, which he won. The parents were both strong-willed and jealous: Humphrey says his mother would not have thought she loved her husband if she had not been a jealous wife. The father's violent streak is an ominous touch. The son recalls once that the family's safety was imperiled on a road trip when a drunken driver almost drove their car off a steep drop. Clarence beat the man insensible. On another occasion he beat up a drunk who spoke in a leering way to his wife on the town square.

Some of the tension in Humphrey's childhood came from the mother's ambitions for her son: She wanted the Humphrey family to rise to the top in two generations. Young Humphrey grew up with a craving for success in school—his mother could see the usefulness of that. And so he worked desperately for good grades. "What spurred me and made me studious and ambitious was insecurity and fear—insecurity about my origins, fear of the times. They were also making me into a little prig, a snob, both social and intellectual" (44). The mother's ambitions and concern with gentility led to conflict with her husband, and the son was caught between them, a situation similar to the tensions in the family of D. H. Lawrence. In his notebook, Humphrey drew the parallel between Lawrence and himself and also mentioned the same theme of ambitious wife and immature husband in Sean O'Casey's *Juno and the Paycock*. Like Lawrence, Humphrey found his father's skills appealing—the tremendous sense of woodlore, the manual dexterity of the born mechanic. One indelible image in the book is Humphrey's father riding on the hood of a car around town to listen to the engine, an image repeated in a novel, *Proud Flesh*. But the younger Humphrey was not permitted to hang around the garage because this might lower him. He envied all the other boys in town who could enter the shop and watch. D. H. Lawrence turned the Oedipal conflicts in his family into a novel, *Sons and Lovers*, which kept close to the realities of his parents and their marriage. In his first novel, *Home from the Hill*, Humphrey presented a kind of sublimated portrait of his father, making him into the rich man in town, the proficient hunter and lover, Wade Hunnicutt.

The actual father's hunting skills are commemorated in the book in chapter three. The segue is from daybreak in the Paris hospital the morning of the accident, which reminds Humphrey of the times he would get up early to go hunting with his father. The son could hunt with his father, but he could not visit the lowly garage although every other boy in town could, an aspect of his mother's social-climbing attitude. The game pursued was progressively more difficult as the boy learned to hunt: quail, doves, wild ducks. This is a traditional rite of passage, especially in southern writing. One of Humphrey's most interesting scenes deals with his father as another kind of hunter: On one occasion he pursued a robber into the heart of the deep woods south of Clarksville known as the Sulphur Bottom. The man had shot a filling station attendant, so the pursuit was perilous. The scene is an imaginative reconstruction, and Humphrey's notebook shows the mind of a novelist at work. His father, he says in the notebook, described the pursuit of the man—who was so terrified in this wilderness that he meekly surrendered—in about twenty words. As Humphrey struggles to flesh out the scene, he remembers that he had turned the situation into fiction for *Home for the Hill*, then rejected it. He begins hunting for the discarded passage. He does not say in the notebook if he found it, but the process is interesting: Life is magnified into art, then the artist realizes that the magnification can become the basis for describing life.

The desire to rise socially required money, and as the Depression deepened, the garage began to fail, creating even more conflict. Pathos arises when the parents, who had little schooling, had to ask their young son to help them with the bookkeeping. Those who are low on the economic scale may get a vicarious triumph from admiring outlaws. William Owens's grandmother admired Jesse James and hoped that her grandson would grow up to be as good as James. Humphrey says of his father: "His heroes were Jesse James, Sam Bass, and, later, Pretty Boy Floyd, Clyde Barrow and Bonnie Parker: robbers of those banks which had foreclosed on his mortgage, closed down on his deposit" (176). Near the end of his life, the father acquired a new habit of keeping a gun and roaming the roads at night. Rumors suggested there might be another woman involved, something likely to cause hostility in a young boy in the Oedipal triangle. Or there might have been some criminal activity to raise money.

The black citizens of Clarksville in the 1930s were even lower on the social ladder than poor whites, and Humphrey's sketch of his father's employee, Wylie, makes that clear. Wylie West was as skilled in car repairs and hunting as his employer; in fact, Humphrey calls him a carbon copy of Clarence—both were short, and stripped to the waist, each seemed a version of the other in a contrasting color, with the black man as a carbon-copy image of the white one. But of course true friendship between the two men was inhibited by the racial barrier. In a brilliant scene, Humphrey describes an alligator hunt the two men went on for fun: Hunting enabled them to treat each other as equals. In his notebook for *Farther Off from Heaven*, Humphrey speculated that his family was actually lower on the social scale than the "niggers." Such a thought would be repugnant to black people, but it reflects the special contempt southerners held for "poor white trash," the classification in which H. L. Mencken placed the Beasleys.

The final chapter of this admirably concise memoir packs powerful emotional scenes into a brief space. We follow the deterioration of the marriage: Clarence Humphrey starts carrying the gun and often staying out nights. His notebook shows Humphrey agonizing over his treatment of the father's gun. As a maker of plots he would be aware of Chekhov's rule: If a gun appears on the stage at the beginning of a play, it must go off before the end, a rule which applies to novels and stories too. But in real life the gun never went off, just as the revolvers are never fired in the memoirs of Gertrude Beasley and Hallie Stillwell. His notebook entry of June, 3, 1975, declares the book finished. Then on June 12, he writes, "Oh yeah?" and complains that he was still not satisfied with the part about the pistol.

The most disturbing scene in the final chapter describes a Sunday dinner: The father arrived late; there was a quarrel; he struck his wife and broke her pearl necklace (glass pearls, of course). After he left, the mother told her son to eat his tomato soup: Sunday decorum must be preserved. A brilliant image captures the boy's desolation: He found a pearl in his spoonful of soup and fled the house crying. The scene is told with admirable restraint. It has a different kind of horror from the last quarrel between Gertrude Beasley's parents, the moment when a blow was struck and the father gets out of bed cursing and exposing his genitals.

Parental misery is not the only subject of Humphrey's last chapter. It also conveys the depth of the boy's love for his mother in some touching scenes. Humphrey's work was influenced heavily by his readings in Freud, and he once translated a fifty-page essay by the psychoanalyst. The Oedipal conflicts in his family are unobtrusively dramatized in the chapter. He loved being cared for by his mother when he was sick or injured, and they shared a profound intimacy, achieving that relationship of mother and son which Freud says in his *New Introductory Lectures on Psychoanalysis* is "the most perfect, the most free from ambivalence of all human relationships."[8] The father became a distant antagonist as the unforeseen date of his death approached.

Information withheld from the reader (and sometimes from young Humphrey) emerges late in the work, like the secret of the birth defect. His supposed drowning is explained to us: The town coroner, who was drunk at the time, filled out a death certificate giving the cause as accidental suffocation, appropriate enough for someone who would be emotionally suffocated by parental conflict. The death certificate was saved but went up in smoke when the family's house burned. A favorite plaything went up too: a carousel horse. In a scene as magical as the carousel scene in Allen's *Southwest*, we learn that the family came upon an extraordinary abandoned merry-go-round on one of their drives. Clarence Humphrey carried off the most splendid horse for his son. When he returned the same evening for the other horses, the carousel was gone. The incident has a symbolic power, an allusion to a lost world of mystery and beauty.

The last chapter tells the story of the father's death and funeral.

The son refused to attend, and the memoirist gives great weight to his decision. The adult Humphrey strives to define his character—to present "metaphors of self" through this refusal, which represented a new view of his own personality. His basic metaphor is to see himself as an artist stepping back from the easel to see a self-portrait of a happy, trusting, confident boy. The death of his father made him rub out that portrait; he became a suspicious, fearful orphan who had to make his solitary way out of the Eden of Clarksville hand in hand with his mother. He decided against his scheduled religious confirmation. Henceforth he felt abandoned by God and his father, a rebel in the universe, or at least an orphan. Humphrey had many friends in adult life, but he shunned publicity and kept a prickly distance from the wider world, just as he refused to go to the funeral. He would henceforth, he says, be guarded and skeptical. He also resolved never to return to Clarksville: He rather melodramatically says he would "go his lone way" in exile. This vow he kept for thirty-two years. It kept the Clarksville of the thirties vivid for him and nourished his early fiction, though by the time of *Proud Flesh* his view of Texas had become obviously dated.

He ends his book in a way similar to the conclusion of Greene's *A Personal Country* by describing his return, dictated at last by the "salmon instinct." The actual occasion was his receiving an honorary degree at Southern Methodist University in 1969. A trip from Dallas to Clarksville was logical enough. He discovered that an area which had essentially been part of the old South, with cotton farming by men in overalls, had become far west, with cattle operations run by men in boots and cowboy hats. The biggest change was the conversion of the near-mythical Sulphur Bottom into grazing land. The writer had believed that the Sulphur Bottom was impenetrable and indestructible. He had once written a letter (August 9, 1958) to his agent, Annie Laurie Williams on behalf of James T. Vaughn (who was planning the locations for the film of *Home for the Hill*), suggesting it would take army tanks to enter the depths of the woods.[9] Once again childish perception, like Thomas Hood's fir trees touching heaven, proved inaccurate.

A return after thirty-two years requires an epiphany, and

Humphrey delivers one. According to his notebook, he thought of writing one elaborate sentence in parentheses—fifteen pages long. It is fortunate that he did not, as this had been done by William Faulkner in *Requiem for a Nun*, and all through his career Humphrey could not shake off the label "Faulknerian." Instead he provides a straightforward account of walking around town with his favorite Varley uncle. He happened to regret aloud the vanished house where he was born. The uncle showed surprise and told him that the house never disappeared. They went to see it, and it turned out to be one of the hovels behind the cemetery. The last family secret was revealed, and it symbolized the shame and ambition that drove Humphrey's parents as they were rising a little in the world. It also encapsulates the misery they must have felt as their economic situation began to collapse. As the town clock tolled, he could put his hometown in new perspective, noting that the cottonseed mill was swept away, that the Confederate monument in the town square had been turned a different direction, that the town now seemed a smaller place, shrunken "like old clothes long outgrown" (241). He measured his loss as the clock struck: Old Red once told him that he had all the time in the world, but time has been passing. The ending is full of emotion but does not lapse into sentimentality.

The book failed in the marketplace, but it remains one of the finest American memoirs, thanks to the author's master of the tools of his trade as a novelist, such as setting, characterization, structure, foreshadowing. He told Ashby Bland Crowder in an interview that "I want any book I read to have the shapeliness that a good work of fiction should have, rather than just be a chronological account of events that are worth reading because they actually happened." His object was to create "not a document, but something with the shapeliness of work of art."[10] Tact is not a literary technique, except perhaps as an aspect of tone. But certainly much of the power of the work comes from his exemplary tact in dealing with his dysfunctional family. He avoided sensationalism and has gained all the more power for that. Mary Karr, as we shall see, listened to the advice of Tobias Wolff, who told her that the memoirist should take no care for her own dignity. William Humphrey shows the power of maintaining not only his own dignity but the dignity of the parents who gave him life and did their best to nurture him in hard times.

Larry McMurtry

10

THE AUTOBIOGRAPHER IN DENIAL: LARRY MCMURTRY

Larry McMurtry's writing skills and his interesting multiple careers as novelist, scriptwriter, and bookstore owner make him the contemorary Texas writer whose full-scale autobiography would be the most interesting to read. He has been writing his life story in a fragmentary form in what Barbara Liss in the *Houston Chronicle* refers to as three "nonautobiographies"[1] in three years, *Walter Benjamin at the Dairy Queen*, *Roads*, and *Paradise*, books of 1999, 2000, and 2001. Liss suggests that "family-memoir-cum-travelogue is the writing form that most appeals to him." McMurtry's misfortune has been to lose his sense of self as a consequence of a heart operation, which has resulted in his experiencing the fragmented personality which postmodernism often posits as the real human condition. Much has been written about the "liberal individual" as an illusion. McMurtry has not found the loss of individuality liberating.

That individual known as Larry McMurtry was born in Wichita Falls in 1936, the city closest to his family's ranch in Archer County. He spent his childhood first on the ranch and then in the county seat, Archer City (present population: 1,993), after his family became commuter-ranchers. He is the best-known Texas novelist today, author of twenty-four novels by 2001, with a Pulitzer Prize in 1986 for *Lonesome Dove*, which became a highly successful television series. A scriptwriter himself, he has an ability to write books which become successful movies. Several of the films are set in towns which resemble his West Texas hometown and two were actually filmed there: *The Last Picture Show* and *Texasville*, both directed by Peter Bogdanovich. And as *Texasville* was being filmed, George Hickenlooper made a documentary (*Picture This: The Times of Peter Bogdanovich in Archer City, Texas*) about the production and the real-life marital conflicts of Bogdanovich,[2] thereby putting Archer City in a remarkably postmodern position at the intersection of life, art, and art about art. Under the names of Thalia and Anarene, the town has inspired five novels, two films, and one documentary, George Hickenlooper's, making it more prominent in American popular culture than the Lambshead Ranch, which has merely served as the setting for a successful series of television commercials. Now McMurtry is creating the world's largest used-book operation in Archer City. No wonder he is featured prominently and proudly on the town's website. He mentions in *Walter Benjamin* that his friend Susan Sontag has told him that he is living in his own theme park (a comment which may contribute to his sense of unreality). It is a mark of change in Texas that a town of just under 2,000, the county seat of a remote ranching area in West Texas, two hours from the Forth Worth/Dallas Metroplex, can become, in McMurtry's own terms, the King Ranch of the book industry.

The most clearly autobiographical of the works is *Walter Benjamin at the Dairy Queen: Reflections at Sixty and Beyond*. He says that it is not an autobiography but an exploration of his relationship to European writers (70), though he also says that understanding the emptiness of the West Texas landscape "is so important to my own self-understanding" (20). He seems to believe that the omission of his marriage and other love relationships keeps it out of the autobiography category: "Of mother, wives, lady loves, and *amitiés amoureuses*—well that's another book" (202). However, *Walter Benjamin at the Dairy Queen* provides a family saga, an account of his childhood and youth in a dysfunctional family, an assessment of his education, and a discussion of his two vocations, bookselling and writing. Jonathan Miles in *Salon* refers to the book as McMurtry's "first dip into the green fields of memoir."[3] One unique quality of this memoir is the author's exploration of the tension between reading and writing in his literary career. Most writers say something about the books they loved, but not about the dialectical tension in their lives between devotion to reading and devotion to writing. A writer must read but cannot write while doing so.

The form of the book is a set of four personal essays in the tradition established by Michel de Montaigne and extended by writers like Virginia Woolf. In the foreword to his brilliant collection of 1968, *In a Narrow Grave: Essays on Texas*, McMurtry speaks of the essay form as a kind of place for rumination (xvii), a good metaphor for a cattleman's son. A major influence on him is Virginia Woolf, whom he refers to as the "Blue Nile of Literature." (Marcel Proust, his other favorite writer, is the "White Nile.") Sometimes McMurtry's segues are not convincing, as when a description of the Rodeo Parade in the "Reading Section" intrudes into the narrative and is followed up by a commentary on the sexism implicit in "ladies' barrel racing." Jonathan Miles called it "a sometimes beautiful ragbag of a book."

The opening essay, "Place—and the Memory of Place," begins nonchalantly in 1980 with the narrator sitting in the Dairy Queen in Archer City on a day of record heat (116º) having a thoroughly Texas drink, a Dr Pepper. But the drink is completely parochial: It is a *lime* Dr Pepper, something unknown at the next Dairy Queen. A local vintage, so to speak, *vin de pays*: a little joke. McMurtry says in the book that his aim is to show his relationship to European culture through reading. Nothing could be less European than lime Dr Pepper. Nor is the Dairy Queen a site redolent of high culture: What could be less European than a franchise restaurant in an isolated town? This essay is clearly important to McMurtry; it originated almost twenty years before, and he discussed it with Patrick Bennett in an interview, "Thalia, Houston and Hollywood" in 1980:

> I'm still writing on that. It's right up there on the mantle. It's a long essay; it'll probably turn out to be a short book. I know I'm after something, but I'm not quite sure yet what. I suppose it's really an essay about storytelling and the way it has changed in the last hundred years. It takes off on a brilliant essay by Walter Benjamin and kind of applies the things he says to my own local experiences in Archer County. I'm not quite sure where that essay is going to end up. I don't think it will be magazine length, though. This is already a hundred pages and hasn't found its channel yet.[4]

The channel found twists and turns a little but the direction is clear. He moves from an inquiry into storytelling to a consideration of the way that place—the family ranch, the history of a ranching family in the place, and his own experiences ranching in that place—led him to a storytelling vocation of his own. One undercurrent is his realization that Archer County is his own *querencia*, to which he has returned after many years away in urban centers like Houston, Los Angeles, and Washington. Unlike Dobie and John Houghton Allen, he has found a way to remain in ranching country. They left their ranch homes to find intellectual stimulation, but in his sixties McMurtry has chosen to bring stimulation to Archer City.

He begins, then, with a scene of reading the German philosopher, Walter Benjamin, on a day so hot that Archer City had to cancel its first-ever marathon race, an unusual event for a town where the rodeo has always been the great diversion. The work he was reading on that day in 1980 was the great essay, "The Storyteller," discussed in chapter two of this study. McMurtry likes coincidences (like any good novelist), and he was struck by the date of the essay, 1936, the year of his own birth. Benjamin suggests that the art of oral storytelling is dying in our world and that the decline is linked with the falling value of experience. McMurtry is a novelist rather than a raconteur, but the essay is ominous for fiction writers as well, especially Texans in touch with the oral tradition. After reading the essay, McMurtry goes on a quest to find out if the storytelling traditions of his county are still alive. He starts with the Dairy Queen, the new meeting place for locals, the equivalent of the town square in William Humphrey's Clarksville or the courthouse in small county seats. In her book of photographs, *Watt Matthews of Lambshead*, Laura Wilson says of Albany: "In earlier times, the courthouse was the community center, but now the ubiquitous Dairy Queen has taken over as the town hangout, dispensing the day's news along with blizzards and burgers."[5] McMurtry thinks that the Dairy Queen could be his Amazon or Olduvai Gorge. In the 1960s, Mary Karr found the source of storytelling at her father's unofficial Liar's Club in the local American Legion bar.

In his youth McMurtry had heard adults on the ranch tell stories before the radio arrived with its static and its substitutes for the anecdote and yarn. But in 1980 he discovered that little of the oral tradition remained. People seemed to remember only a few incidents, like car crashes, which, along with the weather, are favorite topics in small towns. Sports events were preserved as well, but they were even vague about World War II. Ironically, McMurtry discovers for himself the insight of J. Frank Dobie, who said in "Storytellers I Have Known": "I do not believe any young man of parts could today set out to find storytellers and meet them on every hand as I met them between the World Wars. Instead of entertaining each other with tribal lays now, tribesmen listen to radio and look at television" (271).

Like Albany, Archer City has its own historical pageant, although it is not famous like the Fort Griffin Fandangle, and when McMurtry talked to its director, it transpired that the man was no Robert Nail: He was from Brooklyn and made his living directing county historical pageants all over the United States. McMurtry makes it clear that the Archer City event is a poor man's Fandangle, with the struggle of the Scotch-Irish frontiersman in the Indian Wars reduced to a few scuffles (100). The real preservation of Archer County is in McMurtry's novels, it seems.

McMurtry's quest to find a surviving tradition of storytelling in his native region is tied up with his feeling that European writers have culture while he has only geography. He broods over the shortness of the tradition in his region. Archer City is only about a hundred years old, and when he visits the local museum (housed, like Albany's museum, in the old jail), he sees mostly the detritus of farmhouses. This is an old complaint of American writers. In his book on Nathaniel Hawthorne, Henry James wrote a long list of "things absent in American life," including aristocracies, palaces and castles, public schools like Eton and Harrow—a long list. Certainly Proust's Paris has an impasto of culture which Archer City aka Thalia could never match. American writers of the hinterland often feel that, as Gertrude Stein said of Oakland, "there is no there there." In *Wolf Willow*, his memoir of a belated frontier in southern Saskatchewan, Wallace Stegner recalls telling a friend from London about the cultural desert he grew up in, a place with no Tate Gallery, no British Museum, no bookstores, and libraries. The friend remarked that perhaps there were advantages to coming from such an area: "Perhaps you got something else in place of all that."[6] Stegner, whose creative writing program at Stanford helped shape McMurtry as a writer, found ways to work with the very deprivations of the frontier experience, and the Texas novelist has also striven to write in a region which sometimes seemed empty of culture and history. Comedy is always possible, and Thalia is the muse of comedy.

Written stories have their own value, but something is lost when the tradition of oral storytelling fades away. The aim of the oral narrative is to give counsel, Benjamin says, to transmit wisdom. We have a world of information, tidal waves of it, and relatively little wisdom. A comment by Benjamin is particularly relevant: "By now almost nothing that happens benefits storytelling; almost everything benefits information." Most of the stories McMurtry heard in childhood were based on experiences of daily life. They did not have obvious morals directed at the growing child, but they covered lessons of experience: bad choices and good ones, misjudgments of neighbors, and family history. The radio had already penetrated the realm of the family, a harbinger of the devaluation of experience for information that television and the computer would bring about. McMurtry does not mention (but might have) the brilliant discussion of the media in Benjamin's *Illuminations* volume. The essay, entitled "The Work of Art in an Age of Mechanical Reproduction," considers the loss of experience which comes about because of devices like the movie camera. McMurtry makes a similar point when he observes that the movies about Archer City have confused inhabitants about what has happened in life rather than in the movies: "the whole area leaked into the films, as it had into the books" and some individuals have persuaded themselves that they were the models for the characters in *The Last Picture Show*. The author tells us that he is writing this book, unlike his twenty-two previous ones, with a pen, "because I don't want the sentences to slip by so quickly that I don't notice them. They need to be the work of the hand, eye, and ear" (35).

He presents his own family saga as a means of considering what kind of experience might be preserved in "west Texas," as he rather unusually spells it. His grandparents, William Jefferson and Louisa Francis McMurtry, came to Archer County in the 1870s, once the power of the Comanches and Kiowas had been broken. The grandmother had some Sioux blood (65). He tells us that her privations on the frontier were so great that McMurtry's father could never forget them. The ranching life that the family created for themselves was never lavish: They did not have enough land. One thing he learned about from his grandparents and other relatives was their hunger for land, typical of those who opened frontiers. The land the McMurtrys acquired was not nearly as profitable as the ranches on the Clear Fork established by the Reynolds and Matthews families a little southwest of Archer County. Most of the migrants in Archer County were the Scotch-Irish stock so numerous in the Anglo settling of Texas, but the McMurtrys were Scots. There was a German colony not far away at Windthorst. Texas used to be studded with German settlements, even formal colonies. The Germans were hardworking and prosperous, like the Germans the Beasleys knew in Coleman County, the people Gertrude admired for their orderly lives.

McMurtry's grandparents stopped at a place with a "fine seeping spring" and a hill which is as important to McMurtry's imagination as Hallie Stillwell's rock on the sand dune or Jewel Babb's hill at the tie house. "To this day if I attempt a rural setting I invariably reproduce the contours of the hill where I first walked" (46). McMurtry would likely be familiar with Stegner's idea in *Wolf Willow* that we are imprinted with our original landscape in the way that a newly hatched bird is imprinted with the image of the mother bird. McMurtry shares the same feeling about his own native soil. He eventually bought the home place and spent time there on that "customary, familial hill."

Along with the hill, he has been fascinated with the sky. The heavens in McMurtry's native region are magnificent, and he celebrates them in a manner similar to A. C. Greene in *A Personal Country*:

> In the West lifting up one's eyes to the heavens can be a wise thing, for much of the land is ugly. The beauty of the sky is redemptive; its beauty prompts us to forgive the land its cru-

> elty, its brutal power. Most farm and ranch people on the Great Plains are so accustomed to being victims of the skies that they can rarely find the time, or muster the detachment, just to sit on the porch and enjoy the skies for their beauty. "Lord, it's pretty here, on a summer night," one might say, watching a long, lingering many-toned afterglow, but the subtle grays that come with winter are seldom noted. (72)

The work of the rancher is not to contemplate the sky but to struggle with mesquite, drought, and the banks. McMurtry is very moving when he describes his father's struggle to make a go of the ranch in spite of antagonistic natural and economic forces.

The father realized that his son would not be taking over the ranch. The boy preferred reading to raising a prize calf. McMurtry manages in a self-mocking manner to convey his own experiences as a reluctant cowboy. He has some hilarious accounts of what terrified him on the ranch—not stampedes or bulls or rattlesnakes but trees and poultry. The muse of comedy seems to favor self-deprecation. When he was four years old he rode into a mesquite thicket on his pony and dislodged a yellow jacket nest, which left him reluctant to ride into brush. He was terrorized by a peacock kept by his grandmother (an attempt at elegant living common in West Texas) and by "hens, roosters, guineas, turkeys, game chickens" (61). A cousin left a box with nineteen "boys' books" at the ranch when McMurtry was six, and he discovered that the reading lessons he had taken at school could lead to pleasure, a private pleasure.

But ranching left him with a subject—the cowboy myth, which he manages to deconstruct and then to rebuild—and a metaphor for both of his vocations: herding books into stores and herding words into books. He has long been ambivalent about literal cowboys. His classic essay, "Take My Saddle from the Wall," was a fine examination not only of the myth but of the character of the cowboys he has known, including his father and his eight cowboy uncles. In *Walter Benjamin at the Dairy Queen* he goes over the cowboy myth several times, giving the book a repetitive air.

The myth, McMurtry concedes, is indestructible. William Humphrey, the other major novelist in modern Texas, tried to destroy a number of Texas myths, like the oil myth, the cowboy myth, and the myth of the Texas Revolution, and, as I show in my book on him, he was appalled to find that readers believed he was glorifying what he satirized.[7] McMurtry reveals much about his fiction in talking about his father's nostalgia for an open range which was closed before the father's birth. The open range lasted about twenty years and the railroads made trail drives uncompetitive. But McMurtry knew people who had experienced the Old West, like his grandparents. His uncle, Jeffrey Dobbs, saw Geronimo and Quanah Parker when they were held at Fort Sill, Oklahoma, a story worth preserving. The West is not without history.

Along with the hard work of ranching, McMurtry grew up in a dysfunctional family. His grandmother was a silent woman: He does not remember her ever addressing a word to him. His parents were locked in a hateful relationship dating from the moment when his grandmother slapped his mother in some minor dispute. The father, acutely aware of how much his mother had suffered, could not side with his wife. This tortured relationship, which collapsed after forty-four years, is one of the subjects of McMurtry's travel book/family narrative, *Paradise*.

The second essay in *Walter Benjamin*, "Reading," offers insights into McMurtry's growth as both a writer and reader, with some attention to the conflicts between the two activities: Reading is essential to a writer and yet cuts into the time needed to create. Another rancher turned writer, J. Frank Dobie, also devoted much care to describing what he had to read as a child and as a university student. Dobie had more books available at the start because his mother obtained that list of the ten best books for young people. After the McMurtry family moved into town from the ranch, they acquired a *World Book* and an anthology called *My Book House*. The son has some fine reflections on the difficulty in getting books in Archer City. He was not as desperate as William Owens, certainly, for a local drugstore put in a paperback rack where he could find Mickey Spillane, Kathleen Winsor (*Forever Amber*, a bodice-ripping historical romance), and Erskine Caldwell. At Rice University he met his first "great reader," Alan Dugald McKillop, a professor who influenced him in much the way that Albert Shipp Pegues at Southwestern University influenced J. Frank Dobie. The other great readers that McMurtry met over the years were Susan Sontag and Joe Alsop.

The initial discussion of early reading and the tutelary effect of "great readers" modulates into an overlong diatribe against television and the decline of the family dinner as an institution. He then reverts to the early reading theme in the second section of the "Reading" essay by talking about the enormous impact of *Don Quixote* on him as a child. His fellow novelist, William Humphrey, became a writer under the influence of the same work, which he found for five cents in Deep Ellum when he was fourteen.[7] McMurtry has a comic description of his childhood conception of himself as being Sancho Panza to the old family retainer, Jesse Brewer, an incompetent cowboy whose real job was to look after young Larry. A late frontier area like Archer County is so culturally deprived that McMurtry had no awareness that *Don Quixote* was an old book. He also had very little understanding of literary modernism when he went to Rice University, his self-acquired literary background being so spotty. Houston was, he says early in the book, "my first city, my Alexandria, my Paris, my Oxford" (66).

He also remembers the rich man in town, Will Taylor, who was the only other avid reader in Archer City. Taylor would sit in his study all night, by the evidence of his reading lamp, which McMurtry could see from his own bedroom. One day he was looking at the garbage in the gully behind Taylor's house, curious about what the rich would discard. He found a neat stack of discarded catalogs from Francis Edwards, Booksellers, of London. The antiquarian offerings made him aware of the "Aladdin's Cave" of books and contributed to his own choice of career as an antiquarian bookseller. With a craving for symbolic gestures, he naturally bought Taylor's house when he moved back permanently to Archer City. Another even more symbolic gesture was the decision to create an enormous used-book business in his hometown.

He does not neglect descriptions of his education as a writer in the Stanford Writing Program, which was named for Wallace Stegner. McMurtry was a member of the famous class of 1960-1961, which has produced, he says, seventy or eighty books. It included Ken Kesey, Peter Beagle, and the Australian Christopher Koch. McMurtry provides vivid reminiscences of Malcolm Cowley and Frank O'Connor, whose teaching styles were radically different. He also discusses his mixed attitude toward Jack Kerouac's *On the Road*, a book which has influenced not only his fiction but his own book of travel essays, *Roads*. He does miss the opportunity to discuss his complicated friendship with Ken Kesey, who took the hippie road to literature, notoriously dropping by to see McMurtry in Houston when driving to New York in a psychedelic bus, reversing the westward movement.

He eventually throws a surprise into the "Reading" section by discussing his heart operation. In his opening essay, he had one short section mentioning that one day he had hit a cow when driving home to the ranch. This was a week after Labor Day, 1991. He created foreshadowing with this hint: "I was driving a rented Lincoln, and the collision had interesting results—but I'll table that story for now, in the interest of getting back to the Dairy Queen. . . . (29). That laconic "interesting results" refers to the heart operation which cost him his ability to read for almost three years and nearly destroyed his writing career. He thought little of a routine collision with a cow in cattle country, but he developed a cough and felt poorly, which led him to stop off at his doctor when going to town to have the rented Lincoln's faulty air bag checked. He learned that he was having a heart attack and eventually had a quadruple bypass operation in 1991 at Johns Hopkins University in Baltimore.

The operation so changed his state of mind that he could not read for years, a deeply unsettling time. The trauma of the operation was involved with a metaphysical wound, so to speak: He wondered just where he was during the five hours that the heart-lung machine did his living for him. Was the continuity of his personality lost? A. C. Greene's book on his heart transplant discusses the "cardiac blues," a postoperative depression that actually affects heart-valve and bypass patients more often than transplant recipients. If the information flood in our time tends to swamp experience, the high-tech invasion of the body for medical purposes can be even more disturbing. McMurtry seems haunted by the fact that his heart was removed from his body and placed in coolant while machinery performed its functions. It is ironic that he has literally experienced the "death of the author" which Roland Barthes and Michel Foucault have proclaimed. In her influential manifesto, *Critical Practice*, Catherine Belsey says, "Jacques Lacan, Louis Althusser and Jacques Derrida have all from various positions questioned the humanist assumption that subjectivity, the individual mind or inner being, is the source of meaning and of action."[8] Having lost this source of meaning and action, McMurtry found that he could not read for almost three years, and his writing became flat and futile. He returns to this trauma in the memoirs which follow *Walter Benjamin*. Mary Karr's formulation of "Same Self" at the end of *Cherry* is an attempt to suggest that the self can change and yet maintain continuity. But McMurtry seems to find it difficult to feel any self at all. Whether we think of "fictions of self" or "metaphors of self," the autobiographer has to have some confidence in the enterprise of self-definition. So far no one seems to have created an autobiography as a portrait of the artist as decentered subject. McMurtry has come close, as his three books reveal, and he is not happy with what he has become: He has fought to regain his personality (his sense of himself in the old "liberal individual" manner condemned by some postmodernists). The three memoirs are haunted by the ghost of a former self. One reason that he seems reluctant to label these books autobiographies (while feeling it was important to write them) is doubtless his difficulty in feeling an integrity of the self. A review by Thomas Mallon in *The New York Times* complained that the author seems "detached not just about but from his own books."[9]

The third section of his book is an essay on his work as a book scout, his journeys to bookstores to find stock for Booked Up, the store he and Marcia Clark started in Washington, D.C. He prefers selling books to teaching as a second vocation because, as for many writers, he finds teaching is an activity too close to writing. Ranching is his metaphor for writing, while scouting is like exploration: He invokes the great scouts of the early West, including Black Beaver, a Delaware scout for Randolph Marcy who once "camped near our own seeping spring" (155). Besides describing his own career in an unusual occupation, he creates an elegy for the many independent bookstores which have died in recent years: Their names, locations, and stock have a kind of poetry. He has gathered books from twenty-two major stores for his enormous book operation in Archer City, a town now known in the book trade as McMurtryville. His quixotic attempt (Don Quixote, he reminds us, was a bibliophile) to turn Archer City into a book town like Britain's Hay-on-Wye has probably gotten more attention in print than his recent books: There are at least ten articles about his enterprise,[10] including one about his alleged feud with the owner of the Archer City Dairy Queen over a change in cooks. His goal is to place a million volumes in a town two hours from the metroplex of Dallas/Fort Worth.

The final essay, "The End of the Cowboy—The End of Fiction" has a *déjà vu* quality. It echoes sentiments in the opening essay about the decline of the actual cowboy and the durability of the cowboy myth. These ideas were explored more than thirty years ago more incisively in "Take My Saddle from the Wall: A Valediction," his essay in deconstructive family saga which was collected in *In a Narrow Grave*. But McMurtry has a special urgency in the recent essay. He is writing a valedictory to his father, who never quite succeeded as a rancher, and for his own work, which he fears may not endure. He remembers his father's pastoral dream, which foundered on debt, cattle not fit for West Texas (Mexican cattle used in South Texas would have prospered), and the endless struggle with mesquite. His father did not have the resources of the Lambshead Ranch to fight mesquite. His father's religion was grass, but the Bible says that flesh is grass. The Reynolds-Matthews clan eschewed mysticism: After all, they believed that ranching was the conversion of grass into beef cattle at a profit. As Joe B. Matthews, brother of Watt, used to say, "the best place for an old cow is in the bank." Perhaps the less successful rancher needs mysticism to survive.

There is a poignancy in McMurtry's fear that his own work will be impermanent. He ends his book with an amusing story about the transience of fame: Once he was a guest writer at the campus of a modest college in Texas in Uvalde, the hometown of John Nance Garner, the vice president who, McMurtry may know, defined the office as not being "worth a bucket of warm piss"—a good example of the Texas vernacular. McMurtry saw that the local motel had a sign on the marquee saying, "Welcome Larry McMurtry, Author of *Terms of Endearment*." That day he learned that he'd won the Pulitzer Prize for *Lonesome Dove*. But when he next saw the marquee, on his way to a press conference, the sign read "Lunch Special, Catfish: $3.95" (203). Thalia, the muse of comedy, has not deserted him.

One of the finest tributes to this "ragbag" of a book comes from a thoroughly metropolitan source, *Partisan Review*. At the end of a long article on Benjamin, Noah Isenberg praises McMurtry's book as "an elegant memoir which employs Benjamin as means of opening up larger questions about autobiography, storytelling, memory, and the cultural significance of fiction." Isenberg suggests that McMurtry's book is an important step in the reception of Benjamin and thinks that the new collected works of the German scholar in English "will produce yet another generation of Benjamin scholars and readers, maybe even some at the local Dairy Queen."[11]

There have been few kind words for the latest McMurtry nonautobiographies, *Roads* and *Paradise*. In the first book, McMurtry describes a series of long highway drives through America. He deliberately shunned the interesting backroads and stuck to the major highways. In *Walter Benjamin*, he suggested that his compulsive highway driving was an atavistic reflection of the trail-driving instinct. In this book, he compares the interstates to the great rivers. In the preface to *Roads*, he admits that he will not be exploring his personality, which he does not find interesting. He also says with some regret that he lacks what so many travel writers possessed: a delightful companion to add human drama. Nor does he concern himself with talking to people on the way or stopping at major attractions unless it is convenient. The preface carries his habit of self-deprecation too far. The chapter titles, generally like "January The 35 from Duluth to Oklahoma City," are as flat as could be imagined, and the contents are often flat as well.

Nevertheless, the book offers occasional insights into McMurtry, his past, and his fictional characters. He discusses the McMurtry family photograph from the first reunion in 1918, a striking picture which can be found on the inside flap of the *Walter Benjamin* book. He has some scathing comments on the role of the Border Patrol and Texas Rangers when he stops off in Laredo (52-54). His comments on the Lambshead Ranch when he drives by are rather disappointing. Readers of *Interwoven* may not agree that Sally Reynolds Matthews "passes rather lightly over the dangers of the early years of the Clear Fork of the Brazos, though the dangers were real, frequent and often desperate" (58). He likes to discuss places where some of his characters lived or died in Texas. The drive through Los Angeles inspires some very good pages on his dealings with the studios: No one interested in McMurtry's Hollywood career would want to miss those revelations. And his ambivalence toward Washington, D.C., makes fine reading.

The drive through Baltimore leads him to think of his heart operation and the loss of personality which followed it. "Some years back, as the result of heart surgery performed in the great hospital, I inadvertently left a self there—my first self, one that I was mostly comfortable with for fifty-five years" (75). He illustrates the loss of self by describing a day when he inspected the remarkable collection of books up for sale by Jeane Dixon, a clairvoyant who had some years of fame for her prophecies and her connections with celebrities. He found himself unable to take any interest in the books.

The really first-rate essay in the book, "Short Roads to a Deep Place" (a title which may parody Basho's famous *Narrow Road to the Deep North*), has been praised by reviewers like Michiko

Kakutani in *The New York Times.*[12] She complains about the curiously perfunctory tone of the book but sees eloquence in this essay: "the hasty travel chat of the book's earlier portions gives way to something deeper and more moving." The piece is a nostalgic but precise examination of the dirt roads around the McMurtry ranch. He recalls riding with his grandfather to town twice a week to pick up the mail. It would take a half morning: The pace of life has changed immensely, as he documents in the essay. This familiar essay is one of his best; he mixes tones and changes subjects with complete confidence. "Though now, ambitiously, I might take all America as my province, the road that has meant most to me is the sixteen-mile stretch of dirt road that I drive from our ranch house to town" (184). The piece is his best elegy for his father, better than the more sententious comments in the final essay of *Walter Benjamin at the Dairy Queen.* The narrator explores the contrast between his own travels and his father's very circumscribed world, and he even manages a good rattlesnake story. Another *New York Times* commentator, Timothy Foote, complains that the book as a whole is "mostly a jumble of enigmatic glimpses at the Western past, present cultural gossip and now and then a literary perception, offered at flashcard speed by an omnivorous reader,"[13] but he too responds to the dirt road chapter, where McMurtry slows down at last. Foote sees the book as "some kind of therapy," which is an astute observation.

The most recent book, *Paradise*, is surely the weakest of the three, though it has some of the most detailed history of McMurtry's dysfunctional family. He set off on a trip to the South Seas, Tahiti followed by a cruise to the Marquesas. His mother, aged ninety and long widowed, was in a decline at the time. He claims that he wanted to visit the Tahitians "in order to think about my parents, Hazel and Jeff McMurtry" (16) in a place radically different from Archer County, Texas. The Tahitians were said by early anthropologists to be without neuroses, another contrast with his parents. The premises of the book—that an earthly paradise is a good place to contrast with West Texas and that his unhappy parents would contrast well with the Tahitians—seem dubious. The opening section, "My Parents and Polynesia," alternates discussions of the Tahitians with scenes from a marriage, a bitter one. We learn much about the parents, but the approach is analytical and abstract, not dramatic. The scenes do not offer the horror of Gertrude Beasley's family, the passionate angers of Humphrey's increasingly estranged parents, or the sizzling energy of quarrels in Mary Karr's family. We learn that the mother liked to travel, though not far, and the father did not, that in-law tensions (that slap in the kitchen from Louisa Francis) undermined the marriage, and so on. The most interesting scene is Hazel McMurtry's revelation to her son when he went off to Rice University in 1954: She told him that she had been married and divorced before marrying Jeff. With some confusion, she told him he should know lest he find out on his own and suspect that Jeff was not his father, something most unlikely, as his parents were married two years after the divorce. Her sense of shame shows that even in the 1930s—twenty-five years or more after the Beasley parents parted—a divorce was something many people considered disgraceful. McMurtry regrets that an odd sense of respectability kept his parents together as if a divorce would destroy them in the eyes of the few friends who were still alive.

But mostly the book talks about the unhappiness of the family rather than dramatizing it. And the second part is a very routine travel diary about the trip to the Marquesas detailing predictable encounters with people on shipboard. He does conclude with a strong description of his mother's death just after his return to the United States. In her *Houston Chronicle* review, Barbara Liss calls it a tossed-off book and wonders if "the family-memoir-cum-travelogue is the form which most appeals to him."[14] McMurtry has provided some material for a future biographer, but the book hardly succeeds at making his family or the South Seas interesting. Perhaps the author will eventually resolve to write a full account of his life, one which will bring together his origins, his education, his vocations—not to mention his marriage and lady loves. So far he has managed to discuss everything except the love relationships. He has preserved much of the world he grew up in, and at the same time has proved that there is at least one superb storyteller having lime Dr Peppers at the Archer City Dairy Queen.

Pat Mora

Ray Gonzalez

Gloria López-Stafford

11

FROM THE BORDERLANDS: PAT MORA, GLORIA LÓPEZ-STAFFORD, AND RAY GONZALEZ

El Paso is a unique Texas community along a highly permeable border. Gloria López-Stafford's *A Place in El Paso* and Pat Mora's *House of Houses* are complementary works which give a full picture of Chicano family life and the survival of

Mexican customs in an Anglo world which was not very receptive to cultural and racial differences. López-Stafford spent her early years in the Segundo Barrio in south El Paso, while Mora had a comparatively middle-class upbringing on the north side of the city. Although Ray Gonzalez has not written a full autobiography, a number of his essays in *Memory Fever: Beyond El Paso del Norte* supplement Mora and López-Stafford from the perspective of someone who spent formative years in a suburb in northwest El Paso. In these memoirists, as in other Chicano writers such as San Antonio's John Phillip Santos, a people found its voice: It would not be necessary for the paternalistic John Houghton Allen to speak for the Mexican inhabitants of the Southwest.

Texas has a remarkably long border with Mexico. And of course it was once part of that country. Gloria Anzaldúa, the poet and theorist from South Texas, astutely comments on borders and borderlands, calling the American-Mexican border an open wound, "*una herida abierta* where the Third World grates against the first and bleeds."[1] She distinguishes between the border per se and a borderland: "Borders are set up to define the places that are safe and unsafe, to distinguish *us* from *them*. A border is a dividing line, a narrow strip along a steep edge" whereas "a borderland is a vague and undetermined place created by the emotional residue of an unnatural boundary. It is in a constant state of transition" (3). The Chicano theorist, José David Saldívar, calls the two-thousand-mile border a "*Transfrontera* contact zone," which he defines with a surplus of jargon: "This zone is the space of subaltern encounters, the Janus-faced border line in which peoples geopolitically forced to separate themselves now negotiate with one another and manufacture new relations, hybrid cultures, and multiple-voiced aesthetics."[2] Pat Mora and Gloria López-Stafford are excellent examples of individuals who have negotiated new relationships for themselves and achieved a multiple-voiced mode of expression, an English enriched by *dichos* (proverbs) and Spanish expressions.

El Paso, unlike so much of Texas, cannot be considered an extension of the American South. It is more a southwestern city. It is common to speak of the "metro area" of Juarez and El Paso which the municipal government estimates at 2,456,820 people, with only 734,900 of them living in El Paso.[3] The largest ethnic group is classified as Hispanic, with twice as many inhabitants as the Anglo population. Pat Mora entitles her collection of essays *Nepantla: Essays from the Land in the Middle*,[4] using a Nahuatl word which meant "land in the middle." She says in an interview, "Listening to the Desert," that she is grateful for "living in a city where I could see Mexico, the country of my grandparents."[5] She and other Chicano/a writers have lived very much in the middle.

Mexicans inhabited Texas, including El Paso, long before the first Anglos arrived, but the region has had an enormous influx of migrants from Mexico, and the families of these writers were part of that relocation. The most extensive study of Mexican immigration is Mario T. García's *Desert Immigrants: The Mexicans of El Paso, 1880-1920*,[6] a work which documents the social setting which the memoirists know by direct experience or family tradition. It is symptomatic of the Anglo attitudes of the early twentieth century that the first history of El Paso, the boosterish account by Owen P. White,[7] mentions the Mexican population of El Paso only twice and in passing. But that population has its own stories to tell as much as the British stock who created the farms and ranches of Anglo Texas. Gloria López-Stafford's story is highly personal and limited to her immediate family and godparents, while Pat Mora creates a family saga as well as a narrative of childhood.

A number of economic and historical forces brought a large immigrant population into the area. Cheap labor was needed for the railroads and the enormous smelting industry, which began in 1887 with lead and silver ore from Mexico. According to Mario García, in 1906, 1,997 Mexican immigrants arrived in the United States from Mexico. The Mexican revolution and civil war, which began in 1910, increased the numbers dramatically: Legal immigration totals for 1912 were 23, 238. In November 1913, Pancho Villa's army attacked Juarez. Among those who fled that year were Pat Mora's maternal grandfather and his daughters, all of them crossing the cold waters of the Rio Grande in a rickety old carriage, a *guayín*. Three years later, during another crisis in the civil war, her paternal grandparents left the city of Chihuahua and entered El Paso from Juárez, by bridge rather than by fording the river in a carriage. Ray Gonzalez's maternal grandfather, Bonifacio Canales, took part in the battle of Juarez as an unwilling Villa conscript of fourteen. After the battle, he and his wife, Julia, who was also fourteen, fled to the United States.

Pat Mora (1942-), a popular children's writer, is the most anthologized Mexican-American writer in the United States. Among her literary awards are the Pellicer-Frost Bi-national Poetry Award, four Southwest Book Awards, and the Premio Aztlán Literature Award. Her memoir exemplifies Paul John Eakin's concept of the "relational life." If we are social beings, with an identity formed in relation to others, in dialogue with others, then it makes sense to define ourselves in autobiography through relationships. Mora's warm work about her extended family—paternal Moras and maternal Delgados—provides such a definition. Like Tristram Shandy, she gets herself born fairly late in the narrative, which is made up of her memories and the stories she got from her parents and her collateral relatives, like her aunts, Lobo and Chole, and her uncle Lalo. Her book contrasts with the best-known (and most controversial) Chicano autobiography, Richard Rodriguez's *Hunger of Memory*,[8] which describes Rodriguez's estrangement from his language and culture. Mora is trying to reconstitute and preserve, for herself and also for three grown children, who are often present when relatives tell family stories. Mora told me in an E-mail questionnaire (November 30, 2000) that she was not trying to respond to Rodriguez. The questionnaire will be referred to several times in this chapter.

In a subsequent E-mail (December 1, 2000) she listed a number of books which she read before starting to write:

> I glanced at some of the memoirs/autobiographies I had on the shelf before I started to write: [Ved] Mehta's *Mamaji,* [Eva] Hoffman's *Lost in Translation* (an absolutely wonderful book), [Jill Ker] Conway's *The Road from Coorain,* [Annie] Dillard's *An American Childhood,* [Michael] Ignatieff's *The*

> *Russian Album.* I'm not sure when I read the first two but think I read the last three in preparing for *House.* Conway reminded me of the importance of conveying geography and Ignatieff of the importance of details, describing clothes for example, their textures.

Ignatieff is just the sort of intergenerational, crosscultural memoirist: His family migrated from Russia to Canada. Hoffman explores immigration (from Poland to Canada and the United States) and "linguistic dispossession." Mehta is another writer who has moved from one culture to another, in his case from New Delhi to the United States. None of these writers is an overwhelming influence on Mora; her reading of them shows her interest in understanding the genre of autobiography. In the one fairly extensive essay on Mora's book, a review article in *Aztlán*, Hector A. Torres suggests that Isabel Allende's novel, *House of the Spirits,* with its multigenerational scope and abundance of ghosts, may be an influence as well: "As in Allende's novel, so in Mora's, the spirits of the dead continue to commune with the living."[9]

The most obvious formal feature of *House of Houses* is the division of the book into chapters with evocative titles. The first, to the prologue, reads: "House of Houses *Ut rosa flos florum, sic est domus ista domorum.* As the rose is the flower of flowers, so is this the house of houses." The remaining chapters go through the calendar year, with the months given in English and Spanish, beginning with "Enero friolero/Chilly January." Most of the titles are followed by Spanish proverbs, like the one for October: "*La que anda entre la miel, algo se le pega.* Honey clings if you're surrounded by it." The proverbs in the titles and in the text (there is a glossary of proverbs, *dichos,* at the end with translations) emphasize the reality of a folk culture in Mexican-American life. Gloria López-Stafford's book also abounds in *dichos.*

Another aspect of folk tradition in the work is the exploration of holidays and the saints associated with them. Great care is given to describing the flowers associated with a month. It would be possible to compile a concise version of the liturgical calendar and a herbarium from Mora's book. Some of the flowers have folk associations—like their use as remedies or tisanes, lists of which appear in the book. She points out that an enclosed garden is both a private and a communal space. The affirmation of the seasons, like the celebrations of the desert landscape in the book, suggests that it is possible to live harmoniously in the world. She values the desert and the garden equally. Mora's poems have often dealt with the desert and flowers. This book is no exception: "The world's flora nourish, inspire, intoxicate. Rich sources of mystery, magic and mythology; they flavor our dishes, beautify our rooms, soothe our aches, scent our beds, decorate our bodies and altars, perfume our paths and poems; these green lifeforms that rise from the dark tangle of underground life, like our subconscious, fertile and full of promise." (8) Mora's vision is an ecological one, a translation of the traditional love of landscape of a Hallie Stillwell into an awareness of the interrelationship of living beings with themselves and the environment.

Even more important than the evocation of landscape, which is a traditional literary device, is the innovative use of the imaginary house, an ideal southwestern-style house in the desert, in the Rio Grande Valley. The natural setting helps to put human life in perspective, and Mora evokes the geological ages which have gone into making the mountains and desert, and the abundance of plant and animal life that the land supports (45). Her first foreshadowing of the house in the memoir comes in a poem from *Communion*, "My Word-house,"[10] which describes an idealized house in the desert that grows out of the natural setting and is open to anyone who wishes to enter. In this poem, the house seems to represent her poetry itself, which serves as an idealized space for summoning up people and events from the past. It is the house where family bread is always rising, old women teach children to dance, and children wash the feet of the old women (86-87). The house in her autobiography is also a mental construction, on one level her book itself. It is a place where the narrator can meet with all her relatives, including the ones who have died and are now transparent spirits, even the ones she never met but who are preserved in family traditions. They can meet each other: Two great-great-grandmothers who never knew each other trade recipes, while Mora's grown children learn adobe brick-making with the assistance of an ancestor who died long before they were born (96). Further, the English and Spanish, Anglo and Chicano elements in their lives can be reconciled in family celebrations. The house, like the human body as conceived of in the Bible, is described as having a skin of clay, of adobe. Clay, of course, is the substance from which the human race is generated in the biblical creation. The house has a traditional Spanish design, which comes down from Spain and beyond that from the Arab world and, ultimately, Persia, with an inner courtyard containing flowers and a fountain. Early on she quotes Gaston Bachelard's phrase from *The Poetics of Space*,[11] "protected intimacy."

In life, intimacy involves conflict, even in the happiest of families. Mora shows flashes of residual conflict between people who had hostility between them in life, but the emphasis is on harmony, with the writer's mind as mediator. After all, the space of the house is her field of understanding and reconciliation. Conflict is not ignored, because it emerges in some of the stories that characters tell. It is always mediated in the scenes in the house: This is Mora's work of imaginative reconciliation. She tells her dead father Raúl that she is writing a book about the family, and the book itself is a space to "house the spirits I gather, living and dead" (3). And of course, "house" is a trope for family, though it is usually applied to royalty.

The premise of a house where all generations meet is a fantasy but attempts to link the *House of Houses* with magic realism, as Hector Torres and other reviewers have tried to do, are misguided. Her publisher used the term on the dust jacket of *House of Houses*, but moments of fantasy are few. Her father seems to turn into a tree on one occasion, into a bird on another. In one charming scene on St. Rafael's Day, September 29, the archangel himself shows up for the celebration (along with the Virgin of Guadalupe, Mexico's patron saint, and the Christ Child). She responded to the inquiry about magic realism in my questionnaire: "This wasn't a term I applied to my work. It's a trendy term that suggests the lush inventiveness of Latin American writing, the presence of spirits. I feel that I'm describing my reality and am not sure if the label 'magical' makes that reality less concrete." Behind the imaginary houses is the image of the stone house at 704 Mesita where she spent her childhood: Twice she calls it the "house of houses." Bachelard suggests that the original house of childhood is the source of dreams, for it was the place where daydreams began. He maintains that "there exists for each of us an oneiric house, a house of dream-memory. . ."[12] Mora's house of spirits rests on reverie rather than magic.

The favorite form of narrative time in the book is the present tense, which is appropriate for a house in which past and present, living and dead, mingle. When I queried Mora about this tense, she said in an E-mail: "I'm very fond of the present tense and the immediacy it creates. In my children's books also I often begin with it for a first draft. For HOUSE, it seemed particularly important since I was hoping to eliminate time as a dimension that created an impediment to communication"(November 30, 2000). The use of a seasonal pattern frees her from too much dependence on chronology. Some events can be discussed in the context of months appropriate to them, not in strict chronological sequence. Hector A. Torres points out that she begins with the family past: "Chapters 1 through 3, January through March, are a genealogical exposition of how the Delgado and Mora families became Texas-México borderlanders,"[13] but these chapters tell the story of each family separately, Delgados first, which makes a strict chronological order impossible. When the generation-spanning stories of two different families are explored, a year-by-year chronology would be forced. Juxtapositions of events occurring generations apart become possible when the narrative is set in a kind of eternity. Past and present are dealt with using holy days and seasonal changes as markers, often through chains of association rather than temporal development, though broad movements spanning months occur. The story moves toward the present in a roughly linear way.

Through allusions to the church calendar she unites time and eternity, history and the ideal. The climax of the work is the

November section, with its use of the Day of the Dead as a way of uniting the generations in a celebration on All Souls' Day. December, dealing with a celebration of Christmas, offers a joyful ending, an affirmation of life and the family. She affirms the value of family ties and her Catholic heritage by alluding to her use of Aunt Loba's missal to work out details of the church year and saints' days. The missal unites time and eternity.

The house is set in a context of earth, sky, and spiritual presences. Bachelard's *The Poetics of Space* emphasizes our feelings of intimacy and shelter in domestic areas. The house is our "topography of intimate being" and it produces "felicitous space, eulogized space."[14] He rejects, without naming him, the claim of the early Martin Heidegger that we are "cast into the world." But Heidegger later modified his views and discussed the ways that we build on the earth, and the German philosopher's ideas illuminate Mora's project in *House of Houses*. In his essay, "Building Dwelling Thinking," Heidegger suggests that true dwelling requires care for the earth, a willingness to protect and preserve. "Mortals dwell as they save the earth. . . ."[15] Mora's book is particularly mindful of the need to preserve the earth. In "Conserving Natural and Cultural Diversity: The Poetry and Prose of Pat Mora," Patrick D. Murphy has explored the ecological awareness in some of Mora's other works.[16] In *House* the awareness is intense. Mamá Cleta, who shows constant awareness of plants, and Abuelo Gregorio, who says good night to the trees, are exemplars of that caretaking activity.

Dwelling, Heidegger says, requires a reverence for the ways that the fourfold realms of being unfold: the earth, the sky, the mortals, and the deities who represent the godhead. Human beings enact their protective vocation "in saving the earth, in receiving the sky, in awaiting divinities, in initiating mortals." In her "Listening to the Desert" interview with Darwin Henderson, Mora says of the desert: "All kinds of spirits dance on it; the wind dances on it, and the light dances on it."[17] Mora celebrates the earth and sky. She is particularly strong in her descriptions of the sky, something she shares with López-Stafford, who also celebrates the sky of El Paso. Mora also sees the interplay of earth and sky through the symbol of light in a passage from *House of Houses* about the Feast of the Epiphany: "In this land, light descends from above but also rises from the land, *la tierra madre*, reflecting its old bones. When the sun rises over the mountain to the East and pours its light over our heads, a daily grace, the braiding of light from land and sky pours into us, filling us, raising us to greet the day. When I leave this landscape, this light, I feel slighter, diminished"(18).

The divine is represented by the saints whose holy days are described repeatedly. The feast days are a way of anticipating the sacred. When San Rafael, the Virgin of Guadalupe, and the Christ Child come for their visit, they are served a kind of Mexican sacrament of *café con leche* and *pan dulce*. San Rafael leaves a feather behind. His name means "God heals," and his appearance is natural enough in a book which emphasizes peace and harmony. The realm of mortals, whose distinctive quality, according to Heidegger, is their initiation into death, is represented by all the people of the house. Death is a constant subject, and the communion with the dead which plays a large part in the work is not a denial of death but an affirmation of its profound meaning. Mora implies that we can commune with the dead through rituals (like the *Día de los Muertos* which she describes) and memory, but she does not deny that power of death. She presents us with an ideal of life on the earth, one in which proper reverence is felt for earth, sky, and the realm of the spirit, and the dealings of human beings with one another are brought into a state of understanding and commemoration, a harmony of the living and the dead which does not deny suffering and death. As Murphy says, she wants to preserve cultural diversity as well as biological diversity, and her book is genuinely multicultural, with her husband and mixed-culture children adding an Anglo dimension to the house.

The mysterious Mamá Cleta, Mora's paternal great-grandmother (Anacleta Manquera), is the quiet but numinous spirit of the house. A devoted gardener, she is completely attuned to nature and "listens to the secret life of spiders, to beetles burrowing, pods swaying in the trees." Her perception of nature is synaesthetic:

"She touches the yellow columbine, hears its clear soprano melody" (139). Early in the book she complains that the scent of her violets no longer tastes "like round circles," an image combining odor, perceptible shape, taste, and the sense of touch, a complaint which expresses the loss of a unifying perception of the world (59). Synaesthesia is, as Lawrence E. Marks has demonstrated in *The Unity of the Senses*,[18] at the roots of metaphor and suggests a unified view of the reality. Charles Baudelaire, the modern poet most preoccupied with synaesthesia, used it to suggest the unity of nature (228-229), Marks says, a way of conveying that the world is a network of correspondences. In the December chapter, Mamá Cleta reads a prayer for the feast day (December 12) on the patron saint of Mexico, the Virgin of Guadalupe. The Virgin appeared to a shepherd, who brought the viceroy a mantle full of roses in the middle of winter. The mantle bore an image of the Virgin on the side which wrapped the roses. Mamá Cleta says, to everyone's puzzlement, that the roses "tasted round," an image which suggests wholeness in its shape (274).

Mamá Cleta represents a traditional but unforced Catholic piety, exhorting Mora to plant flowers that have religious names: "hers a religious rather than scientific taxonomy" (9). She is full of traditional wisdom, herbs, and proverbs. She has something of the Angel in the House about her, naturally, coming as she does from an earlier society. I suggested to Mora in an E-mail that "earth mother" has the wrong connotations, and she agreed:

> Oh I'm just delighted that you're fond of Mamá Cleta. Since we know little if anything about her, she's the character that provided a totally free range. I'm intrigued by synesthesia and loved giving her that condition, a bit "abuzz" with the senses. I agree that "earth mother" may not be quite right. There's a softness to the term that I don't associate with her. I see her as very erect, independent, resilient, determined. Let me see if a term comes to mind. (November 30, 2000)

Certainly this figure embodies the best qualities of traditional womanhood in Catholic-Spanish terms. She also suggests that common figure in Chicano writing: the curandera, the healer, and her male counterpart, the curandero. Mora has an essay on "Poet as *Curandera*" in *Nepantla*.[19] She suggests that the poet and the herbal doctor can perpetuate traditions and explore attunement with nature. In her essay, "Tradition and Mythology: Signatures of Landscape in Chicana Literature," Tey Diana Rebolledo examines Mora's poem, "Curandera," and suggests that the curandera in Chicano writing is "the repository of past learning, of history. She is also an integral part of the utopic pastoral tradition so strongly evident in Hispanic literature."[20] There is no similar figure in English literature.

Traditional folk medicine may meet resistance from contemporaries: Mora provides a scene in which one of her daughters is under stress from "papers, cases, meetings." Mamá Cleta wants to offer her traditional therapies like a poultice of violets for her feet and a compress of rose petals heated with mint. The young woman responds: "Tell them I don't have time for this stuff, Mom. I don't mean to be rude, but I've got to finish these papers and try to sleep. How do I say I'm sorry in Spanish? Oh to be five again. Those were the days" (59). The scene is imaginary but suggests the complexities of mixing modern and traditional cultures.

The problem of the survival of Spanish is touched on obliquely in this passage. Later we learn that the older inhabitants of the house would like for the young people to speak more Spanish. As the language declines, the culture is likely to decline as well. Mora's work tries to preserve some of the practices which came down from Mexico, like herbal remedies and the use of tisanes (*gordolobo*, *manzanilla*, *canela*, among others—mullein, chamomile, and cinnamon) and folkways like the custom of covering mirrors in a storm because mirrors attract lightning, or making the sign of the cross to drive off bad weather.

Perhaps the most important custom in *House of Houses* is the *Día de los Muertos*, a three-day celebration culminating on November 2, All Souls' Day. The festival begins October 31, though the big events are the commemoration of dead infants on November 1, All

Saints' Day, and the commemoration of the dead in general on November 2, All Souls' Day. The really central day is November 2. The Mexican custom is to go to the cemetery that day, clean the plots and gravestones, and have a picnic. William Humphrey describes a similar southern practice (Graveyard Decoration Day) in two of his novels, *Home from the Hill* and *The Ordways*. The Mexican custom celebrates death in a startling way which goes beyond southern Anglo culture: Children are given candies shaped like skulls or skeletons, and altars are built on graves with offerings of candy and *pan de muerto*, a sweet bread. In "Love Ritual," from her first book, *Chants*, Mora describes the luring of the dead back to a junction with the living: The lures include candles and marigolds, cigarettes and tequila.[21] In an essay about her Aunt Lobo in *Nepantla*, Mora suggests that the purpose of the day, which meant so much to her aunt, was to affirm that "family ties are so strong that not even death can sever them."[22] In *House of Houses*, the "*Noviembre*/November" section is a kind of *Día de los Muertos* with anecdotes of the dead and ghost stories, like the tale of the Indian servant, Dolores, who prankishly covered herself with masa flour and phosphorus to make a very convincing ghost to terrify Lobo and her siblings. Images of light in darkness run through the chapter, most of them more solemn than the story of Dolores glowing in the dark.

The celebration of the Day of the Dead in *House of Houses* has an optimistic tone. We begin with Lobo's story of the time in Mexico when her sister Adelina was thought to be dead, pronounced so by the doctor. Her godfather could not believe that the child had died, so he took a glass of warm water sweetened with sugar and began sprinkling drops on her mouth. She revived. The inhabitants of the house hold a ceremony with marigolds sprinkled on tiered altars that hold *pan de muerto* in such shapes as skulls and bones, and candies shaped like little skulls. Objects likely to lure the spirits of all the deceased members of the family will be placed on the altars: modern items like Bayer aspirin and Big Hunk candy bars as well as mezcal and dried chiles. The most significant is an object for her paternal grandmother, a cassette playing a thoroughly Mexican song, "Cielito Lindo": "*Ay, ay, ay, ay, canta y no llores.*" (270), an invocation to sing rather than cry. And the celebration of the day ends with the launching of votive candles in foil boats down the Rio Grande to commemorate all the dead members of the family. The familial relationship of the living and the dead is affirmed, fittingly enough with a ceremony in which the river that separates/joins two countries and cultures becomes a kind of River Styx. As participants walk back to the house, a final scene commemorates the union of nature and humanity. Mora's son, Bill, sees the most distant Mora ancestor, Gregorio, on his nightly round of speaking to the trees (271). When Bill asks him what he is doing, Gregorio strokes his cheek and says, "*Diciéndoles buenas noches a las almas ancienas de estos arbolotes, hijito.*" While Bill's Spanish may be shaky, his question makes it clear that something of the language has been transmitted: "Did he say he's saying good-night to the old souls of these huge trees?" Indeed, that is what Gregorio said.

The symbolic structure is interesting in itself, with the counterpoint of the calendar year and the festivals of the liturgical year. However, the substance of most of the work is family history. In fact, the conversations that Mora has with her relatives about the earlier periods of the history are an attempt to construct a family saga, to record significant events, most of which, in Boatright's terms, have a social value, though it is not always made explicit. The Moras and Delgados have histories in Mexico which are roughly parallel in the beginning, and they intersect with the marriage of Mora's parents. The family narratives explore life in Mexico, the flight to the United States, the history of the Mora-Delgado marriage, and the childhood and youth of Mora herself.

A favorite subject for family sagas is the account of how the family came to the place where they live, particularly if the circumstances were dramatic. Emigration during a revolution is dramatic enough. The sources for these stories are the favorite aunts of the narrator: Aunt Lobo on the maternal side, the family which came first; and Aunt Chole on the paternal side. Lobo's full name is

Ignacia Delgado, known in childhood as Nacha, then renamed "Lobo," or "wolf," by her nieces (Patricia, Cecilia, and Stella) and nephew (Roy), because she used to call them her "lobitos" or little wolves.

Lobo is one of the best-drawn characters in the book, strong willed, immensely generous, with an aversion to men and sex. Mora has her tell the story of her childhood. She was the daughter of a judge in a mining district in Chihuahua. Mora uses her to narrate the journey the family had to make into the mountains where the father went to settle an estate case in Ocampo. The journey had a strangeness that grows naturally out of the exotic locale and the child's eye view: No magic realism is needed. The journey was by mules on steep trails, with a pregnant mother along and the two smallest children in panniers on one mule. We are promised that the story will culminate in a scream, and Mora delivers it: When they reached the guest house, the mother entered the bedroom and saw a snake curled up on the white bedspread. A harmless snake, it turned out. The trip was a disaster, for the father was stung by a parasitic insect and spent eight months in a fever. Fearing that he would die in the bleak mountain country, he insisted he be taken to lower altitudes. He recovered; and the lesson that Mora draws from this part of the family saga involves the profound tie between health and a beloved landscape.

The narrative of the flight to El Paso in a rickety carriage follows, emphasizing timeliness—the judge had to be implored to leave by an almost archetypal figure, a resourceful servant woman—and the value of a good reputation, as the family was saved when someone recognized him at the river and offered assistance. The family's first refuge was a house on Second Street, in the district known at the time as Chihuahuita, or Little Chihuahua, so named from the Mexican state bordering on El Paso. The house had forty-six people living it. The early years in El Paso were difficult, especially for the judge, who knew no English. He had a large interest in a silver mine, La Minerva, but he was forced to sell it for less than half its value to a man who had influence with Pancho Villa and could have taken it all. One of the functions of a family saga, Boatright points out, is to explain the failure of a family to have wealth. In Texas, worldly success is particularly esteemed—so many have become wealthy. Mora also tells the story of her grandmother's lost inheritance, a sum left to her by her Basque sea-captain father. Judge Delgado insisted that the money be sent from Spain to his brother in Mexico City, who would know how to take care of the matter. But the brother-in-law claimed that the money never arrived: This bit of the family saga has a feminist point.

The family lived in El Paso for reasons of safety, while the father continued to practice law in Juárez. Lobo recalls that immigration officials made the poor crossing from Mexico bathe in gasoline as a disinfectant. A Mr. Calisher treated all Mexicans who shopped in his store as thieves. The store burned down one night, and when he opened another he called it "Everybody," an apparent change of heart. The Calisher incident was treated in Mora's poem about immigration from *Chants*, "1910," in which the store owner's name is given as Upton.[24]

In 1917 Lobo went off to work at the Popular Dry Goods Store, whose owner believed that Mexican women could work for less because their standard of living was low. She remained an employee for forty-five years. The book assumes that family traditions are established and tested through dialogue. As Lobo tells the story of the flight to the United States, two of Mora's listening children object to their great-aunt's politics, criticizing the older generation's support of the dictator, Porfirio Díaz, and their opposition to Pancho Villa, who was, after all, something of a popular hero. For Lobo, Villa was a murderer and robber. She did not romanticize his soldiers as John Houghton Allen does so luridly in *Southwest*.

As an eyewitness, Lobo could tell the story of the judge's remarriage to Pat Mora's grandmother, Amelia. We get some perspective on the beloved aunt via Estela, Mora's mother, who told her daughter that Amelia suffered from conflicts with Lobo, her stepdaughter. At one point an argument was so bitter that the judge slapped his daughter and his wife. Along with domestic conflicts, English began to creep into the household as the children born to Amelia and her husband brought it home from school, though parts of the house were an English-free zone. The judge attempted for years to master English but never really succeeded. He eventually suffered a stroke, and Raúl Mora, a young man courting Mora's mother, helped with his care. The judge was beyond realizing who Raúl was. According to Estela he never would have approved of her marrying a dark-skinned man. Mora is quite frank about this kind of color discrimination within the Mexican community.

Ironically, one of Estela's brothers, Uncle Lalo, suffered discrimination from Anglos precisely because his skin was fair. His surname did not make sense to immigration authorities when he crossed into El Paso after trips to Mexico. He was informed that he could not be a Delgado. The problem was a persistent one. He was told by his army sergeant that he didn't look like a Delgado and that he could have a desirable job if he changed his name. There are problems with banks. "It is annoying that people think that we all have to look a certain way. Even some of us think that" (221). In the more common situation, Mora's own father suffered discrimination because his skin and features were so obviously Mexican. He told his daughter that when he took Anglos out to lunch the bill was never brought to him. "I have a map of Mexico on my face." Her mother, like her brother Lalo, was very fair, so she too discovered the arbitrariness of race: She was quite acceptable as long as her name is unknown, an experience she shared with Gloria López-Stafford, whose father was Swedish. She told her daughter Pat about a school trip where a café had a sign all too common in an earlier Texas: "NO DOGS OR MEXICANS" (177).

The Mora side of the family came to El Paso in 1916. Mora's father was four at the time, but he (or at least his spirit) tells that story, the events having clearly been indelible. His own father, Lázaro Mora, was a tailor in Chihuahua, traditionally an occupation of the timorous, and Mora presents him as being no match for his strong-willed wife, Natividad Pérez. Raúl remembered passing dead bodies on the way to church, and once the Villistas came to the house wanting the use of an axe so that they could break into the Chinese grocery across the street. Allen wrote about the hostility of the Villistas to the Chinese. Villa's henchman Little Blood would murder the *chinos* by tying their pigtails together and then burning them alive. Raúl's resourceful mother sent the Villistas away by offering them her sewing scissors, which were obviously of no use.

She decided that the large family would take the train to Juárez and then cross into El Paso. Their story is similar to the Delgados. Much of it comes through the reported reminiscences of Mora's other favorite aunt, Chole (Soledad Mora), who, like Lobo, worked at a department store, El Paso's other large one, The White House. Her deepest regret is that she never finished school. Chole was an eccentric, obsessed with pet birds, and like Lobo she never married. Mora speculates about a story of lost love, elaborating family legend. After she was old and blind she called a radio announcer on a request show one day, which led him to avow his love for her constantly on his program for three months. There is a tragicomic tone in this story of the blind woman being courted by an announcer who has never met her, and Mora captures it very well: The situation is ridiculous, but the aunt is described with an affection that keeps her from being absurd. Her eccentric piety makes a good contrast with the extreme traditionalism of Mamá Cleta. Chole was on close personal terms with God, whom she calls "*mi diosito*," "my little God," a very droll diminutive, and with the Holy Spirit, who often talked to her and gave advice about daily life. She could report quite casually on having a vision of Jesus in her living room. The three Garcia sisters, the aunts and grandmother of John Phillip Santos, manifested a similar mysticism, which he attributes to their origins in a culture under the dispensation of the Virgin of Guadalupe, a spell which has faded in the United States.

Mora is acutely aware of thwarted human lives, especially when the waste is caused by discrimination. Aunt Chole is not the only figure who fails to finish her education. Mora's mother, Estela, did very well in elementary school in spite of a principal who resented any distinction by Mexican-Americans. Her Anglo appearance created identity problems for her. In a painful scene, her mother came to her school one day to watch a Maypole festival. Estela tried to ignore her, and when she spoke to her daughter in Spanish and put a sweater over her shoulders on the cool day, she was snubbed. A boy turned to Estela and says, "I didn't know you're a spik" (170). Mora captures her mother's confusion well. In high school she called herself Stella and tried both to excel and to blend in, an impossible task. She made a gesture at affirming her Mexican heritage by doing her speech on Lorenzo de Zavala, a Mexican official who came to Texas and took part in the revolution against his own country, eventually becoming vice president of the Republic. She was aware of the contradiction in her desire to recognize a Texas hero who was Mexican but also, in a sense, a traitor to his country of birth. Gloria López-Stafford had an even more difficult time with Texas history at Houston School.

Mora's mother gave up her education after high school and went to work in a department store, where her teachers would sometimes express surprise at seeing her there instead of at college. Her potential is conveyed by Mora's use of a passage from her diary expressing her desire to be a writer and also puzzling over the question of race, wondering if "Mexican" is a race. Uncle Lalito found himself unable to go to Texas Western College in spite of the encouragement of one of his teachers, who suggested he could raise his tuition by working at the college gym. But he had to work to support his mother. Mora is aware of the irony in this story: She later became an administrator at the institution where he could not afford to be a janitor (219-20).

Her father's story is one of extremely hard work and mixed success. He is described with affection and frankness, a big man with a strong temper but not a violent one. He became an optician and worked a decade for an El Paso branch of Bausch & Lomb. He started his own optical company in 1949. Mora implies that business was difficult for a Mexican-American, but she does not give many details. After bankruptcy, he started again as an employee of an ophthalmologist in Santa Monica. In 1991, he suffered a mysterious collapse that deprived him of full use of his faculties. He suffered from hallucinations and growing aphasia. The onset of his illness took place in April, so Mora keys it to Good Friday, which often occurs in April. His decline is described with sympathy and frankness and also with restraint.

Her own life does not escape attention, but as a relational autobiography the work pays the most attention to the nexus of human relations that produced her. We learn about her childhood in "Octubre/October," a section which gives glimpses of her memories, like playing at four with her mother's perfume and lipstick and playing games in the backyard with her siblings. She describes her school days at St. Patrick's Elementary School and Loretto Academy, her high school, where she found the nuns inspirational: no heretical Stephen Dedalus she. She traces her early reading habits. Some of this material is presented through journals in which she tries to recall the past, with a saying by Ingmar Bergman in mind: "The doors between the old man today and the child are still open, wide open. . . . I can move from my bed at night to my childhood in less than a second" (248). She gives the most space to journal entries reconstructing two significant moments in her relationship with her father: In one passage, she remembers his temper through an occasion when she let a door slam and was punished by having to open and shut the door a hundred times while everyone waited for dinner. In the other, he went to a great deal of trouble (and apprehension on his wife's part) teaching his small daughter to catch herself when falling. The scene is remarkably suspenseful for a small incident, which shows her ability to convey the terrors of childhood. The passage suggests that she has gained the skill to trust herself when she needs to: "he's taught me to take care of myself, to catch myself, to fall into my own hands" (252). In the long run, she learned to take care of the entire family in the symbolic realm of art, gathering them all into her house of houses. The book ends with Christmas, which enables her to stress harmony and peace. At the end, the whole family, real and ghostly, is sleeping: "Gradually our breaths become one."

Mora's poems often deal with what theorists like José David Saldívar and José Limón refer to as "resistance," a refusal to accept the authority of the dominant culture. In her *Communion* volume, for example, she deals with the situation of illegal aliens and recalls the mysterious burning of the five-and-dime store owned by the racist Upton in the 1910s. In her recent collection, *Aunt Carmen's Book of Practical Saints*,[24] she has wryly appropriated a title by T. S. Eliot and put it to her own humorous purposes, the usual situation in which the subaltern's voice is appropriated by the dominant culture is reversed. For all her interest in resistance, perhaps her strongest impulses are expressed by book titles like *Communion*, and *House of Houses*. Hers is an imaginative utopia, a place which is "nowhere," to use the root meaning of utopia, an imaginary space of reconciliation with the reconciliation expressed through festivals like the Day of the Dead and Christmas.

The autobiography of Gloria López-Stafford (1937-) is a straightforward chronological narrative without the elaborate framework and encompassing family narrative of Pat Mora's *House of Houses*. López-Stafford provides a rich picture of life in south El Paso, in the notorious Segundo Barrio (the Second Ward) as the Chihuahuita area was eventually known. Mora's grandparents stayed in Chihuahuita only briefly, but López-Stafford lived there from 1940, when she was three, to 1947, and most of the time she was in the heart of the district, the Alamito Projects on St. Vrain Street. The Segundo Barrio has produced several poets, such as Abelardo Delgado and Ricárdo Sánchez. López-Stafford's account is the richest to appear in any form, preserving a unique social history. Anyone who wants a detailed picture of daily life in the barrio will find it in her book. She observes her childhood "is tucked away in special place in my mind. In my memory, everything is huge compared to what it was in reality" (6). This encapsulation of her childhood perhaps comes from her having left it suddenly at ten for another way of life, just as William Humphrey's departure from Clarksville after the death of his father left the town frozen in his memory.

There is no secondary literature on Gloria López-Stafford. When her book appeared, the *El Paso Times* ran a lengthy article by Ramon Renteria, "A Look Back," with a useful chronology.[25] López-Stafford is a retired professor of social work at Texas Tech

University who now lives in Santa Teresa, New Mexico, just outside of El Paso. When asked to list her favorite writers she mentioned Pat Mora, Sandra Cisneros, and Maya Angelou. She told the reporter: "I had to negotiate and find my place. . . . I'm half Mexican and half *gringa*." Her work is a fine illustration of the complexities of living in a border situation. Mexican Americans in El Paso are especially aware of the ambiguities of living on a fluid border where they are influenced by two cultures and two languages. The situation was perhaps more acute for an individual of dual parentage. López-Stafford had to learn to see that ambiguous situation as a strength. For much of the work she presents her younger self in conflict with her dual heritage, and only through the guidance and acceptance of her peers does she resolve the problem.

Born in Juárez, across the Rio Grande from El Paso, she was the product of an unusual couple. Her father, Charles Palm, was a Texan, of Swedish descent, from Brownsville. He was a merchant who, as she puts it, tired of a Baptist middle-class life. On a business trip to Piedras Negras, across from Laredo, Texas, he met a much younger Mexican woman, Francisca "Panchita" López and deserted his wife and children for her. He tried to make a living in Piedras Negras by chicken farming, but his operation was destroyed by a storm, so they moved to Juárez, where a third child, Gloria, was born after two sons, Oscar and Carlos. Palm was sixty-five at the time, his wife in her early twenties. López-Stafford has only sketchy information about her mother. When Palm got a divorce and married Panchita, he could take the family across the river to El Paso, where he made a marginal living as a used clothing dealer.

The mother died after an unsuccessful operation in Juárez when her daughter was about six, leaving her elderly and impoverished husband to raise three children. An occasional visitor in the household was the children's maternal grandfather, López, who is one of the richest characterizations in the book. López, whom she describes as an "old Indian," was a *brujo*, a witch, and a *curandero*, an herb doctor. He is a more interesting figure than Palm, who is usually described as a thin and weary man. López got into serious trouble as a *brujo*, because he practiced healing "to fulfill his carnal wishes" as in this incident which happened in El Paso:

> There was a young married woman in the neighborhood who thought herself *embrujada,* hexed. My grandfather performed a *limpia,* a cleansing, with his herbs and massages. He also swept around her with a broom and rubbed her body with an egg as part of the treatment. But because the woman was passionate, the cleansing got out of hand and her husband walked in and caught them in each other's arms. My grandfather fled toward Juarez with the husband in pursuit. On Stanton Bridge, the man fired a shot from his gun at my grandfather. Fearing the Mexican custom officers at the end of the bridge, the jealous husband threw the gun into the río and my grandfather escaped into the streets of Juárez. (10)

The grandfather always enlivens the book when he appears, but he faded from her life after her godparents adopted her, and she learned of his death from tuberculosis in 1949 a full month after it happened.

With such a background, it is understandable that Gloria López-Stafford offers little family history beyond her own life—so much would be untraceable. When her father died, one of the members of his first family said, "You can throw him in the Rio Grande for all we care" (8). She would find her extended family in the barrio, first in the Alamito Projects and then in the tenement where she lived with a foster mother, María. She has written a kind of relational autobiography in which the family reaches beyond her fragile biological nexus and encompasses a whole community.

At the time López-Stafford lived there, the Segundo Barrio stretched from Second Avenue to the Rio Grande, where the Stanton Street and Santa Fe Street bridges crossed into Mexico. Until the Chamizal Treaty, implemented in 1967, put the river into a concrete channel and ceded much of the barrio to Mexico, the river was broad. She remembers the boys on the Mexican side who would ask tourists crossing the Santa Fe bridge to throw coins into the water for them to dive after. Such scenes define the relations of Anglo America and Mexico rather clearly. In the early days of Chihuahuita, the housing in the area was mostly adobe *jacales* (huts) and tenements. In *Desert Immigrants*, Mario García makes it clear that the tenements, the first of which went up in 1916, were thought to be an advance, though they had one toilet and one water hydrant for every fifteen families. López-Stafford spent some months in one of these tenements at the end of her time in the barrio and describes life there brilliantly.

The intended showpiece of the barrio was the Alamito Projects. In his *Power and Politics in a Chicano Barrio*, Benjamin Marquez provides the background. The projects were completed in 1941 and would have been new when Palm and his family moved in. There were 349 units and for the time, the Alamito must have seemed progressive: "The facilities included a library, and provided for classes in homemaking, hygiene, first aid, the use of appliances, food preparation and general home management for the new Mexican American tenants."[26] But Marquez points out that the projects were only 2.3 percent of the accommodation on the south side of El Paso, and it would be thirty-three years before any new public housing was built. The apartments did not solve the problem of poverty. López-Stafford describes a world in which the chief amusement of the children was playing in a *tartana*, a convertible jalopy which Ignacio, the son of the widow Alma, left parked on the street when he went off to war.

She gives a vivid sense of the community which people from villages all over Chihuahua and Mexico created for themselves in the very un-Mexican setting of the projects. In effect, they created their own village. In that village she was naturally called "Yoya" by everyone, the usual nickname for "Gloria." She points out that the border hardly exists, which is a commonplace of studies of the border. For many, the border is a legal fiction. Mexican events like the Day of the Dead were observed (she describes three of them) and the sixteenth of September, Mexican Independence Day, was a major holiday. One of her set pieces is the description of the combined celebration of her September birthday and *Dieciséis de Septiembre*, a wonderful jumble of birthday customs like the piñata, and the *Grito*, the dramatic moment when a senior member of the community would be called on to give the *Grito de Dolores*, the shout of freedom: *Viva México!* At López-Stafford's party, Don Benito, the neighbor who usually gave the shout, was too old to perform the task, so the privilege was claimed by her grandfather, López. One person who felt uneasy at the party was Padre Luna, the priest who is present at most significant moments in Gloria's childhood. He was born of Spanish parents, and López-Stafford uses his experiences to bring out the prejudice felt toward Spaniards in the Mexican community. He declined to join in with the partygoers who spoke admiringly of Pancho Villa and the Revolution, remembering the persecution of priests, including the time that revolutionaries hanged a priest who had just hidden him and another novice.

The author carefully explains the aspects of her culture which would be unfamiliar to many of her readers. There are discussions of diminutives and nicknames, of godparenthood, of the favorite saints of Mexico (like the Virgin of Guadalupe), of the polite country manners of Mexican immigrants, of the role of the *dicho* (proverb) in the folk culture, of the concept of overwhelming sexual passion—*naturaleza*—which results in the *hijo natural*, or "natural child," a circumstance regarded with tolerance. The explanations often come at the beginnings of chapters, like the explanation of Mexican holidays in chapter six, and López-Stafford often uses the second person address to the reader, creating a feeling of intimacy.

Not everything in her barrio community was traditional and benign like the *Dieciséis de Septiembere* celebrations. One response of the young men to new conditions in America was to form gangs, to become in the slang phrase, *pachucos*. López-Stafford had an extremely unpleasant experience when a *pachuco* tattooed her initials on her arm with ink that he said would wash off. But it turned out to be India ink and the marks remained until her adoptive parents had them burned off with acid. She was almost raped by another *pachuco*, the son of Señora Olga, the *tamalera* or tamale-maker. And she relates the time that a young man named Chango fired a homemade pistol, a zip gun, at someone, and the priest had to lecture the parents. The son of Señora Luz was killed by a *pachuco* called El Pajaro Prieto, who was sent to prison for the crime. Señora Luz becomes a police informer in retaliation for the death of her child.

The portraits of the neighbors are indelible. Señora Alma, a kindly neighbor who had lost two sons in the war, often fed the malnourished Gloria. The portrait of Señora Olga, the *tamalera*, is particularly vivid. She had three sons: Juan, who was wounded in the war; Eduardo the child molester; and the tragic Luís, who fell in love with a young woman named Teresa—she passed him over for a *pachuco* named Chillon, who impregnated and abandoned her. The disconsolate Luís went to Juárez where he was struck by a car, probably an act of suicide. The devastated *tamalera* went into mourning, or *luto*. When Teresa had a hard labor and was in danger of dying, her mother had to go to Señora Olga, a skilled midwife, and beg for help. The *tamalera* slammed the door in her face but gave in later when Señora Alma asked her, "How many more children must we lose?" And, inevitably, she comes to love the baby she has saved. The story suggests a *telenovela*, a Mexican soap opera, but many people's lives are indeed soap operas.

One of the most effective motifs in the book is the use of the "silver moment." Throughout the work, López-Stafford finds vivid ways to describe the distinctive sky of El Paso, its sudden mountain sunsets, its summer afternoon when sunlight on tiny particles of sand catch the light and give an effect "like peeling a lemon and having the light catch tiny particles of mist flying in the air" (183). She tells us that there is "a silver glow in the atmosphere that happens seconds before it rains in West Texas" (35). The silver moment is used to symbolize moments of epiphany: "The silver moment is similar to the one I described to you just before it rains. It's the moment when all the colors in the atmosphere become one single silver color and allow you to see a situation as it really is" (63). Gloria's father married again, to a much younger woman from

Delices in the state of Chihuahua, perhaps in order to give his children a mother. Carmen worked out poorly. In chapter seven, "Plata," she uses the symbol to convey her realization at eight that there is something wrong with the marriage of Palm and Carmen. For her, one such moment comes when she hears them address one another using the formal pronoun for "you," *usted* instead of *tu*. But she realized that her father was not ready for his silver moment. In chapter ten, "Sayings and Secrets," she tells how she accompanied Carmen to Juárez to visit her stepmother's family. She saw Carmen kiss a young lover. "Heaviness overtook my body as I realized my silver moment" (93). And when she tells her father what she has seen, he too has a silver moment and the marriage is over.

The problem faced by her father was how to provide a maternal figure for his daughter. His solution was to board her with a warm and lively Indian woman, María, who lived in a tenement two blocks from the river. Part II of López-Stafford's book, "The Tenements," contains some of her most powerful writing. María was poor and lived with her two daughters, *hijas naturales*, products of passion by different fathers. She supported herself by whatever work she could find: housecleaning, fortunetelling, caring for the sick, picking cotton in season, tortilla making. On the Day of the Dead, María took Gloria with her to pick cotton; the child, like young William Owens, found it tough going.

The tenement building was brick, with houses in two rows of five with a breezeway between them and one toilet for the ten units. The tenement was full of bizarre characters who have little and just hold on to life: "*En la miseria* is a good description of life in the tenements. The atmosphere was many times like a carnival because there was always a great deal going on" (116). One neighbor was a prostitute whose jealous husband would sometimes stand outside his door and howl like an animal; another was a mad woman whom little Gloria had to calm down in a terrifying scene.

The tenement chapters show people whose lives are less acculturated to the United States than the inhabitants of the Alamito: the tenements, close to the river, were a first stop for many immigrants. Yoya was surprised to find that María referred to Palm as a *norteamericano*, or non-Mexican; it had never occurred to her before that her father could be a *gabacho*, the street term for an American. María deplored this slang term for Anglo as crude but concurred with the meaning. López-Stafford would eventually be troubled by her ambiguous heritage. She became more fully imbued with Mexican culture in her life with her foster mother. In the tenements, Mexican folklore—riddles and songs—abounded, and the city of Juárez played a big part in Gloria's life, with trips to the colorful and pungent Cuauhtemoc market across the river.

Near her new school she became aware of the notorious Franklin Canal, which conveys water from the Rio Grande to the fields of El Paso. It is deep and fast-running, and drownings are not unusual. Her fear of the canal was compounded by hearing the story of *La Llorona* from a new friend, Lupita. *La Llorona*, "the Weeper," is one of the most celebrated folklore figures in Mexico. She is the ghost of a woman who drowned her children and must wander by waterways searching for them and weeping as she goes. As she mentioned in chapter two, the story was retold in J. Frank Dobie in *Tongues of the Monte*. Pat Mora's poem, "Llantos de La Llorona" in *Agua Santa=Holy Water*[27] transforms the legend, giving it a feminist twist, as does Sandra Cisneros's short story, "Hollering Woman Creek."[28] The effects of the pure legend in a small child who has lost her mother can be imagined. Lupita told Gloria that the drowning and haunting were particular to the Franklin Canal.

López-Stafford provides her own later adult interpretation of the story, observing that the stream is dangerous when confined to a concrete channel but becomes life-giving when it spreads out in the valley. Symbolic interpretation is fine for an adult, but a child perhaps needs symbolic action. Gloria's way of coping with the story in childhood was rooted in Mexican folklore: She and María carried out a ceremony nightly with holy water and the smoke of burning herbs to ward off the ghost. All four walls had to be blessed by María before the child could sleep.

Life with María offered Gloria a mother substitute but did nothing for her malnutrition. People meeting her always thought she was years younger than she really was. When her godparents learned that she was living in a tenement, they intervened, insisting that she live with them. She was torn at having to leave María, whom she called *mi india*, but a new phase of her life began, bringing her life in the barrio to an end. The portrait of the artist as a member of a Mexican community ends as she entered a more traditional search for identity in a nuclear family, a quest which takes up the third and fourth parts of her book. In her case, the problem was to create a self as a person aware of two worlds—the Mexican social life of her first ten years and the Anglo world in which she suddenly had to find her way. As a person of mixed heritage, both genetically and culturally, she had to cope with a divided subjectivity and find her true place in El Paso.

Her godparents, Fred and Martha Justus, took her in at the age of ten. They clearly felt the profound obligation of *compadrazgo*, the relation of godparent to godchild which comes out of Spanish culture (155). One oversight in the book is the lack of information about the relationship of the godparents to Gloria's parents. The godparents in this case were an unusual pair: Fred Justus was not Mexican himself, but a German-American from Missouri. He married a Mexican woman from Torreón who was thirty years younger than himself. Fred Justus had retired and he and his wife lived behind his former place of business on Alameda, some distance from the barrio but still in south El Paso. The brief third section, "Alameda Street," deals with the short stay there. They moved away after an incident at Beall School, where the students, who were mostly Mexican in origin, were brutally sprayed with insecticide because lice had appeared on a few of them. Gloria came home with her eyes swollen almost shut. So the family moved to a place on Pershing Drive, in the Five Points area, a considerable distance from south El Paso. The final section, "A Home," deals with this new phase in López-Stafford's life, one in which her usual name is no longer Yoya but Gloria. Houston School had a fifty percent Anglo enrollment, giving her unfamiliar circumstances to cope with. Besides Anglos and Mexicans, the school had a number of Syrian students, a blanket term for Syrian and Lebanese immigrants: Lebanon was not a political entity until 1919 and most of the immigrants came between 1880 and the First World War, hence the use of the term "Syrian." El Paso has a large "Syrian" population, most of them Maronite Christians. In a publication from the Institute of Texan Cultures, John L. Davis estimates that there are about 30,000 Lebanese and Syrian Texans, another diaspora, like the Mexican Chinese of El Paso who came over the river during the Revolution.[29]

As a child, López-Stafford had resisted learning English and jokingly referred to it as Chinese. She had been chagrined when Palm's Anglo son came to visit from San Antonio and she couldn't speak with him. Early in the book she describes being punished for speaking Spanish to a school friend: Both were forced to stand in a closet during recess. They were fortunate not to have to kneel on stones, a common punishment. Her inability to learn the Pledge of Allegiance was a serious problem, and she and her friends found amusing devices to teach it to her by rote, such as conducting a pretend firing squad complete with blindfold when she missed any words.

After she moved from the barrio, she quickly became aware that the Anglos looked down on Spanish speakers, asking them to say "chocolate" and "chicken" because the Spanish "ch" sound resembles an sh, so that Anglos heard "shocolate" and "shicken," to their amusement. Those words were a "shibboleth" in the biblical sense. And the general image of the Mexican in American culture could be summed up by "the *campesino*, a rural person usually depicted sleeping with a sombrero over his face" (167). López-Stafford actually begins her book with a prologue about a moment in school when the students watched *The Battle of the Alamo*. Houston School, like several others in El Paso, was named for the hero of the Texas Revolution, Sam Houston. The movie presented the Mexicans, Santa Anna in particular, in a bad way, and the lesson following the movie was an indoctrination in the standard Texas view of history: Mexicans who didn't fight fair, heroes like Bowie and Crockett, a great victory at San Jacinto, and the glorious history of the Texas Rangers. One student interjected, "And Texas is for Texans." López-Stafford and her friend Linda had cheered for the Mexicans. The teacher ended the lesson by saying, "Remember the Alamo!" leaving López-Stafford confused and tearful.

López-Stafford notes that the Spanish-speaking children had a knowledge of two languages while the Anglo children had no need for more than English. As a fair-skinned and freckled person, she was not considered Mexican until she spoke, creating a series of unpleasant moments. She was thrown into perplexity about her own identity, and her home life hardly helped. Her godfather was not that removed from his German background. Her godmother was very proud of having become an American citizen but hardly knew any English and even felt uncertainty about her own Mexican identity because she was half French. Her godparents wanted to provide a good, middle-class American home for her, complete with oatmeal in the morning, but their only expedient for helping her learn English was to let her watch many films in the Pershing Theater nearby. They had rejected Catholicism, a large part of young Gloria's Mexican identity, on the grounds that the religion had done harm to Mexico.

As a result, she was uncertain about her *lugar*, a term first used by one of her friends about Señora Olga, the *tamalera*, who remained unhappy at the end of her mourning for her son Luís. A friend, Flaco, quotes his father: "My father says that *ella no puede hallar su lugar*, she can't find her comfortable place" (54). "Comfortable place" is a good translation, as it carries the emotional connotations of a word that literally means just "place." *Lugar* in López-Stafford's book has the same kind of intensity as Dobie's *querencia*, but her place had be found or created, not inherited. She was immersed in Mexican culture in the Alamito and the tenements and then introduced to the dominant American society by going to live with parents whose own American identity was wobbly. Naturally she was uncomfortable.

The situation of the mestizo in a border area like the juncture of Texas and Mexico has received considerable attention. The border is more than geographical: There are divisions of race and culture, and at the same time there are blurrings of boundaries, overlapping cultures, and multiple identities. In *Migrant Song*, a study of

Chicano literature, Teresa McKenna has looked carefully at poems by Pat Mora which explore the border situation, like "Sonrisas," a poem from *Borders* in which the speaker sees herself in a doorway between two worlds, one of Anglo academia, with talk of tenure and the other containing señoras who drink sweet milk coffee. "I live in a doorway/between rooms," Mora says.[30] McKenna suggests that "this middle space of divisions in which we attempt to find meaning can also affirm connections."[31] In his brilliant study of early autobiographies by Mexican Americans in California, *My History, Not Yours*, Genaro M. Padilla suggests that recent Chicano writers show an awareness of multiple cultural possibilities in the borderland situation, suggesting that some of them "premise a condition of empowered multiple identity that is a result of living in the marginal space to which history (and the dominant society) has consigned them."[32] It is toward a multiple identity that López-Stafford moves in her struggle to find her comfortable place. To repeat José David Saldívar, the "*transfrontera*" condition calls for negotiations of hybrid identities, which is precisely what López-Stafford describes in the latter part of her memoir. "Negotiate" is the term she herself uses for her attempts to find an identity.

The struggle was painful and even humiliating, and in the middle of her quandaries her grandfather and father died only a few months apart. In school, she was drawn toward a new student, Barbara, who was blonde and pretty. Barbara was momentarily friendly until she realized that Gloria was "Spanish," which was long a polite term in Texas for Mexican. Barbara quickly became popular and was surrounded by an Anglo clique who show their distinctiveness by speaking in pig Latin. The implied irony is the Anglos ignore Mexican Americans who speak a language descended from Latin. Gloria had her own friends, Jane and Linda. Jane was a red-haired Protestant; Linda a Mexican and a neighbor. Significantly, Gloria played with Linda at home and with Jane at school, school being the arena where she felt that being Mexican was a liability.

Her rebuffs by Barbara led to an emotional crisis. In the barrio days, her emotional problems were often expressed through nightmares that dramatized the conflicts, but now she had to work out problems in the real world, confront her nightmares wide awake. She sought adult advice, first by quizzing her stepmother about racial identity, then by talking to her old parish priest, Father Luna. His advice pointed her toward the solution. He was sympathetic with a twelve-year-old girl who says, "*No puedo hallar mi lugar*. I can't find my comfortable place" (202). He pointed out his own problems with being a Mexican with Spanish parents and then observed that she has two "bloods," but they were inseparable. She could not say that one side of her body is Anglo and one side Mexican or that her head was Anglo and her heart and lungs Mexican. Gloria Anzaldúa suggests in *Borderlands / La Frontera* that the *mestiza* "learns to juggle cultures. She has a plural personality, she operates in a pluralistic mode—nothing is thrust out, the good, the bad, and the ugly, nothing rejected, nothing abandoned."[33] Anzaldúa is one of the Chicano writers who like to speak of "code switching," a term which originated among linguists to describe the ability of bilingual people to move from one language to the other. Gloria López-Stafford needed to be confident at code switching in the broadest sense.

This was a good theoretical conception, but it was with her peers that she worked out the problem and accepted a metaphor of herself as a person of dual heritage, one who could sing Christmas carols with Protestants and still pray to the Virgin of Guadalupe. In conversations with her schoolmate Ahmad, who described himself as half Syrian and half Lebanese and a Catholic as well, she learned that her conflicts were not unique. Ahmad's ability to speak English, Arabic, and Spanish struck her as a strength.

Finally, Gloria went Christmas caroling with young people in Jane's church. She was disturbed when she realized that they would be stopping at her adoptive mother's house, and it would become clear to Jane's church friends that she and her godmother Martha were both Mexican in ancestry. Jane told her that if she ran away that would be the end of their friendship. Further, Jane made it clear that everyone in the group knew her ancestry anyway. Gloria—Yoya—found herself able to go to the door and publicly acknowledge her godparents and therefore her own ancestry.

She decided that, like a sparrow in a mulberry tree, she would take and defend her place in the world against all comers. She felt good for the first time in a long while and said a prayer to the Virgin of Guadalupe in her head, in the middle of a Protestant group of carolers. Not long after, when she and Jane and Linda discussed the husbands they would like, Gloria said, "I want to marry a man who can sing like a *mariachi* and dance the two-step like a Texan, I said as I stood up and yelled like a *mariachi*" (212). She accepted her multiple identity. In the terms of Mora's "Sonrisas," she was willing to live in a doorway between the rooms of Mexican and Anglo identity. Her last word in the book is an interjection, the yell of the mariachi repeated: "AyyAyyAyyAyy!" The expression is defiantly Spanish but not a Spanish word; a purely human utterance. Perhaps the interjection symbolizes the solution.

Pat Mora and Gloria López-Stafford have written full accounts of life in El Paso. Some of the essays in *Memory Fever: A Journey beyond El Paso del Norte*, a collection by poet Ray Gonzalez (1952-) explore his El Paso experiences. Some essays are just sketches about his love of 1960s rock and roll, his times hanging out in his father's pool hall, and his youthful binges. He provides some journalistic insights into ethnic food and drink: tamales, menudo (this traditional hangover remedy is a soup made of hominy and tripe), and mescal, and he reflects on interesting southwestern sites like White Sands and Taos. He touches on other Chicano themes: the Day of the Dead, the role of the rosary, and stories about weeping saints' images in the lives of his older relatives. The desert around El Paso is often his subject: He writes about his dreams of rattlesnakes and his boyhood obsession with killing lizards. He has a good essay on discovering his vocation as a poet when he attended Robert Burlingame's class at the University of Texas at El Paso. Burlingame was also a mentor to Pat Mora, who completed an M.A. under his supervision.

Gonzalez recalls racial discrimination in the classrooms and playing fields of his schools. The Chicano boys were expected to play Indians in the games of cowboys and Indians at Putnam Elementary School. He eventually learned to have contempt for Davey Crockett and other Anglo icons. In high school he was passionate about football and became manager (a fancy term for water boy) for the team at Coronado High School. Anglo team members ridiculed him for his weight and his Mexican ancestry.

He misses the chance to describe in detail his visits to his grandparents in the barrio, but he has two revealing essays on the illegal alien situation. In "Peace Grove" he narrates an evening walk to a place across the river from the grove of cottonwoods planted by Pancho Villa to commemorate his battle for Juárez. The idea of Villa planting a peace grove obviously charmed Gonzalez. He talks a little about one of his grandfathers, Bonifacio Canales, who fought for Villa at the age of fourteen, before leaving Mexico for Arizona with his wife Julia. On the walk, Gonzalez is stopped by *La Migra*, the Border Patrol. Gonzalez does a fine job of communicating the situation in which any American of Mexican descent is liable to challenge by the Border Patrol, especially near the river. The essay ends with Gonzalez overhearing a conversation between two genuine *mojados* ("wet ones" or wetbacks) whom he last sees crouching midway across the river. And at that point he is challenged by another Border Patrol officer. The ironies of the event are implicit in the essay: the peace grove planted by a man of war, the American citizen challenged twice as a wetback while the real wetbacks wade across. In the following essay, "Crossing to America," he gives a shirt to a *mojado* who shows up soaking wet at his house near the river. For Hallie Stillwell, the Border Patrol was just a nuisance for anyone using wet Mexican laborers. In one episode in *I'll Gather My Geese* she dodges the *chota* while driving with one of the "wet" Mexicans who worked for her. The anxieties from the point of view of the Mexican laborer did not seem to occur to her (137-40). Anzaldúa's claim that "a borderland is a vague and undetermined place created by the emotional residue of an unnatural boundary" fits the situation described by Gonzalez quite well. Gonzalez shows what it feels like to live in a borderland and to cope with the emotional residues of fear and prejudice.

Some of the Gonzalez's read like sketches for a full autobiography of growing up in El Paso. It would be good if he wrote such a book. He has a new collection of essays on El Paso and the changes in it forthcoming from the University of Arizona Press. The book's title is *The Underground Heart: Essays from Hidden Landscapes.* The open wound of the border has not closed. Fortunately, to paraphrase W. H. Auden's elegy for Yeats, it can hurt people into poetry, or into excellent prose.

Mary Karr

12

MARY KARR'S FAMILY SIDESHOW

Mary Karr's memoirs, *The Liar's Club* and *Cherry*, achieved a success denied to Humphrey. *The Liar's Club* dominated bestseller lists and helped to create what has been called the memoir explosion. In an article in a special issue of *The New York Times Magazine* devoted to memoirs, James Atlas said: "The triumph of memoir is now an established fact," and his prize exhibit was Mary Karr.[1] The Penguin Books website lists a series of awards won by their author: the PEN/Martha Albrand Award, the Texas Institute of Letters Nonfiction Prize, and a finalist position for the National Book Critics Circle Award.[2] Popular success is indicated by its selection as a best book of the year by *Time*, *People*, *The New Yorker*, and *Entertainment Weekly*, an interesting set of magazines. The rights to *The Liar's Club* have been sold to Hollywood. One sign of Karr's success is the proliferation of materials about her, in interviews and reviews, on the World Wide Web. Her perspective on her own work, which helps to shape its reception, can be downloaded in quantity, though the interviews overlap a great deal and the same witticisms are repeated too often. This is a new dimension of literary life in our time, the shaping of reader response through interviews and reading group guides with the imprimatur of the publisher.

Before this extraordinary success, Mary Karr (1955—)was known as a poet with two books to her credit, *Abacus* and *The Devil's Tour*, and she has since published another, *Viper Rum*.[3] All three poetry collections have poems about her family. Her memoirs come out of the zeitgeist, which seems to be an age of the troubled family. Americans found that the books expressed their traumas and dilemmas, their preoccupation with family breakdown. We live, after all, in an age of therapy, confessions, and the public display of psychic wounds on talk shows. In "The Family Sideshow," an article originally published in *The New York Times Magazine* special issue on memoirs and now included in her publisher's reading group guide, Karr defines a dysfunctional family as "any family with more than one person in it."[4] Karr managed to appeal to a large audience with a work set in an area not previously dealt with in literature, the Gulf Coast of Texas, and she made good use of the racy Texas demotic, which she sees as a heritage from her father. She has never stated any particular interest in Texas writers: The only one mentioned in her interviews is a passing reference to Cormac McCarthy, but she has listened to Texas speech.

In the "Author Interview" included in the reading group guide, she praises her father's speech, "the densely poetic idiom I grew up with in East Texas. To say 'it's raining like a cow pissing on a flat rock' is to utter a line of poetry. The phrase is metaphorical."[5] Lucy Jane Beasley's phrase comes to mind, that some people chatter "like the clatter bone of a duck's ass." Karr's comment on the pissing cow image is revealing: She notes that it is accurate as a description of rainstorms off the Gulf, "plus it works at the bounds of social propriety, which is where writers often go to find difficult truths that haven't been written to death already." In another interview, with Karen Olsson in the *Texas Observer*, she suggests that the Texas simile is never far removed from reality: "It never doesn't have something to do with some kind of bodily function or the milieu and the noise of it, like a cow pissin' on a flat rock."[6] In her second memoir, *Cherry*, she pushed the bounds of propriety pretty far, with a title which alludes, of course, to the hymen. She makes casual use of the word "pussy," which was one of the words Beasley used in an effort to exorcise her horror of sexual terms.

Karr's memoir was written out of deep understanding of the autobiographical tradition as well as personal experience and a fluency in the Texas idiom. She has taught courses in memoir since 1985, and in her interviews she constantly mentions writers like Vladimir Nabokov, Maxine Hong Kingston, Mary McCarthy, Maya Angelou, Harry Crews, and Frederick Exley, whose *A Fan's Notes* she admires for being a memoir pretending to be a novel. This saturation in precedent is common enough to writers, and the academic world intensifies the process. Writers have always learned from traditions and then peers, but now we have authors giving courses on their genre.

While the world visualizes cattle or oil fields when Texas is mentioned, Karr writes about an industrial area. It is not the production of petroleum which dominates her region—the Port Arthur area/Beaumont/Orange "Golden Triangle"—but its transformation into gasoline and chemicals. True, oil production began at Spindletop, near Port Arthur and Beaumont, but by the time she was born in Groves in 1955, wealth came from processing: refineries and chemical plants. Groves is a community of around 16,000 just north of Port Arthur. It was originally called Pecan Grove, then The Groves, and finally just Groves. In her memoirs, the community is called Leechfield, which explains her attitude: It is not a pastoral setting. She says she chose a fictional name to protect the privacy of her mother in Groves for many years. The mother, Charlie Marie Karr, died in May 2000. There is no question of a *querencia* in Karr, who used to dine out on stories about the miseries of Leechfield. According to her literary agent, Amanda Urban, quoted by Robert Draper in *Texas Monthly*: "She could tell these incredible stories . . . and never once felt sorry for herself. Not only was she thriving, she was making dinner party chatter out of it."[7] It is no wonder that the anecdotes in her first book are so polished.

The Port Arthur region is a blue-collar area, and ethnically mixed. Many Cajuns came from Louisiana to work in the refineries, and names in the memoirs include Boudreaux and Fontenot. There is a large Mexican-American community as well as many African Americans. We are far from the Big Bend of Hallie Stillwell, the Brush Country of Dobie and Allen, the heavily Anglo West Texas of Matthews and Greene. Karr grew up in Texas after the great shift of population from country to urban life. The industrial blight created by petrochemical industries is evoked with chokingly strong details. Her home area produced Agent Orange for the Vietnam War, and the air was always filled with fumes.

Her father, J. P. (Pete) Karr, came from Buna, in Jasper County, about sixty miles from Port Arthur, in the celebrated Big Thicket region. His family as described in *The Liar's Club* were pretty typical rural East Texans, people who would not have seemed out of place in Pin Hook. Her mother, Charlie Marie, came from a cotton farm near Lubbock. She was leaving her fourth husband, Paolo, when she blew a tire and stopped at the service station where Pete Karr was working, covering for his friend, Cooter, who was in the middle of a crap game in Baton Rouge. She fell in love with Karr immediately. She was in a Marxist phase, and he was a ruggedly handsome working man. Thus began some thirty years of a difficult but passionate union, interrupted once by a divorce, which was followed by remarriage. The marriage produced two children, Mary Marlene and her sister Lecia, who was two years older.

Once we spoke of unhappy families. Now we speak more clinically of "dysfunctional families." A. C. Greene's family was dysfunctional but not on the scale of Humphrey's and Karr's. She suggests in "The Family Sideshow" that the enormous popularity of "coming-of-age memoirs" is "precisely because they offer some window into other people's whacked-out families, with which nearly everyone born in the fractured baby-boom era can identify." In an interview with Dwight Garner published by the online magazine *Salon*,[8] she says that her tour with *The Liar's Club* taught her that readers like memoirs because they see the survival of the author as a value and therefore a cause for hope. Further, the voice from a memoir has a kind of reality that a fictional voice does not. As she told an interviewer for Wisconsin Public Radio,[9] the truth offered by memoir is subjective, but the reader understands the subjectivity and accepts it. One of her favorite phrases is, "we lead with our corruption." This kind of compact with the reader neutralizes some of the skepticism that a memoir can arouse if it purports to be the literal, documentary truth. A title like *The Liar's Club* announces that the contents of the book may be fictionalized. William Harmon's admiring review, "Mary Karr, Mary Karr, Mary Karr, Mary Karr," suggests that on a secondary level the "Liar's club is the whole human race,"[10] though on the primary level the club is a group of working men, friends of Pete Karr, who gathered in bars and pool halls to tell stories. His daughter loved to come along, an obvious way to become a part of her father's life. As Freud's theory of the Electra complex predicts, she even takes on a feminine role to please him by spreading liquid cheese on crackers, making her a good little 1960s housewife in miniature. As the psychologist Christopher F. Monte puts it, the outcome of the Electra complex is "identification with female behaviors to appeal to the father."[11]

The stories are a triumph of the book. The South is known for the vividness of its oral tradition, and Pete Karr is presented as an artist, a Gulf Oil worker with limited education who created brilliant tall tales with a remarkable grasp of the vernacular. His daughter listened eagerly to lies that, she came to realize, could convey the truth. The most outrageous lie, which she realizes is a way for her father to insulate himself from too much intimacy with his friends, was the story of how his own father "hung hisself." Little Mary knew very well that her grandfather was still alive in Kirbyville, Texas. In "This Personal Maze Is Not the Prize," Eric Murphy Selinger calls her reaction "a defense of poesy."[12] Karr says: "I've plumb forgot where I am for an instant, which is how a good lie should take you. At the same time I'm more where I was inside myself than before Daddy started talking, which is how lies can tell you the truth" (124).

One of the delights of *The Liar's Club* is the dramatic evocation of the storyteller and audience. Dobie realized that describing the scene of storytelling could be as interesting as the story itself. In a similar way, Karr shows how stories create a reciprocal relationship with the audience: The storyteller depends on listener response and even adapts his narration to any perceived boredom in his hearers. In her father's circle, the "straight man" was Cooter, who "always asks the next question," and the skeptic was Shug, the one black man. Cooter's unspoken racism made him uneasy with Shug, which added tension to the stories.

This lie about the hanged grandfather, which creates a powerful emotional reaction in the listeners, is a little different from the father's usual stories. But in all of them he is, in a way, creating his own family saga in fictional terms. The imagined hanging of a father gone simple surely reflects tension over the physical and mental breakdown of his mother-in-law. A more conventional story tells how young Pete ran away from home. It has tall-tale elements but dramatizes an ambivalence of the young, who wish for adventure and yet long for security. Pete was sent out to buy coffee but hopped a freight train instead. It was winter and the listeners (and the reader) were treated to some typical southern tall tales about a cow on the stock car giving popsicles of frozen milk and a dead migrant having frozen farts in his pants. The story ended with the return of the prodigal, whose father merely said, "You git the coffee?" The story functions as family saga by teaching this lesson, and another: "To Mother, such stories showed that Daddy offered steadiness. He always returned to the logging camp at the end of whatever journey, and coming back was something she'd begun to need from a man, badly. He was a rock" (18).

Something about marriage (a social value, in Mody Boatwright's terms) is taught by a bit of family history told to Mary on a fishing trip. She tells us that her father did not believe in divorce: "In his world, only full-blown lunatics got divorced. Regular citizens in a bad marriage just hunkered down and stood it" (35). He told of his uncle, Lee Gleason, and his wife, Annie, who didn't speak to one another for forty years. They developed a strange telepathic sympathy that compensated for their silence, each knowing what the other was thinking or wanted. Finally, after ten years, they had the house sawed in two, or so the father said. The story created deep anxiety in the daughter.

The anxiety grows out of witnessing the fragility of her parents' marriage and the angers that ran through the house. She has lots of precedents for depicting this kind of misery. She met Tobias and Geoffrey Wolff when she was in school at Goddard College, and Tobias was later a colleague of hers at Syracuse University, where she still teaches. The Wolff brothers uniquely managed to write from different halves of a broken home: Geoffrey, author of *The Duke of Deception,*[13] was raised by his father, and Tobias, author of *This Boy's Life,*[14] was brought up by his mother.

In her essay, "A Memoirist's Apology," Karr says that Tobias Wolff wrote to her with advice which "was a vaccine that I took daily against my self-protective vanity."[15] Among other things Wolff told her not to be afraid of "appearing angry, small-minded, obtuse, mean, immoral, calculating, or anything else. Take no care for your dignity." He also cautioned her not to be didactic. "Tell your stories, and your story will be revealed." She follows the precedent of Wolff's own memoir, and reveals her humiliations and her faults with a merciless frankness.

The powerful opening scene of her book was based on a memory she had mostly suppressed, and she has said that it took her months to reconstruct it. Reconstruction of long-past events inevitably involves some reinvention and even fictionalization, but the scene is true to the vision of the book as a whole and to our sense of the people in it. She also vouches for her intention to tell the truth by providing parenthetical confessions and corrections that rectify the limitations of her child's-eye narrator. This kind of reflexiveness is also practiced by Gertrude Beasley, but Karr's own source is Mary McCarthy's *Memories of a Catholic Girlhood*, a book she has praised in print.[16] In a long interview with Mary Park ("Don't Mess with Texas") published on the Amazon.com website,[17] Karr observes that while McCarthy had to go to some lengths to provide passages of correction of her memories, a contemporary writer can do it quickly and parenthetically: A convention has been established. Gertrude Beasley used this technique seventy years before Karr and thirty-five years before McCarthy, but her book was largely unread.

The root cause of the dysfunction in Karr's family was her mother's "nervousness," a euphemism for mental illness. The ultimate cause of the illness is kept a secret from the children and from the reader and it drives the book. At the end we follow the narrator into the attic looking for more of her father's papers. She blunders into the family secret. But Karr makes the reader wait to find out just what the secret was. She begins in the midst of things, with the culmination of her mother's nervousness. The opening scene is brilliant in its suspense. The work begins in a traditional memoirist's way, with her sharpest memory. She was seven; it was night; she was in a Texas bluebonnet nightgown; and the family doctor was examining her for marks. She tells us that "it took three decades for that instant to unfreeze" (3). The reader is left wondering for some time what has happened: sexual abuse, a beating? The sheriff was present, which heightens the suspense. It turned out that she was not injured. The mother was taken away and spent some time in a mental institution. Karr delays giving us the full story for 143 pages, until near the end of the first section.

That entire opening section of *The Liar's Club*, "Texas 1961," is a masterful collection of scenes. It is hard to pick out the best episodes but perhaps the finest are: the chapters dealing with the maternal grandmother's illness; the long description of Hurricane

Carla; the attack on her sister by a stinging jellyfish, a Portuguese Man-of-War; and her mother's nervous breakdown. The story of her grandmother starts with Charlie Marie and her daughters driving to West Texas after a quarrel between husband and wife. The region is not presented with the sympathy of A. C. Greene: "How the westward settlers decided to keep moving in the face of all that nothing, I can't imagine. The scenery is blank, the sky total" (26). The only lively moment along the road was provided by a vast cloud of locusts, something different from a more traditional dust storm.

Eventually the grandmother came to live with the Karrs. She had cancer, and it is typical of the contemporary memoir that we are given a series of horrifying images of sickness and decay. The doctors tried to treat a cancerous leg with injections of mustard gas. The result was a deeply disgusting gangrene and the loss of the leg—not before the patient suffered extreme agony of mind and body. The progress of the illness is documented in unsparing detail, and the grandmother's total decline into irrationality is documented as well.

The limits of decorum have been widened in the last two decades. Poets like Sharon Olds describe the cancer deaths of parents with details that would have been thought inexcusably tasteless before. The reader can expect shocking accounts of dissolution in memoirs. Tubes coming into and out of the suffering body are now standard properties, even clichés. Karr certainly captures the repulsion that a child can feel for a deranged and mangled adult. It comes at the cost of her dead grandmother's dignity. Karr does concede that her older sister saw the grandmother quite differently.

The unhappiness generated by the mother's "nervousness" was compounded by alcohol abuse by the parents. Karr's father drank heavily, and the mother could put away a fifth of vodka a day. She would often take to bed for days in depression or behave in a manic way. In such an atmosphere quarrels were a certainty, and the neighbors were repelled by what they saw and heard, which increased the isolation and defiance of the family. In a rather droll scene, one Sunday morning Mary hung naked from the cast iron curtain rod over her window in a chin-up contest with her sister when the next door neighbors—a whole truckload—drove up and were open-mouthed at what they'd seen. For Karr, nakedness is an act of defiance, and there are comparable scenes in *Cherry*. The family ate in one big bed and sometimes slept there, with no suggestion of incest, but there is a suggestion of an oppressively close family atmosphere.

The children reacted in typical ways to their family situation. One of the most popular forms of counseling children of dysfunctional families, alcoholic families in particular, is to interpret their responses by means of birth order, a theory derived from the family order theory of Alfred Adler.[18] The oldest child often becomes the Hero, abnormally mature and responsible. A younger child may become the Rebel. This pattern certainly fits Karr's family. She presents her sister, who was two years older, as bossy and extremely capable. It was Lecia who tried to talk their mother out of suicide when the nervous breakdown hit. Mary herself knew that during her mother's binges she should hide the car keys and tie up the phone so that Charlie Marie could not call teachers or neighbors to insult them. And she stealthily poured her parents' alcohol down the sink. But Mary was still the rebel, a licensed rebel in most cases: Attempts to discipline her rarely succeeded.

Just before the grandmother's death, the father's refusal to accompany his wife, daughters, and mother-in-law in their escape from Hurricane Carla intensified the rift between the parents. Karr has a fine gift for describing action, and her treatment of this notorious hurricane (which hit the mainland on November 10, 1961) is a powerful set piece. The father was supposed to remain at work, so he watched the hurricane, one of the most powerful of the twentieth century, from the Gulf refinery while his family drove in high wind and rain over the Orange Bridge, which crosses the Sabine River, on their way to take refuge with his relatives in Kirbyville in Jasper County.

The mother's growing mental illness became clear on Mary's birthday not long after the hurricane. Charlie Marie spent a huge sum in preparation, charging items the family could not afford. The family went off to have barbecued crabs (a favorite Gulf Coast delicacy) at Bridge City. On the way home, Charlie Marie attempted to drive the car off the Orange Bridge and the father had to knock her unconscious.

A mother bent on self-destruction and willing to take her family with her was clearly on the edge of a breakdown, and the breakdown is described near the end of the first section. The mother had artistic aspirations and was a fanatical reader who loved Sartre and taught her daughter to pronounce Camus. She inherited a huge sum from her deceased mother—oil rights on the West Texas farm—and this made her restless rather than happy. One day she destroyed most of the family's possessions in a gasoline fire in the backyard and then approached the children with a twelve-inch knife. This moment is a child's deepest nightmare, surely, but she did not stab them. Karr's mastery of style drives this scene to tremendous tension. She describes how her mind coped with terror by reducing her mother, her sister, and herself to stick figures in her mind like the ones she had put on her Mother's Day card one week before. Fortunately, the mother put down the knife and called Dr. Boudreaux, the family physician. She told him that she had stabbed both of her children to death, which explains the scene with which the book began. The aftermath was painful, with the mother institutionalized for a while. Mary dealt with the children who teased her about her mother by taking shots at them with a BB gun, one of her typical fierce gestures.

The second section, "Colorado, 1963" has less emotional tension because the parents had a divorce interregnum. Newly affluent from the grandmother's inheritance, they set out with their daughters for the Seattle World's Fair, but got only to Colorado, where the mother was entranced by the setting and the children could take up horseback riding. It is amusing that a book about a Texas childhood brings in ranches and riding only in the mountains of Colorado. The parents decided to divorce, and the daughters stayed with the mother because they feared that left alone, "she'd get in capital-T trouble" (193). But of course she did get into trouble, buying a bar, which was capital-T trouble for an alcoholic, as she had become. She married the Mexican bartender, Hector. While married to Hector, Charlie Marie Karr ran through nearly a million dollars in a year.

One of Karr's metaphors of self is to present herself as a forthright and fierce individual, a scrapper with a bad temper and worse mouth, a survivor as we like to say nowadays. She conveys her growing toughness when she describes a fight with an older girl in her Colorado school. The fight ended in a comic moment when she tore open the girl's blouse exposing her white training bra, part of the nakedness motif which runs through the work. But she had no resources for dealing with an adult male baby-sitter who forced her to perform fellatio on him. The appalling experience is conveyed in more detail than seems necessary, which might make some readers feel that Karr is writing a virtuoso piece rather than reliving a trauma. In contemporary writing the boundary between frankness and the prurient is often unclear. She had been raped when she was seven by an adolescent boy, an experience which is described more concisely and has emotional impact from its brevity and the callous efficiency of the rapist.

The Colorado sojourn collapsed when the mother's building anger with the incompetent Hector led her to threaten to shoot him. The feckless Hector seems to have been inadequate in every way, including sexually. The scene following is both suspenseful and comic, a fine cinematic piece of writing. The daughters disliked Hector but did not want their mother to kill him. Mary flung herself in front of Hector, and Lecia tried to reason with her mother, first with the tones of a Yankee newscaster, to convey rational arguments, then in an accent which was "pure Texan, straight from what you might call the Ringworm Belt." Finally, Mary ran for help at her principal's house. She returned with the principal, and they were greeted by a calm Charlie Marie, another sign of her emotional volatility. That night, Lecia, the Hero of the family, called her father and told him with complete authority that he must send two air tickets immediately. She was completely convincing, and the two girls returned to Texas and their father.

Charlie Marie showed up in Leechfield one day with Hector, planning to pick up some clothes. This was a tense moment, and when Hector said something demeaning about Charlie Marie, Pete demolished him in a fight that Mary Karr admits she enjoyed watching. She calls the scene a filmstrip, and she certainly knows how to block a scene. Her descriptions of violent actions call to mind what cinema critics have called "blood ballet" in discussing John Woo's films. We hear cartilage crunch and ribs crack. The result of the fight was a happy and passionate reunion between Charlie Marie and her ex-husband.

The third section of the book is a fast-forward to 1980 and her father's stroke. She begins not with the stroke itself but an explanation of the process whereby she and her father grew apart. Then she describes returning home, and she does not spare us the clinical details of his illness. In 1980, after the insurance money for his care ran out, Karr ascended into the attic to try to find documentation of a war wound so that he could qualify for veterans' benefits. The attic search led to a trunk where she was shocked to see her grandmother's artificial leg, which could still terrify her after so many years. The important find was her mother's collection of wedding rings, which revealed that her mother had been married many times. Seven, it turns out, counting the two marriages to J. P. Karr. The family secret was about to come out of the attic, even more dramatically than the revelations of the Humphrey family secrets.

When confronted, her mother responded typically by going to bed for days and taking her prescription drugs. There was a scene of revelation at a Mexican restaurant where mother and daughter drank margaritas. Karr skillfully counterpoints the revelations with events in the restaurant: The waiter refilled salt shakers in the restaurant as the mother wept, and at the end the mother and daughter staggered out like cartoon characters in a hallucinatory atmosphere created by the piñatas hanging in the restaurant.

The revelation has been prepared for. In her mental decline, the grandmother called Lecia "Belinda" several times, and in one scene she showed Mary photos of children she referred to as Tex and

Belinda. We now learn that the mother married young and had two children. Her ambitions took her and her unwilling husband from Texas to Manhattan, where she wanted to study art. Her husband could not understand why she wanted to paint naked strangers. Her hostile mother-in-law joined them, and in a "shameless" act the young mother took a full-time job making drawings for the Bell Laboratory, an act not approved of in Lubbock of the 1940s. One day she returned home to find her house empty and her husband, mother-in-law, and two children gone.

The multiple marriages were attempts to find a man who would help her get the children. The immediate effect of the revelation was not liberation and joy, though understanding would come of it. The "Liar's club" has been dissolved, so to speak. Driving home (drunk, apparently) they passed a stretch of bluebonnets filled with fireflies that somehow managed to survive the pollution of the Gulf Coast petrochemical industries. That image is hopeful, but not overemphasized. It also echoes the first page of her book, in which the little girl in a bluebonnet nightgown was being examined in a dark room. Only in retrospect does she feel that the "clear light of truth" should have liberated them. She modulates that image skillfully into an evocation of the reports of near-death experiences, then travels into light where "all your beloveds hover before you, their lit arms held out in welcome" (320). Reconciliation and reunion can at least be imagined; the darkness of her first indelible memory is relieved by the vision of escaping darkness into light.

In *The Liar's Club* Karr emphasizes her childhood in the first two sections, then provides two brief ones about her father's stroke and its aftermath. Originally she had planned to cover her adolescence as well, but the chosen structure enables her to keep the focus on her parents. It also left room for a sequel, *Cherry*, the story of her adolescence, which suffers from the downplaying of the extraordinary parents and their tumultuous marriage. Instead she focuses on her sexual coming of age and her absorption into the hippie and surfer cultures of disaffected Gulf Coast youth.

In the "Don't Mess with Texas" online interview with Mary Park, Karr illuminates her attitude toward the sequel. In the first book, she had the advantage of her "this great inherited idiom—my daddy's idiom, the idiom I grew up with—as well as this milieu that no one had ever written about." But her problem in the second book was "that there's no language to write about a girl being sexual." Her solution, which does not in fact seem radically original, is to filter sexual feeling through the lens of romantic, sexually vague language: ". . . my fantasies at the time weren't being thrown down and boffed into guacamole; they were in the courtly mode that I write about in the book." The phrase "boffed into guacamole" is a good example of her racy and transgressive idiom, that tendency to work at the bounds of social propriety. However, the language of the book is often the language of romance novels but given a sexual tinge: romantic language adapted to describe physical sensations in the pelvis. Gertrude Beasley used a similar technique but the language was more clinical.

However, this kind of language is not exclusive to young girls. The romantic feelings in James Joyce's *A Portrait of the Artist as Young Man* are equally vague and lush, as in the reverie in which Stephen Dedalus dreams of a young woman he loves: "Her nakedness yielded to him, radiant, warm, odorous and lavish-limbed, enfolded him like a shining cloud, enfolded him like water with a liquid life: and like a cloud of vapour or like waters circumfluent in space the liquid letters of speech, symbol of the element of mystery, flowed forth over his brain."[19]

Karr describes her nascent desire by saying "cool fire circled more in my abdomen than between my legs, and it was vague and smoke gray," and she says that a forceful light was glowing "nonspecifically from my solar plexus" (46). As if to compensate for this kind of diction, she also loves expressions like "johnson" (surfer slang) for penis, and she has titled her book *Cherry*, a term for the hymen and an expression used, she told Jesse Kornbluth, "about bright shiny new cars and virgin girls . . . which I was, theoretically, if not in fact."[20] Terms like "dick" and "fuck you" are used on a scale which would disturb poor Gertrude Beasley, for whom the terms were a purgation rather than casual slang.

In the "Don't Mess with Texas" interview, Karr explained why she chose to write much of the book in the second person. Memory is not "a hard drive" with a folder to "download an experience. The way it gets remembered is shaped by who you are at the time you're remembering it." But adolescents, she says, with perhaps a touch of exaggeration, "lack a self to remember through." She was "assembling a self" in adolescence, as most people do, trying out a variety of contradictory roles (as she says in the interview: potential cheerleader, hippie, girlfriend, or badass). Considering her raucous and chaotic childhood, the role of badass came easiest to her as an adolescent. She is in effect explaining how she tried out various metaphors or fictions of self. "Don't mess with Mary Marlene" would be a good subtitle for the book. The lack of a stable identity explains the frequent use of the second person pronoun: She is alienated from herself. Another effect is to assert the reality of feminine experience: The universalizing "you" invites the reader to identify with experiences which are, in fact, female, thereby asserting the equality of women's experience with men's.

The "Prologue" is in that second-person mode and uses the present tense for immediacy, as she often does in this book. The opening inverts normal narrative order, beginning the memoir at its climax, the moment when Karr and her friends took off for Los Angeles in a truck in the typical fashion of the hippie period, 1972 in this case. But this will not be an *On the Road* narrative: The rest of the book shows how she got to this point. She raised money by every means except "selling your spanking new pussy" (3), an idiom inconceivable for casual use among earlier memoirists.

Karr's leave-taking was virtually ignored by her family. Her father had retreated from the family, her mother was preoccupied with an art history book, and her sister, as was the non-hippie fashion at the time, was teasing her platinum blonde hair after filling the air with Aqua Net hair spray. The older sister was, as in *The Liar's Club*, the premature adult. In a classic situation defined by Freud in his essay, "Family Romances," she had chosen to pretend that she was not the child of her parents. Freud suggests that such attitudes begin with an Oedipal conflict, a rivalry with the parent of the same sex for the attention of the other parent. The next stage is what Freud calls an "ambitious" rather than erotic one: ". . . the child's imagination becomes engaged in the task of getting free from the parents of whom he now has a low opinion and replacing them by others, who, as a rule, are of higher social standing."[21] This is precisely what Lecia did, for she spent as much time as possible with other families and looked, Mary Karr says, as if she were riding an imaginary parade float. She had her own dreams of elegance, identifying herself with Queen Guinevere and John Cleary, a boy she had a crush on, with Sir Lancelot defending her honor.

Karr herself vacillated between wanting to be accepted and wanting independence. After the prologue, the opening chapter of the first section of the book shows her in a skating rink toilet at the end of the fifth grade, striving desperately to be accepted by other "popular" girls. Her one real friend, Clarice, had "outlaw tendencies" like Karr. Clarice climbed a flagpole on a playground one day and mooned the onlookers. She then went further and showed "her hairless pudendum" (33). When the adult Mary Karr asked her long afterward why she did it, the reply is: "Because I could, I guess. . . . Wasn't anybody around to stop me" (34). A few chapters later, when Mary wanted a training bra, she made a point with a similar gesture, riding her bicycle around the block topless. Female assertiveness is one of the values Karr wants to affirm. We should recall the moment in *The Liar's Club* when she shocked the pious neighbors by hanging naked in the window.

Much of the work deals with her junior and senior high school days in the Port Arthur area. In a scathing review in *Texas Monthly*, "The Pits," Don Graham has complained that the structure tends toward a monotonous recitation of what happened to her in each grade: a school timeline as structure.[22] A reviewer in *The New Statesman* suggested that *Cherry* would be a good book if it had a plot,[23] and Karen Olsson's introduction to her interview with Karr also complains about the lack of plot. In *The Liar's Club*, Karr did have a plot, one turning on a destructive family secret, and she had two highly original parents to describe. Everyone who has been to school during Karr's lifetime (and even a little before it) will recognize the situations she covers. The crackle and sizzle of the earlier book, provided by the parents and their struggles, are largely missing. The authentic Texas idiom is not so apparent either. In yet another negative review, Clay Reynolds notes that the dialogue of her adolescent characters is full of anachronistic expressions like "tube top ho" and "all hat, no cattle," which he says "smack more of late-eighties, early-nineties *patois* than anything that might have been uttered in, say, 1970."[24]

Karr attended the Port Neches-Groves High School. She saw the social milieu there as conformist, boring, and "mind crushing," with sex and drugs as the only escape. This view of adolescent life in the area has been promulgated in a number of popular biographies of Janis Joplin, who attended high school in Port Arthur itself, and has been supported by the first scholarly Joplin biography, *Scars of Sweet Paradise*, by Alice Echols.[25] Karr joined the girls' drill team, the sort of authorized female exhibitionism popular in Texas, where cheerleading and baton-twirling still have high status. She was actually punished with removal from her academic classes when she quit the team; punishment for her uppityness.

In *Cherry* Karr writes a *kunstleroman*, an account of the growth of an artist: She discovered her vocation as a writer very early. Credibility is stretched when she suggests that at the age of eleven she imagined her writing would be "1/2 poetry and 1/2 autobiography" (25). Her real support comes from a highly intellectual friend, Meredith. When they first had a conversation, they discovered that they both had memorized the same poem by Howard Nemerov (145). Later she made another friend, Stacy, who had a great knowledge of T. S. Eliot. Clay Reynolds is skeptical about the depth of knowledge presented by these young women who were "surrounded by 'bubbas,' thick-necked football jocks, semi-literate pipe-fitters, and ignorant Cajuns,"[26] but we have to take Karr's word for it.

Much of the narrative deals not with art but with various crushes, particularly a boy she calls John Cleary, whose name (perhaps only by coincidence) calls to mind Joyce's Emma Clery in *Stephen Hero*, the first version of his autobiographical novel, *A Portrait of the Artist as a Young Man*. One of the best scenes in the book describes the excruciatingly exciting moment when John's parents asked her to massage his legs after football practice. She wound up straddling his thighs as if he were a horse, and she remembered her excitement riding an actual horse in Colorado. The effect of this "horseback ride" was unequivocally sexual; it is not uncommon for a real horseback ride to cause an adolescent girl to have a first orgasm. No longer did she have unfocused sensations in the pelvis: She went home and found that her panties were soaked through. However, she still had vaguely romantic fantasies rather than visions of explicit sex.

Female desire is an important concern in contemporary literature and criticism, and Karr's account of her own experience is valuable because it tries to balance the romantic and the physical. She knows that male desire has traditionally been preoccupied with immediate sexual experience, and she acknowledges some of the paradoxes of desire between the sexes. She went out with a Cajun boy in order to test her power to arouse desire. When she kissed him, "some unnamed luster" rushes into her pelvis "with swirling star colonies and nebulae" (132). A more serious relationship with a young man named Phil showed her the power to fascinate, and that ability acted like a drug on her. "Your fleshly image of yourself is deriving from what he sees" (168). In this period, a woman was still expected to arouse desire and yet preserve her virginity. To arouse desire too forcefully and persistently was to be a "prick tease." The balance was hard to maintain. To some extent, she was caught in the traditional pattern defined by Samuel Taylor Coleridge: "The man's desire is for the woman, but the woman's desire is rarely other than for the desire of the man." But she also emphasizes agency and makes her own decision to offer herself to Phil. The language used to describe the decision emphasizes her choice: She "booked" her "official deflowering" (181), making the event a rather clinical moment, with her friends Meredith and Stacy waiting in the living room, playing chess.

A new ethos was forming because of the sexual revolution brought about by oral contraceptives. Karr's own mother took her to a physician in Houston (to avoid gossip) to have the Pill prescribed. Other currents were swirling through the Port Arthur area, like drug use and iconoclastic rock music. Janis Joplin, the rock singer who died of a heroin overdose in 1970, set an ambiguous example of freewheeling sexual behavior. Karr describes the concerts at The Towne House, a converted warehouse on the edge of a swamp where groups like ZZ Top (which is still recording: Indeed, they played for George W. Bush's inauguration) appeared. Karr's treatment of the period is influenced by Tom Wolfe's *Electric Kool-Aid Acid Test*,[27] a book which encouraged her to leave for California. Wolfe's favorite expression for violence, to "tear somebody a new asshole" is one that Karr likes.

Much of this material is a predictable if well-written saga of the hippie era: locker searches, police cars waiting to stop teenagers, the obligatory description of a drug bust. She does give the descriptions of drug taking with her friends a Gulf Coast flavor, as many of them are in the local surfing culture. The drug bust took place in the Piney Woods of East Texas. Karr escaped charges because the judge in the case turned out to know her mother. She was not an especially dedicated badass. The familiarity of this kind of hippie memoir was noted by some reviewers, and the subordinate role of the parents also caused some disappointment.

The last few chapters have a brief and rushed quality, covering topics like transcendental meditation and an affair with a musician nicknamed "Little Hendrix," after Jimi. The real set piece is the penultimate chapter, describing the time when Karr and two friends went to a black juke joint called Effie's Go-Go in Beaumont. The subject matter—a drug-amplified nightmare of paranoia and weirdness—is familiar enough from memoirs of the hippie period. The hallucinations (like the doorknob of the club, which disappears once they enter) are evoked with skill, and both the seediness and the menace of the club come through. Rather predictably, the full truth of the episode turns out to be ineffable: "for on nights like this the greatest truths can't be uttered. Certainly not right off, maybe never" (271).

However, the book does close with an insight, mixed with comedy. In the final chapter, she tells the story of the night at Effie's to Meredith, when she said, "There's no place like home." Meredith, who is a confidante with common sense, pointed out that the motto is from *The Wizard of Oz*. Then, while eating Froot Loops, Meredith told her that she accomplished a great thing: "You're your Same Self," an insight that might have come out of *The Electric Kool-Aid Acid Test*, in which members of Ken Kesey's Merry Pranksters tend to utter crashing banalities. But Karr sees this saying as an epiphany, albeit a Froot Loop epiphany, which ironizes it. She has finally started to assemble a self, to forge an identity out of her multiple roles. There is no reference to the "Same Self" idea in *The Liar's Club,* though she supposedly discovered it in her adolescence. It is perhaps a new and fictional formulation imposed on the past to understand its lessons. "That odd catch phrase will serve as a touchstone in years to come, an instant you'll return to after traveling the far roads" (276). She does not define that self, but the reader knows some roles which she has tried and repudiated (a drill-team member, a popular girl) and some which she is (a rebel, a badass, a poet). She is only halfway, in truth, to creating "an immoveable self," if such there can be, but she will try to "will Same Self into being." She concluded *The Liar's Club* with an image of gliding into a luminous womb. The sequel ends with light as well:

> What's inalterable as bronze, though, is the image of your radiant friend that morning barefoot on the porch with suns in her rampant hair. She's holding out that bowl of Froot

> Loops and touching your shoulder as if to bestow the right name upon you, the one you'll bear before you through the world, each letter forged into a gleaming shield. (276).

The suggestion is that the girl who dreamed of herself as Guinevere being defended by Sir Lancelot now sees herself as a female equivalent of Lancelot. She seems ready to go into the world on whatever quest appeals to her. California would do for a start. No doubt there will be a sequel to *Cherry*, another installment in a serial autobiography. Karr hasn't even finished with the 1970s yet, and it is already the twenty-first century.

John Phillip Santos

13

THE MEXICAN DIASPORA AND JOHN PHILLIP SANTOS

His soul had approached that region where dwell the vast hosts of the dead. He was conscious of, but could not apprehend their wayward and flickering existence. His own identity was fading out into a grey impalpable world: The solid world itself which these dead had one time reared and live in was dissolving and dwindling

James Joyce, "The Dead"

In *Places Left Unfinished at the Time of Creation* John Phillip Santos (1957-) has written a profound exploration of Mexican-American life. The work, which was shortlisted for the National Book Award, is a relational biography similar to Pat Mora's—his aunts and uncles are his chief informants. Like Mora's book, this probes into migration during the time of Pancho Villa, with the migration of his paternal forebears from Coahuila, the Mexican state bordering South Texas from the tip of the Big Bend almost to Laredo. He goes even further into the past than Mora, pushing his quest to understand his ancestry by searching the landscape and the history of Mexico back to the time of the Conquest and beyond. Through Aztec mythology and the almost suppressed history of Mexico before and after Cortés, he puts the experience of his family in the context of a diaspora within a diaspora: Mexico itself was part of the great Spanish migration which reached from the Americas to the Philippines. In an act of piety similar to Aeneas carrying his aged father on his back, Santos seeks to overcome what he calls the "empire of forgetting." In the process, he preserves much of the history of San Antonio and its "lost mestizo city," an emigré society hidden within the larger community. He also illuminates the *Tejanos*, the Mexicans who lived in Texas before the Mexican Revolution, as his mother's ancestors go all the way back to 1757. The reader needs the genealogical charts (which are even more elaborate than Pat Mora's) to keep the relatives straight.

Santos's background prepared him to write such a book. Born in 1957, the year of *Sputnik*, he grew up in the suburbs of San Antonio with frequent contacts with the aunts and uncles through whom he tells much of his story. Originally he hoped to be a poet, but he wound up a documentary maker, with more than forty documentaries for CBS and PBS to his credit. Two of them, on AIDS and on Mexican-American spirituality, were nominated for Emmy awards. He now works in New York as a program officer for the Ford Foundation. In *Places Left Unfinished*, he manages to use both the skills of a documentary maker and a poet. His ability to synthesize his vivid experiences in Texas and Mexico with his research is one side of his achievement. The other is his ability to explore visionary experience, though here perhaps he falters from time to time, relying too heavily on rhetorical questions, on flowery words like "myriad," and on rhetoric adapted from Beat poetry. The New Age mysticism of Carlos Castaneda's Don Juan books seems to have left a mark as well in scenes like the final journey through Manhattan in a car of air.

The tone is set by the opening: His ninety-year-old paternal great-aunt, named Tomasa but called Madrina, obsessively asked the question, "Are all the Santos dead yet?" To which his Aunt Connie (Consuelo), with whom she lived, replied one day, "All of the Santos are dead." They were not of course: At the inception of the work Santos's father and Uncle Roger were alive, and Santos and his two brothers are still living. But Santos said that he also replied that "All of the Santos are dead," by which he meant that the older generation is quickly passing away, the generation which came to the United States from Coahuila in 1914 to escape Pancho Villa. In a way, the book is the narrator's own *Día de los Muertos*; he even refers to it as a "Mexican Book of the Dead" (39). In the Penguin Reader's Guide which is included in the paperback edition, he says: "*Places Left Unfinished at the Time of Creation* is a memoir with a poetic intent, a conversation with the dead."[1] The elegiac spirit gives the book a definite fin de siècle feeling: The millennium was approaching as he wrote. He even alludes to the Aztec belief that the "Fifth Sun" or epoch will be the last, and to the Mayans, who carried their vast calendar only up to August 2112 in the belief that the world would not endure beyond that date. He alludes several times to Pedro Calderón de La Barca (1600-1681), whose play *La vida es sueño* asserts that life is only a dream. Melancholy is a trait of the Santos men, we are told, a weakness in the line.

His awareness of a dying tradition of family stories has made him eager to preserve them. Living in New York for so long, he is still conscious of the elderly women in San Antonio who entrusted him with their narratives: "They are keeping a vigil over the stories they told to me as if they are a *compromiso*, a promise that has been handed on" (18). He says that "the unstoppable carousel of stories was our parallel history of San Antonio, part of another history of Texas, another history of Mexico" (96). As he says, "We may be later-day Mexicanos, but we are still connected to the old story, aren't we?" (4) His putting the idea as a question shows how threatened the oral tradition is. As a maker of documentaries, he could be considered part of the threat information makes to storytelling. But his training enables him to ride that carousel of stories. He can move from one story to another suddenly or with a gentle modulation. He has those parallel histories to convey—his family's life in Mexico and Texas. Each chapter has a dominant subject but always contains other related material, which may in turn branch into more subjects, all with a subtle thematic relationship.

There are four titled sections of three chapters each. Like Mora, he uses bilingual chapter titles: Each main title, printed in bold, is either in English or Spanish, with an italicized subtitle in the other language. The first section, "Testimonio," stresses family history, and its opening chapter is called "*Tierra de Viejitas:* Land of Little Old Ladies." The women in his family tended to outlive the men, and he re-creates the atmosphere of their houses with a sensuous immediacy which recalls Pat Mora's constructed ambiance in *House of Houses*. One theme of the first chapter—and a dominant one in the book—is the difficulty of reconstructing the past through its material traces. He says that his relatives were prone to losing mementos. Santos believes that the forgetting has its origins in Mexican history: Mexicans would like to forget that their culture was founded on conquest and the eradication of a civilization, and that the mestizo people are the descendants of Indian women who had children fathered on them by Spaniards—repeated acts of violation.

Much space is devoted to the women of the Garcia family, his paternal grandmother's relatives. Less is given to his mother, Leandra Lopez (née Vela), who came from an old *Tejano* family in

Cotulla, Texas. The Santos and Garcia families resided there for a while as they sought to make a life in Texas. He is most fascinated with the three Garcia sisters: Tía Madrina, Tía Pepa (full name, Josefa), and Margarita, his grandmother (usually referred to as Uela, short for *abuela* or grandmother). The three sisters grew up in Palaú, Coahuila, about one hundred miles from the Rio Grande and three hundred miles from San Antonio. They were mystics, students of the Rosicrucians. Madrina became a healer herself after a *susto*, or deep fright, she received after the family had moved to Texas. She saw a buggy conveying a dead girl who was covered with a shroud. The buggy hit a bump and the shroud fell away, revealing a body devastated by consumption. Madrina saw the dead girl's soul leave the body at that moment. She fell into a seizure, and her mystical insights increased. The experience parallels the seizures that turn people into shamans in circumpolar and Native American cultures.

The *susto* is a well-documented folk disease found in Latin American countries (and in Taiwan and the Philippines). In Mexican culture, it is treated by *curanderos*. It has been the subject of an intensive medical study, *Susto: A Folk Illness*, by Arthur Rubel and his colleagues,[2] and is discussed in all studies of *curanderismo*. The susto has an emotional rather than physical basis and usually arises in individuals under social stress. The supposed mechanism of a *susto* in folk belief is the loss of vital essences in the body as a result of fright. The research by Rubel does not turn up any gain in supposed psychic powers by the victims, but the massive questionnaires were not aimed at anything but documenting pathology.

Her second seizure came later in San Antonio in an incident redolent of Texas life. She saw a caged and emaciated wolf in the back of a truck marked "Wolf Brand Chili." This particular brand is a Texas favorite with a long history. She was reminded of the wolves in her native state of Coahuila, wild beings outside human control. When the wolf looked at her, she had another susto and on reviving saw the relatives who surrounded her in a mysterious light. Enigmatically, Santos reports her reaction: "We have been taken to Purgatory, she told herself. And soon the chastisements would begin." The following chapter, on the death of John Phillip's grandfather, helps to explain that statement.

Tía Pepa had a vision also, and it is described even more vividly than Madrina's *sustos*. One night when the Garcia family was sharecropping at Creedmore, Texas, before they settled in San Antonio, she had a vision of "a slow-moving cascade of numberless luminous pears" in the sky, green and fruit which entered the bodies of the sleeping family. Something close to a hundred of them entered her heart, and afterward "she slept her first real sleep since leaving Mexico" (103). The experience is described vividly and without an attempt to read its symbolism, which seems tactful here: It was not his dream. It has an emotional pressure similar to Coleridge's equally mysterious dream vision, "Kubla Khan."

The mysticism of the Garcia sisters comes out of a Mexico which lived under the spell of the Virgin of Guadalupe, he says, and that spell is fading. He believes that the magic of that epiphany is vanishing as Mexico collapses (the "crísis" brought on in part by deluded economic policies of technocrats), so that when Madrina asked if the Santos are all dead yet, she was asking if her world had vanished.

His grandmother and her sisters gave a precedent for his own symbolic readings of experience. As Rosicrucians, they imbibed some historically dubious but poetic teachings. As he explains, the Rosicrucian doctrines do in fact encourage a reading of symbolism into the events of life. "Since all creation was part of the same manifestation of God, everything the world presented was part of the story of something larger taking place, revealing the ultimate meaning of the world" (101). Santos began by wanting to be a poet, and poets read the world for its symbolism. His more elaborate visions, like the visit of the dead Uncle Raul to his New York apartment, are out of literary convention, like Chaucer's dream vision poems, as is his final epiphany in the book, which imagines Mexican dancers on a building in Manhattan.

He supplements the Rosicrucian habit of seeing symbols in nature with the Aztec concept of the *inframundo*, the realm where all exists simultaneously, the living and the dead, humans and gods, a kind of equivalent of Jung's collective unconscious. In the *inframundo* dwell his ancestors, he says, and they ask him where their forebears came from, what "they have amounted to in this world," and "where are we headed, like an arrow shot long ago into infinite empty space?" (9) Santos does tend to pose cosmic rhetorical questions which he rarely answers, an honest but sometimes overworked strategy.

His second chapter deals with paternal ancestors: "Códices de los Abuelos: *Grandfather Codices*." The "codex" is an important motif in the work: The Aztec codices were written records incorporating pictures. Most of them were destroyed by the Spaniards. In contrast with the mystical Garcia women, the Garcia men were attuned to the practical, skilled in the use of machinery. Uncle Frank (Francisco), the oldest brother of the Garcia sisters, was a distinguished inventor. But origins of the Garcia family can be traced back to a great-great grandfather, "el abuelo Teofilo Garcia," whose story is more magical than rational. His life was passed down as family saga. He was kidnapped as a child by the Kikapu Indians, who have a homeland in the mountains of Coahuila. Wounded in a skirmish after he was an adult, he was taken in by a Mexican couple. He knew no Spanish, but one day he began to sing, and the song was a lullaby which the wife had taught her own son—and of course the wounded Indian turned out to be the long-lost child as in any number of folk tales. In the horror versions, the parents unwittingly kill their son. The lesson of the saga, according to Uncle Frank, is that "abuelos can be lost and found."

It is a lesson that Santos tries to follow himself: The book turns on the exploration of a traumatic family secret about a grandfather. Mother's Day has supplanted the Mexican Day of the Dead, he observes, and on Mother's Day when he was seventeen he went with his family to see the family graves. While looking at the headstone for Uela and her husband, Juan José Santos, he suddenly realized what no one has ever mentioned: The dates, 1890-1939, represent an early death. The family had kept something concealed, the apparent suicide by drowning of his grandfather on a foggy day in San Antonio. His grandfather was found in the river on a foggy New Year's morning; fog was a common occurrence in San Antonio. And the family tried to befog the circumstances of the death out of a feeling of shame.

Santos never quite dispelled the fog around his grandfather's death. He read old newspapers on microfilm; he questioned relatives; he even looked up the fireman who found his grandfather's body, only to find that the man was senile. His best informant would have been his own father, who evaded the issue. As with the memoirs of Humphrey and Karr, the family has been damaged by secrets. The grandfather was an object of deliberate forgetting: an erasure. As Santos says, "Sometimes, for me, it felt as if he had taken our entire past with him" (128). He makes an excellent distinction between two effects of the disclosure of a secret, saying there are secrets which emerge "like a great island from the sea," and secrets which "appear like whispered fragments you've heard many times before but never understood" (45). The Santos family secret remains fragmentary. The secrets in the families of William Humphrey and Mary Karr are in the more dramatic category.

One key to understanding the dead ancestor lay in understanding his origins in Mexico; another was in explaining the move to the United States and the experiences of the immigrant families. In chapter three of the book, "*Valle De Silencio*/Valley of Silence," Santos describes his dream of Uncle Raul, his father's eldest brother. The vision took place in Manhattan, a place as remote from Mexico as could be imagined. Raul recited a series of Spanish words, beginning: "Mariposa. Canela. Atole." (butterfly, cinnamon, porridge) and ending, "Benidiciones y benidiciones. Siempre. Siempre. Siempre" (blessings and blessings, forever, forever, forever). This cultural mantra seems aimed at resisting the tendency to forget the Mexican heritage: "a prayer against forgetting," the ghost said, but a prayer which has to be recited forever, as a heritage must be preserved by effort. And Raul's advice about learning the origins of the family was to tell his nephew to ask the primordial realities, like the stars and the earth and fire. In effect, the dream suggested that John Phillip should get in touch with the sheer physical reality of Mexico.

This third chapter is a kind of overture, touching in brief episodes on Mexican themes which will be explored later in the book. Santos gives a first glimpse of the Aztec world view, the realm of sorcerers and the *inframundo*, and a first description of the events which initiated the American phase of the family's journey, the immigration in the time of the Revolution, with the great-uncle Francisco Garcia (Uncle Frank) as the first family immigrant, followed later by most of the Garcia and Santos families. The way that family history becomes a family saga (he actually uses the term) is dramatized by the contradictory descriptions of the train ride into Piedras Negras. Madrina recalled an attack by Pancho Villa's men with bullets hitting the sides of the cars, while Tía Pepa remembered a peaceful journey.

One story about Mexico illustrates that you can't go home again. It is one of those treasure-hunting tales that J. Frank Dobie liked to collect. Decades after the move to the United States, the senior Garcia, Jacob, son of the Kikapu captive, sent the narrator's father and two of his uncles, Raul and Rudy, back to Mexico to find a lost mine at "*la Loma de los Muertos,*" the hill of the dead. Their quixotic adventures with a flashy beige Hudson which managed to die on the only railroad track in the desert are amusing if not quite the folkloric sign of a curse or supernatural opposition. They had to abandon the search (as usually happens in such stories). The symbolic meaning of the story is quite clear, and the name of the hill reverberates in a book filled with ghosts. The lost treasure is surely Mexico, and it can no longer be possessed, especially by exiles in an expensive American car, the kind of car made famous in *On the Road*.

The most interesting anecdote in this heavily anecdotal chapter comes after the lost treasure story: Tía Madrina's story of a valley in Coahuila, between Palaú—the city where the Garcias and Santoses lived before their departure to the United States—and the Sierranía del Burro, the mountain range where the Garcia patriarch lived with the Kikapu Indians before his miraculous return to his parents. In this valley there was no sound, making it "el Valle del Silencio." It lies, of course, near the Loma de los Muertos. The soundlessness her father attributed to its being, as in the title of the book, one of the places left unfinished at the time of creation. One of the questions in the Penguin Readers Guide hints that the unfinished nature of such a place implies that the Mexican-American journey (that diaspora within a diaspora) is perpetually unfinished. Certainly this suggestion is true to the book.

This bit of myth-making is followed by a childhood memory of the San Antonio Hemisfair when he first saw *voladores*, practitioners of a rope dance with pre-Columbian origins. The dance becomes a key symbol of the book, recurring eight times. The volador ("flyer") dance involves a pole and five performers who wear wings trimmed with eagle feathers. Four stand on the edges of a revolving wooden platform atop the pole. The remaining volador stands on the pole blowing an eagle bone whistle and beating a hide drum while saluting the four directions of the universe. The four dancers on the platform eventually descend on spiraling untwisting ropes to the ground. Santos says that he attended many performances of the *voladores* in San Antonio. He seeks the origins of the dance in the depths of Mexico, as if they hold the key to primordial Mexican culture. Randall Holdridge says in the *Tucson Weekly* this mystical structure "requires lengthy flats in which momentum sometimes falters, suggesting that not even the author takes this heavy dose of pre-Columbian mysticism literally."[3] Santos does make himself vulnerable to the criticism that he offers a series of wild goose chases after the *voladores* and the insoluble mystery of his grandfather's death.

The quest for the Mexican earth ends with the realization that he has been on dead-end trail, that interrogating the Mexican sun and sky and earth does not yield answers to the meaning of Juan José's life—or to the family's pilgrimage. But he does describe some experiences at the Rancho Los Generales of the Guerra family in the Serranía del Burro where he spent time in his youth. In the *New York Times*, Suzanne Ruta complained in a generally admiring review[4] that class inequities are never properly addressed in the book: The inequities have impelled immigration but the paternalistic structure of life at the ranch, with its many servants, is never questioned. Santos might reply that he wants to evoke traditional Mexican life, not critique it.

The first vignette from the ranch introduces Alejo, the foreman of the ranch, a vaquero who as he develops in the book calls to mind similar vaqueros in Dobie's *Tongues of the Monte* and John Houghton Allen's *Southwest*: a man of the earth, simple and straightforward. He and Santos went searching for wild pequín chiles, the ferociously hot peppers which the Kikapu Indians claim were the place where God hid the fire "with which he had created the world, leaving it with us to remind us where everything came from" (60). They saw the lairs of pumas or perhaps even bears and finally came across huge hives of wild bees: The narrator was in touch with the wildest aspects of the Mexican earth. And in the next brief sketch, on a day when the monarch butterflies were migrating, he descended with Alejo into what the vaquero called "*El Valle de los Ancianos*," the Valley of the Ancestors. In the wild beauty of the scene, he felt the imminent presence of some ancestral wisdom, some memory of the earth itself. But if he did receive it, the experience is incommunicable: "The Mexican earth is alive, but mute" (62). Hence, the next section of the book considers the human realm.

That section, "Mexico Viejo" opens with a chapter on the mixed ancestry of Mexicans, "Cuento Mestizo: *Mestizo*." The chapter actually gives more space to Texas than to Mexico, but that reminds us that there were Mexicans in Texas before the Anglos arrived. The Lopez and Vela lines of Santos's mother were *Tejanos* dating back to the eighteenth century, long before the Texas Revolution. The focus of the chapter is Uncle Lico (Ludovico Lopez), the brother of John Phillip's mother and an avid genealogist who sat in his study listening to Mexican music on his stereo system and compiling elaborate charts of all the families allied to his own. He was the product of two old *Tejano* families (Lopez and Vela) in Cotulla, Texas, near Laredo, and made himself the keeper of the last bit of the Lopez land grant, which had been bestowed by a viceroy.

Uncle Lico's researches introduce the theme of the mestizo, as genealogical research into Mexican lines almost inevitably runs into dead ends because people of mixed ancestry often did not know who their Spanish fathers were. This trauma of the conquest, a kind of rape, is still a subject of shame in Mexico. The Indian woman who served as interpreter and mistress for Cortés, Malinche, or Malintzín, is the emblem of betrayal, as Octavio Paz points out in his famous book on Mexico, *The Labyrinth of Solitude*,[5] and she was betrayed herself by Cortés, who abandoned her when she was no longer useful. Paz sees her as a counterpoise to the Virgin of Guadalupe, the Mexican Madonna. One explanation of the *La Llorona* legend claims that the ghostly weeping woman is Malinche, who supposedly killed her son by Cortés when the conqueror wanted to take him to Spain.

The chapter has a brilliant scene, the funeral of Santos's grandmother, Leandra Lopez (born Vela), who had requested a highly traditional funeral in Laredo, with a professional mourner. Unfortunately, the mourner, "señora Rosa, Queen of the *Pésames*" (pésame: condolence) mourned with such "unfettered caterwauling" that no one could keep a straight face (82). Some cultural practices cannot be preserved. A sad counterpart to this scene comes much later at the funeral of Uncle Lico. The archaic funeral of grandmother Leandra Lopez was farcical in its way, with the howling mourner, but the ceremony for her son was absurd in a contemporary way, presided over by a minister in a paisley tie who claimed that Lico had secretly been born again. At the grave the minister's suitcase-sized boom box played Nashville gospel music (198), an implied contrast with Uncle Lico's love of traditional Mexican music played on a fine stereo system.

Chapters five and six expand on the migration of the Garcia and Santos families to Texas. "The Flowered Path: *El Sendero Florida*," gets its title from Rosicrucian studies of the three Garcia sisters: Santos's grandmother, Margarita Garcia, gave Madrina a 1602 Spanish Bible with an inscription referring to the "flowered path" of Rosicrucianism. The flowered path is also the route to the United States, which offered the families a refuge from the growing lawlessness of the Mexican Revolution. The prejudice and hardships the families often faced give an ironic tinge to the "flowered path" motif.

The move began with a cavalcade of wagons headed toward the railway that could take them into Piedras Negras, across the river from Eagle Pass, Texas. For some time the families rode along with a group of Chinese (who were especially victimized by Pancho Villa's followers). But the Chinese, who had been brought into Mexico by the deposed dictator Porfirio Díaz to build the railways, flew a banner with his image on it, and the senior member of the Garcia/Santos group, Abuelo Jacobo Garcia, decided it was too dangerous to travel with a group flaunting their antirevolutionary feelings; and they parted company.

The following chapter, "From Huisache to Cedar: *De Huisache a Cedro,*" looks at the new way of life in Texas. But it begins with a retrospective glimpse at Mexico through a family anecdote which is subjected to the scrutiny of reason. Santos says that several of his relatives (his father and several uncles and aunts) told a similar story about returning to Mexico on a visit and seeing an impoverished Mexican or Kikapu Indian walking down the road with a donkey. "In each version of the tale, they ended by turning to one of their traveling companions, whether brother, sister, cousin, uncle or aunt," and saying, "If we hadn't moved to Texas . . . that would be you!" (105) The story is in effect a bit of family saga, and probably apocryphal—its uncertain provenance is a clue—but it teaches the lesson that moving to Texas was worth it, whatever problems might have arisen.

In the early days the families found that their sharecropping on a hilly pecan farm was not successful, so they moved to San Antonio where the Garcias and Santoses shared a house in Fernridge, the estate where Juan José worked as a gardener for Colonel George Brackenridge, who had splendid greenhouses. Juan José's brothers-in-law, Uncle Jesse (that is, Jesús, a name usually anglicized in Texas at the time) and Uncle Gilbert (Gilberto) started school in the area and were the only Mexicans enrolled. They were persecuted, had bicycle tires slashed, and were taunted as "Meskins," a deplorable but once-common expression.

The city job of Juan José had its country parallel: His Garcia uncle, Abrán, twin brother of his grandfather, Jacobo, had pursued the free life of charcoal burner in Mexico, using huisache—the tree immensely common south of the Nueces River and mentioned by Dobie and Allen as a feature of their landscape. He did not come to Texas with the big family group, but he grew tired of having his wagons robbed by revolutionary soldiers and immigrated to the Texas Hill Country, where cedar is common and makes good charcoal. Most of the people who cut cedar sell the trunks as fence posts. The chapter has a virtuoso description of the making of charcoal, writing which rivals any of the scenes of folkways in Owens. The passage is so vivid the reader may forget that Santos was not an eyewitness but got the story from great-uncle Gilbert, the son of Jacobo Garcia.

The third major section, "Peregrinaje" ("pilgrimage") deals with the death of Juan José. The pilgrimage is essentially an exploration of San Antonio, not of a distant place. The opening chapter, "*Zona de Niebla*: Zone of Fog," deals with the January morning when Juan José was found in the river and the circumstances leading up to his death. No great mystery is solved: The fatal day remains shrouded in fog. But we learn much about Juan José's struggles with depression and the ups and downs of his life in San Antonio. He even consulted a *curandero* in an attempt to treat his melancholy. His drowning in the San Antonio River was ambiguous: It could have been suicide, an accident (perhaps a heart attack causing the man to fall into the river), or even a racist murder.

Santos tries rather hard to elevate his grandfather's death into a symptom of a greater malaise by pointing out that 1939 was a terrible year in Europe, which perhaps stretches the significance of one family's misfortune. More important is the fact that in 1939 San Antonio seemed to be trying to erase the Mexican presence in the city by closing down the celebrated chili queens of the Mexican mercado on Haymarket Square. The chili queens sold *picadillo* in booths. The dish has been called the forerunner of the chile con carne of which Anglo Texans are so proud and which has generated such wry frivolities as the Terlingua Chile Cook-Offs. The square was full of life, and singers like the famous Lydia Mendoza performed alongside the chile stands. The health department also banned the funeral processions which, like their counterparts in New Orleans, were accompanied by music: in San Antonio, by musicians dressed like Mexican peasants and playing such traditional instruments as the trumpet, the violin, the accordion, and the *bajo sexto* (134).

The significant erasure happened within the family: Juan José was virtually canceled out. Santos says rather profoundly that deliberate forgetting subtracts something from the universe: "His bundle of years, his every *abrazo* and breath, were rendered a perfect absence, a photo negative of memory, a tear in the fabric of the world" (128). One aim of *Places Left Unfinished at the Time of Creation* is to restore the dead grandfather to the family history, which has been mutilated by the willful forgetting. The most important informant, Santos's father (also named Juan José, as a reviewer, Dorothy Cole,[6] rather irrationally complained—a memoirist is stuck with his family's names), evaded talking about the event until near the end of his life.

After discussing his grandfather's death, Santos turns in his next chapter, "Aztec Theatre/*Teatro Azteca*" to a rich portrait of San Antonio from the founding to the present. The oldest family still extant in Santos's youth was that of Don Demostenio Zuniga and his sister, Doña Herlinda, both in their eighties, whose ancestry could be traced back to the Canary Islands. He would see them in church, looking "shipwrecked and abandoned in an alien century" (143).

Santos himself did not feel that he was in an alien century. He grew up in an Anglo suburb—a last migration, so to speak—and grew with rock and roll, the "Beverly Hillbillies" and a trip to Disneyland. But he clearly laments the progressive loss of history and culture in a city where, as he says, the Hard Rock Cafe offers a "virtual cantina" and Planet Hollywood is "quaintly Spanish-styled." The old mercado, gutted by the health department in 1939 and demolished in the 1970s, was rebuilt as a kind of theme park "made from bricks the color of a Ramada Inn." The Alamo itself has been restored and the famous battle is the subject of an IMAX film nearby: *The Battle for Freedom*. Santos points out that in the film Davy Crockett is wearing a wristwatch, a Chicano documentary maker's critique of dubious Anglo propaganda.

The Texas of his youth offered no virtual cantinas and the dominant ethos was heavily Anglo. Mexicans were called "greasers, "wetbacks," or "taco benders," and the racist frame of mind was assimilated by the victims, who felt powerless. He describes the annual Battle of the Flowers, a euphemistic term for a celebration of the victory of Anglo Texas over Mexican Texas at the battles of San Antonio and San Jacinto. The Anglo pioneer, Mary Maverick, was one of the organizers of the original festival. The two-week festival is presided over by "King Antonio," who is chosen by an all-Anglo organization, the Cavaliers. Santos recalls that King Antonio would show up at Sacred Heart School with a face so white he appeared to have been treated with talcum powder, wearing a grotesque military uniform in turquoise and magenta, with knee-high boots. In a fine touch, the white caricature gave the brown students wooden nickels.

Santos moves smoothly into the twentieth century by suggesting that the Mexicans "lived in the ruins of that time" of conquest, which has attenuated into "mirages and echoes." His chief exhibit is the Aztec Theater, a magnificent movie palace built in 1926. It was decorated with Aztec and Mayan images which the architect had assistants copy from ruins all over Mexico. The curtain itself had a painting of the key moment in Mexican history, when Cortés met Montezuma, which would lead to the fall of the Aztec empire. One of Santos's great-uncles went to the opening of the theater, where the fatal moment was reenacted in a pageant in front of that curtain. Images of images: a brilliant way to evoke the ruins of time and the loss of a heritage. The theater is now derelict, and even the copied images are vanishing.

The succeeding "Rain of Stones" chapter turns from a plasticized San Antonio back to the Mexican earth, with scenes of the Guerra family's Rancho Los Generales, which Santos visited during his college summer vacations. He learned about genuine ranch life there, including such morbid details as a dead cow covered with vultures which "shook out their rugs of wings." He was in love with poetry and the vocation of poet in those years and says that one of his journal entries described himself as "a laughing vaquero poet at end of twentieth century" (171). The omitted "the" in the last phrase probably grew out of his readings in Beat Generation literature: It is one of Allen Ginsberg's mannerisms.

One of the best scenes is a storytelling night on the ranch. The tales of the monte at Los Generales were mostly ghost stories, which suits this book rather well. The celebration of the Day of the Dead in Mora's *House of Houses* comes to mind, along with the fictional stories at Dobie's Hacienda de Las Cinco Llagas (placed in Coahuila, like the real ranch of the Guerra family). One Guerra uncle described a mysterious rain of stones, and three sisters jointly told a story of the exorcism of a ghost in Sabinas by a spiritualist who lured it out of the house and back to the cemetery with a trail of "orange petals of *zempaxuchitl* flowers" (173). Santos recited his favorite "life is a dream" passage from Calderon de la Barca, the play in which an imprisoned prince is briefly allowed to rule his father's kingdom to test a prophecy which said he would ruin it. When the prophecy was clearly confirmed, the prince was taken back to his prison to dream away his life: The story adds to the fin de siècle atmosphere of Santos's book, the suspicion that life is a mere illusion.

Near the end of "Rain of Stones," he narrates his first journey to the heart of the country, Mexico City itself, once known as Tenochtitlán, the ancient capital of the Aztec empire. There are two routes into the heart of Mexico. One from the north, the route taken by the wandering tribes who left their legendary homeland of Aztlán long before the Conquest, the other from the east, the route taken by Cortés. In this chapter he takes the northern approach, recording a visit to Mexico City with his family in 1976. San Antonio was a large city with a kind of Mexican city concealed in it: The real thing overwhelmed him with its vastness, and it turned out to be a Mexican city with an Aztec city buried in it. The trip was made on the four-lane Mexican Highway 57 which has, he says, replaced the legendary route taken by the Aztecs from their mythical origins in Aztlán to the valley of Mexico.

Aztlán was a utopian construct in the early writings of the Chicano movement, as Rafael Pérez-Torres explains in *Movements in Chicano Poetry: Against Myths, Against Margins*.[7] Sometime around 820 A.D. the god of the Aztecs, Quetzalcoatl, is said to have instructed his people to head south until they saw a portent, the famous scene perpetuated on the Mexican flag, an eagle eating a snake and resting on a cactus. The journey took centuries, but it led to the founding of the great capital, Tenochtitlán, on a lake which was drained for the purpose. Ironically, this legendary path southward has received more attention until recently than the historical route Cortés took from Veracruz to Tenochtitlán in the Conquest of Mexico, another example of forgetting. But Aztlán has a cultural weight as a symbol of origins for Chicanos trying to make sense of the Mexican diaspora.

The peculiar tendency of buildings to sink in Mexico City, which was built on a lake bed, offers him an excellent metaphor for the theme of forgetting in the book. Churches are built over churches that were built on the sites of Aztec temples and pyramids: The past is obliterated, though not beyond imaginative retrieval. At Chapultepec Park he and his family saw *voladores* performing and were told by their guide that the dance enacts the patterns of the ancient Mexican calendar. That calendar assumes that the world is either renewed or destroyed at the end of each fifty-two year cycle. At the end of each cycle, new pyramids would be built on the sites of the old ones to commemorate the survival of the world.

The most important site he visited in 1976 was Tepeyac, where in legend the Virgin of Guadalupe appeared to the Indian Juan Diego. The hill at Tepeyac was sacred to the mother Goddess Tonantzín. The miracle whereby the Indian Juan Diego's cloak bore the imprint of the Virgin's face (an Indian face) was the means by which Catholicism could be built over the foundations of Aztec religion: the Mother of God superimposed on the Mother Goddess. A series of shrines on the spot have sunk and been replaced. The Virgin's image now resides in an ultramodern building which Santos compares to a space ship. The pious can see it by riding one of three moving sidewalks, an astonishing juxtaposition of ancient pilgrimage and modern technology. Canny pilgrims know how to jam the mechanism of a sidewalk so that they get a longer glimpse of the sacred image. An ironic action: Traditional piety finds a way to stop the movement of modern machinery in order to get a better view of an ancient holy image.

The trip to Mexico City was followed by a return to the Rancho Los Generales, where the monarch butterflies were making their journey deep into Mexico. Santos is fond of alluding to the monarchs, who make their own pilgrimages to and from the United States and Mexico. At the ranch he had a series of strange apocalyptic dreams with rather forced symbolism: These are not Santos's best writing. The chapter ends with the narrator feeling that he never wants to leave Mexico, but he says that in fact he did not return for ten years.

The swerve the work makes next is brilliant: The "Volador" section, the last one, opens with a chapter called "*Exilio:* Exile." It takes Santos to England as a Rhodes scholar. Just before he left he had a conversation with his Uncle Beto, who had married Santos's Aunt Margie (Margarita Santos) and is something of an exile himself, having emigrated from Nueva Rosita, Coahuila, some decades before: the Mexican diaspora continues well after 1914; indeed it is not over yet. The uncle talked about Socrates while making the traditional tripe and hominy soup, *menudo*. He attributed a saying he liked, "*Todo se acaba. Todo se extermina*" (everything ends, everything is exterminated"), to the Greek philosopher, thereby affirming the apocalyptic end-of-the-world feeling of the book, a note anticipated in the previous chapter by the Aztec belief in world cycles. At the time of his scholarship, Santos was studying analytical philosophy, which demands an approach to truth and language quite different from his memoir, which relies on image and symbol and suggestion. The analytical philosophers rule out myth and metaphysics: no *inframundo* or ghosts for them.

One thing that Santos did in his exile was look up a surviving pre-Conquest codex of the Aztecs, which resides in a library in Oxford. Comically, he made a trek across the library floor in his Tony Lama boots, which had started to rot in the damp climate and squeak, causing elderly scholars to tell him to be quiet. In the codex he found an astonishing image: a little picture of *voladores*. He eventually made a sacrifice of the boots by throwing them off the "bridge of exile" into the Thames.

The most complex and personally revealing chapter in the book is "*La Ruta*: The Route." One of his key metaphors has been the road or path, especially as a means of talking about the long journey of the Santos/Garcia families in the twentieth century. His personal journey in life has involved television journalism, a new kind of story collecting done not around a campfire but with cameras and microphones. The negative side of the career has been his inability to do more than tell stories when dealing with terrible human suffering: He remembers the starving in Sudan (who remind him of the poverty his family escaped from in 1914). Back in New York, he edited the scene on a monitor: "Now, as I watched the story unfolding, in sequences of playback and record, I realized that when asked for relief, all I could do was to offer to tell a story" (225).

He juxtaposes a return to San Antonio on a truth-seeking mission with the dubious spirituality of the notorious Chevrolet Madonna. On a visit to interview the fireman who found his grandfather, he heard about the Madonna, one of those odd miracles that cause hysteria among the credulous. The Chevrolet Madonna involves a supposed image of the Virgin Mary kneeling in prayer (and perhaps reading the Bible), an image thrown onto the wall of house by a porch light reflecting off the fender of a 1975 Chevrolet Impala. The discoverer was a teenage Chicano boy emptying the garbage one night. Soon people were coming on crutches and wheelchairs, until the man whose house had the apparition projected on it decided to end the farce by shining mercury vapor lights on the image to drown it out. Santos brilliantly contrasts his quest for journalistic truth in his interview with Pompa, who turned out to be senile, with the credulity of the pious in the suburb. He notes that this was a Madonna who had nothing to say. The spell of the Virgin of Guadalupe seems to have dissipated into farce.

But in one of the almost subliminal transitions that he excels in, Santos immediately takes the reader on a return trip to the Virgin's magical realm, which constitutes the heart of his "La Ruta" chapter. He wanted to follow the eastern route into Mexico which he calls the umbilical journey. During the Revolution of 1910 all the monuments to Cortés in Mexico City were destroyed, but his invasion route is now signposted for tourists and advertised in tourist literature. *La Ruta de Cortés* is an "erased journey" (239) but, like a ruin in the waterlogged soil of Mexico City, it seems ready to rise again. This trip enabled him to watch *voladores* in the mountains where the rite is said to have origins. In the ancient center of Yohualichan, he ran into an anthropology professor from the University of Puebla. For a moment it appeared that he would learn the secret of the *voladores*, but she put him off with New Age babble and gave him an odd blessing, rubbing his forehead and clothing with spittle. She told him to leave something of personal value behind, and he buried his walkman, a good choice for a media journalist. A subsequent meeting with a *volador* dancer yielded no answers.

He reached Mexico City on the Day of the Dead. The remains of the Templo Mayor have (an irony of history) now been uncovered by the most contemporary sort of enterprise, the building of a subway. Since his first visit in 1976, archaeologists had learned that the sites destroyed by the Spaniards at the Conquest were merely the latest layers of many. The oldest of the pyramids seems to exist under "an ancient moat of water," the remains of the ancient lake under Tenochtitlán. It is inaccessible to contemporary digging techniques and may be unreachable.

After Mexico City he returned to the Rancho Los Generales, to wild Mexican landscape. At the ranch he was hit by a *remolino*, an enormous whirlwind of dust, and a bee the size of his fist landed on his mouth, a moment reminiscent of Isaiah's mouth being touched by a coal of fire. Words resounded in his head, and they are recorded for the reader. They don't measure up to the description of the *remolino* itself. The last few phrases are an adequate sample: "Indistinct knowledge as a Papaya. As Frijol. Eyes like mirrors. Heart like wind. Sangria by the gallons. River of souls. Songs pull toward the earth like a magnet. Lost friends. Dead grandfathers, grandmothers, uncles, and aunts. Holy. Holy. Mystical Revolutions. Five hundred years." (256). The influence of the Beats is perhaps too strong here: Allen Ginsberg's litany of "Holy" things in "Footnote to Howl" comes to mind. The phrases heard in the whirlwind become the basis for the rather weak poem that serves as a prologue for the whole book.

After this high-pitched mystical experience, a more effective chapter, "*Una Canción*: A Song," deals with his quest to learn the truth about Juan José's death from his father. John Phillip Santos believes that the mystery of his grandfather's journey in the fog leaves "the question of our destiny in Mexico and Texas unresolved. . . ." (265) He persuaded his father to go to the cemetery one year on the anniversary of the death, and he finally got the father's story. However, it was inconclusive; the son of Juan José was not sure just what happened. More might have come into memory if they entered into the cemetery, but they were delayed in traffic and arrived to find the gates closed. To increase the portentousness of the moment, Santos mentions that they encountered shoppers at Las Palmas Mall, getting ready for the feast of the Three Kings, "the last celebration of the sacred calendar in Mexican Christmas tradition" (270). He does not mention it, but the feast is an Epiphany celebration. There was no epiphany at the locked cemetery nor at the ersatz fiesta at the shopping mall, but back home his shy father agreed to sing a few of his songs, and he ended with "Corrido de Múzquiz," about the town from which the patriarch of the family in Coahuila had been kidnapped by the Kikapu Indians. In a perfect dying fall, the narrator queried his father's suggestion that he would like to die in Múzquiz. The fictive element found even in art which commemorates experience is brought out by his father's reply: "That's just the story, John Phillip. That's just the story in the song" (274).

The epilogue to the book is highly fictional, just a "story in the song" itself: an attempt to find a positive direction in the diaspora. Nowadays there is a large Mexican presence in New York City. Santos uses a vision to convey a positive element in this extension of the Mexican journey to New York—and into the wider world. Santos was interested in the works of Carlos Castaneda in his youth. Castaneda, an anthropologist born in Peru (or perhaps in Brazil: He cultivated mystery), wrote books about a Yaqui Indian sorcerer named Don Juan. The works, with their proto-New Age atmosphere, had a cult following in the 1960s and 1970s. The reliability of the books is highly doubtful but they put a mythical overlay on the Mexican-American border with their tales of magical events in a realm which seems very much like the *inframundo*.

Santos describes returning to his New York apartment, where in his absence guests had seen a ghostly presence in the living room, like a silvery smoke. One person even saw a man in white, like Uncle Raul in the earlier vision. In a climactic dream vision, he describes the reappearance of Uncle Raul, who takes his nephew on a journey in a car made of air, which is rather hard to visualize. They fly past the towers of the World Trade Center (which, unfortunately, did not long survive the millennium) to a building on the Upper East Side, where *voladores* perform their ritual on the roof. They eventually fly out over the city, referred to as "Babylon-on-the Hudson," doubtless an allusion to the Israelite diaspora of Psalm 137, where the exiles hang their harps on willows, unable to sing the songs of Zion in a strange land. It is as if Santos is saying, "If I forget thee, O Mexico, let my right hand forget her cunning." Babylon has more ominous apocalyptic associations too, as the city at the end of the world. The meaning of the dream, the author tells us, is that in New York "Mexico's invisible enchantment is underway" (279). A diaspora can be a dissemination of a culture, though it can also be a dissipation of the authentic, something the upbeat ending does not address.

With this epilogue, the story has ceased to be a Texas/Mexico chronicle and looks toward the so-called global village. The ending places an upbeat spin on the attenuation of Mexican culture and goes counter to the elegiac burden of the book. It lacks the imaginative power and the meticulous recall of the earlier narrative, but it is understandable that Santos would want to turn from the recurring dirge, "all of the old Mexicans are dying," to suggest that the story of his family, the Mexican and mestizo story, will have survived into the new century, that the book need not end with fin de siècle sadness in spite of the family melancholy which often appeared in it. His afterword, "Tent of Grief," does add to the tone of sorrow by observing that his father died five days after *Places Left Unfinished* was finished and that Madrina is now completely senile. But the family saga is not yet finished. His next book, he told Pamela Coloff in an interview for *The Texas Monthly*, will trace his family's roots in the Basque Country of Spain. The title at the moment is *The Farthest Home Is in an Empire of Fire*.[8]

Naomi Shihab Nye

CONCLUSION:
ARE TEXANS STILL TEXANS?

At the start of the twenty-first century it seems reasonable to ponder whether Texans are still Texans rather than Americans who happen to live in one politically defined territory. Of course, the political boundaries are a reminder that the state has had a very particular history, the effects of which are still felt. Migrations, war with Mexico, brief nationhood, slavery, the Indian Wars, the Civil War, the Mexican diaspora of the twentieth century: These events have contributed to Texas exceptionalism. The groups represented by the authors I have discussed are diverse enough to make it clear that there has never been a typical Texan embodying a Lone Star exceptionalism. Some writers in this book, like Hallie Stillwell and J. Frank Dobie, became public figures because they fit an image of the Texan, an image that has always been Anglo, as if Texas had no vaqueros or African-American oil-field workers.

Farmers and ranchers are relatively scarce: The shift from rural to urban witnessed by Owens and Beasley and McMurtry has left Texas heavily urban. The shopping malls of Dallas and Houston are generic, as are the outlet malls of San Marcos and New Braunfels. Texans today watch national television rather than tell stories around campfires or the fireplace. No wonder the supply of "originals"—out of the Anglo traditions of the American South—seems to have run out. John Graves elegized the type in his portrait of the Old Fart in *Hard Scrabble.* The difficult conditions of life in pre-urban Texas probably fostered rugged individualism. But writers who see themselves as products of dysfunctional families, whatever their background, will be, in their own way, as stubbornly idiosyncratic as anyone "from the old rock": Consider Mary Karr's combative sense of self, John Houghton Allen's *coraje*, or William Humphrey's feeling that his father's "abandonment" in death left him a rebel and an orphan in the universe. Gertrude Beasley's willful combination of aggressiveness and neurosis seems prophetic. Tolstoy claimed in the opening of *Anna Karenina that* all unhappy families are unhappy in their own way; perhaps we can go on to say that all children of dysfunctional families are unhappy in their own way. Humphrey chose isolation and reticence. There are many ways to assert a stubborn sense of self. Larry McMurtry's melancholy work shows the cost of losing that sense of wholeness.

If any group in Texas has declined in influence it must be the Anglo Texans, the group most closely identified with the mystique of Texas and its images: the Alamo, the Texas Rangers, the ranchers and oil men. The Anglos have not vanished, of course, but they belong to an increasingly multicultural society, one in which they likely will be a minority in a quarter of a century. Paradoxically, the memoirists most aware of the Anglo-Texas tradition today seem to be Mexican-Americans, who experienced the Anglo hegemony and recall its prejudices: Pat Mora, John Phillip Santos, Ray Gonzalez, and Gloria López-Stafford remember the Alamo very well, though their views on it would not delight Mary Maverick. The black memoirists, Annie Mae Hunt and the Reverend Charlie C. White, show a similar awareness of the problems of growing up in an Anglo world: One interest of their books lies in the ways that they found to act in Texas history as well as to suffer it, Annie Mae through Democratic party politics, Charlie White through negotiations on civil rights in his community. All these writers, Chicanos and blacks, are Texans as much as anyone whose ancestors fought in the Texas Revolution or the Civil War. Of course, it is easy to overlook that *Tejanos* died at the Alamo and that the first cowboys were vaqueros.

One of the interesting trends in Texas memoirs is the cyclical role of family saga and family history, stories in which the experience of pioneering times in Texas are preserved. The earlier Anglo writers show an intense interest in family stories. Sallie Reynolds Matthews is representative, with her controlling metaphor of interwoven families, the ones incorporated in her name. For Mora and Santos and Gonzalez, the pioneering days do not go back so far as with Matthews and Greene and Lomax. Their families mostly came to Texas in the 1910s.

No doubt other groups will add their family sagas now that Texas is adding new strands to its interwoven society. Naomi Shihab Nye (1952-), a major American poet and a good friend of John Phillip Santos, has not yet written a full-length memoir, but some of the essays in her collection, *Never In a Hurry*,[1] deal with the Arab diaspora. She tells the story of her Muslim father's emigration from Palestine to the United States, where he decided briefly to become a Christian minister. Eventually he had a successful career as a newspaper editor. Nye's Lutheran mother sent the children to a Vedanta Society in St. Louis and to a Unity Sunday School. Nye says that she called herself a Hindu when anyone asked about her religion. She spent a year in Jerusalem, where she was a student in an Armenian school. In the essay called "One Village," she has written movingly about her visit as an adult to the village where her grandmother was living. Since her teens she has lived in San Antonio, and many of her essays are based on the neighborhood where she lives on South Main. She is thoroughly multi-cultural by birth, origins, and commitment, and has compiled ethnic collections of poetry and writings for children. This history seems perfectly normal in twenty-first century America, where cultural pluralism is so widespread, where being part of a diaspora is increasingly common.

James Clifford notes in a fine study that "the discourse of the diaspora is replacing, or at least supplementing, minority discourse. Transnational connections break the binary relation of *minority* communities with *majority societies.*[2] The sudden popularity of the concept of the diaspora in academic studies represents a shift in cultural consciousness, an awareness that ethnic groups in America (aside from Native Americans) are part of a process of immigration, and that in some cases they still have important ties with the originating group, ties which can be maintained through modern communications. The Scotch-Irish in America, who are often described as the driving force in the settlement of Texas, are a diaspora whose origins in the history of Ulster are mostly forgotten, but John Phillip Santos and Naomi Shihab Nye show that it is possible to return to the originating country to inquire into history and identity. What is theoretical in academic circles is experience for such writers.

In his conclusion to *Places Left Unfinished at the Time of Creation*, Santos suggests that the Mexican diaspora will continue, from the Mexican border to New York and beyond. It is fascinating to see him envisioning a limitless evolution of the Mexican presence in the world, the diaspora moving onward. In *Border Matters*, José David Saldívar suggests that it will be important to understand the Chicano diaspora in relation to other diasporas.[3] Texas, with its enormous resources and its move to a highly urban society, is increasingly a site where the workings of various migrations, Asian as well as Mexican and African American, can be traced as well as in New York City.

Of course, sociologists and anthropologists can study diasporic groups at will with statistics and interviews. Those who seek a literary understanding, a rendering of experience into art, must wait for the writers. It would be possible to assemble a wish list of memoirs: accounts by Vietnamese Catholics and Buddhists from the Port Arthur area, or narratives by Mexican Americans who grew up in South Texas, like Gloria Anzaldúa, a sixth generation *Tejana*. These groups have stories to tell, and some members are likely to want to tell them.

Of course, the next major autobiography to come out of Texas may not be written by a member of an identifiable ethnic group at all: It could be written by an Anglo, perhaps even one who sees being a Texan as no more significant than being a Pennsylvanian or a Nebraskan. Or it could be written by a Hindu working for Digital in Austin. Mary Karr comes close to this point of view: She is not particularly interested in the history of the state. Texas exceptionalism has, to return to Benjamin Soskis's "Lone Star Joining," declined. It has not vanished, however, and strangely enough, the minority groups long resident in Texas are by virtue of their history most aware of it. The residual influence of the American South and the links with Mexico make the demographic mixture in Texas distinctive: California has the Mexican influence but not the southern heritage. The landscapes of the state remain, whatever the changes in society, and writers will always respond to those: the desert of the Trans-Pecos, the enormous sky of West Texas, the red soil of northeast Texas, the thorny world of the Brush Country. Texas has enough exceptionalism to last for a while yet.

NOTES

Introduction

1. Benjamin Soskis, "Lone Star Joining," *The New Republic* 4,470 (18 September 2000): 23-27.

2. William Humphrey, *Farther Off from Heaven* (New York: Knopf, 1977).

3. Craig Clifford, "Horseman, Hang On: the Reality of Myth in Texas Letters," *Range Wars: Heated Debates, Sober Reflections, and Other Assessments of Texas Writing*, eds. Craig Clifford and Tom Pilkington (Dallas: Southern Methodist University Press, 1988), 54.

4. William A. Owens, *This Stubborn Soil: A Frontier Boyhood* (New York: Scribner's, 1966; Revised edition with an introduction by John Graves and an afterword by Owens; New York: Lyons Press, 1986. Page citations are to the revised edition); *A Season of Weathering* (New York: Scribner's, 1973).

5. Mary Karr, *The Liars' Club* (New York: Viking, 1995); *Cherry* (New York: Viking, 2000).

6. Hallie Crawford Stillwell, *I'll Gather My Geese* (College Station: Texas A&M University Press, 1991).

7. Larry McMurtry, *In a Narrow Grave: Essays on Texas* (Austin: Encino Press, 1968; New York: Simon and Schuster, 1989), xiv.

8. _______, *Walter Benjamin at the Dairy Queen: Reflections at Sixty and Beyond* (New York: Simon & Schuster, 1999); *Roads: Driving America's Great Highways* (New York: Simon & Schuster, 2000); *Paradise* (New York: Simon & Schuster, 2001).

9. A. C. Greene, *Sketches from the Five States of Texas* (College Station: Texas A & M University Press, 1998).

10. _______, *A Personal Country* (New York: Knopf, 1969; Revised edition, with a preface by Larry L. King and an afterword by the author: College Station: Texas A & M University Press, 1998).

11. Dorothy Redus Robinson, *The Bell Rings at Four: A Black Teacher's Chronicle of Change* (Austin: Madrona Press, 1978).

12. Annie Mae Hunt and Ruthe Winegarten, *I am Annie Mae: An Extraordinary Black Texas Woman in Her Own Words* (Austin: Rosegarden Press, 1983; Austin: University of Texas Press, 1996.)

13. C. C. White and Ada Morehead Holland, *No Quittin' Sense* (Austin: University of Texas Press, 1969).

14. Dave Oliphant, *Memories of Texas Towns & Cities* (Austin: Host Publications, 2000).

15. J. Frank Dobie, *Some Part of Myself* (New York: Little, Brown and Co., 1967).

16. John Houghton Allen, *Southwest* (Philadelphia: Lippincott, 1952; reprint, Albuquerque: University of New Mexico Press, 1977).

17. Pat Mora, *House of Houses* (Boston: Beacon Press, 1997).

18. Gloria López-Stafford, *A Place in El Paso: A Mexican American Childhood* (Albuquerque: University of New Mexico Press, 1996).

19. Sallie Reynolds Matthews, *Interwoven: A Pioneer Chronicle* (privately printed, 1936; second edition, El Paso: Carl Hertzog, 1958; third edition, College Station: Texas A & M University Press, 1982. Page citations are to the third edition).

20. Gertrude Beasley, *My First Thirty Years* (Paris: Contact Editions, 1925; reprint with an afterword by Larry McMurtry; Austin: Book Club of Texas, 1989. Page citations are to the reprinted edition).

21. John Phillip Santos, *Places Left Unfinished at the Time of Creation* (New York: Viking Penguin, 1999; reprint, with Reader's Guide, 2000).

22. Jewel Babb, *Border Healing Woman: The Story of Jewel Babb/as told to Pat LittleDog* (Austin: University of Texas Press, 1985; second edition with a new epilogue by Pat LittleDog,1994).

23. John A. Lomax. *Adventures of a Ballad Hunter* (New York: Macmillan, 1947).

24. Gloria Anzaldúa, *Borderlands/La Frontera: The New Mestiza* (San Francisco: Aunt Lute, 1987; second edition, 1999), 52.

25. Ray Gonzalez, *Memory Fever: A Journey Beyond El Paso del Norte* (Seattle: Broken Moon Press, 1993; reprint, Tucson: University of Arizona Press, 1999).

26. Ron Rozelle, *Into That Good Night* (New York: Farrar, Straus and Giroux, 1998; Huntsville: Texas Review Press, 2000), 47.

27. John Graves, *Hard Scrabble: Observations on a Patch of Land* (New York: Alfred A. Knopf, 1974), 114-140.

28. Some of J. Frank Dobie's sketches of "originals" were collected in *Out of the Old Rock* (New York: Little, Brown and Co., 1972).

29. L. Langness and Gelya Frank, *Lives: An Anthropological Approach to Biography* (Novato, California: Chandler & Sharp, 1981), 117-155.

30. James Olney, *Metaphors of Self: The Meaning of Autobiography* (Princeton: Princeton University Press, 1972).

31. Paul John Eakin, *Fictions in Autobiography: Studies in the Art of Self-Invention* (Princeton: Princeton University Press, 1985).

32. Barrett Mandel, "Full of Life Now," *Autobiography: Essays Theoretical and Critical*, ed. James Olney (Princeton: Princeton University Press, 1980), 58.

33. Ibid., 66.

34. Paul John Eakin, *How Our Lives Become Stories: Making Selves* (Ithaca and London: Cornell University Press, 1999), 69.

35. Américo Paredes, *With His Pistol in His Hand: A Border Ballad and Its Hero* (Austin: University of Texas Press, 1958).

36. Sylvia Grider, "Memories that Never Were," *From Texas to the World and Back: Essays on the Journey of Katherine Anne Porter*, eds. Mark Busby and Dick Heaberlin (Fort Worth: TCU Press, 2001), 225-237.

37. Mody C. Boatright, "The Family Saga as a Form of Folklore," *The Family Saga and Other Phases of American Folklore* (Urbana: University of Illinois Press, 1958), 1-19.

38. James McNutt, *Beyond Regionalism: Texas Folklorists and the Emergence of a Post-Regional Consciousness* (Ann Arbor, Michigan: University Microfilms International, 1982).

39. Ernest B. Speck, "Mody Coggin Boatright," *The Handbook of Texas Online*, <http://www.tsha.utexas.edu/handbook/online/articles/view/BB/fbo1.html> (15 February 1999, 13 May 2001).

40. Sandra K. Stahl, "The Oral Personal Narrative in Its Generic Context," *Fabula* 18 (1977): 32-34.

41. Tom Pilkington, *State of Mind: Texas Literature and Culture* (College Station: Texas A & M University Press, 1998), 10-18.

42. Mary A. Maverick, *Memoirs of Mary A. Maverick*. (Privately printed,1896; San Antonio: Alamo Printing Co., 1921).

43. Paula Mitchell Marks, "Mary Ann Adams Maverick," *Handbook of Texas Online*,<http://www.tsha.utexas.edu/handbook/online/articles/view/MM/fma82.html> (15 February 1999, 10 September 2001).

44. Amelia E. Barr, *All the Days of My Life: An Autobiography, The Red Leaves of a Human Heart* (New York and London: D. Appleton and Company, 1915).

1. Sallie Reynolds Matthews

1. Frances Mayhugh Holden, *Lambshead before Interwoven: A Texas Range chronicle, 1848-1878* (College Station: Texas A & M University Press, 1982).

2. Lawrence Clayton, *Watkins Reynolds Matthews: A Biography* (Abilene: Hardin-Simmons University Press, 1990).

3. Frances Mayhew Holden, "George Thomas Reynolds," *Handbook of Texas Online*,<http://www.tsha.utexas.edu/handbook/online/articles/view/RR/fre31.html>(15 February 1999, 9 July 2001).

4. Cynthia Rose, "Lottie Deno," *The Handbook of Texas Online*, *<http://www.tsha.utexas.edu/handbook/online/articles/view/DD/fde59.html>* (15 February 1999, May 23, 2001).

5. Deborah Bloys Hardin describes the event and its history in "Bloys Camp Meeting," *The Handbook of Texas Online*,<http://www.tsha.utexas.edu/handbook/online/articles/view/BB/ibyl.html> (15 February 1999, 13 May 2001).

6. *The Texas Almanac 2000-2001*, millennium edition (Dallas: *Dallas Morning News*, 1999), pp. 257, 267.

7. Kenneth F. Neighbours, "Elm Creek Raid," *Handbook of Texas Online*, <http://www.tsha.utexas.edu/handbook/online/articlesview/EE/bte1.htm> (15 February 1999, 13 May 2001).

8. Wallace Stegner, *Wolf Willow: A History, a Story, and a Memory of the Last Plains Frontier* (New York: Viking, 1955), 26.

9. "The History of the Old Jail Art Center," Albany, Texas: Attractions, n. d., <http://www.albanytexas.com/attractions/artcenterhist.html> (13 May 2001).

10. Robert E. Nail, *The Fandangle, A People's Theater* (Albany, Texas: The Fort Griffin Fandangle Association, 1970).

11. Laura Wilson, *Watt Matthews of Lambshead* (Austin: Texas State Historical Association, 1989).

12. Ethel Matthews Casey, *Reminiscences* (n. p.: privately printed, 1985 by Carl Hertzog).

13. Watt Matthews, *Lambshead Legacy: The Ranch Diary of Watt R. Matthews*, ed. Janet M. Neubegauer, with an introduction by Frances Mayhugh Holden (College Station: Texas A & M University Press, 1997). The introduction gives a superb overview of the history of the ranch (which was built by piecemeal acquisitions of land) and its current operations. The work of Watt Matthews in preserving his family's legacy is described in abundant detail.

2. John A. Lomax and J. Frank Dobie

1. James McNutt, *Beyond Regionalism: Texas Folklorists and the Emergence of a Post-Regional Consciousness* (Ann Arbor, Michigan: University Microfilms International, 1982), 19-22.

2. J. Frank Dobie, "The Tournament in Texas" *Publications of the Texas Folklore Society* (Austin: Texas Folklore Society, 1926), 93-103.

3. Burton Bledstein, *The Culture of Professionalism* (New York: Norton, 1976).

4. Nolan Porterfield, *The Last Cavalier: The Life and Times of John A. Lomax 1867-1948* (Urbana and Chicago: University of Illinois Press, 1996), 142.

5. John A. Lomax, ed. *Cowboy Songs and Other Frontier Ballads* (New York: Sturgis and Walton, 1910).

6. J. Evetts Haley, *George W. Littlefield: Texan* (Norman: University of Oklahoma Press, 1943), 243.

7. William A. Owens, *Three Friends: Roy Bedichek, J. Frank Dobie, Walter Prescott Webb* (Austin and London: University of Texas Press, 1975).

8. Ronnie Dugger, ed., *Three Men in Texas: Bedichek, Webb, and Dobie* (Austin and London: University of Texas Press, 1967).

9. Winston Bode, *A Portrait of Pancho: The Life of a Great Texan*. (Austin: The Pemberton Press, 1965).

10. Lon Tinkle, *An American Original: The Life of J. Frank Dobie* (New York: Little, Brown and Co., 1978).

11. Francis Edward Abernethy, *J. Frank Dobie*, Southwest Writers Series no. 1 (Austin: Steck-Vaughn, 1967), 2.

12. Don Graham, "Pen Pals." *Texas Monthly* (March 1996): 100-107.

13. James Ward Lee, "Arbiters of Texas Literary Taste," *Range Wars: Heated Debates, Sober Reflections, and Other Assessments of Texas Writing*, eds. Craig Clifford and Tom Pilkington (Dallas: Southern Methodist University Press, 1988), 125.

14. Gregory Curtis, "Curse of the Coots," *Texas Monthly* (February 1993): 206.

15. Américo Paredes, *George Washington Gómez: A Mexicotexan Novel* (Houston: Arte Público Press, 1990).

16. José E. Limón, *Dancing with the Devil: Society and Cultural Poetics in Mexican-American South Texas* (Madison: University of Wisconsin Press, 1984).

17. Pilkington, *State of Mind*, 18.

18. J. Frank Dobie, *Tongues of the Monte* (Garden City, New York: Doubleday, 1939; reissued with the 1947 introduction by Dobie, Austin: University of Texas Press, 1980. All citations are to the 1980 edition).

19. Tinkle, *An American Original*, 147.

20. Roy Bedichek, *Karánkaway Country* (Austin: University of Texas Press, 1950.)

21. Limón, *Dancing with the Devil*, 45.

22. J. Frank Dobie, *Coronado's Children: Tales of Lost Mines and Buried Treasures of the Southwest* (Dallas: Southwest Press, 1930); *Apache Gold and Yaqui Silver* (Boston: Little, Brown and Co., 1939). In *Coronado's Children*, "Pancho" devotes a chapter to Fort Ramirez and the fate of the Ramirez family.

23. *Texas: A Guide to the Lone Star State*, American Guide Series (Austin: Texas Highway Commission, 1940); reissued as *The WPA Guide to Texas*, with a new introduction by Don Graham (Austin: Texas Monthly Press, 1986), 89.

24. The sixth chapter of McNutt's *Beyond Regionalism*, "J. Frank Dobie's Romance of the Border," (166-212) is a superb and balanced inquiry into Dobie's racial attitudes. McNutt discusses aspects of Dobie's life and prejudices which Lon Tinkle ignored or overlooked.

25. J. Frank Dobie, *A Vaquero of the Brush Country*, (Dallas: Southwest Press, 1929), 60.

26. Tinkle, *An American Original*, 30.

27. J. Frank Dobie, "Guilt by Rumor," *Southwest Review* 35 (Summer 1950): 211-212.

28. Ralph W. Yarborough, *Frank Dobie: Man and Friend* (Washington, D.C.: Potomac Corral of the Westerners, 1967).

29. J. Frank Dobie, *A Texan in England* (Boston: Little, Brown and Co., 1945).

30. Limón, *Dancing with the Devil*, 51.

31. Walter Benjamin, "The Storyteller: Reflections on the Works of Nicolai Leskov," *Illuminations: Essays and Reflections*, ed. with an introduction by Hannah Arendt (New York: Schocken, 1968), 83.

3. Gertrude Beasley

1. At the time that Larry McMurtry was preparing the Book Club of Texas edition of *My First Thirty Years*, Patrick and Shay Bennett collected documents pertaining to Beasley, including her marks at Hardin-Simmons University and her application for a reader's card at the British Library. They have generously shared these with me. Other sources of information which I have discovered include her passport applications, 1920, 1922, and 1924, (National Archives and Records Administration.) There is so little information about Beasley that they are particularly valuable. The 1920 application, dated May 1, 1920, Bellingham, Washington, contains her mother's affidavit certifying the place and date of her birth. The 1922 (April 17) application, prepared in Peking, is more interesting, as it gives some details of her whereabouts in Japan and China in 1920-1922. She also filed an Application for Registration—Native Citizen on February 2, 1922 in Peking (National Archives and Records Service).

2. Gilbert Grosvenor, letter to Gertrude Beasley, February 21, 1922 (*National Geographic* Archives) accepting "Something about Work in Japan." Grosvenor's letter also mentions four other articles, including one on Korea, which he was forwarding to the magazine, *Asia*, for its consideration. None of this work appeared in print.

3. Don Graham, "A Woman of Independent Means," *Texas Monthly* (July 2000): 22.

4. Sigmund Freud, *Three Essays on the Theory of Sexuality* and *On Sexuality*, (First published in English translation, 1905; The Penguin Freud Library, vol 7, London: Penguin, 1991).

5. H. L. Mencken, "A Texas School Marm," *The American Mercury* 7.25 (January 1926): 124.

6. One confusion of the book is her tendency to refer to older siblings by their ordinal number: "my second brother," "my third sister," and so on. On the basis of the memoir itself and various online genealogical sources, it is possible to work out their birth order and approximate birth dates (and sometimes dates of death) for readers and future commentators. It is easier to track dates of birth than of death in some cases. Where possible I have given both: Wiley Thomas (1880), Willie Abigail (c. 1881), Reuben (c. 1882 or 1883), Rush (c. 1884), Corrie (c. 1886), Emma Mae (1887-1986), Ruel (1889), Sumpter (1891-1977); the dates for the

younger children are: Roger (1894), Martha (c. 1897), Alta (c. 1899), and Major McKinley (1902-1994).

7. E. Gertrude Beasley, "Moving," *The American Mercury* 9.34 (October 1926): 227-232.

8. Gertrude Beasley, "Birth Control in Russia," Part I and Part II. *The Birth Control Review* (December 1924 and January 1925): II, 18.

9. Dudley R. Dobie Jr., E-mail to the author, 12 February 2001. Mr. Dobie, relying on his memories of his father's account, does not have an exact date for the incident.

10. A good overview of Lee Scarborough's life and work is "Lee Rutland Scarborough," Southern Baptist Historical Library and Archives 1998, <http://ww.sbhla.org/bio scarborough.htm> (15 May 2001).

11. Eakin, *Fictions in Autobiography*, 7.

12. Virginia Woolf, "Professions for Women," *Collected Essays*, vol. 2 (London: Hogarth Press, 1966), 288

13. Havelock Ellis, *Studies in the Psychology of Sex* (Philadelphia: F. A. Davis, 1901-14). This is the edition of a constantly evolving and expanding work which Gertrude Beasley is most likely to have read.

14. Steven Watson, *Strange Bedfellows: The First American Avant-Garde* (New York: Abbeville Press, 1991), 15.

15. Robert Crunden, *American Salons: Encounters with European Modernism 1885-1917* (New York: Oxford University Press, 1993).

16. Rachel P. Maines, *The Technology of Orgasm: Hysteria, The Vibrator and Women's Sexual Satisfaction* (Baltimore: Johns Hopkins University Press, 1999).

17. Robert McAlmon, *Being Geniuses Together* (London: Secker & Warburg, 1938), 57-58.

18. All letters from Gertrude Beasley to Bertrand Russell are from the Bertrand Russell Archives, William Ready Division of Archives and Research Collections, McMaster University Library, Hamilton, Ontario, Canada. The letter to Russell from Paul Bousfield is from the same collection.

19. Bertrand Russell, *The Autobiography: 1914-1944*, vol. 2 of *The Autobiography of Bertrand Russell* (London: George Allen and Unwin, Ltd., 1968), 275-76.

20. Phyllis Grosskurth, *Havelock Ellis: A Biography* (New York: Alfred A. Knopf, 1980), 340-41.

21. Havelock Ellis to Françoise Lafitte, September 2, 1925, Havelock Ellis Collection, Library of Congress.

22. The letters of E. W. Camp and other customs officials concerned with *My First Thirty Years* can be found in Folder 16, Box 701 of the series Customs Case Files, 1908-1938, Record Group 36, National Archives and Records Administration.

23. Jim Sanderson, "Art in the Desert," *A West Texas Soapbox* (College Station: Texas A & M University Press, 1998), 16-27.

24. Dudley R. Dobie Jr., E-mail, 12 February 2001.

25. Gertrude Beasley, letter to Sylvia Beach, 6 August 1927. Yale Collection of American Literature, Beinecke Rare Book and Manuscript Library.

26. Sylvia Beach, *Shakespeare & Company* (Lincoln: University of Nebraska Press, 1991), 131.

27. Gertrude Beasley, postcard to the American Councler [sic], 19 August 1927. Transcribed and sent in an E-mail by Sally Kuisel, National Archives, Archivist, Civilian Records, 17 May 2001.

28. Gertrude Beasley to the Secretary of State, 7 January 1928, Civilian Records, National Archives and Records Administration.

29. Jay A. Gertzman, *Smuthounds and Bookleggers: The Trade in Erotica 1920-1940* (Philadelphia: University of Pennsylvania Press, 1999). In her letter from the S. S. *Republic,* Beasley seems to link Roth with the Dawn Publishing Company. Professor Gertzman tells me that he has not seen an imprint of Roth's with that name, but as a wily purveyor of erotica, Roth had many publishing imprints.

30. *My First Thirty Years, Casanova Jr's Tales*. 1.1 (April 1926): 17-47; 1.2 (July 1926): 199-235; 1.3 (October 1926): 295-346; 1.4 (509-72).

31. An ad mentioning the $20-$50 selling price of the original Contact Editions version appears in the unpaginated endpapers of *Two Worlds Monthly* 3 (April 1927) and a reference to the work as "still the sensation of Paris" was printed in an ad on the back cover of 2 (December 1926). Various ads mentioning Beasley's work run throughout the 1926-1927 issues.

4. Hallie Stillwell

1. *Texas Monthly*, October 1997.

2. Robert McG. Thomas Jr., "Hallie C. Stillwell, a Rancher and Texas Legend, Dies at 99," *New York Times*, 24 August 1997, section 1, 34.

3. Alan Fisher, writer and producer, *Change in the Bend*, 55-minute video documentary (Austin: Austin Community College, 2000); Heather Gilmour, writer and producer, *Not a Clinging Vine*, 27-minute video documentary (Austin: Chip Taylor Productions, 1993).

4. Virginia Madison, *The Big Bend Country of Texas* (Albuquerque: University of New Mexico Press, 1955; revised edition, New York: October House, 1968), 165.

5. ——— and Hallie Stillwell, *How Comes It's Called That? Place Names in the Big Bend Country*, (Albuquerque: University of New Mexico Press, 1958; revised edition, New York: October House, 1968).

6. *Hallie Stillwell 1897-1997*, "Tumbleweed" Smith, compiler. Hallie's Hall of Fame, Alpine, Texas, audiocassette, one hour. Mr. Smith has a syndicated radio show, "The Sound of Texas."

7. Dobie, *Coronado's Children,* (Dallas: Southwest Press, 1930),158-162.

8. Madison, *The Big Bend Country*, 164-165.

9. Rosemary Williams, "The Marfa Lights—A Mystery," *Texas Highways*, (August 1993): 39.

10. Helen Thorpe, "Hallie and Farewell," *Texas Monthly* (October 1997), 140.

11. Joe S. Graham, "Tradition and the Candelilla Wax Industry," *Some Still Do: Essays on Texas Customs*, ed. Francis Lee Abernethy (Austin: Encino Press, 1975), 43.

12. Bess Whitehead Scott, *You Meet Such Interesting People* (College Station: Texas A & M University Press, 1989).

5. Jewel Babb, Charley C. White, and Annie Mae Hunt

1. Griffin Smith Jr., "Texas West of the Pecos," *National Geographic* 165 (February 1984): 210-135. A photograph of Jewel Babb appears on 230-31.

2. Langness and Frank, *Lives*, 117-155.

3. John O. West, *Mexican-American Folklore: Legends, Songs, Festivals, Crafts, Tales of Saints, of Revolutionaries, and More,* (Little Rock: August House, 1988.)

4. Jewel Babb, *Goat-Lore: A Book of Folklore & Folklife from the Rio Grande* (Edgewood, Texas: Slough Press, 1980).

5. Pat LittleDog, *Afoot in a Field of Men* (New York: Atlantic Monthly Press, 1988).

6. William A. Cloud, "Indian Hot Springs," *Handbook of Texas Online* <http://www.tsha.utexas.edu/handbook/online/articles/view/II/rpi1.html>(15 February 1999, 22 July 2000).

7. Joe S. Graham, "The Role of the *Curandero* in the Mexican American Folk Medicine System in West Texas," *American Folk Medicine: A Symposium*. ed. Wayland D. Hand. (Berkeley: University of California Press, 1976), 175-189.

8. Ariel Kiev, *Curanderismo: Mexican-American Folk Psychiatry* (New York: The Free Press, 1968).

9. Reported in Limón, *Dancing with the Devil*, 88.

10. Jeff David Titon, "The Life Story," *Journal of American Folklore* 93 (July-September, 1980): 283.

11. James W. Lee, "The Old South in Texas Literature," *The Texas Literary Tradition: Fiction, Folklore, History*, ed. Don Graham, et. al. (Austin: The College of Liberal Arts, The University of Texas at Austin, and The Texas State Historical Association, 1983), 56.

12. The ensemble musical and the one-woman play version have not been published but productions have been successful. Naomi Carrier's one-woman play is described in an advertisement in the back of the University of Texas edition. The video is available: Cynthia Salzman Mondell and Allen Mondell, *Guts,*

Gumption and Go-Ahead: Annie Mae Hunt Remembers, 24-minute video production (Dallas: Media Projects, 1993).

13. Ruthe Winegarten, *Black Texas Women: 150 Years of Trial and Triumph* (Austin: University of Texas Press, 1995); *Black Texas Women: A Sourcebook* (Austin: University of Texas Press, 1996).

14. Stephen Butterfield, *Black Autobiography in America* (Amherst: University of Massachusetts Press, 1974), 3.

6. William Owens

1. Mody C. Boatright, "Hard Times and Good in Old Pin Hook" *Southwest Review* 40 (Winter 1967): 99.

2. Tom Pilkington, "William A. Owens," *My Blood's Country: Studies in Southwestern Literature* (Fort Worth: TCU Press, 1973), 129. First published as *William A. Owens*, Southwest Writers Series, No. 17 (Austin: Steck-Vaughn, 1968).

3. William A. Owens, *Walking on Borrowed Land* (New York: Bobbs-Merrill, 1954).

4. William A. Owens, *Slave Mutiny: the Revolt of the Schooner Amistad* (New York: John Day Company, 1953; reprint, under the title *Black Mutiny*, Philadelphia: United Church Press, 1968).

5. T. R. Fehrenbach, *Seven Keys to Texas* (El Paso: The Texas Western Press, 1983), 83.

6. *Texas: A Guide*, 233.

7. T. R. Fehrenbach, *Lone Star: A History of Texas and the Texans* (New York: Macmillan, 1968), 595-612.

8. William A. Owens, *Swing and Turn: Texas Play-Party Games* (Dallas: Tardy Publishing Company, 1936).

9. William A. Owens, *Tell Me a Story, Sing Me a Song. . .* (Austin: University of Texas Press, 1983).

10. Mody C. Boatright and William A. Owens, *Tales from the Derrick Floor: A People's History of the Oil Industry* (Garden City, NY: Doubleday, 1970).

7. John Houghton Allen

1. Dian Leatherberry Malouf, *Cattle Kings of Texas* (Hillsboro, Oregon: Beyond Words Publishing, 1991), 47.

2. Elmer J. Edwards, "Randado" *The Handbook of Texas Online*, <http://www.tsha.utexas.edu/handbook/online/articles/view/RR/hrrt5/html> (15 February 1999, 15 May 2001).

3. Richard Harding Davis, *The West from a Car-Window* (New York: Harper & Brothers, 1892), 132.

4. Tom Lea, *Randado* (El Paso: Carl Hertzog, 1941).

5. Tom Lea, *Tom Lea: An Oral History*, eds. Rebecca Craver and Adair Margo (El Paso: Texas Western Press, 1995), 61.

6. Joe S. Graham, *El Rancho in South Texas: Continuity and Change from 1750* (Denton: University of North Texas Press, 1994).

7. Orlan Sawey, "Introduction," *Southwest*, by John Houghton Allen (Albuquerque: Zia Books Edition, University of New Mexico Press, 1977), vii.

8. John Houghton Allen, "The Long Ride," *Southwest Review* 53 (Autumn 1968): 417-422. Editor's note citing Allen on 438.

9. John Houghton Allen to Harold Bugbee, 6 June 1960, Harold Bugbee Archive, Panhandle-Plains Museum.

10. Allen to Bugbee, 18 March 1948.

11. John Houghton Allen, "Shining Hour at A&M", *Southwest Review* 46 (Autumn 1961): 329-31.

12. John Houghton Allen, "That Was Randado," *Holiday* 43 (December 1956). The essay was published as *That Was Randado* (Dallas: Somesuch Press, 1956), a miniature book issued by Stanley Marcus. The book is fascinating as a feat of printing, but it is too small and too tightly bound to read with much comfort.

13. Malouf, *Cattle Kings of Texas*, 50.

14. John Houghton Allen, "Rodeo." *Southwest Review* 49 (Summer 1964): 259-264; "The Gentleman's Game," *Holiday* 41 (September 1954): 52-55, 86-88.

15. John Houghton Allen, *The Poetry of John Houghton Allen* (privately printed, 1944).

16. *Song to Randado* (Dallas: Kaleidograph Press, 1935); *Four Tales* (privately printed, 1943); *San Juan* (privately printed, 1945).

17. Jerald Underwood, "The Vaquero in South Texas with an Interpretation by John Houghton Allen." *West Texas Historical Association Year Book* 68 (1992): 93-99.

18. John Houghton Allen, *The Minor Testament of John Houghton Allen* (Dallas: privately printed, 1941); included in *The Poetry of John Houghton Allen*.

19. Allen to Bugbee, 27 November 1944.

20. John Houghton Allen, "The Low River," *Southwest Review* 48 (Winter 1963): 30.

21. Allen to Bugbee, 21 October 1944.

22. Malouf, *Cattle Kings of Texas*, 47.

23. G. C. Spivak, "Can the Subaltern Speak?" *Marxism and the Interpretation of Culture*, ed. C. Nelson and L. Grossberg (Basingstoke: Macmillan Education, 1988), 271-313.

24. John Houghton Allen, "Always a Brave River," *Southwest Review* 50 (Autumn 1965): 349.

25. Friedrich Katz, *The Life and Times of Pancho Villa* (Stanford: Stanford University Press, 1998), 269.

26. John Houghton Allen, *A Latin-American Miscellany* (privately printed, 1943), 60-63.

27. Allen to Bugbee, 25 March 1949.

28. A. C. Greene, "Polo Fever, 1904," *Sketches from the Five States of Texas*, (College Station: Texas A&M University Press, 1998), 154-55.

29. John Houghton Allen, "Little Pinto: being a loveletter to a polo pony," *Southwest Review* 46 (Winter 1961): 1-15.

30. J. Frank Dobie, *Guide to Life and Literature of the Southwest*, rev. ed. (Dallas: Southern Methodist University Press, 1952), 95.

31. John Houghton Allen, "Horse Cavalry," *Southwest Review* 51 (Spring 1968): 161-166

32. _________, "The Low River," 29.

33. Ibid., 35.

34. Allen, "Always a Brave River," *Southwest Review*: 352.

8. A. C. Greene

1. Patrick Bennett, "Molding the Past into Art." Interview with A. C. Greene. *Talking with Texas Writers: Twelve Interviews*, ed. Patrick Bennett (College Station: Texas A & M University Press, 1980).

2. Chris Ohan, "Biographical Sketch," Guide to the A. C. Greene papers 1923-Present,<http://libraries.uta.edu/SpecColl/findaids/AR409.htm>(August 1999, February 2000). Ohan provides an excellent summary of Greene's activities and I am indebted to him.

3. Walter Prescott Webb, *The Great Plains* (1931; New York: Grosset & Dunlap, 1977).

4. John Graves, *Hard Scrabble: Observations on a Patch of Land*, (New York: Alfred A. Knopf, 1974), 32-35.

5. John Graves, *Goodbye to a River* (New York: Curtis Publishing Co., 1959; New York: Alfred A. Knopf, 1976).

6. A. C. Greene, "A. C. Greene," *Growing Up in Texas: Recollections of Childhood* (Austin: Encino Press, 1972), 76-85.

7. T. R. Fehrenbach, *Lone Star*, 81-92.

8. Maude E. Cole, *Wind Against Stone: A Texas Novel* (Los Angeles: Lymanhouse, 1941).

9. A. C. Greene, *Taking Heart* (New York: Simon & Schuster, 1990).

9. William Humphrey

1. Ian Parsons, "Outstanding Merit," *The Bookseller*, 7 January 1978: 45.

2. William Humphrey, *Home from the Hill* (New York: Alfred A. Knopf, 1958); *The Ordways* (New York: Alfred A. Knopf, 1965); *Proud Flesh* (New York: Alfred A. Knopf, 1973); *No Resting Place* (New York: Delacorte/Seymour Lawrence, 1989).

3. Horton Foote, *Farewell: A Memoir of a Texas Childhood* (New York: Simon & Schuster, 1999), 28-34.

4. William Humphrey, Notebook for *Farther Off from Heaven* ("Father of the Man," 1975), William Humphrey Collection. Harry Ransom Humanities Research Center, University of Texas.

5. Bert Almon, *William Humphrey, Destroyer of Myths* (Denton: University of North Texas Press, 1998), 271.

6. Phillipe Lejeune, *On Autobiography* (Minneapolis: University of Minnesota Press, 1989), 188.

7. William Harmon, "Mary Karr, Mary Karr, Mary Karr, Mary Karr," *Southern Review* 33 (Winter 1997): 150-55.

8. Sigmund Freud, *New Introductory Lectures on Psycho-Analysis*, vol. XXII of the New Standard Edition (1933; London: Hogarth Press, 1964), 133.

9. William Humphrey, letter to Annie Laurie Williams, 9 August 1958, Annie Laurie Williams Archive, Columbia University.

10. Ashby Bland Crowder, "William Humphrey on Writing," *Writing in the Southern Tradition: Interviews with Five Contemporary Authors* (Amsterdam & Atlanta, GA: Rodopi, 1990), 21.

10. Larry McMurtry

1. Barbara Liss, "McMurtry: Rumination Lite in Paradise," *Houston Chronicle*, 22 August 2001, "Zest" section, 19.

2. Mark Busby's *Larry McMurtry and the West: An Ambivalent Relationship* (Denton: University of North Texas Press, 1995) has a useful chapter on "McMurtry and the Movies: Film Flam," 277-300.

3. Jonathan Miles, "Walter Benjamin at the Dairy Queen," *salon.com*, <http://www.salon.com/books/review/1999/11/29/mcmurtry/> (29 November 1999, 11 October 2001).

4. Patrick Bennett, "Thalia, Houston and Hollywood," *Talking with Texas Writers* (College Station: Texas A&M University Press, 1980), 19.

5. Wilson, *Watt Matthews of Lambshead*, 88.

6. Stegner, *Wolf Willow*, 24-25.

7. Almon, *William Humphrey*, 9-10.

8. Catherine Belsey, *Critical Practice* (London and New York: Routledge, 1980), 3. Belsey's work is cited merely as a representative formulation of ideas widespread in the academy.

9. Thomas Mallon, "Even Cowboys Get the Blues," *New York Times*, 21 November 1999, section 7, 14.

10. The most interesting articles about McMurtry's store, "BookedUp," are: John Schwartz, "Secondhand Book Wrangler; a Pulitzer Prize Winner Is Also a Profitable Bookseller," *New York Times*, 23 July 2001, C1; David Streitfield, "Lonesome Trove," *The Washington Post*, 22 February 1998, E01

11. Noah Isenberg, "On Walter Benjamin's Passages," *Partisan Review* 68 (Spring 2001): 263.

12. Michiko Kakutani, "As a Ribbon Unfurls Into Infinity," *New York Times*, 6 July 2000, E40.

13. Timothy Foote, "Life in the Fast Lane," *New York Times*, 16 July 2001, sec.7 col.1 p.5.

14. Liss, "Larry McMurtry: Rumination Lite," 19.

11. Pat Mora, Gloria López-Stafford, and Ray Gonzalez

1. Gloria Anzaldúa, *Borderlands/La Frontera: The New Mestiza*, (St. Paul, MN: Consortium Books Sales & Dist.,1999) 3.

2. José David Saldívar, *Border Matters: Remapping American Cultural Studies*, (Berkeley: University of California Press, 1997), 13-14.

3. City of El Paso, Quick Facts, <http://www.ci.el-paso.tx.us/demograph.htm> (24 January 2002, 27 January 2002).

4. Pat Mora, *Nepantla: Essays from the Land in the Middle* (Albuquerque: University of New Mexico Press, 1993).

5. Darwin T. Henderson, "Listening to the Desert: A Conversation with Pat Mora," *Ohio Journal of English Language Arts*, vol. 41 (Fall 2000): 12.

6. Mario T. García, *Desert Immigrants: The Mexican of El Paso, 1880-1920* (New Haven and London: Yale University Press, 1981)

7. Owen P. White, *Out of the Desert: The Historical Romance of El Paso* (El Paso: The McMath Company, 1923).

8. Richard Rodriguez, *Hunger of Memory: The Education of Richard Rodriguez* (Boston, MA: David Godine, 1982).

9. Hector A. Torres, "House of Houses," *Aztlán* 23 (Fall 1998): 236.

10. Pat Mora, *Communion* (Houston: Arte Público Press, 1991), 86.

11. Gaston Bachelard, *The Poetics of Space*, trans. Marie Jolas, 1958. (Boston: Beacon Press, 1994), 3.

12. Ibid., 15.

13. Torres, "House of Houses," 14.

14. Bachelard, *The Poetics of Space*, xxxv-xxxvi.

15. Martin Heidegger, "Building Dwelling Thinking." *Basic Writings: Martin Heidegger*, revised and expanded edition, ed. David Farrell Krell (London: Routledge, 1993), 352.

16. Patrick D. Murphy, *Farther Afield in the Study of Nature-Oriented Literature* (Charlottesville and London: University Press of Virginia, 2000).

17. Henderson, "Listening to the Desert," 12.

18. Lawrence E. Marks, *The Unity of the Senses: Interrelations among the Modalities* (New York: Academic Press, 1978).

19. Mora, *Nepantla*, 124-131.

20. Tey Diana Rebolledo, "Tradition and Mythology: Signatures of Landscape in Chicana Literature." *The Desert Is No Lady: Southwestern Landscapes in Women's Writing and Art*, ed. Vera Norwood and Janice Monk (New Haven: Yale University Press, 1987), 121.

21. Mora, *Chants* (Houston: Arte Público Press, 1984), 28.

22. Mora, *Nepantla*, 77.

23. Mora, *Chants*, 38-39.

24. Mora, *Aunt Carmen's Book of Practical Saints* (Boston: Beacon Press, 1997).

25. Ramon Renteria, "A Look Back," *El Paso Times*, 21 April 1996, F1.

26. Benjamin Marquez, *Power and Politics in a Chicano Barrio: A Study of Mobilization Efforts and Community Power in El Paso* (Lanham, MD: University Press of America, 1985), 63.

27. Mora, *Agua Santa = Holy Water* (Boston: Beacon Press, 1995), 74-77. The poem is part of a sequence on Malinche.

28. Sandra Cisneros, "Woman Hollering Creek," *Woman Hollering Creek* (NY: Random House, 1991), 43-56.

29. John L. Davis, *Texans One and All* (San Antonio: University of Texas Institute of Texan Cultures at San Antonio, 1998), 78-79.

30. Pat Mora, *Borders* (Houston: Arte Público, 1986), 20.

31. Teresa McKenna, *Migrant Song: Politics and Process in Contemporary Chicano Literature* (Austin: University of Texas Press, 1997), 119.

32. Genaro M. Padilla, *My History, Not Yours: The Formation of a Mexican American Autobiography* (Madison: University of Wisconsin Press, 1993), 238.

33. Gloria Anzaldúa, *Borderlands / La Frontera*, 101.

12. Mary Karr

1. James Atlas, "The Age of the Literary Memoir Is Now," *New York Times Magazine* (11 May 1996): 25-27. A counter opinion on the memoir boom is Charles Baxter's reference to the mud slides of autobiographies in the introduction to his anthology, *The Business of Memory: The Art of Remembering in an Age of Forgetting*, ed. Charles Baxter (Saint Paul: Greywolf Press, 1999), vii.

2. Penguin Putnam Books Reading Group Guide for *The Liar's Club*, <http://www.penguinputnam.com/clubppi/reading/kar/content.htm> (10 October 2000, 15 May 2001).

3. Mary Karr, *Abacus* (Middletown, CT: Wesleyan University Press, 1987); *The Devil's Tour* (New York: New Directions, 1993); *Viper Rum* (New York: New Directions, 1998).

4. Karr, "The Family Sideshow," reading group guide.

5. Karr, "Author Interview," reading group guide.

6. Karen Olsson, "Refinery Daze, Part Two," *The Texas Observer*, 8 December 2000, 20.

7. Robert Draper, "Mary Karr Comes Clean," *Texas Monthly*, September 1996, 109.

8. Dwight Garner, "A Scrappy Little Beast," salon.com, <http://www.salon.com/May97/Karr970521.html> (21 May 1997, 19 May 2001).

9. "Memory: An interview with Mary Karr, on "To the Best of Our Knowledge," Wisconsin Public Radio, 20 April 1997, audiocassette.

10. William Harmon, "Mary Karr," 153.

11. Christopher F. Monte, *Beneath the Mask: An Introduction to Theories of Personality* (Fort Worth: Harcourt Brace College Publishers, 1995), 86.

12. Eric Murphy Selinger, "This Personal Maze Is Not the Prize," *Parnassus: Poetry in Review* 24.2 (2000): 116.

13. Geoffrey Wolff, *The Duke of Deception* (New York, Random House, 1979).

14. Tobias Wolff, *This Boy's Life* (New York: Atlantic Monthly Press, 1989).

15. Mary Karr, "A Memoirist's Apology," *Parnassus: Poetry in Review* 20.1/2 (1995): 97.

16. Mary McCarthy, *Memories of a Catholic Girlhood* (New York: Harcourt, Brace, 1957).

17. Mary Park, "Don't Mess with Texas: An Interview with Mary Karr." Amazon. com., <http://www.amazon.com/exec/obidos/tg/feature/95141/103-3957227-2660612> (19 May 2001).

18. Monte discusses family-order theory in *Beneath the Mask*, 379-380. Mary Karr and her rival sibling show some of the traits predicted by Adler's birth order scheme, like the independence of the first child and the envy and feelings of incompetence of the second.

19. James Joyce, *Portrait of the Artist as a Young Man*, (1914, New York: Penguin, 1992), 242.

20. Jesse Kornbluth, "Mary Karr," *The Book Reporter* <http://www.bookreporter.com/brc/author.asp?author=104> (6 March 1997, 19 May 2001).

21. Sigmund Freud, "Family Romances," *On Sexuality*, The Penguin Freud Library, vol. 7 (1909; London: Penguin, 1991), 238-239.

22. Don Graham, "The Pits," *Texas Monthly*, October 2000, 72.

23. Jennie Bristow, "Teenage Confessions," *The New Statesman* 130 (25 May 2001): 51.

24. Clay Reynolds, Review of *Cherry*, *Southwestern American Literature* 26 (Spring 2001): 125.

25. Alice Echols, *Scars of Sweet Paradise: The Life and Times of Janis Joplin* (New York: Metropolitan Books, 1999).

26. Reynolds, Review, 126.

27. Tom Wolfe, *The Electric Kool-Aid Acid Test* (New York: Farrr, Straus and Giroux, 1968).

13. The Mexican Diaspora and John Phillip Santos

1. "A Penguin Reader's Guide to *Places Left Unfinished at the Time of Creation*," 4. It is part of the literary culture of our time for publishers to provide study guides for reading groups. The paperback of Santos's book is unusual in printing the study guide in the same volume as the text, with separate pagination.

2. Arthur Rubel, et al, *Susto, a Folk Illness* (Berkeley: University of California Press, 1984).

3. Randall Holdridge, "Bordering Cultures," *Tucson Weekly* (online), <http://multihome.www.desert.net/ww/02-21-00/tw_book.html> (21 February 2000, 23 January 2001).

4. Suzanne Ruta, "North Toward Home," *New York Times*, 5 December 1999, Section 7, 53.

5. Octavio Paz, *The Labyrinth of Solitude: Life and Thought in Mexico* (1950; New York: Grove Press, 1961), 85.

6. Dorothy Cole, "El Inframundo," *Weekly Alibi*, <http://multihome.www.desert.net/ww'09-20-99/alibi_art1.html> (20 September 1999, 23 January 2001).

7. Rafael Pérez-Torres, *Movements in Chicano Poetry: Against Myths, Against Margins* (Cambridge: Cambridge University Press, 1995), 56-96.

8. Pamela Coloff, "John Phillips Santos," *Texas Monthly*, September 2000, 162.

Conclusion

1. Naomi Shihab Nye, *Never in a Hurry: Essays on People and Places* (Columbia: University of South Carolina Press, 1996).

2. James Clifford, *Routes, Travel and Translation in the Late Twentieth Century*, (Cambridge: Harvard, 1997), 255.

3. José David Saldívar, *Border Matters: Remapping American Cultural Studies.* (Berkeley: University of California Press). 196.

A Note on Spanish Orthography

The Spanish orthography in the books discussed here is inconsistent. I have endeavored to follow each author's practice in deciding whether to write Juarez or Juárez, Garcia or García. John Phillip Santos is especially inconsistent.

BIBLIOGRAPHY

Archives and Manuscripts

Allen, John Houghton. Letters to Harold Bugbee, 1944-1963. Harold Bugbee Archive, Panhandle-Plains Museum.

Beasley, [Edith] Gertrude. Application for Registration—Native Citizen. 2 February 1922. National Archives and Records Service.

———. Letters to Bertrand Russell. Bertrand Russell Archives. William Ready Division of Archives and Special Collections. McMaster University.

———. Letter to Gilbert Grosvenor. 16 January 1922. *National Geographic* Archives.

———. Letter to Sylvia Beach, Beinecke Collection, 6 August 1927. Collection of American Literature, Beinecke Rare Book and Manuscript Library.

———. Passport Applications, 1 May 1920, 17 April 1922 and 9 June 1924. National Archives and Records Administration.

———. Postcard to the "American Councler [sic]." 19 August 1927. Record of the American Consular General, London, England. U.S. Department of State. Civilian Records.

———. "Something about Work in Japan." Unpublished typescript. *National Geographic* Archives.

Bousfield, Paul. Letter to Bertrand Russell. 30 June 1925. Bertrand Russell Archives. William Ready Division of Archives and Special Collections. McMaster University.

Camp, E. W., Director of Customs. Letters to the Collector of Customs in New York. 13 May 1926 and 7 March 1927. Old Civilian Records. Textual Archives. National Archives and Records Administration.

Ellis, Havelock. Letter to Françoise Lafitte. 2 September 1925. Havelock Ellis Collection. Library of Congress.

Grosvenor, Gilbert. Letter to Gertrude Beasley. 21 February 1922. *National Geographic* Archives.

Humphrey, William. Letter to Annie Laurie Williams. 9 August 1958. Annie Laurie Williams Archive, Columbia University.

———. Notebook for *Farther Off from Heaven* ("Father of the Man," 1975). William Humphrey Collection. Harry Ransom Humanities Research Center, University of Texas.

Primary Works

Allen, John Houghton. "Always a Brave River." *Southwest Review* 50 (Autumn 1965): 345-54.

———.*Four Tales*. Privately Printed, 1943.
———. "The Gentleman's Game." *Holiday*, September 1954, 52-55, 86-88.
———. "Horse Cavalry." *Southwest Review* 51 (Spring 1968): 161-166.
———. *A Latin-American Miscellany*. Privately printed, 1943.
———. "Little Pinto: being a loveletter to a polo pony." *Southwest_Review* 46 (Winter 1961): 1-15.
———. "The Long Ride." *Southwest Review* 53 (Autumn 1968): 417-422.
———. "The Low River." *Southwest Review* 48. (Winter 1963): 29-36.
———. *The Minor Testament of John Houghton Allen*. Privately printed, 1941.
———. "Parable." *Southwest Review* 48 (1963): 279-284.
———. *The Poetry of John Houghton Allen*. Privately printed, 1944.
———. "Rodeo." *Southwest Review* 49 (Summer 1964): 259-264.
———. *San Juan*. Austin, TX: Privately Printed, 1945.
———. "Shining Hour at A&M" *Southwest Review* 46 (Autumn 1961): 329-31.
———. *Song to Randado*. Dallas: The Kaleidograph Press, 1935.
———. *Southwest*. Philadelphia: J. B. Lippincott, 1952; Albuquerque: University of New Mexico Press, 1977.
———. "Tales of Diego." *Southwest Review* 55.2 (Spring 1970): 177-188.
———. "That Was Randado." *Holiday*, (December 1956): 38-47); *That Was Randado*. Dallas: Somesuch Press, 1956.
———. *Translations*. Privately Printed, 1945.

Babb, Jewel. *Border Healing Woman: The Story of Jewel Babb as told to Pat LittleDog*. Austin: University of Texas Press, 1985. Second edition with a new epilogue by Pat LittleDog. 1994.
Barr, Amelia E. *All the Days of My Life: An Autobiography, The Red Leaves of a Human Heart*. New York and London: D. Appleton and Company, 1915.
Beasley, E. Gertrude. "Birth Control in Russia," Part I and Part II. *The Birth Control Review* (December 1924 and January 1925): 341-42 and 364; 17-19 and 30.
———. "Moving." *The American Mercury* 9.34 (October 1926): 227-232.
———. *My First Thirty Years*. Paris: Contact Editions, 1925. Reprint, *Casanova Jr's Tales*. 1.1 (April 1926): 17-47; 1.2 (July 1926): 199-235; 1.3 (October 1926): 295-346; 1.4 (509-572); Reprint, with an afterword by Larry McMurtry. Austin: Book Club of Texas, 1989.

Casey, Ethel Matthews. *Reminiscences*. N. p.: Privately printed by Carl Hertzog, 1985.

Dobie, J. Frank. *Apache Gold and Yaqui Silver*. Boston: Little, Brown, 1939.
———. *Coronado's Children: Tales of Lost Mines and Buried Treasures of the Southwest*. Dallas: Southwest Press, 1930.
———. *Out of the Old Rock*. New York: Little, Brown and Co., 1972.
———. *Some Part of Myself*. Boston: Little, Brown and Co., 1967.

———. *A Texan in England*. Boston: Little, Brown and Co., 1945.
———. *Tongues of the Monte*. Garden City, NY: Doubleday, 1935; Austin: University of Texas Press, 1980.
———. *A Vaquero of the Brush Country. "Partly from the Reminiscences of John Young."* Dallas: Southwest Press, 1929.
Foote, Horton. *Farewell: A Memoir of a Texas Childhood*. New York: Simon and Schuster, 1999.

Gonzalez, Ray. *Memory Fever: A Journey Beyond El Paso del Norte*. Seattle: Broken Moon Press, 1993; Reprint ,Tucson: University of Arizona Press, 1999.
Greene, A. C. "A. C. Greene" *Growing Up in Texas: Recollections of Childhood*. Austin: Encino Press, 1972. 76-85.
———. *A Personal Country*. 1979. New York, Knopf, 1969; Revised edition with a preface by Larry L. King and an afterword by the author, College Station: Texas A&M Press, 1998.
———. *Sketches from the Five States of Texas*. College Station: Texas A&M.Press, 1998.
———. *Taking Heart*. New York: Simon & Schuster, 1990.

Humphrey, William. *Farther Off from Heaven*. New York: Knopf, 1977.
———. *Home from the Hill*. New York: Alfred A. Knopf, 1958.
———. *No Resting Place*. New York: Delacorte / Seymour Lawrence, 1989.
——— *The Ordways*. New York: Alfred A. Knopf, 1965.
———. *Proud Flesh*. New York: Alfred A. Knopf, 1973.
Hunt, Annie Mae, and Ruthe Winegarten. *I Am Annie Mae: An Extraordinary Black Texas Woman in Her Own Words*. Austin: Rosegarden Press, 1983. Austin: University of Texas Press, 1996.

Karr, Mary. *Abacus*. Middletown, CT: Wesleyan University Press, 1987.
———. "Author Interview." Penguin Putnam Books Reading Group Guide for *The Liar's Club*. (10 October 2000, 15 May 2001) <http://www.penguinputnam.com/clubppi/reading/kar/content.htm>.
———. "Chats and Events," Barnes & Noble interview. (16 October 2000, May 15, 2001) <http://www.barnesandnoble.com/community/archive/transcript.asp?/eventId=2327>
———. *Cherry*. New York: Viking, 2000.
———. *The Devil's Tour*. New York: New Directions, 1993.
———. "The Family Sideshow." Penguin Putnam Books Reading Group Guide for *The Liar's Club*, (15 May 2001, 10 October 2000) <http://www.penguinputnam.com/clubppi/reading/kar/content.htm>.
———. *The Liars' Club*. New York: Viking, 1995.
———. "A Memoirist's Apology." *Parnassus: Poetry in Review* 20.1/2 (1995): 96-107.
———. *Viper Rum*. New York: New Directions, 1998.

Lomax, John A. *Adventures of a Ballad Hunter*. New York: Macmillan, 1947.
López-Stafford, Gloria. *A Place in El Paso: A Mexican American Childhood*. Albuquerque: University of New Mexico Press, 1996.
Matthews, Sallie Reynolds. *Interwoven: a Pioneer Chronicle*. Privately printed, 1936. Second edition, El Paso: Carl Hertzog, 1958. Third edition, College Station: Texas A & M Press, 1982. Page citations are to the third edition.
Matthews, Watt R. *Lambshead Legacy: The Ranch Diary of Watt R. Matthews*. Edited by Janet M. Neubegauer, Introduction by Frances Mayhugh Holden. College Station: Texas A & M University Press, 1997.
Maverick, Mary A. *Memoirs of Mary A. Maverick*. Privately printed, 1885. San Antonio: Alamo Printing Co., 1921.
McMurtry, Larry. *In a Narrow Grave: Essays on Texas*. Austin: The Encino Press, 1968; Second edition, with a new preface. New York: Simon and Schuster, 1989.
———. *Paradise*. New York: Simon and Schuster, 2001.
———. *Roads: Driving America's Great Highways*. New York: Simon and Schuster, 2000.
——— *Walter Benjamin at the Dairy Queen: Reflections at Sixty and Beyond*. New York: Simon and Schuster, 1999.
Mora, Pat. *Agua Santa = Holy Water*. Boston: Beacon Press, 1995.
———. *Aunt Carmen's Book of Practical Saints*. Boston: Beacon Press, 1997.
———. *Borders*. Houston: Arte Público, 1986.
———. *Communion*. Houston: Arte Público, 1991.
———. "Confessions of a Latina Author," *The New Advocate* 11 (Fall 1998): 279-90.
———. *House of Houses*. Boston: Beacon Press, 1997.
———. *Nepantla: Essays from the Land in the Middle*. Albuquerque, University of New Mexico Press, 1993.

Nye, Naomi Shihab. *Never in a Hurry: Essays on People and Places*. Columbia: University of South Carolina Press, 1996.

Oliphant, Dave. *Memories of Texas Towns & Cities*. Austin: Host Publications, 2000.
Owens, William A. *A Fair and Happy Land: A Chronicle of Frontier America*. New York: Scribner's, 1975.
———. *A Season of Weathering*. New York: Scribner's, 1973.
———. *Tell Me a Story, Sing Me a Song. . .* Austin: University of Texas Press, 1983.
———. *This Stubborn Soil: A Frontier Boyhood*. New York: Scribner's, 1966; Revised edition with an introduction by John Graves and an afterword by Owens, New York: Lyons Press, 1986. Page citations are to the revised edition.

———. "Writing a Novel: Problem and Solution." *Southwest Review* 40 (Summer 1955). 254-61.

———. *Walking on Borrowed Land* (New York: Bobbs-Merrill, 1954).

Robinson, Dorothy Redus. *The Bell Rings at Four: A Black Teacher's Chronicle of Change*. Austin: Madrona Press, 1978.

Rozelle, Ron. *Into That Good Night* New York: Farrar, Straus and Giroux, 1998; Huntsville: Texas Review Press, 2000.

Santos, John Phillip. *Places Left Unfinished at the Time of Creation*. NY: Viking Penguin, 1999. Rpt. "with Readers Guide," 2000, paginated separately, 1-18.

Scott, Bess Whitehead. *You Meet Such Interesting People*. College Station: Texas A&M Press, 1989.

Stillwell, Hallie Crawford. *I'll Gather My Geese*. College Station: Texas A & M Press, 1991.

———. *Hallie Stillwell 1897-1997*, "Tumbleweed" Smith," compiler, "Hallie's Hall of Fame, Alpine, Texas. Audiocassette.

White, C. C., and Ada Morehead Holland. *No Quittin' Sense*. Austin: University of Texas Press, 1969.

Other Works

Abernethy, Francis Edward. *J. Frank Dobie*. Southwest Writers Series. no. 1. Austin: Steck-Vaughn, 1967.

Almon, Bert. *William Humphrey, Destroyer of Myths*. Denton: University of North Texas Press, 1998.

Anzaldúa, Gloria. *Borderlands / La Frontera: The New Mestiza*. San Francisco: Aunt Lute, 1987.

Atlas, James. "The Age of the Literary Memoir Is Now," *The New York Times Magazine*, 11 May 1996.

Bachelard, Gaston. *The Poetics of Space*. Trans. Marie Jolas. 1958. Boston: Beacon Press, 1994.

Baxter, Charles. *The Business of Memory: The Art of Remembering in an Age of Forgetting*. Saint Paul: Greywolf Press, 1999.

Beach, Sylvia. *Shakespeare & Company*. 1956. Lincoln: University of Nebraska Press, 1991.

Bedicheck, Roy. *Karánkaway Country*. Austin: University of Texas Press, 1950.

Belsey, Catherine. *Critical Practice*. London and New York, Routledge, 1980.

Benjamin, Walter. "The Storyteller: Reflections on the Works of Nicolai Leskov." *Illuminations: Essays and Reflections*. Ed. and with an introduction by Hannah Arendt. 83-109.

Bennett, Patrick. "Molding Past into Art." Interview with A. C. Greene. *Talking with Texas Writers: Twelve Interviews*. College Station: Texas A & M Press, 1980. 37-62.

———. "Thalia, Houston and Hollywood." Interview with Larry McMurtry. *Talking with Texas Writers: Twelve Interviews*. College Station: Texas A&M Press, 1980.

Blackburn, Regina. "In Search of the Black Female Self: African-American Women's Autobiographies and Ethnicity." Ed. Estelle C. Jelinek. *Women's Autobiography: Essays in Criticism*. Bloomington: Indiana University Press, 1980.

Bledstein, Burton. *The Culture of Professionalism*. New York: Norton, 1976.

Boatright, Mody C. "The Family Saga as a Form of Folklore." *The Family Saga and Other Phases of American Folklore*. By Mody C. Boatright, et al. Urbana: University of Illinois Press, 1958. 1-19.

———. "Hard Times and Good in Old Pin Hook." *Southwest Review* 40 (Winter 1967): 99-101.

———, and William A. Owens. *Tales from the Derrick Floor: A People's History of the Oil Industry*. Garden City, NY: Doubleday, 1970.

Bode, Winston. *A Portrait of Pancho: The Life of a Great Texan*. Austin: The Pemberton Press, 1965.

Bristow, Jennie. "Teenage Confessions." *The New Statesman* 130 (25 June 2001): 51.

Busby, Mark. *Larry McMurtry and the West: An Ambivalent Relationship*. Denton: University of North Texas Press, 1995.

Butterfield, Stephen. *Black Autobiography in America*. Amherst: University of Massachusetts Press, 1974.

Cisneros, Sandra. "Woman Hollering Creek." *Woman Hollering Creek and Other Stories*. New York: Random House, 1991. 43-56.

City of El Paso, Quick Facts. (24 January 2002, 27 January 2002) <http://www.ci.el-paso.tx.us/demograph.htm>.

Clayton, Lawrence. *Watkins Reynolds Matthews: A Biography* Abilene: Hardin-Simmons University Press, 1990.

Clifford, Craig. "Horseman, Hang On: The Reality of Myth in Texas Letters." *Range Wars: Heated Debates, Sober Reflections, and Other Assessments of Texas Writing*. Ed. Craig Clifford and Tom Pilkington. Dallas: Southern Methodist University Press, 1988. 43-57.

Clifford, James. *Routes: Travel and Translation in the Late Twentieth Century*. Cambridge: Harvard University Press, 1997.

Cloud, William A. "Indian Hot Springs," *Handbook of Texas Online*. (15 February 1999, 20 July 2000) <http://www.tsha.utexas.edu/handbook/online/articles/view/II/rpi1.html>.

Cole, Dorothy. "El Inframundo," *Weekly Alibi*.(20 September 1999, 23 January 2001) <http://multihome.www.desert.net/ww'09-20-99/alibi_art1.html>.

Cole, Maude E. *Wind Against Stone: A Texas Novel* Los Angeles: Lymanhouse, 1941.

Coloff, Pamela. "John Phillips Santos." *Texas Monthly*, September 2000, 160-163.

Conway, Jill Ker. *When Memory Speaks: Exploring the Art of Autobiography*. New York: Vintage, 1999

Cook, Spruill. *J. Frank Dobie Bibliography*. Corsicana, TX: Privately Printed, 1968.

Crowder, Ashby Bland. "William Humphrey," *Dictionary of Literary Biography*. Second Series. Volume 212: Twentieth-Century American Western Writers,. Edited by Richard H. Cracroft. Detroit: The Gale Group, 1999. 126-132.

———. "William Humphrey," in *Dictionary of Literary Biography*. Third Series. Volume 234: American Short-Story Writers Since World War II. Edited by Patrick Meanor, and Richard E. Lee. Detroit: The Gale Group, 2001. 142-152.

———. "William Humphrey on Writing". *Writing in the Southern Tradition: Interviews with Five Contemporary Authors*. Amsterdam, Atlanta, GA: Rodopi, 1990. 19-34.

Crunden, Robert. *American Salons: Encounters with European Modernism 1885-1917*. New York: Oxford University Press, 1993.

Curtis, Gregory. "Curse of the Coots." *Texas Monthly*, February 1993, 206.

Davis, John L. *Texans One and All*. San Antonio: University of Texas Institute of Texan Cultures at San Antonio, 1998.

Davis, Richard Harding. *The West from a Car-Window*. New York: Harper & Brothers, 1892.

Dobie, J. Frank. *Guide to Life and Literature of the Southwest*. Rev. ed. Dallas: Southern Methodist University Press, 1952.

———. "The Tournament in Texas." *Publications of the Texas Folklore Society*. Austin: Texas Folklore Society, 1926. 93-103.

Draper, Robert. "Mary Karr Comes Clean." *Texas Monthly*, September 1996, 109-111.

Dugger, Ronnie, ed. *Three Men in Texas: Bedichek, Webb, and Dobie*. Austin and London: University of Texas Press, 1967.

Eakin, Paul John, ed. *American Autobiography: Retrospect and Prospect*. Madison: University of Wisconsin Press, 1991.

———. *Fictions in Autobiography: Studies in the Art of Self-Invention*. Princeton: Princeton University Press, 1985.

———. *How Our Lives Become Stories: Making Selves*. Ithaca and London: Cornell University Press, 1999.

Echols, Alice. *Scars of Sweet Paradise: The Life and Times of Janis Joplin*. New York: Metropolitan Books, 1999.

Edwards, Elmer J. "Randado, Texas." *The Handbook of Texas Online*. (15 February 1999, May 17 2001) <http://www.tsha.utexas.edu/handbook/9online/articles/view/RR/hrrt5/html>.

Ellis, Havelock. *Studies in the Psychology of Sex*. Philadelphia: F. A. Davis, 1901-14.

Fehrenbach, T. R. *Lone Star: A History of Texas and the Texans*. New York: Macmillan, 1968.

———. *Seven Keys to Texas*. El Paso: Texas Western Press, 1983.

Fisher, Alan, writer and producer. *Change in the Bend*. Video production. Austin: Austin Community College, 2000.

Foote, Timothy. "Life in the Fast Lane," *New York Times*, 16 July 2001, Sec.7, col. 1, p.5

Freud, Sigmund. "Family Romances," *On Sexuality*, The Penguin Freud Library, vol. 7. 1909; London: Penguin, 1991.

———. *New Introductory Lectures on Psycho-Analysis*. Vol. XXII of the New Standard Edition of the Works of Sigmund Freud. 1933; London: Hogarth Press, 1964.

———. "Three Essays on the Theory of Sexuality." *On Sexuality*. First published 1905. The Penguin Freud Library, vol. 7. London: Penguin, 1991.

García, Mario T. *Desert Immigrants: The Mexican of El Paso, 1880-1920*. New Haven and London: Yale University Press, 1981.

Garner, Dwight. "A Scrappy Little Beast." *Salon.com*, (21 May 1997, 15 May 2001) <http://www.salon.com/May97/Karr970521.html>.

Gertzman, Jay A. *Smuthounds and Bookleggers: The Trade in Erotica 1920-1940*. Philadelphia: University of Pennsylvania Press, 1999.

Gilmour, Heather. *Not a Clinging Vine*. Profiles of Hallie Stillwell, Beverly Weyerts, and Kay Love. 27 minute video. Austin: Chip Taylor Productions, 1993.

Graham, Don. *Giant Country: Essays on Texas*. Fort Worth: TCU Press, 1998.

———. "Pen Pals." *Texas Monthly*, March 1996, 100-107.

———. "The Pits." *Texas Monthly*, October 2000, 70-74.

———. "A Woman of Independent Means." *Texas Monthly*, July 2000, 22.

Graham, Joe S. *El Rancho in South Texas: Continuity and Change from 1750*. Denton: University of North Texas Press, 1994.

———. "The Role of the *Curandero* in the Mexican American Folk Medicine System in South Texas." *American Folk Medicine: A Symposium*. Ed. Wayland D. Hand. Berkeley: University of California Press, 175-189.

———. "Tradition and the Candelilla Wax Industry." *Some Still Do: Essays on Texas Custom*. Ed. Francis Lee Abernethy. Austin: Encino Press, 1975. 39-57.

Graves, John. *Goodbye to a River*. New York: Curtis Publishing Co., 1959; New York: Alfred A. Knopf, 1976.

———. *Hard Scrabble: Observations on a Patch of Land* New York: Alfred A. Knopf, 1974.

———. "Introduction," *This Stubborn Soil*, by William A. Owens. New York: The Lyons Press, 1986. Pp. ix-xii.

Grider, Sylvia. "Memories that Never Were." *From Texas to the World and Back:*

Essays on the Journey of Katherine Anne Porter, ed. Mark Busby and Dick Heaberlin. Fort Worth: TCU Press, 2001. 225-237.

——— and Lou Hassell Rodenberger, eds. *Texas Women Writers: A Tradition of Their Own*. College Station: Texas A & M University Press, 1997.

Grosskurth, Phyllis. *Havelock Ellis: A Biography*. New York: Alfred A. Knopf, 1980.

Haley, J. Evetts. *George Littlefield, Texan*. Norman, University of Oklahoma Press, 1943.

Harmon, William. "Mary Karr, Mary Karr, Mary Karr, Mary Karr." *Southern Review* 33.1 (Winter 1997): 150-155.

Hardin, Deborah Bloys. "Bloys Camp Meeting," *The Handbook of Texas Online*. (15 February 1999, 10 May 2001). <http://www.tsha.utexas.edu/handbook/ online/articles/view/BB/ibyl.html>.

Heidegger, Martin. "Building Dwelling Thinking." *Basic Writings: Martin Heidegger*. Revised and expanded edition. Ed. David Farrell Krell. London: Routledge, 1993. 343-63.

Hemingway, Ernest. *The Sun Also Rises*. New York: Scribner's, 1926.

Henderson, Darwin. "Listening to the Desert: A Conversation with Pat Mora," *Ohio Journal of English Language Arts* 41 (Fall 2000): 12-17.

Hinojosa, Rolando. *The Valley*. Ypsilanti, MI: Bilingual Press, 1983.

"The History of the Old Jail Art Center." Albany, Texas: Attractions. N.d. (13 May 2001).<http://www.albanytexas.com/attractions/artcenterhist.html>.

Hogan, Ron. "Mary Karr." The BEATRICE Interview: 2000. N. d. (20 May 2001). <http://beatrice.com/interviews/kar/>.

Holden, Francis Mayhugh. *Lambshead Before Interwoven: A Texas Range Chronicle 1848-1878*. College Station: Texas A&M Press, 1982.

Holdridge, Randall. "Bordering Cultures." *Tucson Weekly* (online). (21 February 2000, 23 January 2001). <http://multihome.www.desert.net/ww/02-21-00/tw_book.html>.

Isenberg, Noah. "On Walter Benjamin's *Passages*." *Partisan Review* 58 (2001): 254-263.

Isle, Ray. "Three Days in McMurtryville," *Stanford Magazine*. (November / December 1999, 10 August 2001) <http://www.stanfordalumni.org/news/magazine/1999/novdec/articles/mcmurtry.html>

Jelinek, Estelle C., ed. *Women's Autobiography: Essays in Criticism*. Bloomington: Indiana University Press, 1980.

Kakutani, Michiko. "As a Ribbon Unfurls into Infinity." *New York Times*, July 6, 2000.

———. "The Carefully Examined American Life, Continued." *New York Times*, September 26, 2000.

Kanner, Ellen. "Mary Karr: Remembering the Agonies and Ecstasies of

Adolescence." *First Person Bookpage*. BookPage Interview October 2000: Mary Karr. (20 May 2001). <http://www.bookpage.com/0020bp/mary_mary.karr.html>.

Katz, Friedrich. *The Life and Times of Pancho Villa*. Stanford: Stanford University Press, 1998.

Kiev, Ari. *Curanderismo: Mexican-American Folk Psychiatry*. New York: The Free Press, 1968.

Kornbluth, Jesse. "Mary Karr." *The Book Report*. (6 March 1997, 19 May 2001) <http://www.bookreporter.com/brc/author.asp?author=104>.

Langness, L. L., and Gelya Frank. *Lives: An Anthropological Approach to Biography*. Novato, California: Chandler & Sharp, 1981.

Lea, Tom. *Randado*. El Paso: Carl Hertzog, 1941.

———. *Tom Lea: An Oral History*. Ed. Rebecca Craver and Adair Margo. El Paso: Texas Western Press, 1995.

Lee, James W. "Arbiters of Texas Literary Taste." *Range Wars: Heated Debates, Sober Reflections, and Other Assessments of Texas Writing*. Ed. Craig Clifford and Tom Pilkington. Dallas: Southern Methodist, 1988. 123-136.

———. "The Old South in Texas Literature." *The Texas Literary Tradition: Fiction, Folklore, History*. Ed. Don Graham, et al. Austin: The College of Liberal Arts, The University of Texas at Austin, and The Texas State Historical Association, 1983. 46-57.

———. "Porter and Dobie: The Marriage from Hell." *From Texas to the World and Back: Essays on the Journeys of Katherine Anne Porter*. Ed. Mark Busby and Dick Heaberlin. Fort Worth: TCU Press, 2001. 66-77.

———. "William Humphrey." *Dictionary of Literary Biography*. Vol. 6: *American Novelists since World War I*, Second Series, ed. James E. Kibler. Detroit: Gale Research Co., 1980. 148-153.

"Lee Rutland Scarborough" Southern Baptist Historical Library and Archives. N. d. (23 May 2001) <http://ww.sbhla.org/bio_scarborough.htm>.

Lejeune, Philip. *On Autobiography*. Minneapolis: University of Minnesota Press, 1989.

Limón, José E. *Dancing with the Devil: Society and Cultural Poetics in Mexican-American South Texas*. Madison: University of Wisconsin Press, 1984.

Liss, Barbara. "McMurtry: Rumination Lite in Paradise." *Houston Chronicle*. August 22, 2001.

LittleDog, Pat. *Afoot in a Field of Men*. New York: Atlantic Monthly Press, 1988.

Lomax, John A. *Cowboy Songs and Other Frontier Ballads*. New York: Sturgis and Walton, 1910.

Madison, Virginia. *The Big Bend Country of Texas*. Second ed. New York: October House, 1968.

——— and Hallie Stillwell. *How Come It's Called That? Place Names in the Big Bend Country*. Albuquerque: University of New Mexico Press, 1958; Revised edition, New York: October House, 1968.

Maines, Rachel P. *The Technology of Orgasm: Hysteria, The Vibrator and Women's Sexual Satisfaction*. Baltimore: Johns Hopkins University Press, 1999.

Mallon, Thomas. "Even Cowboys Get the Blues." *New York Times*, 21 November 1999, sec.7, 14.

Malouf, Dian Leatherberry. *Cattle Kings of Texas*. Hillsboro, Oregon: Beyond Words Publishing, 1991.

Mandel, Barrett. "Full of Life Now." *Autobiography: Essays Theoretical and Critical*. Ed. James Olney. Princeton: Princeton University Press, 1980. 49-72.

Marks, Lawrence E. *The Unity of the Senses: Interrelations among the Modalities*. New York: Academic Press, 1978.

Marks, Paula Mitchell. "Mary Ann Adams Maverick." *Handbook of Texas Online*. (15 February 1999, 10 September 2001).<http://www.tsha.utexas.edu/handbook/online/articles/view/MM/fma82.html>.

Marquez, Benjamin. *Power and Politics in a Chicano Barrio: A Study of Mobilization Efforts and Community Power in El Paso*. Lanham, MD: University Press of America, 1985.

McCarthy, Mary. *Memories of a Catholic Girlhood*. New York: Harcourt, Brace, 1957.

McKenna, Teresa. *Migrant Song: Politics and Process in Contemporary Chicano Literature*. Austin: University of Texas Press, 1997.

McMurtry, Larry. "Afterword." *My First Thirty Years*, by Gertrude Beasley. Austin: Book Club of Texas, 1989. 233-41.

McNutt, James Charles. *Beyond Regionalism: Texas Folklorists and the Emergence Post-Regional Consciousness*. Ann Arbor, Michigan: University Microfilms International, 1982.

"Memory: An Interview with Mary Karr," on "To the Best of My Knowledge," Wisconsin Public Radio. 20 April 1997. Audiocassette.

Mencken, H. L. "A Texas School Marm," *The American Mercury* 7.25 (January 1926): 123-125.

Miles, Jonathan. "Walter Benjamin at the Dairy Queen." *Salon.com* (29 November 1999, 11 October 2001). <http://www.salon.com/books/review/1999/11/29/mcmurtry/>.

Mondell, Cynthia Salzman, and Allen Mondell. *Guts, Gumption and Go-Ahead: Annie Mae Hunt Remembers*. Video production. Dallas: Media Projects, 1993.

Monte, Christopher F. *Beneath the Mask: An Introduction to Theories of Personality*. Fort Worth: Harcourt Brace College Publishers, 1995.

Murphy, Patrick D. "Conserving Natural and Cultural Diversity: The Prose and Poetry of Pat Mora." *Farther Afield in the Study of Nature-Oriented Literature*. Charlottesville and London: University Press of Virginia, 2000.

Nail, Robert E. *The Fandangle—A People's Theater*. Albany, Texas: The Fort Griffin Fandangle Society, 1970.

Neighbours, Kenneth F. "Elm Creek Raid," *Handbook of Texas Online*. (15

February 1999, 13 May 2001). <http://www.tsha.utexas.edu/handbook/online/articlesview/EE/bte1.htm>.

Ohan, Chris. "Biographical Sketch." Guide to the A. C. Greene papers 1923-Present. (August 1999, 10 February 2000). <http://libraries.uta.edu/SpecColl/findaids/AR409.htm>

Olney, James, ed. *Autobiography: Essays Theoretical and Critical.* Princeton: Princeton University Press, 1980.

———. *Memory and Narrative: The Weave of Life Writing*. Chicago: University of Chicago Press, 1998.

———. *Metaphors of Self: The Meaning of Autobiography*. Princeton: Princeton University of Princeton Press, 1972.

Olsson, Karen. "Refinery Daze," Part Two. *The Texas Observer*, 8 December 2000,rf 18-20.

Owens, William A. *Slave Mutiny: the Revolt of the Schooner Amistad*. New York: John Day Company, 1953; reprint, under the title *Black Mutiny*, Philadelphia: United Church Press, 1968.

———. *Swing and Turn: Texas Play-Party Games*. Dallas: Tardy Publishing Company, 1936.

———, ed. *Three Friends: Roy Bedichek, J. Frank Dobie, Walter Prescott Webb*. Austin and London: University of Texas Press, 1975.

Padilla, Genaro M. My *History, Not Yours: The Formation of Mexican American Autobiography*. Madison: University of Wisconsin Press, 1993.

Paredes, Américo. *George Washington Gómez: A Mexicotexan Novel*. Houston: Arte Público Press, 1990.

———. *With His Pistol in His Hand: A Border Ballad and Its Hero*. Austin: University of Texas Press, 1958.

Park, Mary. "Don't Mess with Texas: An Interview with Mary Karr." *Amazon.com*. N. d., (19 May 2001). <http://www.amazon.com/exec/obidos/tg/feature/95141/103-3957227-2660612>.

Parsons, Ian. "Outstanding Merit." *The Bookseller*. 7 January 1978, 45.

Paz, Octavio. *The Labyrinth of Solitude: Life and Thought in Mexico*. 1950; New York: Grove Press, 1961.

Penguin Books Reading Group Guide for *The Liar's Club*. N. d., (15 May 2001). <http://www.penguinputnam.com/clubppi/reading/kar/content.htm>.

Pérez-Torres, Rafael. *Movements in Chicano Poetry: Against Myths, Against Margins*. Cambridge: Cambridge University Press, 1995.

Pilkington, Tom. *State of Mind: Texas Literature and Culture*. College Station: Texas A & M Press, 1998.

Pilkington, William T. *Imagining Texas: The Literature of the Lone Star State*. Boston: American Publishing Company 1981.

———. *My Blood's Country: Studies in Southwestern Literature*. Fort Worth: Texas Christian University Press, 1973.

———. *William A. Owens*. Southwest Writers Series, No. 17. Austin: Steck-Vaughn, 1968. Reprinted in *My Blood's Country*, 123-162.

Porterfield, Nolan. *The Last Cavalier: The Life and Times of John A. Lomax 1867-1948*. Urbana and Chicago: University of Illinois Press, 1996.

Rebolledo, Tey Diana. "Tradition and Mythology: Signatures of Landscape in Chicana Literature." *The Desert Is No Lady: Southwestern Landscapes in Women's Writing and Art*. Ed. Vera Norwood and Janice Monk. New Haven: Yale University Press, 1987. 96-124.

Renteria, Ramon. "A Look Back." *El Paso Times*, 21 April 1996.

Reynolds, Clay. Review of Mary Karr, *Cherry*, *Southwestern American Literature*, 26 (Spring 2001): 125-127.

Rifkind, Donna. "She Who Has Suffered." *New Times Los Angeles Online*. (5 September 2000, May 19, 2001). <http://www.newtimesla.com/issues/2000-10-05/ink.html>.

Rodríguez, Miguel. "Memories without Borders: John Phillip Santos' San Antonio Recollections." *The Texas Observer* (online). (18 February 2000, 24 December 2000). <http://www.texasobserver.org/Archives/000218_rodriguez_on_santos.htm>.

Rodriguez, Richard. *Hunger of Memory: The Education of Richard Rodriguez*. Boston: David Godine, 1982.

Rose, Cynthia. "Lottie Deno." *The Handbook of Texas Online*. (15 February 1999. 13 May 2001). <http://www.tsha.utexas.edu/handbook/online/articles/view/DD/fde59.html>.

Rubel, Arthur J., et al. *Susto, a Folk Illness*. Berkeley: University of California Press, 1984.

Russell, Bertrand. *The Autobiography: 1914-1944*, vol. 2 of *The Autobiography of Bertrand Russell*. London: George Allen and Unwin, Ltd., 1968.

Ruta, Suzanne. "North Toward Home," *New York Times*. 5 December 1999.

Saldívar, José David. *Border Matters: Remapping American Cultural Studies*. Berkeley: University of California Press, 1997.

———. "Chicano Border Narratives as Cultural Critique," *Criticism in the Borderlands: Studies in Chicano Literature, Culture and Ideology*. Ed. Héctor Calderón and José Saldívar (Durham and London: Duke University Press, 1991. 167-80.

Saldívar, Ramón. *Chicano Narrative: The Dialectics of Difference*. Madison: University of Wisconsin Press, 1990.

Sanderson, Jim. "Art in the Desert," *A West Texas Soapbox*. College Station: Texas A&M University Press, 1998, 16-27.

Sawey, Orlan. "Introduction," *Southwest*, by John Houghton Allen. Albuquerque: Zia Books Edition, University of New Mexico Press, 1977. v-xi.

Sayers, Valerie. "Tattletale." *Commonweal* 127 (3 November 2000): 27-28.

Schwartz, John. "Secondhand Book Wrangler; a Pulitzer Prize Winner Is Also a Profitable Bookseller," *New York Times*, 23 July 2001.

Selinger, Eric Murphy. "The Personal Maze Is Not the Prize." *Parnassus: Poetry in Review* 24 (2000): 77-117.

Smith, Jr., Griffin. "Texas West of the Pecos," *National Geographic* 165 (February 1984): 210-135.

Soskis, Benjamin. "Lone Star Joining." *The New Republic* 4,470 (18 September 2000): 23-27.

Speck, Ernest B. "Mody Coggin Boatright," *The Handbook of Texas Online*. (15 February 1999, 13 May 2001). <http://www.tsha.utexas.edu/handbook/online/articles/view/BB/fbo1.html>.

Spivak, G. C. "Can the Subaltern Speak?" *Marxism and the Interpretation of Culture*. Ed. C. Nelson and L. Grossberg. Basingstoke: Macmillan Education, 1988, 271-313.

Stahl, Sandra K. "The Oral Personal Narrative in Its Generic Context." *Fabula* 18 (1977): 32-34.

Stegner, Wallace. *Wolf Willow: A History, a Story, and a Memory of the Last Plains Frontier.* New York: Viking, 1955.

Stone, Albert E. "Modern American Autobiography: Texts and Transactions." *American Autobiography: Retrospect and Prospect*. Ed. Paul John Eakin. Madison: University of Wisconsin Press, 1991.

Streitfield, David. "Lonesome Trove," *The Washington Post*, 22 February 1998, E01.

Texas: A Guide to the Lone Star State. American Guide Series. Austin: Texas Highway Commission, 1940; reissued as *The WPA Guide to Texas*, with a new introduction by Don Graham. Austin: Texas Monthly Press, 1986.

Texas Almanac 2000-2001. Dallas: Dallas Morning News, 1999.

Thomas, Robert McG., Jr. "Hallie C. Stillwell, a Rancher and Texas Legend, Dies at 99." *New York Times*, 24 August 1997, Section 1, 34.

Thompson, Jerry. "Juan Nepomuceno Cortina." *The Handbook of Texas Online*. (15 February 1999, 30 May 2001). <http://www.tsha.utexas.edu/handbook/online/articles/view/CC/fco73.html>.

Thorpe, Helen. "Hallie and Farewell." *Texas Monthly*, (October 1997), 132-140.

Tinkle, Lon. *An American Original: The Life of J. Frank Dobie*. Boston: Little, Brown and Co., 1978.

Titon, Jeff David. "The Life Story." *Journal of American Folklore* 93 (July-September 1980): 278-92

Torres, Hector A. Review of Pat Mora, "House of Houses." *Aztlán* 23 (Fall 1998): 233-38.

Trotter II, Robert T., and Juan Antonio Chavira. *Curanderismo: Mexican American Folk Healing*. Second Edition. Athens, Georgia: University of Georgia Press, 1997.

Two Worlds Review. 2 (December 1926); 3 (April 1927).

Underwood, Jerald. "The Vaquero in South Texas with an Interpretation by John Houghton Allen." *West Texas Historical Association Year Book* 68 (1992): 93-99.

Watson, Steven. *Strange Bedfellows: The First American Avant-Garde*. New York: Abbeville Press, 1991.

Webb, Walter Prescott. *The Great Plains*. 1931. New York: Grosset & Dunlap, 1977.

———. *The Texas Rangers: A Century of Frontier Defense*. Boston and New York: Houghton-Mifflin, 1935.

West, John O. *Mexican-American Folklore: Legends, Songs, Festivals, Crafts, Tales of Saints, of Revolutionaries, and More*. Little Rock: August House, 1988.

White, Owen. *Out of the Desert: The Historical Romance of El Paso*. El Paso, TX: The McMath Company, 1923.

Williams, Rosemary. "The Marfa Lights—A Mystery." *Texas Highways*, August 1993, 36-39.

Wilson, Laura. *Watt Matthews of Lambshead*. Austin: Texas State Historical Association, 1989.

Winegarten, Ruthe. *Black Texas Women: A Sourcebook*. Austin: University of Texas Press, 1996.

———. *Black Texas Women: 150 Years of Trial and Triumph*. Austin: University of Texas Press, 1995.

Wolfe, Tom. *The Electric Kool-Aid Acid Test*. New York: Farr, Straus and Giroux, 1968.

Wolff, Geoffrey. *The Duke of Deception*. New York, Random House, 1979.

Wolff, Tobias. *This Boy's Life*. New York: Atlantic Monthly Press, 1989.

Woolf, Virginia. "Professions for Women." *Collected Essays*. Vol. 2. London: Hogarth Press, 1966. 284-89.

Yarborough, Ralph W. *Frank Dobie: Man and Friend*. Washington, D. C.: Potomac Corral of the Westerners, 1967.

Zeidner, Lisa. "Fresh Fruit" *Salon.com*, (25 September 2000, 13 May 2001). <http://www.salon.com/books/feature/2000/09/25/karr/index.html>.

INDEX

** Note: The work of each author discussed in the book can be found at the conclusion of her or his entry.*